Lonely Planet Publications
Melbourne | Oakland | London

D1025827

Sara Benson

Las Vegas

The Top Five

1 Gambling
Don't leave without chancing your arm at the tables (p35)

2 Dining
Sample the delicacies at Circo (p106)

3 Fremont Street Experience
Gape at the Glitter Gulch canopy, Fremont St (p82)

4 The Strip
Survey the Strip from Stratosphere Tower (p79)

5 Production shows
Savor the color and spectacle of a Vegas show (p142)

Contents

Published by Lonely Planet Publications Pty Ltd
ABN 36 005 607 983

Australia Head Office, Locked Bag 1, Footscray,
Victoria 3011, ☎ 03 8379 8000, fax 03 8379 8111,
talk2us@lonelyplanet.com.au

USA 150 Linden St, Oakland, CA 94607,
☎ 510 893 8555, toll free 800 275 8555,
fax 510 893 8572, info@lonelyplanet.com

UK 72–82 Rosebery Ave, Clerkenwell, London,
EC1R 4RW, ☎ 020 7841 9000, fax 020 7841 9001,
go@lonelyplanet.co.uk

© Lonely Planet 2006
Photographs © Ray Laskowitz and as listed (p247)
2006

The Authors

Sara Benson

Awestruck by the Luxor pyramid's 40-billion-candlepower beacon, Sara first stumbled into Las Vegas many moons ago during a cross-country trip from Chicago to California. That serendipitous one-night stand became a torrid love affair with Sin City. Of course, gambling already ran deep in her veins, as few in her Irish American family have ever said no to a friendly card game. Now she travels down to the Nevadan desert every chance she gets, always taking time to stroll the Strip and roll through downtown's classy carpet joints with her mini entourage before escaping into the natural wonderlands of Southern California, Arizona and Utah. The veteran author of several city guidebooks, Sara's travel writing has also featured in newspapers from coast to coast, including the *Miami Herald, Las Vegas Review–Journal, Los Angeles Times* and *San Francisco Chronicle*.

CONTRIBUTING AUTHOR
JONATHAN GROTENSTEIN

Jonathan wrote about poker and blackjack for the Gambling chapter. A writer and professional poker player living in Los Angeles, he cowrote *Poker: The Real Deal* with Phil Gordon and is a frequent contributor to *All In* magazine. His most recent book is *All In: The (Almost) Entirely True History of the World Series of Poker*.

PHOTOGRAPHER
Ray Laskowitz

Ray has been making pictures for almost 30 years in the United States, through most of Asia and a bit of Europe. His imagery is a unique blend of photojournalistic decisive moments and artistic feeling and movement. For Ray, working in Las Vegas was enjoyable since many of his images depend on light and intense color for their impact. Even during the daylight hours Las Vegas certainly is a colorful city.

SARA'S TOP SIN CITY DAY

Nobody's an early riser in Vegas. I get up just in time to make the breakfast buffet at Le Village (p111) and maybe a free gambling lesson (p36). Shaking off the Rabelaisian fête of the night before, I devote the afternoon to shopping in the vintage clothing stores and galleries of the downtown arts district (p177) or dipping into a spa (p164). As the sun sets, it's time to zoom up the Stratosphere (p79) for thrill rides and drinks at the Top of the World Lounge (p136). Scoring a dinner reservation at Rosemary's (p128) justifies a detour before heading back to the Strip after dark. Then let the gaming begin, first on the Strip and eventually ending up downtown, where I get myself into an Old Vegas mood at the Golden Nugget (p83), then cruise by the Neon Museum (p84) and into the poker room at Binion's (p81). After having the Fremont Street Experience (p82), I head out to a nightclub like Ice (p152) or tangerine (p153). After hours, I drop by Mr Lucky's (p124) and play the rock 'n' roll slots at the Hard Rock (p87) before catching a little vampirish shut-eye back at my hotel. At noon, it starts all over again.

Introducing Las Vegas

As ambitious as a starlet vying for your affections, fabulous Las Vegas is a wild ride – an outrageous fantasy that'll never let you down. According to Hollywood legend, some ramshackle gambling houses, tumbleweeds and cacti were all there was the day mobster Bugsy Siegel drove into the Mojave Desert and decided to raise a glamorous, tropical-themed casino under the searing sun. Nobody thought anyone would ever come here. But everybody couldn't have been more wrong.

In Sin City, fate is decided by the spin of a roulette wheel. It's a place where the poor feel rich and the rich lose thousands. In this high-octane desert oasis, all that glitters is likely gold. Glamour's sweet stench is as thick as the cigarette smoke rolling off the fingers of a blue-haired grandmother feeding nickels into the slot machine and slugging gin-and-tonics. Vegas wasn't built to last, but it does. Like the shifting sand dunes of the Mojave Desert, what's hot and what's not can change in the blink of an eye. Thankfully, what never changes is the eternal cool of the city itself.

Euphoria is Las Vegas' defining mood, from the silver miners of yesteryear hoping to strike the mother lode to the giddy torrent of mobsters, movie stars, showgirls and crooners through the 1950s and '60s. As the 20th century raced toward its end, megaresorts began to spike the skyline of the Strip. Every decade has made Vegas more of a boomtown than ever before. Now it's time to come see it for yourself.

Even if you don't shell out big bucks, you'll still leave town convinced you've had the time of your life. It doesn't matter if you play the penny slots or drop a bankroll each

LOWDOWN

Time zone Pacific Standard Time (PST)

Metro area population 1.8 million

Annual number of visitors More than 37 million

Marriage licenses issued each year 120,000

Monorail single-trip ticket $3

Cost of a drink while you're gambling Free (don't forget to tip)

Steak-and-eggs graveyard special Less than $10

Three-star hotel room From $80/150 per weekday/ weekend night

Ticket to a megaproduction show Around $100

Average visitor's gambling budget $500

and every night – short-skirted cocktail waitresses democratically comp drinks for all gamblers, whether you're a high roller or a novice. Careening from one opulent casino to the next, looking for the next red-hot table, downing martinis, smoking stogies and devouring rich steaks – you'll pinch yourself and ask, does this ever have to end? Nope.

Time is irrelevant here. There are no clocks, just never-ending buffets and ever-flowing drinks. A bible-toting Elvis kisses a dizzy couple who just pledged eternity in the Chapel of Love. Acrobats spiral above the blackjack tables at Circus Circus, fountains burst outside the Bellagio, and go-go dancers heat up svelte ultra lounges at the MGM Grand. The Strip just never stops, and neither does ol' downtown, where authentic cowboy flavor and a revival of Rat Pack style collide, making flashy Fremont St ripe for an urban revival.

Vegas is the ultimate escape. Give it a few days, and it'll give you the world. Any whim can be gratified instantly. Indulge in a spa after midnight, slip past a nightclub's velvet ropes after hopping out of a stretch limo, or taste the five-star offerings of America's top chefs. Emptying your wallet never felt so damn good. You can reinvent yourself a hundred times over or hide out with your lover in a hotel room for days. Sin City keeps all of your naughty secrets, because (sing it, sister) what happens here, stays here.

Do like locals do. Admit Vegas has flaws – it's far from 'civilization,' it can be seedy, and it's an unforgiving place when you're down and out – but love it anyway. Buy a drink for a retired showgirl and hear how she remembers kissing Elvis. Sidle up to a degenerate gambler and reminisce about the hurly-burly years when the mob really ran things. Hang out with artists and hipsters at the frayed edges of downtown. And always milk the city for every last freebie, discount and promo deal, of which there are hundreds.

Finally, when you tire of the ding-ding-ding of the slot machines, rejuvenation is no further than just outside the city limits. Not a road leaves Vegas that doesn't pass through the sparse, wind- and water-carved landscapes of the Southwest's famous desert. Begin with Red Rock Canyon and the Valley of Fire. Gape in awe at the Grand Canyon and Hoover Dam. Head east to lose yourself in the spires of Zion and Bryce National Parks, or west into the solitary beauty of Death Valley and the Mojave National Preserve.

Then it's time to head back into the belly of the beast. Viva Las Vegas, baby! Where everyone lives like the King.

ESSENTIAL LAS VEGAS

- The Strip (p48)
- Fremont Street Experience (p82)
- Rodeos (p163)
- Atomic Testing Museum (p87)
- Leaving Las Vegas (p207)

City Life

City Life

LAS VEGAS TODAY

Just like the King, Las Vegas is all shook up. Change here is as sudden and unpredictable as a Southern Californian earthquake. Ever since the start of the 20th century, every decade has morphed this southern Nevada metropolis, much maligned by the rest of the nation. But it's an undeniable adrenaline rush just to be here: to watch the neon Strip reach dizzying heights, to feel the revival of Old Vegas in downtown, to witness the hurly-burly battles of politicos and casino impresarios, and to be catered to by celebrity chefs, entertainers, athletes and fashionistas. Having thrown itself a knock-out centennial bash in 2005, Sin City now is raring to zoom ahead into the future, one with a Silver State lining.

CITY CALENDAR

Las Vegas is a nonstop party 24/7, so organized celebrations are almost superfluous. But that doesn't stop anyone. Holidays (p240) especially are taken to the max, with New Year's Eve along the Strip seeing the biggest crush of humanity this side of Times Square. Most production shows are 'dark' (shut down) the week before Christmas, and many shops close on 25 December. The only other times that the city slows down are in the dead of winter (January and February) and during the sweltering height of summer (June, July and August). For climate details, see p237.

HOT CONVERSATION TOPICS

You'll never believe who I saw! At last, Sin City is 'in' again from Hollywood to the Big Apple. Celebrities are making surprise appearances at hot nightclubs on and off the Strip. Some are even plunking down money for condos in the new casino, hotel, shopping and residential megacomplexes that are starting to rise on and off the Strip. It's time for a Vegas revival, baby.

Uh-oh, what did Mayor Goodman do now? Set to lead the city until 2007, former mob lawyer Oscar Goodman is a lightning rod for controversy, whether it's him getting in hot water by being a celebrity photographer for *Playboy* or telling elementary school students that if he were stranded on a desert island and could only take one thing with him, it'd be gin. The self-proclaimed 'happiest mayor in the world' has also been quoted saying, 'I drink to excess, I gamble with both fists and when I eat, I eat like a gourmand. I can do whatever I want.' Kind of sounds like what every tourist on the Strip wants, don't it?

What's up with downtown? Even though the **Fremont Street Experience** (p82) has been up and running for over a decade, downtown boosters and naysayers still disagree about whether the area really is making a comeback. The dynamic duo Tim and Tom of *Casino* reality-TV fame have just sold off the **Golden Nugget** (p83), the new owners of **Binion's** (p81) are relatively unknown players and – well, everyone's a bit worried about the Glitter Gulch along Fremont St.

Urban planning. You're joking, right? Encompassing some of America's fastest growing cities, the metro Las Vegas area continues to sprawl into the desert. The problem isn't so much that land isn't available; it's infrastructure that's lacking, which you'll notice as you drive around town, where highways are jammed day and night. So are local surface streets, much to the frustration of commuters. Those new high-rise condo developments aren't exactly going to ease the traffic problems, either.

Culture and the arts...wait, let me think a sec. Downtown's arts district and the 'Cultural Corridor' on Las Vegas Blvd N sound more impressive than they actually are, and the planned Las Vegas Performing Arts Center hasn't been able to get off the ground. Meanwhile, funding for the arts has flown out to more moneyed suburbs such as Summerlin.

You'll want to avoid Sin City during a big convention. The colossal crowds are off-putting, not to mention costly, as hotels jack up room rates and dinner reservations or show tickets become impossible to get. Major sports events, such as championship boxing and Nascar races, also pack the city to a full house.

The exact days, weeks or months when annual conventions and special events are held shift from year to year. Promoters have been known to move their 'shows' as finances dictate. Contact the **Las Vegas Convention & Visitors Authority** (LVCVA; p245) to obtain a current calendar of convention dates and major special events. The following info is highly subject to change.

JANUARY & FEBRUARY
LAUGHLIN DESERT CHALLENGE
☎ 702-298-3321, 800-452-8445; www.score-international.com; Laughlin Events Center Park, Laughlin; tickets $15-35
It's the closest you can get to the off-road desert racing in *Fear & Loathing in Las Vegas*. The short, brutal circuit races are held over a three-day weekend in mid-January in **Laughlin** (p228).

CHINESE NEW YEAR
☎ 702-221-8448; www.lvchinatown.com; Chinatown Plaza, 4255 Spring Mountain Rd, Las Vegas; adult/child 6-12 $2/1; bus 203
Day-long festivities feature entertainers from throughout Asia and the Pacific Rim, with dragon dances, calligraphers, traditional folk music and martial arts, all to mark the beginning of the Chinese lunar new year, falling between late January and mid-February.

COLORADO RIVER BLUEGRASS FESTIVAL
☎ 702-298-3321, 800-452-8445; www.coloradoriverbluegrassfestival.com; off Hwy 95, Laughlin; admission per day adult/child 7-17 $13/5, campsite per night $5
In mid-February, **Laughlin** (p228) showcases local bluegrass fiddlers and old-timey musicians all the way from back east. The Sunday morning gospel hour is a revelation. Bring your own blanket and cash for the craft and food booths.

MARCH
NASCAR WEEKEND
☎ 702-644-4444, 800-644-4444; www.nascar.com, www.lvms.com; Las Vegas Motor Speedway, 7000 Las Vegas Blvd N, North Las Vegas; ticket prices vary; bus 113A
Nascar fans descend on the 1.5-mile oval at the **Las Vegas Motor Speedway** (p162) for the Sam's Town 300 (Busch Series) and the UAW-DaimlerChrysler 400 (Nextel Cup Series) in mid-March.

ST PATRICK'S DAY
Downtown Las Vegas and Henderson have raucous parades, replete with floats and Celtic music, every March 17. Notice the color of the beer in most of the casinos along Fremont St on this day: green. Yikes! Meanwhile, New York–New York's **Nine Fine Irishmen** (p135) stages a Celtic Féis festival.

APRIL
LAUGHLIN RIVER RUN
☎ 800-357-8223, tickets 714-694-2800; www.laughlinriverrun.com; Laughlin
More than 60,000 hogs roar into **Laughlin** (p228) over a long, long weekend in late April for a Harley-Davidson trade show, motorcycle stunts, charity poker games, concerts and a ride along Route 66 (p217).

UNLVINO
☎ 702-876-4500; www.unlvino.com; advance tickets $50, admission at the door $75
For more than 30 years, this one-day annual wine-tasting extravaganza in late April has brought together oenophiles and more than 300 winemakers from around the world. All proceeds, including from the wine and art auction, benefit the University of Nevada, Las Vegas (UNLV).

TOP FIVE UNUSUAL HOLIDAYS & EVENTS
- Aviation Nation (p12)
- CineVegas (p10)
- Helldorado Days (p10)
- National Finals Rodeo (p12)
- World Series of Poker (p10)

MARDI GRAS

Elaborate New Orleans–style carnivals – held for your convenience in early April, instead of on Fat Tuesday before Lent – feature Cajun food, parades and stage shows at the Rio (p91), Orleans (p90) and Fremont Street Experience (p82).

MAY
LEI DAY

☎ 702-385-1222; California, 12 E Ogden Ave; www.alohavalley.com; events admission free-$25; bus 301, 302

For the Hawaiian *ohana* (extended family) of island expats living in the Las Vegas Valley (p13), this Polynesian and Pacific Rim block party comes alive on the weekend closest to May 1 with parades, food vendor stalls, and live music and dance shows, everything from Tahitian hula to Jawaiian (Hawaiian-style reggae). It's held at the California (p81).

CINCO DE MAYO

On May 5, Mexico's victory over French forces in 1862 at the Battle of Puebla is remembered. But Cinco de Mayo is basically an excuse for a party. Day-long celebrations around town feature Latin American entertainers, including mariachi bands, *ballet folklorico* and, if you're lucky, maybe even Lucha Libre (Mexican stunt wrestling).

HELLDORADO DAYS

Dating back to the 1930s, this historic four-day hoedown has been revived. Expect rodeo events, barbecue, country fiddlers and a re-creation of an Old West frontier town, though the rowdy kangaroo court is no longer a festival institution. Most of the action happens downtown from mid-May to early June, usually near the Fremont Street Experience (p82).

JUNE & JULY
CINEVEGAS

☎ 702-507-4849, 888-898-3427; www.cinevegas.com; Palms, 4321 W Flamingo Rd; festival passes $100-500; bus 202, 807

This nine-day film festival in early to mid-June showcases indie films, first-time directors and some major Hollywood names like Nicolas Cage and also Dennis Hopper, who currently chairs its creative board. The action revolves around the Brenden Palms Casino (p159) movie theaters.

WORLD SERIES OF POKER

☎ 702-777-7777, 800-342-7724; www.worldseriesofpoker.com; Rio, 3700 W Flamingo Rd; free Strip shuttle

High-stakes gamblers, casino employees and celebrities match wits in more than 40 tournaments running from early June to mid-July. The four-day final championship, held at the Rio (p91), earns the winner a cool $5 million; buy-ins cost just $10,000. Free public viewing allowed.

REGGAE IN THE DESERT

☎ 702-455-8200, tickets 702-474-4000; www.reggaeinthedesert.com; Clark County Amphitheater, 500 S Grand Central Pkwy; admission $20; bus 106, 108

The Clark County Amphitheater (Map p261) hosts this upstart summer festival that brings together musicians, arts vendors and roots-reggae, ska and Jamaican dance hall fans for a starry night of Caribbean celebrations.

LAS VEGAS INTERNATIONAL FOLK FESTIVAL

☎ 702-455-7340; www.co.clark.nv.us; Winchester Cultural Center, 3130 S McLeod Dr; adult/senior & child per night $7/5; bus 111, 112

Three days of folk music, dancing and costumes with flair from around Europe, Asia and Latin America at the Winchester Cultural Center (Map p260). Performances from Latino communities around the USA include Las Vegas' own Mexico Vivo Dance Company (www.angelfire.com/folk/mexicovivodc/).

FOURTH OF JULY

You can catch fireworks on this all-American holiday at Clark County's Red, White 'N Boom Celebration (☎ 702-455-8200; www.redwhitenboom.com; Desert Breeze Park, 8275 W Spring Mountain Rd; admission adult $12, child under 13 free; bus 203), which has headliner rock bands and carnival games; Summerlin's Star Spangled Spectacular (☎ 702-895-2787; www.summerlin.com; Hills Park, Hillpointe Rd; adult/child 6-18 $15/10), with the Las Vegas Philharmonic (p158); Rockets Over the River in Laughlin (p228); and the old-fashioned Damboree in Boulder City (p210).

DEF CON

www.defcon.org; admission $80 (cash only)
The nation's largest conclave of underground computer hackers takes place over one long, heavily caffeinated weekend in late July, usually at **Alexis Park Villas** (p204), with cutting-edge speakers, new tech tools, book signings, artwork contests, even a dunk tank. Just FYI, so you know why all those geeks are skulking on the Strip around then.

AUGUST

CLARK COUNTY FAIR

☎ 888-876-3247; www.ccfair.com; 1301 W Whipple Ave, off NV 160, 5 miles east of I-15 exit 93, Logandale; fair only adult/child 5-12/senior $8/5/6, carnival & fair $20
Not too far from **Valley of Fire State Park** (p212), this old-fashioned county fair boasts four days of pro rodeo events, yummy barbecue, 4-H farm exhibits and demonstrations, and retro carnival rides and games.

NEVADA POLICE & FIRE GAMES

☎ 702-259-6350, 800-863-9676; www.npaf.net
Cops and firefighters from around the world compete in 22 events at various venues during a five-day period. These mini-Olympics aren't likely ever to overshadow the real Games (here events include billiards and poker), but hey, it's fun – and free to watch.

SEPTEMBER

GREEK FOOD FESTIVAL

☎ 702-221-8245; St John the Baptist Greek Orthodox Church, 5300 El Camino Rd; adult $5, child under 13 free
Opa! The name says it all. Held in late September or early October at **St John the Baptist Greek Orthodox Church** (Map p260), this festival features Greek music, dancing and loads of à la carte food stalls with cheese, breads, *dolmathes* (stuffed vine leaves) and more.

LAS VEGAS AQUAFINA SHOOTOUT

☎ 702-693-5000, 800-693-7625; www.avp.com; Hard Rock, 4455 Paradise Rd; tickets $10-30; bus 108
This three-day event on the annual pro beach volleyball tour features two-person male and female teams (even Olympians Kerri Walsh and Misty May once played here) competing round-robin style for $250,000 in prize money. The competition takes place on 350 tons of sand in the parking lot of the **Hard Rock** (p87).

OCTOBER

OKTOBERFEST

www.lasvegasoktoberfest.com
From late September through the end of October, Las Vegas' all-you-can-drink festival is endorsed by real Bavarians. Raise your beer stein at restaurants and casinos all over town, notably **Cafe Heidelberg** (p123),

Crazy Girls statue, Riviera (p76)

the Hofbräuhaus (p138), Gordon Biersch (p139) and the German-American Social Club (☎ 702-649-8503; 1110 E Lake Mead Blvd, North Las Vegas; bus 113, 210).

HALLOWEEN
Haunted houses, masquerade and fetish balls, ghoulish outdoor bashes and Houdini séances make spending October 31 in Las Vegas a cool idea, especially given the costume rental options (who doesn't want to dress up in a white Elvis jumpsuit?).

VIVA! LAUGHLIN
☎ 702-298-3321, 800-452-8445; www.visitlaughlin .com/viva; Laughlin; admission varies
During Latino Heritage Month, Laughlin (p228) puts on a four-day fiesta of Latin musicians, dancers, comedians, and variety shows, plus hot fashions on the catwalk, and parties with south-of-the-border themes.

NOVEMBER
AVIATION NATION
☎ 702-652-2750; www.aviationnation.org; Nellis Air Force Base, North Las Vegas; admission free; park at Las Vegas Motor Speedway, then bus ($2) to Nellis AFB
On a weekend in mid-November, arguably the nation's most famous military and

civilian air show is attended by more than 100,000 people at Nellis Air Force Base (Map p260). Keep your eyes peeled for the Thunderbirds, an aerial demonstration team often scheduled to zoom in on the last day.

DECEMBER
LAS VEGAS INTERNATIONAL MARATHON
☎ 888-543-7223; www.lvmarathon.com; entry fee $95
This 26.2-mile race begins and ends at the south end of the Strip. It draws up to 15,000 competitors from dozens of countries. Watching the race is free.

NATIONAL FINALS RODEO
☎ 702-702-739-3267, 866-388-3267; www.nfr experience.com; Thomas & Mack Center, 4505 S Maryland Pkwy; tickets from $36.50; bus 108, 109, 201, 213, 804
This hugely popular 10-day event, held at the Thomas & Mack Center (Map p265), features the top 15 pro rodeo performers competing in events such as steer wrestling and bull riding. Tickets are tough to get (for more details and helpful hints, see p163). Vegas gets taken over by real cowboys at this time, and a highlight among all the hoopla is the 'Downtown Hoedown,' a free honky-tonk party at the Fremont Street Experience (p82).

LAS VEGAS BOWL
☎ 702-739-3267, 866-388-3267; www.lvbowl.com; Thomas & Mack Center, 4505 S Maryland Pkwy; tickets $10-100; bus 108, 109, 201, 213, 804
This college football game kicks off at the Thomas & Mack Center (Map p265) around Christmas Eve, when the second-place Mountain West Conference (MWC) finisher competes against the fifth-best team out of the Pac-10 Conference.

NEW YEAR'S EVE
The Strip becomes a huge party scene every December 31, as thousands turn out to hear live music, watch fireworks and fights break out, and see people faint. Did we mention 'drink like fish'? They do that, too. Celebrations go on at the Fremont Street Experience (p82; admission $35), which is entirely blocked off to traffic.

GOT LUCKY?

When Hawaii residents go on vacation, they go to…Las Vegas. Perhaps blasé about tropical scenery, a surprising number of islanders enjoy the artificial glitz, theme-park casinos, nearby golf courses, all-you-can-eat buffets and the chance to win big (gambling is illegal in only two states: Hawaii and Utah).

The Honolulu–Vegas circuit has become a well-oiled machine, and companies such as **Sam Boyd's Vacations-Hawaii** (www.boydvacationshawaii.com/home/index.asp) offer discounted packages that keep residents of Hawaii coming back – often multiple times annually. Most stay downtown by Fremont Street at casino hotels like the **California** (p81), rather than at the upscale resorts on the Strip.

Over the years, Hawaii has considered ending its gambling ban, but opposition abounds from a bipartisan coalition of politicians, religious groups and the general public. Despite the state's financial woes and the local penchant for playing the slots, island gambling remains taboo.

A sizable community of Hawaii expatriates now lives in Vegas, largely due to the low cost of living. Surf the scene at www.alohavalley.com and don't miss **Lei Day** (p10). Many locals back in Hawaii shake their heads, though, in disbelief. Vegas is fun, but the islands are always *mo' bettah.*

CULTURE

For the lowdown on arts and architecture, turn to p20.

IDENTITY

The population of Las Vegas is over half a million, and if you count the outlying suburbs and independent cities, the total number of people in the metro valley area is fast approaching two million, almost double what it was just 10 years ago. Visitors outnumber locals 20:1, and most tourists have no idea what residents are really like.

So, let's talk about that. Vegas is a youthful city. The vast majority of locals were not even born in Nevada. Most are twenty- or thirtysomethings who moved here within the last five years. The city has slightly more women than men, but the ratio is far more balanced than during frontier days, when there was just one woman for every 15 men. More than half of all residents are white. More than a quarter identify themselves as Latino. Nearly one in 10 is African American, and a growing number (over 6%) are Asian American. Fewer than 1% of Las Vegans are Native Americans, the valley's original inhabitants.

Sin City's bad reputation precedes, overwhelms and obscures the reality of what the place is like. Infamous historically for its mob ties, Nevada's biggest metropolis today is best known for the naughty-minded marketing slogan: 'What happens in Vegas, stays in Vegas.' Often considered America's dirty little secret, Las Vegas is a bastion of hangover-inducing weekends for people from all walks of life and all over the country (though mostly Southern California), and even the world.

But all that belies what is, at heart, a conservative cow town. Prostitution, all images to the contrary, is illegal in Clark County. Gay and lesbian life is often hidden for the sake of the town's majority view. Racism has a long history in southern Nevada, and it wasn't until the 1960s that the color line at Las Vegas casinos was first crossed.

All that said, if the city's friendliness was measured on a scale from one to 10, with 10 being 'most friendly,' then Las Vegas would rate a solid 10. Everywhere you go in town people ask how you are doing, ask if they can be of assistance, stop and say hello. Sure, the city is service-oriented. Sure, it counts on repeat visitors to keep its casinos filled. But spend a few days here and you'll likely leave as so many people do, feeling that Sin City has more than its share of genuinely big-hearted folks.

LIFESTYLE

For most Las Vegans, the lifestyle is suburban. People tend to come here when they're young, looking for the American dream. And many find it. The median family income is $50,000 per year, with almost half of all households run by married couples. Births outpace

GIRLS! GIRLS! GIRLS!

More than 100 pages. That's the length of the Entertainers section in Las Vegas' yellow pages. Businesses that advertise there are not fronts for prostitution run by a handful of rich people as Las Vegas police officers have testified on numerous occasions. They can't be; prostitution is illegal in Sin City and the rest of Clark County. Has been for years.

Prostitution was banned in Las Vegas in the 1940s, when the US Air Force built a base nearby and forced the closure of the city's brothels. But the number of the city's red-light entertainers has soared. These services offer, in their own words, entertainment for adults only in your hotel room. But do these off-duty 'full-service Barbie girls' and 'barely legal Asian playmates' do more than take their clothes off and then leave again?

Absolutely not, they testify. But no one would blame you if you got the wrong idea. In 1997, the police proposed outlawing escort services in Clark County; the bill failed, but the services voluntarily toned down their advertisements as a result. Now they only show exploding skyrockets, strawberries with whipped cream, cheerleading uniforms and so on, but no actual women – you know, because they aren't offering sex. No doubt their singing and dancing skills (in fact, usually nonexistent) justify their $300-an-hour rates.

Not everyone hates the idea of prostitution in Las Vegas. Mayor Oscar Goodman has gone on record with his pro-prostitution stance, saying that legalizing prostitution here would 'turn old motels into beautiful brothels,' and speculating about how Fremont Street might advantageously be turned into Nevada's Little Amsterdam.

And then there's George Flint, an ordained minister who is Nevada's only paid lobbyist for the state's legal bordellos. His job is to see that attempts to end legal prostitution in Nevada, where it is permitted in 10 of the state's 17 counties, don't get too far. The good minister, who has been working for the Nevada Brothel Owners Association for two decades, says, 'Other than family, who was Jesus' best friend? She was a young woman named Mary from a town on the Sea of Galilee called Magdala.'

It's true. You can look it up in that other book found in many Vegas hotel rooms.

deaths at a ratio of two to one, with the residential boom concentrated in outlying suburbs like Henderson, not downtown or along the Strip, where new high-rise condo complexes are being snatched up instead by visitors who plan to make a mint by subletting them, and by celebrities who need a crash pad for their entourage.

Of course, Lady Luck does not smile on everyone here. In 2003, Las Vegas was ranked as the 'meanest city in America' in which to be homeless. If you wander east of the Fremont Street Experience or south into the Naked City stranded between downtown and the Strip, it won't take five minutes before you run into someone in desperate need of help: crack whores looking to score, babbling schizophrenics pushing shopping carts full of garbage bags, and degenerate gamblers drunk off 40oz beer cans in crumpled paper bags. More often exploited than dangerous, these folks are oft-overlooked in talk about urban revival.

Nevada has the second-highest percentage of high-school dropouts in the country, often attributed to the fact that the local economy is fueled by low-wage workers, so teens think higher education won't help them get ahead. Las Vegas has two academic institutions: the University of Nevada, Las Vegas (UNLV) and the Community College of Southern Nevada (CCSN), neither of which is very competitive on a national scale.

For such a sinful city, religion is surprisingly alive. There are more than 600 houses of worship in the metro area, which also has one of the nation's fastest-growing Jewish communities. Many tourists seeking religious services visit Catholic **Guardian Angel Cathedral** (p76), just off the Strip. Founders of Las Vegas' first religious mission, the Mormon church in 1989 erected a spired modernist **temple** (p79). It's up in the hills on the eastern outskirts of town and is well attended.

FOOD & DRINK

When you think of food in Las Vegas, chances are it's all-you-can-eat buffets and $5 steaks that come to mind. As for drinks, you're imagining watered-down drinks served free to any gambler inside the casinos, right? Well, it's true: Vegas has all of those things.

But these days, the foodie scene is on fire. Thank Wolfgang Puck, the first star chef to charge into Sin City in the early 1990s, when he opened a branch of Spago at Caesars Palace. Since then, a vainglorious parade of as-seen-on-TV chefs from America's most revered restaurants have dallied here, from Bobby Flay to Charlie Palmer to Nobu Matsuhisa to the Brennan family of Commanders Palace fame from down N'awlins way.

What's the attraction? Being bankrolled by a casino megaresort, for one. Then, there's the little-known factoid that Vegas is actually closer to the bountiful farmlands of California than either of the culinary meccas of San Francisco or Los Angeles. Both of these factors contribute to the incredibly delicate and rare ingredients you'll find on menus across town, usually with high-roller prices to match.

Some restaurants (p133) have taken the art of wine to new heights, literally at **Aureole** (p115). Brewski fans will find a sea of microbrews to try (p139), too. To dive right into the dining scene, turn to p104.

FASHION

When movie stars first landed in Las Vegas in the 1950s, no lady would be caught dead in anything less than an evening gown once the cocktail hour arrived, and even off-duty showgirls aspired to dress like starlets. Meanwhile, Sy Devore tailored European-style suits for the Rat Pack. In the early days of the Flamingo even the janitors wore tuxedos.

However, things changed in the late 1960s when Circus Circus opened its doors and Vegas began to sell itself as a family-friendly destination. Since then, casual attire has become the new norm. These days, dress codes exist only at high-end restaurants and more exclusive nightclubs.

Vegas invites fashion designers the world over to set up shop. Most of the to-die-for names in fashion hailing from Europe, New York and Los Angeles have boutiques inside casino shopping arcades or malls, such as the **Forum Shops** (p174), **Wynn Esplanade** (p175), **Via Bellagio** (p175) or the **Fashion Show Mall** (p173). Outlet shopping is rampant, too.

Most of the designs that Vegas can call its own, though, are made for the stage. Liberace indulged in a fabulous excess of velvet, fur, sequins and feathers when performing, and some of his costumes are still on display at the **Liberace Museum** (p88). For his comeback in 1969 at the International (now the Las Vegas Hilton), Elvis wore a karate *gi*–inspired white jumpsuit designed by Bill Belew. Only in Vegas.

Most famous maybe are what Las Vegas' famous showgirls wear (or don't wear, as the case may be). Bob Mackie's original designs for *Jubilee!* (p145) are still used in the show today. The female dancers must be at last 5ft 8in tall to support the elaborately beaded and feathered costumes and headdresses weighing as much as 35lb. To get your own feather boa, visit **Rainbow Feathers** (p179).

During **National Finals Rodeo** week (p12), the gambling halls downtown fill with cowboys and cowgirls all dudded up in embroidered dress shirts with bolo ties, crafted silver belt buckles influenced by Native American designs, and hand-stitched cowboy boots made from exotic leathers – just like in the days when Las Vegas was a dusty Old West frontier town.

TOP FIVE CITY LIFE BOOKS

- *Brothel: Mustang Ranch and Its Women* (2001) Alexa Albert's conflicted, disturbing and highly personalized account of the last days of Nevada's most famous cathouse.
- *Cult Vegas: The Weirdest! The Wildest! The Swingin'est Town on Earth* (2001) Mike Weatherford, an entertainment reporter for the *Las Vegas Review–Journal*, reveals all the offbeat trivia and celebrity gossip you could ever want, and then some.
- *Fabulous Las Vegas in the '50s: Glitz, Glamour & Games* (1999) This book, by Fred E Basten and Charles Phoenix, has loads of retro-modern photos, fun facts and nostalgic memorabilia.
- *Skin City: Uncovering the Las Vegas Sex Industry* (2004) A resident of 30 years, Jack Sheehan, interviews madams, strippers and XXX-film stars for this tell-all exposé.
- *The Last Honest Place in America: Paradise and Perdition in the New Las Vegas* (2005) A featherweight outsider, Marc Cooper, reflects on Sin City in a book that's as full of fluff and illusions as the city itself. Perfect poolside reading for a lazy afternoon.

SPORTS

This is a city of die-hard sports fans, and there are scores of race and sports books inside casinos to prove it. The problem is, there aren't any professional home teams to root for. Most of the betting action surrounds the national franchise teams, although UNLV college sports are big business. Monday night football is huge at bars all over town, and Vegas' most famous sportsperson is tennis champ Andre Agassi.

Everyone gets revved up for 'Fight Night,' too, when championship boxing matches are staged. Nascar weekends flood the Las Vegas Motor Speedway and the Strip. True to the town's ranching roots, pro rodeo events take place throughout the year. Or grab cheap tickets to a minor-league game played by baseball's Las Vegas 51s or hockey's Las Vegas Wranglers.

For more details on spectator sports in Las Vegas, turn to p162.

MEDIA

Most of the media in Las Vegas is spun toward tourists, from in-room advertorial TV channels to freely available glossy magazines and brochures promoting the casino industry. Even the *Las Vegas Review–Journal* local newspaper and the free weekly tabloids *CityLife* and *Las Vegas Weekly* don't ruffle many feathers. For more independent media, pick up a national newspaper like the *Los Angeles Times* or surf online. For more on local media, see p242.

ECONOMY & COSTS

Tourism and gambling drive the Las Vegas economy. That's no surprise given that most of the 37-million-plus tourists per year gamble away hundreds of dollars here. More than 50% of the city's workforce is employed in the service industry, mostly in minimum-wage jobs.

The city's economic stability fluctuates with the US economy. The worldwide travel decline after 9/11 hurt Las Vegas. Air travel plummeted. Hotel occupancy plunged. An estimated 15,000 casino workers lost their jobs, and tens of thousands more had their work schedules reduced. Recently, job growth in the Las Vegas metro area has been among the most robust in the nation.

When planning your trip to Las Vegas, take time to scout around for the best hotel

HOW MUCH?

Local in-room phone call	$1
Valet parking	Free (but tip $2)
US gallon of gas (liter of petrol)	$2.40 (63¢)
Small bottle of water	$2.50
Pint of local microbrew	$4
Souvenir Las Vegas T-shirt	$5
Average taxi ride on the Strip	$10
Typical club cover charge	$20
High-end hotel dinner buffet	$25
Cirque du Soleil ticket	$75 to $150

deals, especially if you're visiting on weekends or during a major special event. Airfare and accommodations take the biggest bite out of your budget, at least initially. Then all sorts of incidental expenses, whether a $5 cup of coffee, room-service champagne or a big poker buy-in that goes bust, will quickly max out your credit cards.

You can save money by shopping at discount pharmacies like Walgreens or CVS (p242) for everyday snacks and essentials, rather than buying them at hotel shops. When you're hungry, skip room service and head down to your casino hotel's 24-hour coffee shop. Know your financial limits before you start gambling, and stick to 'em. For tipping practices, see p244.

GOVERNMENT & POLITICS

Citizens of Las Vegas elect six council members and a mayor who make up the city council. The mayor is elected at large by all the voters of the city and each council member is elected from one of six wards. The mayor and council members serve four-year terms. A city manager, hired by the council, is responsible for day-to-day operations.

View of the Strip from Mandalay Bay (p62)

In 1999, in a major blow to official efforts to clean up Sin City's image, Las Vegas voters picked long-time criminal defense lawyer Oscar Goodman to be their mayor. Goodman, who gained fame defending mafia czars such as Meyer Lansky and portrayed himself in the movie *Casino,* caught voters' fancy with a populist platform that called for developers to pay fees to help solve city traffic and air pollution woes.

The alleged 'barrister to butchers,' as an editorial in the *Las Vegas Review–Journal* first described him, makes no effort to hide his past. Indeed, he loves to talk about the old days. As Lansky's attorney, Goodman got the mafia's financial genius dropped from a casino-skimming trial because of Lansky's failing health. In his defense, Goodman also devoted much of his practice to the poor and the dispossessed, often pro bono.

Overwhelmingly re-elected to a second term in 2003, Goodman is still enjoying enormous popularity. He frequently uses the mayoral pulpit for fiery comments on many issues, such as prostitution and the storage of nuclear waste at Yucca Mountain, that fall outside the purview of municipal government but are always on the minds of Las Vegans. Goodman is also a tireless proponent of the need to redevelop the urban downtown core.

ENVIRONMENT
For climate information and charts, turn to p237.

THE LAND
Las Vegas lies inside the 200,000-sq-mile Great Basin, a vast region that includes most of Nevada and many neighboring states. In the parched rain shadow of the Sierra Nevada mountains, it's called a 'basin' because rivers here drain into inland lakes, marshes, salt flats and sinks, not a sea. The geographic area of the Great Basin around the city is the 15,000-sq-mile Mojave Desert, which covers parts of southern Nevada, southeastern California, northwestern Arizona and southeastern Utah. The relatively flat city of Las Vegas (Spanish for 'the meadows') sits on natural springs in the middle of a valley that rises more than 2000ft above sea level and is surrounded by 10,000ft-plus mountain ranges for hundreds of miles.

AN ATOMIC FUTURE

The US government stopped underground nuclear explosions at the Nevada Test Site in 1992, but that hasn't meant the end of a possible nuclear future for state residents. In 1998, a US Department of Energy report recommended Yucca Mountain, near the test site and about 90 miles northwest of Las Vegas, as the best location for the nation's only long-term high-level nuclear waste repository.

Did we say long-term? The proposed site, which would eventually hold 77,000 tons of used reactor fuel from nuclear power plants across the nation, could remain deadly for 300,000 years. In that time, Earth could experience another ice age, and then Yucca Mountain, currently one of the driest and most remote places in the USA, would no longer be a desert.

And that's a problem. Scientists agree that water poses the greatest risk to radiation leakage at the site – a far more serious risk than earthquakes or volcanic eruptions. If groundwater seeps down and contacts the nuclear waste buried below the surface, it could carry radiation relatively quickly – in less than 50 years, some studies have found – into the underground water basin that flows through the tri-state countryside.

The Department of Energy acknowledges this risk, but maintains that the corrosion-resistant metal casks will last for at least 10,000 to 100,000 years, even if they get wet. Maybe so. However, no one is arguing that the containers won't deteriorate. And, once they do, the only thing keeping the radiation from spreading is the bone-dry mountain rock – so long as it stays dry. Would anyone care to predict the weather 200,000 years from now?

Not surprisingly, Nevada officials are fighting the proposed waste site tooth and nail. The problem is that US nuclear power plants already have enormous piles of spent fuel rods and radioactive waste that have to be put somewhere. Although the Yucca Mountain repository was approved by Congress, its opponents in Nevada, Utah, California and the Shoshone Nation have filed federal lawsuits aimed at stopping the project. Bureaucratic mismanagement, falsified scientific data and fraud by project employees have given environmentalists even more ammo for stalling the proposed dump.

Should it get the go-ahead, the Yucca Mountain repository would begin taking nuclear waste in 2010. Click to www.yuccamountain.org for updates. To learn more about Nevada's nuclear age, visit the **Atomic Testing Museum** (p87).

GREEN LAS VEGAS

Las Vegas is an environmentalist's nightmare.

Water usage is the chief concern. The Las Vegas Valley is expected to use its entire water supply by the year 2022. It presently shares the Colorado River with California, Arizona, Utah, New Mexico, Colorado and Wyoming, and none of the communities that currently take water from the river want to give up any of it. Las Vegas residents use, on average, more than 300 gallons of water per day; this figure includes the tremendous quantities of water used by casino hotels and golf courses. This situation is particularly alarming when you consider that Las Vegas is one of the fastest growing metro areas in the country.

Pollution is another big problem. Despite being the largest artificial lake in North America, Lake Mead is experiencing rising levels of water pollution. Air pollution is another unpopular subject in Las Vegas. The city is surrounded by mountains that trap hazardous particulates. Formerly, the view of those mountains was crystal clear on a sunny day; now most days the sky above Las Vegas has a dirty inversion layer that's occasionally so thick you can't even see the mountains. With average daily traffic and the number of takeoffs at McCarran International Airport on the rise, it looks a lot like LA.

URBAN PLANNING & DEVELOPMENT

The Las Vegas metro area contains some of the fastest-growing cities in the US, such as Henderson and North Las Vegas, with more than 5000 newcomers arriving every month. Every year or so it seems another casino-hotel megaresort with several thousand guestrooms opens. Vegas is currently experiencing a boom in high-rise residential condos that will take the city's skyline in a vertical direction. While the new housing supply is predicted to far outstrip demand, local officials still haven't solved the enormous challenges of traffic congestion, water conservation, and keeping water and air pollution at acceptable levels.

Arts &
Architecture

Arts & Architecture

If art imitates life, then Las Vegas must be a masterpiece, as it imitates just about everywhere else on earth. Better called the Great Impostor, Sin City has its ersatz Eiffel Tower, replica Egyptian tombs and temples, and Greek statuary copied from the masters. Meanwhile, critics have interpreted the city through their own lens. Auteurs, gonzo journalists and reality-TV producers have explored its seamy underbelly – and a few have even seen the city for what it really is. From fawning facades to birth narratives and from absurdly romantic to awfully tacky, Las Vegas obligingly lives up to its reputations, both devilish and angelic. Digging down through these obfuscating, larger-than-life images, you'll find a tight-knit, creative local arts and music scene, though. For more on entertainment, turn to p142.

CINEMA & TV

Hollywood raves about Sin City, which is no surprise when Las Vegas is just four hours by car from Los Angeles. Maybe it's the sheer cinematic quality of the Strip, which looks like a giant movie set, and its close proximity to vast stretches of empty desert. Or perhaps it's because screenwriters can push their limits in a city where absolutely anything seems possible, and every side of America can be shown. Not coincidentally, the world's largest motion-picture-industry convention, ShoWest, is held in Las Vegas every year.

More than 130 motion pictures have been filmed in and around the valley since 1932, when director John Ford made *Airmail*, a routine story of pioneer airmail pilots. Some movies shot in or near Las Vegas function as time capsules of this ever-changing place, including *Wild Is the Wind* (1957), with a Nina Simone soundtrack; *The Professionals* (1966), partly shot in Valley of Fire State Park (p212); *The Gauntlet* (1977), directed by Clint Eastwood; and Sydney Pollack's *The Electric Horseman* (1979), with Robert Redford as a washed-up rodeo star and Jane Fonda as a pill-popping reporter. Even *Pay It Forward* (2000), a sentimental mash-up of Kevin Spacey and Helen Hunt, tells home truths about Las Vegas in spite of itself. Most recently, the high-stakes poker flick *Lucky You* (2005), with Robert Duvall and Drew Barrymore as a struggling singer, was filmed on location here.

The **Nevada Film Office** (☎ 877-638-3456; www.nevadafilm.com) liaises with more than 600 film and TV projects each year. Even with profits from casino filming locations yet to be disclosed, Las Vegas has earned more than a billion dollars from film, a big incentive to diversify the economy beyond tourism and gambling. Popular locations, at least historically, have been the **Stardust** (p78) and **Riviera** (p76) casino hotels on the North Strip, as well as downtown's **Fremont Street** (p79) for its vintage gambling halls. The glitterati of

---

WHEN THE LIGHTS WENT OUT

Casino chieftains have turned off their marquee lights on only seven occasions so far. The first was in 1963, following the assassination of President John F Kennedy, but almost every instance since then has been to honor famous stage performers.

The casinos remained open for business when Sammy Davis Jr died of throat cancer on May 16, 1990, but their marquee lights were shut off in unison for 10 minutes. Lights were dimmed again for two more Rat Pack brothers – when Dean Martin succumbed to acute respiratory failure on December 25, 1995, and after Frank Sinatra was silenced by a heart attack on May 14, 1998. The Strip also went dark when legendary comedian George Burns passed away after his 100th birthday in 1996.

In the 21st century, Strip casinos dimmed their lights after the tragic 9/11 attacks on the World Trade Center in New York City and the Pentagon in Washington, DC. The most recent moment of darkness came in 2004, when former US president Ronald Reagan died. The former Hollywood actor performed in a song-and-dance show at the Last Frontier on the Strip in the 1950s.

Hollywood show up every summer for **CineVegas** (p10), a rising star among film festivals, while Boulder City's quirky, independent **Dam Short Film Festival** (www.damshortfilm.org) takes place in February.

Reality TV hit Las Vegas like an epidemic. First, there was MTV's *Real World: Las Vegas*, where a group of painfully untalented twentysomethings cavorted in a penthouse at the **Palms** (p90); the suite was custom-built for the show by casino owner George Maloof as a wildly successful marketing ploy. When Internet wunderkinds Tim Poster and Tom Breitling bought downtown's **Golden Nugget** (p83), they inked a deal with the Fox network and *Survivor* producer Mark Burnett to make *Casino*, in which America followed the travails of Canadian lounge singer Matt Dusk. Then came *The Entertainer*, a cross between *American Idol* and *The Apprentice*, but starring genial Wayne Newton instead of grumpy Trump. *American Casino*, filmed at **Green Valley Ranch** (p202), took a macabre turn when a casino executive died of a drug overdose, after which A&E still added *Caesars 24/7* to its reality TV lineup. Among the few TV dramas set here, *CSI: Crime Scene Investigation* is the most famous, with a cast of characters that includes a former stripper, a gambling addict and a scientist who loves to ride New York–New York's roller coaster.

LITERATURE

'Should I go to heaven, give me…a vaulting red-walled casino with bright lights, bring on horned devils as dealers. Let there be a Pit Boss in the Sky who will give me unlimited credit…[and] decree that the Player have for all eternity, an Edge against the House.'

– Mario Puzo, *Inside Las Vegas*

The few famous literary works set in Las Vegas have been turned into films already. Most books about the city or by Las Vegans tend to focus on one of two topics: beating the casinos at their own game or doing Vegas on a dime.

Gonzo journalist Hunter S Thompson satirically recounts his 1971 trip to cover the Mint 400 off-road biker race in *Fear and Loathing in Las Vegas*, a dope-addled pursuit of the broken-down American dream, which takes Thompson and his partners in crime from the Flamingo to the middle of the Mojave Desert. This book defined the counterculture of its day and, in many minds, is the only major literary work linked to the city. Tom Wolfe's *Kandy-Kolored Tangerine-Flaked Streamline Baby* probes the swinging '60s, and some say its fantastically titled essay on Vegas was a precursor to *Fear and Loathing*.

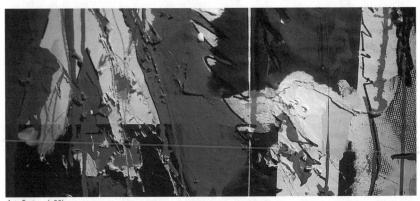

Arts Factory (p80)

TOP 20 VEGAS FILMS

Here's a look at some of the most famous and infamous movies featuring Sin City.

Love, Vegas-Style

Viva Las Vegas (1964) Elvis Presley's the guitar-playin' race-car driver and redheaded Ann-Margret is the sexy dancer. Can Elvis win the race and the girl? Of course! But only after a few musical numbers. Watch for the Sy Devore suit worn by the King poolside.

Leaving Las Vegas (1995) Nicolas Cage plays an alcoholic bent on drinking himself to death in Vegas, and Elisabeth Shue is the victimized prostitute who tries to save his skin in this disturbingly violent yet brilliant movie.

Honeymoon in Vegas (1992) Nicolas Cage must love this town. Here, he's a detective on the brink of losing his bride, Sarah Jessica Parker, to sleazy Vegas mobster James Caan. The climax of this engaging farce features the Flying Elvi.

Swingers (1996) With the huzzah of 'Vegas, baby!', this film starred in and written by Jon Favreau is about hipsters from Los Angeles looking for love. The opening features the Stardust's famous sign, but interiors were shot at downtown's Fremont casino hotel.

The Cooler (2003) William H Macy plays a no-luck gambler who falls in love with a cocktail waitress and pisses off casino owner Alec Baldwin. Mostly filmed in Reno.

Betting the Farm

Rain Man (1988) In an Oscar winner directed by Barry Levinson, Tom Cruise takes his autistic savant brother (Dustin Hoffman) on a cross-country road trip that ends with a triumphant round of cards at Caesars Palace.

Ocean's 11 (1960) This is the movie that gave birth to the Rat Pack: Frank Sinatra, Sammy Davis Jr, Dean Martin, Peter Lawford, Joey Bishop and friends attempt to rob five casinos at once. Though overlong and sometimes dull, it's still a quintessential Vegas film, plus the bonus DVD features are ace. Filmed at the Sands and Riviera.

Ocean's Eleven (2001) This Stephen Soderbergh remake features a host of big-name actors, including George Clooney, Matt Damon, Brad Pitt, Andy Garcia and Julia Roberts, but it's almost as monotonous as the first. The Bellagio steals the scene.

Lost in America (1985) This hilarious film starring Albert Brooks, who also wrote and directed it, is about a middle-class couple looking to escape their yuppie lifestyle, only to lose their nest egg at the Desert Inn after driving a Winnebago across America.

Vegas Vacation (1997) The epitome of bad taste, this Chevy Chase romp has a few redeeming moments: Wayne Newton trying to steal away Mrs Griswold,

Siegfried and Roy on stage at the Mirage, and the comically deadpan Hoover Dam tour guide.

Indecent Proposal (1993) High roller Robert Redford offers $1 million to a desperate married couple (Demi Moore and Woody Harrelson) if the wife will agree to a romantic tryst with him. This wishy-washy blockbuster was filmed partly at the Las Vegas Hilton.

Mobsters & More Bad Guys (and Girls)

The Godfather (1972) There's a brief Vegas interlude in this Oscar-winning tale of an East Coast mafia family, based on the book written by self-admitted degenerate gambler Mario Puzo.

Bugsy (1991) Another Barry Levinson film, starring Warren Beatty and Annette Bening, it takes great pains to re-create the original Flamingo, but glosses over the background of modern Las Vegas and gangster Benjamin 'Bugsy' Siegel.

Casino (1995) This Martin Scorsese film follows casino chief Robert De Niro as Las Vegas changes from a mob-run heaven to a family-fun theme park. Sharon Stone shines amid a heavyweight cast, and Mayor Oscar Goodman portrays himself as a mob lawyer.

Diamonds Are Forever (1971) – Sean Connery is up to his usual tricks and sexual hijinks as Agent 007 in this dull James Bond comic-book adventure, which has retro scenes in Circus Circus and the Las Vegas Hilton, and a car chase down Fremont Street.

Showgirls (1995) – Voted the worst movie ever made about Vegas, it's so untrue-to-life that Sin City's real exotic dancers and showgirls still complain that this film was ever made (mostly shot in Cheetah's strip club).

Weird & Wacky Las Vegas

Mars Attacks! (1996) Martians attack Earth in this Tim Burton farce, and Sin City is a prime target. Watch Jack Nicholson, Tom Jones and a bevy of Vegas oddballs fend for their lives. The chase includes shots of the sign graveyard of the Neon Museum.

Fear and Loathing in Las Vegas (1998) This hallucinogenic Terry Gilliam flick starring Johnny Depp and Benicio Del Toro actually helps the Hunter S Thompson book make sense. Most filming was done at the Stardust and the Riviera instead of at the Flamingo.

The Amazing Colossal Man (1957) In this camp thriller, a man turned into a giant by a nuclear explosion terrorizes Vegas. Extremely silly, but there's footage of the Strip and Hoover Dam.

3000 Miles to Graceland (2001) Ex-cons Kurt Russell and Kevin Costner rob the Riviera during an Elvis convention. It's really a test of your tolerance for bad taste and brutality.

From the hard-bitten author of the *Godfather*, Mario Puzo's *Inside Las Vegas* is a razor-sharp, if dated, look at what makes Sin City tick from a self-admitted degenerate gambler's perspective. It's full of tough-guy ruminations on showgirls, slot-playing grannies and the world of casino pit bosses in the '70s. It also has some hilarious vintage photos that alone are worth this coffee-table book's weight in casino chips.

Nicholas Pileggi's *Casino: Love and Honor in Las Vegas* tracks the true-crime story of the Chicago mafia's move to take over Vegas. It features accounts of bribery, book-making, mistresses and shootings in the dead of night – all of which led into a downward spiral to disaster. Martin Scorsese made it into a movie, just as he did for *Goodfellas,* based on another real-life page-turner by this same New York crime reporter, *Wiseguy: Life in a Mafia Family.*

The landmark 1995 anthology *Literary Las Vegas: The Best Writing about America's Most Fabulous City,* edited by Mike Tronnes, comprises some two dozen essays and short stories spanning 40 years, from atomic bomb–viewing picnics to Joan Didion on the wedding-chapel industry. Scores of pulpy biographies have been written about the gangsters, movie stars and entertainers who pushed this dusty Nevada town into the national spotlight, from Bugsy Siegel to the Rat Pack to Elvis and beyond.

MUSIC

To many people in Las Vegas, singers like Frank Sinatra (aka 'The Chairman') and his Rat Pack pals built this town. For years they weren't merely legendary headliners; they were also the darlings of gossip columnists from Los Angeles to New York, and their all-night partying and tumultuous lives entertained millions of readers daily. Their antics in Las Vegas brought adoring fans, especially dames, movie stars and politicians, by the planeload.

Today, Joey Bishop is the only surviving member of the Rat Pack, and many of the other legendary headliners who built Vegas – Elvis among them – are no longer entertaining crowds here on Earth. Even 'Mr Las Vegas' himself, Wayne Newton, has opted out of a lifetime contract at the Stardust.

But Las Vegas continues to book legendary entertainers. Rock 'n' roll deities appear at the M-Bay's **House of Blues** (p156), the Hard Rock's **The Joint** (p157) and other state-of-the-art venues (p157). Country music superstars? Big-band sounds? Jazz and blues? Outrageous karaoke? Las Vegas has got all that, too. The **UNLV Performing Arts Center** (p159) is a stop for hundreds of touring acts each year, from classical orchestras to experimental composers to world music performers.

Most of the tuneful talent has traditionally been imported. While a few breakthrough local rock bands have catapulted onto the national scene, like the neo-punk Killers, most of these successes had to leave Vegas to make it happen, as did electronica masters the Crystal Method. The local live-music scene is practically underground, as the venues for local bands come and go (p155). For the lowdown on Sin City's newest sounds, tune into at 92.3FM (KOMP) for Laurie Steele's long-running 'Homegrown Show,' which showcases local bands from 10pm till midnight on Sundays, or listen online at www.yourlocalscene.com.

TOP FIVE VINTAGE VEGAS TRACKS

- 'Luck Be a Lady,' as recorded by Frank Sinatra
- 'You're Nobody till Somebody Loves You,' as recorded by Dean Martin
- 'Viva Las Vegas,' as recorded by Elvis Presley
- 'I've Got You under My Skin,' as recorded by Keely Smith & Louis Prima
- 'Ace in the Hole,' as recorded by Bobby Darin

…or just about anything from Capitol Records' *The Rat Pack: Live at the Sands* album or the *Live from Las Vegas* series. For a red-light burlesque groove, the rare *Las Vegas Grind* series from Crypt Records (www.cryptrecords.com) should satisfy all your bad-girl urges.

VISUAL ARTS

Touring masterpieces are displayed at the Venetian's **Guggenheim Hermitage** (p58), designed by Dutch architect Rem Koolhaas. Just up the Strip at **Wynn** (p59), casino impresario Steve Wynn will soon install his multimillion-dollar private collection of art, previously at the

WHERE HAVE ALL THE LOUNGE LIZARDS GONE?

The heyday of Las Vegas lounge acts was the 1950s and early '60s, when Rat Pack singers and their imitators attracted big gamblers, who would pack the casinos. In fact, the famous 'Summit' shows with Frank, Dean, Sammy, Peter and Joey went on even during the filming of the original *Ocean's 11*. It was during those days that this two-bit Nevada railroad town was transformed into an entertainment mecca.

Sure, there were some flops, even back then: Elvis' first performance at the New Frontier in 1956 barely registered. But casino showrooms were still where it was at. People like **Wayne Newton** (p147) have kept the older traditions going, but quality lounge acts are a rarity these days. So, what happened? In the late '60s, casinos began knocking down the showroom walls to keep them open to the casino, and the stars left after they realized that the frenetically gambling audiences were now only half paying attention.

A handful of showrooms have survived into the 21st century, such as the Stardust's **Starlight Lounge** (p156) and the Sahara's **Casbar Theatre Lounge** (p155). You can occasionally catch crooners like Tony Bennett at the Golden Nugget's **Theatre Ballroom** (p157). Some of the local musicians from the fabulous '50s and '60s are still around, too; they play sets some nights at the **Bootlegger Bistro** (p155), south of the Strip. A few casino hotels are inventing new lounge sounds, too, like at New York–New York's **Big Apple Bar** (p134) and the Golden Nugget's **Oasis Lounge** (p137). Also look out for the cheesiest lounge singer ever to strut the Strip, Mr Cook E Jarr, at Harrah's **Carnaval Court** (p131).

Bellagio. Or take a free peek inside Mandalay Bay's **House of Blues** restaurant (p116), where outsider folk art hangs on the walls, and **THEhotel** (p193), which has Richard Serra artworks in the lobby.

But the Strip doesn't hold all the cards when it comes to art in Las Vegas. There are dozens of private and nonprofit galleries spread across the valley. South of downtown, the **Arts Factory** (p80) is a landmark of the Gateway Arts District. Drop by on 'First Fridays' (p81) for gallery openings, live music and more. North of downtown, the city-sponsored **Reed Whipple Cultural Center** (p81) has free temporary exhibitions by local artists. So does the **POST Modern** (p86), a cultural center inside a former US post office, just off Fremont Street. Contemporary artists influenced by the Southwest's stark desert landscape exhibit at the $20-million **Las Vegas Art Museum** (p92), an architectural oasis in the suburb of Summerlin, where funding for the arts is more readily available.

Kitschy Las Vegas is also fertile ground for pop art. The **UNLV Performing Arts Center** (p159) has a monumental piece called *The Flashlight* by Claes Oldenburg – a jet-black, three-story-tall flashlight pointed oddly into the ground just outside the building. Of course, casino hotels like Caesars Palace and the Luxor have their unintentionally pop-art copies of sculptural icons such as *Venus de Milo* and the Sphinx, which we think Andy Warhol would've loved, too.

ARCHITECTURE

Buildings come in all sizes, shapes and designs in the city of cash and flash, where 'Pardon Our Dust' signs greet visitors all over town. Ongoing blockbuster construction projects include the $1.4-billion Encore next to Wynn and the $1.6-billion Palazzo next to the Venetian. Sans irony, bankrupt casino owner Donald Trump is raising a megabucks 64-story hotel-condo tower near the New Frontier, while his ex-wife Ivana is rumored to be lending her name to a new condo high-rise across from the Sahara that will be nine stories taller. Straight out of Miami Beach, Fontainebleau is set to break ground on a Florida-themed casino hotel just north of the Riviera. Thanks to the opening of Wynn, the direction of development on the Strip is now optimistically headed northward.

But Las Vegas doesn't have any masterpieces of architecture per se. Monoliths along the Strip celebrate just about every metropolis and epoch, except modern-day Nevada. There is a faux pyramid of ancient Egypt at the Luxor, miniature replicas of the famous high-rises of the Big Apple at New York–New York, and an Eiffel Tower at Paris–Las Vegas, all of which you can see in a day on one of the walking tours in this book (p94). The predominant architectural style has been branded with the labels expressionist modern, post-modern, populist, symbolic, iconographic, mimetic, neo-constructivist and simply vulgar. Pure spectacle is often the goal, and often buildings are not built to last. Like, for instance, the now-demolished Glass Pool Inn, which once stood south of the Strip, welcoming dusty desert travelers with its bizarre vision of an above-ground, glassed-in, peekaboo swimming pool.

But what's wrong with architecture that people just love to look at? That was the argument of the ground-breaking 1972 book *Learning from Las Vegas: The Forgotten Symbolism of American Architectural Form* by Robert Venturi and others. The irreverent and playful Venturi, a Pritzker Prize–winning architect from the East Coast, is often quoted as saying, 'Less is a bore.' The architectural firm he runs with his wife, Denise Scott Brown, has worked on projects ranging from Disney World to the Seattle Museum of Art (check out their engaging online portfolio at www.vsba.com). Their classic book is now available in a revised version updated in 1993. That same year, Californian architectural critic Alan Hess published *Viva Las Vegas: After Hours Architecture*, which explores how Sin City architecturally represents modern America.

Some of the most innovative architecture can be seen at branches of the Clark County Public Library. Many of these buildings look as though they arose from the encircling desert environment, but open up inside to naturally lit public spaces with glorious atriums, skylights, panoramic windows and other elements only rarely seen in Vegas, where casinos are designed to shut out the sun. For lovers of modern design, the 1944 **Huntridge Theatre** (1208 E Charleston Blvd), once owned by movie stars Irene Dunn and Loretta Young, is a splendid example of Streamline Moderne architecture, a style of clean, austere lines born in the 1930s. It is the only full-scale art-deco structure in the city. However, all you have to do is take a quick ride outside the city limits, cruising by the mid-century modern motels of **Boulder City** (p210), to reach that art-deco masterpiece of the desert, **Hoover Dam** (p209). Before going

TOP FIVE IMITATION BUILDINGS ON THE STRIP

- **Luxor** (p61) The best views of the pyramid are from the tram station, but go inside to see the Temple of Ramses II.
- **New York–New York** (p64) You can walk across Brooklyn Bridge in mere minutes here.
- **Stratosphere Tower** (p79) The tower is the highest structure in the USA west of the Mississippi River; it looks a lot like Seattle's Space Needle.
- **Paris–Las Vegas** (p57) This proudly imitates everything from the Arc de Triomphe to the opera house to the Hotel de Ville.
- **Venetian** (p58) A real canal with gondoliers runs through the Venetian, while its Rialto Bridge has a moving walkway.

TOP FIVE SPOTS FOR NEON

Las Vegas didn't invent neon signage – a Frenchman named Georges Claude did before this town was even founded – but today there are more than a dozen miles of neon tubing in the city. Many of the most famous casino hotel signs were made by Utah's Young Electric Sign Company (www.yesco.com), including 75ft-tall Vegas Vic, who used to wave to railroad passengers from his perch in downtown's Glitter Gulch, and the **Welcome to Fabulous Las Vegas sign** (p62), which still stands south of the Strip.

Elsewhere, see Sin City's biggest neon spectaculars with your own eyes:

- Outside the Stardust, Riviera and Circus Circus on the **North Strip** (p75)
- Fanning out from the blindingly bright Flamingo on the **Center Strip** (p49)
- Downtown in Fremont Street's **Glitter Gulch** (p79) – don't miss the Neonopolis, Vegas Vic and Vegas Vickie (aka Sassy Sally)
- The **Neon Museum's sign graveyard** (p84), a short drive north of downtown
- Along the main drag in **Boulder City** (p210), where some vintage neon signs have been around almost as long as Hoover Dam itself

For a virtual visit to the Strip after dark, browse photos from UNLV's documentary neon survey at http://gaming.unlv.edu/v_museum/neon_survey/.

HERE TODAY, GONE TOMORROW

Structures that predate 1960 cling to Las Vegas like a trailer park during a tornado. Historic buildings are regularly blown to pieces with dynamite or slammed apart by wrecking balls, all to make way for new casino megaresorts and condo high-rises.

Much like mushroom cloud–viewing parties during Nevada's atomic age, modern-day implosions have been an excuse to party on the Strip. Out with a bang, not a whimper, is the motto. Everyone is so eager to know what's next on the chopping block, in fact, that there are websites devoted entirely to Las Vegas casino 'death watches.' Fans can buy videos of famous implosions from decades past and learn all about the tricky technical matters requiring hundreds of pounds of explosives.

But the ghosts of casinos past still linger, and not only in the minds of pop-culture historians. Las Vegans and visitors alike still wax nostalgic about 1950s casino hotels that have bitten the dust, including the Rat Pack–era Sands (where the Venetian now stands); the Dunes, which stirred things up with Vegas' first topless showgirls (on the site of the Bellagio's Lake Como); and the Desert Inn, where Howard Hughes hid for years (demolished in 2000 to make way for Wynn).

You can see and even buy memorabilia pieces from legendary casino hotels at the **Lost Vegas Historic Gambling Museum** (p178), which also sells videos of how they all went ka-boom.

over Railroad Pass, stop off en route at the **Clark County Museum** (p91), a walk-through outdoor repository of Nevada architecture from frontier days of the late 19th century through the first half of the 20th century. To see reconstructions of unusual buildings from the Nevada Test Site, visit the **Atomic Testing Museum** (p87).

Perhaps the most celebrated architect of the American Southwest was Mary Jane Colter (1869–1958), who designed the grand railroad hotels called Harvey Houses on **Route 66** (p217). Colter also created the rustic, archetypal national-park style that can be seen today on the Grand Canyon's **South Rim** (p216), especially in well-preserved Grand Canyon Village.

History

History

What history, you ask. Unlike the rest of the ruin-laden Southwest, traces of Las Vegas' early history are scarce. Native Americans inhabited the valley, the last part of the country to be penetrated by Anglos, for almost a millennium before the Spanish Trail was blazed through. And, contrary to Hollywood legend, colorful characters have sought their fortunes here in Sin City both before *and* after celebrated gangster Benjamin 'Bugsy' Siegel opened the Flamingo casino hotel in 1946.

THE RECENT PAST

The 1990s saw the boom on the Strip get even bigger. **Excalibur** (p61), a giant medieval castle–themed casino hotel complete with moat and staffed with valiant knights and fair damsels, ushered in the decade with trumpets blaring. The **MGM Grand** (p63) reappeared, reclaiming its status as the largest hotel in the world. The same year, the Luxor's black pyramid rose from the desert, and Treasure Island launched its pirate battle on the Strip. Even downtown started reaching for the stars with its canopied **Fremont Street Experience** (p82) in 1995.

Even more impressive were the later arrivals: **Stratosphere Tower** (p79), the tallest building in the western United States; **Bellagio** (p51), one of the most opulent hotels in the world, built on the site of the 1950s Dunes; **Mandalay Bay** (p62), which has taken 'bundling' into new territory with gourmet restaurants and boutique hotels; the **Venetian** (p58), replete with canals and splendid Italian architecture, and **Paris–Las Vegas** (p57), home to an Eiffel Tower and a host of fine French restaurants.

The 21st century started off with a bang, as Steve Wynn blew up the vintage Desert Inn (p26), then spent five years crafting his new resort, **Wynn** (p59). It opened in 2005, just as Las Vegas celebrated its centennial. On the darker side of local goings-on, the trial over the murder of Ted Binion, son of legendary casino owner and high-stakes gambler Benny Binion (see p81), began all over again after the conviction of Ted's exotic-dancer girlfriend and her lover was overturned in 2000.

Las Vegas today boasts all but a few of the world's 20 biggest hotels, attracts more than 37-million visitors each year and rakes in an annual gaming revenue exceeding $5 billion (that's almost $10,000 every 60 seconds!). A blushing bride and groom say 'I do' every five minutes, on average, in this city. And at any time of day or night, you can get a divorce, rent

---

TOP FIVE HISTORY BOOKS

- *Neon Metropolis: How Las Vegas Started the 21st Century* (2002) A professor from the University of Nevada, Las Vegas, Hal Rothman, deconstructs all the successes and failures of Sin City.
- *Rat Pack Confidential: Frank, Dean, Sammy, Peter, Joey and the Last Great Show Biz Party* (1999) Shawn Levy's book echoes the hip stylings of the era, and dishes all the dirt.
- *Running Scared: The Life and Treacherous Times of Las Vegas Casino King Steve Wynn* (1995) Who can resist this racy book written by John L Smith once you know Wynn sued and bankrupted the publisher? See also opposite.
- *The First 100: Portraits of Men and Women Who Shaped Las Vegas* (2000) AD Hopkins and KJ Evans' book offers historical profiles, from early pioneers to Bugsy to Steve Wynn. These are available online at www.1st100.com.
- *The Money and the Power: The Making of Las Vegas and Its Hold on America* (2002) A lyrical, haunting investigation of the city's underbelly by Sally Denton and Roger Morris. Think the mobsters have left town and Vegas has been Disneyfied? Think again.

TIMELINE	1100 AD	1855
	Southern Paiute people begin to inhabit the Las Vegas Valley on a seasonal basis	Mormon missionaries arrive, build a fort, then abandon it just two years later

a date, hire a stretch limo or strike a jackpot. There's no place in the world like Las Vegas, and no city even pretending to be.

FROM THE BEGINNING
PREHISTORY TO THE PAIUTES

It was almost 1000 years ago that the Southern Paiutes followed the Colorado River across the jutting peaks of the Black Mountains and down into the Las Vegas Valley. The tribe belonged to the Uzo-Aztecan language family, among whom are the better known Shoshone Nation, whose territory included parts of northeastern Nevada and southeastern California (p224).

The Paiutes seasonally camped around the natural-springs oasis (p91) on which the city stands today. Indigenous to the desert, they roamed the Mojave, harvesting seeds, roots and berries, and hunting wild game such as rattlesnake, elk, deer and

Comstock Lode monument (p31), Virginia City

antelope, and practiced flood-plain farming. To protect their skin against the blistering sun, they applied red paint to their bodies; to insulate their feet from the broiling earth, they wore yucca-fiber sandals.

In the unforgiving desert, the Paiutes not only endured, but advanced as a culture. They adhered to certain practices without exception. It was believed that one couldn't enter the afterlife without ear piercings, and facial tattoos were favored. Although marriage ceremonies were not very intricate, funerals lasted for days as the corpse was cremated or buried in a cave, precious animals were sacrificed and families fled their homes forever.

WYNN: THAT GUY JUST CAN'T LOSE

You might as well call him the man with the golden touch, even if Steve Wynn doesn't exactly look like the evil mastermind from a Bond movie.

Wynn started visiting Vegas in the 1950s with his dad, a bingo-parlor owner who loved to gamble at the Flamingo and the Sands. After marrying Miss Miami Beach and graduating from the titans-of-business training ground of the University of Pennsylvania, the younger Wynn sank money into the **New Frontier** (p76), which was then bought out by billionaire Howard Hughes (p33). After some more 'flipper' land deals, Wynn assumed enough stock to insinuate himself into Downtown's **Golden Nugget** (p83), which he transformed into a multimillion-dollar moneymaker.

Moving over to Atlantic City next, he honed his skills at scoring big with living legends (he hired Frank Sinatra, for example) and seducing talent away from nearby casino hotels. When Wynn refocused his attention on the Strip, it was to build the miraculous **Mirage** (p54), which was financed mainly with junk bonds, and was forced to make a million dollars a day from the time it opened. Four years later, his daughter Kevin was kidnapped, but, after Wynn paid a handsome $1.45-million ransom, she was returned at McCarran airport physically unharmed. Wynn just kept going, opening the high-falutin' **Bellagio** (p51) with $300 million worth of art from his personal collection. He sold both of his megaresorts to business rival **MGM Grand** (p63) in 2000, paving the way for his newest creation, the vainglorious **Wynn** (p59).

What's next? Nobody knows, but whatever it is, it'll probably be what pundits like to call a Wynn-win proposition.

1905	1920
Railroad between Los Angeles and Salt Lake City finished; city of Las Vegas founded beside the tracks	Las Vegas' first airport opens; passenger services to Salt Lake City and Los Angeles begin soon afterward

Just how forbidding was the Paiutes' territory? The Spanish, who were the first Europeans to claim jurisdiction over Nevada, skirted this region during their extensive exploration of North America in the 16th and 17th centuries. They were content to leave sections of their 'domain' uncharted, calling the blank space on their maps the 'Northern Mystery.' Despite its proximity to well-trodden Mexico and California, the valley was the final area of the USA to be penetrated by white settlers.

TRAILBLAZERS, TRAPPERS & TRADERS

Except for infrequent raids by Navajo and Ute slave traders during the 18th century, the Southern Paiutes lived a peaceful if arduous existence around the Las Vegas Valley for more than 750 years. Their undoing as the dominant people of the region began with the arrival of Europeans.

During the 1820s anybody who was anybody in Europe wore a beaver-pelt hat, while a secretion from the animal's musk glands was thought to be a cure-all, and American fur traders went to extreme lengths to meet the demand. One of those traders was Jedediah Smith, who abandoned his usual stomping grounds to blaze a trail toward the Pacific Ocean. Leaving what is now Utah by the Virgin River, he became one of the first Europeans to set foot in present-day Nevada. Smith also opened up much of the Spanish Trail later used by traders journeying between Santa Fe and Los Angeles. Much of the trail, which lasted from 1830 until the 20th century, was paved over to become freeway I-15.

Most of the people who ventured into the 'Northern Mystery' were traders. Some were settlers anxious to get to California, and all were looking for greener pastures of one kind or another. These Las Vegas had in abundance, and travelers' diaries from the time describe lush, spring-fed *las vegas* (Spanish for 'the meadows') that, along with cottonwood and willow trees, provided grazing and much-needed shade for the caravans. In 1829 Rafael Rivera, a scout for a Mexican trading expedition, was the first to discover a spring in this valley.

Among the most celebrated travelers on the Spanish Trail was John C Fremont, an army officer who spent several years exploring and mapping the area around Las Vegas after 1845. Downtown's main artery, Fremont St, today bears his name. When California gold was discovered in 1849, the Spanish Trail was flooded by rough-and-tumble miners, who then quickly abandoned it in favor of more direct east–west routes.

MORMONS ON A MISSION

Amid the hard-scrabble legions of miners was a group of men hell-bent on doing God's work in Indian country. These were Mormons, sent from Salt Lake City on May 10, 1855, by leader Brigham Young to colonize the expanding state of Deseret, as Mormons called their spiritual homeland. The faithful were to help make secure a string of settlements that church leaders dreamed would stretch all the way from Utah to the Pacific Ocean.

The young missionaries kissed their families goodbye and set out on the Mormon Trail, also used by traders between Salt Lake City and California. To keep the Paiutes 'in check,' Young instructed the missionaries to convert them to Mormonism. Sensibly, the first order of business was planting crops and building a fort, the remains of which still stand (p86). The Mormon settlers then caught mining fever, thinking that Potosi Mountain could bring forth riches of silver. They offered the Paiutes only a little clothing and food in exchange for digging thousands of pounds of ore out of the mountain. The Native Americans hauled only one load of rock on their backs before they realized they had been fooled.

A power struggle developed between two church officers, William Bringhurst and Nathaniel Jones. Bringhurst was among the original colonists, whereas Jones had been dispatched from Salt Lake City after Brigham Young was informed about the possible riches in the mines. Bringhurst didn't want to relinquish control and dissension arose within the

1931	1935
Nevada legalizes casino gambling and drops the state's divorce residency requirement to six weeks	Boulder (later Hoover) Dam, once the world's tallest, completed ahead of schedule

ranks of the missionaries. After violence broke out, the Mormons lost credibility with the people they had hoped to evangelize.

Then came the news that Young had decided to excommunicate Bringhurst. A handful of missionaries had begun mining the silver themselves, but the work was back-breaking and the heat intolerable; Jones abandoned the mine and returned to Salt Lake City. Young closed the mission in February 1857, less than two years after it was established. Although the Mormons failed in all of their objectives, they paved the way for future non-Native settlement of southern Nevada.

THE SILVER STATE & A GOLDEN SPIKE

In 1859, the richest vein of silver ever discovered in the USA, the Comstock Lode, was struck at Virginia City in northern Nevada. Many gold miners en route to California via the Spanish Trail heard about both the lode and also the silver in Potosi Mountain as they passed through Las Vegas. During 1860 secular miners expertly worked the mountain, extracting so much silver that when they headed back to Los Angeles (LA) for provisions and showed off huge chunks of ore they fueled even more excitement about the mine. Soon dozens of miners were arriving every day at Potosi. Some got rich. Most did poorly. A few took to farming in Las Vegas Valley afterward.

The Potosi silver boom was over by late 1861. After the beginning of the Civil War the same year, the Paiutes once again had the valley to themselves, only interrupted by military expeditions. When peace arrived in 1865, a miner named Octavius Decatur Gass descended on the old Mormon fort and replanted the fertile fields. The resulting 2000-acre Las Vegas Ranch flourished for the rest of the century, with travelers paying for the privilege of stopping overnight by the oasis; Gass' success encouraged other settlers to stake claims in the valley.

No railroads crossed southern Nevada in 1900, but plans had been made to link Los Angeles and Salt Lake City by rail, with a stop in Las Vegas. In January 1905, the final spike, a golden one, was driven into the line and train service commenced. By this time, Las Vegas was more than just a ranch ringed by cacti and barren foothills. A post office had opened, as had a newspaper office, a general store and a hotel.

During the winter of 1904–05, 'sooners' (early arrivals) shivered in their canvas tents by the river, waiting for housing lots to go on sale. On May 15, 1905, the railroad company finally put the town on the auction block. During two frenzied days, local settlers and real-estate speculators from LA and the East Coast bid for the land, and the barren lots sold for twice to 10 times their original price. The railroad company made a killing on the town site, which sprawled outward from the corner of Fremont and Main downtown, near today's **Plaza casino hotel** (p86).

As the dust settled, the city of Las Vegas was officially founded as miners' burros (pack donkeys) ran amok on the streets. By the start of WWI, ranches and small farms flourished throughout the valley, and the Downtown area was rapidly developing. Sin also took root in the infamous red-light district known as Block 16, located on First St, just north of Fremont St between Ogden and Stewart Aves. Home to gambling, booze and prostitution, this row of saloons, with their makeshift 'cribs' out back, survived Nevada's 1911 ban on gambling and the supposedly 'dry' years of Prohibition.

THE BEST TOWN BY A DAMSITE

Prosperity, or at least opportunity, soon embraced everyone – except the Paiutes, that is. Unable to speak English and pressured into giving up their land, the Native Americans withdrew from the Las Vegas Valley. Today, most Paiutes live in reservations scattered across the state – all of which would easily fit within the Nevada Test Site, a desert area used by the US Air Force for weapons testing.

1946	1950
Mobster Benjamin 'Bugsy' Siegel opens the Flamingo hotel	The lavish Desert Inn opens on the Strip, heralding the heyday of Las Vegas (aka the 'Fabulous Fifties')

Many small American cities managed to duck the socioeconomic bullets that struck the US during WWI, but few escaped the country's Great Depression, which began with an unprecedented stock-market crash in 1929. One of the lucky cities was Las Vegas, thanks to **Boulder (later Hoover) Dam** (p209). The world's tallest dam at the time, it was built on the 1450-mile-long Colorado River, 35 miles east of Las Vegas. The dam not only provided a reliable source of water to seven states through which the river runs, but also ended widespread annual flooding.

A virtual army of well-paid construction workers lived in the area for five years until the dam's completion in 1935. They flocked to Las Vegas at night to partake in the flowing illegal booze, the rampant prostitution and the numerous, newly legal gambling halls that quickly sprouted on flashy downtown Fremont St. After 1936, as construction forces left, the dam and newly created Lake Mead looked set to become big-time tourist attractions, and the federally funded supply road gave Vegas easy access to them.

Los Angeles hotelier Thomas Hull, more than anyone else, deserves credit for Las Vegas as it is today. In 1941 Hull opened the city's first casino hotel, El Rancho Vegas, south of town along the two-lane Los Angeles highway that eventually became Las Vegas Blvd, aka the Strip. At about the same time, the economy got a boost from the army: when the country entered WWII, the US military opened an aerial gunnery school, 10 miles northeast of downtown. Initially, the site contained only a few shacks, but a large complex was soon constructed to train personnel for combat duty in Europe and the Pacific. That same year, a $150-million magnesium plant was built in Henderson, 15 miles southeast of Las Vegas. Metallic magnesium is the key component of incendiary bombs, which were widely used by the Allies to destroy targets in Germany and Japan.

THE FABULOUS FIFTIES

Along with the rest of America, after WWII Las Vegas felt like a glorious boomtown again. Casino hotels arose at an ever more rapid pace, with everyone – gamblers and owners alike – trying to strike it rich.

In 1950, the lavish $4.5-million Desert Inn set the tone by throwing Las Vegas' biggest party yet for its grand opening. The hotel was run by Wilbur Clark, a small-time gambler who wanted to bring Palm Springs style to the Strip, but it was funded and primarily owned by Moe Dalitz, head of a Cleveland-based crime syndicate. A full-blown federal investigation

THANKS, BUGSY!

In the 1940s, El Rancho Vegas attracted a new element to the desert – Hollywood movie stars, who enjoyed gambling and rubbing elbows with the 'characters' it attracted.

One of these characters was mobster Benjamin 'Bugsy' Siegel, who, along with partner Meyer Lansky, had a dream of building an even more luxurious resort in the desert that would, as Lansky said, draw high-rollers from all over the world.

Backed by Lansky's East Coast mob money, Siegel took over Hollywood gossip columnist Billy Wilkerson's bankrupt construction project and completed the $6-million **Flamingo** (p53) hotel in 1946. With its pastel paint job, tuxedoed janitors, Hollywood entertainers and eight-story flashing neon–covered towers out front, it became the model for the Las Vegas to come.

Unfortunately for Siegel, the Flamingo didn't make a profit immediately, and that was too long to wait as far as Siegel's backers were concerned. On June 20, 1947, he was gunned down by his associates at his mistress' mansion in Beverly Hills.

But the resultant national scandal had a curious effect: more people than ever came to Las Vegas to see its stunning gaming palaces and to consort with their notorious patrons and owners. An explosion of new casino hotels erupted along the Strip, which has continued with only a few short pauses to this day.

1967	1973
Elvis Presley marries Priscilla Beaulieu at the Aladdin resort hotel on the Strip	The magnificent $107-million MGM Grand becomes the world's largest resort

made an emerging trend crystal-clear: the Vegas casino industry enjoyed ties to, and the hidden backing of, mobsters from across the nation.

And why not? The mob loved Las Vegas. It gave them a legitimacy and a glamorous cachet they had never experienced before, and by fixing the games, fixing the local politicians and skimming profits both under and over the table, they were getting rich in a hurry. Las Vegans, for their part, loved them back. Everyone, from low-rolling 'grinds' to Tinseltown starlets, flocked to the desert town to soak up the glittering, extravagant spectacle – a gangster's vision of paradise – and the promise of instant wealth.

After the raging success of the Flamingo and the Desert Inn, every new casino hotel in Las Vegas tried to best the rest in size, flash, style, amenities and entertainment extravaganzas. Revenue from the gaming tables let casinos feature the biggest names in show business, which in turn made them appeal to gamblers and nongamblers alike. The Sands hired Frank Sinatra and Dean Martin, and later the entire Rat Pack to headline the Copa Room, while the **Riviera** (p76) nabbed Liberace and more movie stars.

By the mid-1950s, Vegas had overbuilt, and a number of casinos had gone under or changed hands, but that didn't hold back new ones from opening, each one topping the last. In 1957 the Dunes grabbed the spotlight when it introduced bare-breasted showgirls in its revue, *Minsky Goes to Paris,* then the next year **Stardust** (p78) grabbed it back when it boasted that it had *real* French showgirls in its bare-breasted revue, *Lido de Paris,* not to mention the world's biggest electric sign out front, too.

Throughout the decade, racial segregation was in full force on the Strip. African American performers entertained at casino showrooms and lounges, but were not allowed to sleep overnight in the adjacent hotels. The situation was so notorious that Las Vegas earned the nickname 'Mississippi of the West.' The city's first integrated casino, the Moulin Rouge, opened in 1955. Even though it was a favorite Rat Pack hangout, it lasted only a few months. In 1960, civic and NAACP leaders gathered at the now-shuttered casino to broker a historic deal on desegregating the Strip. Restoration of this historic casino was almost complete when arsonists set fire to it in 2003, leaving only the fabulous sign still standing at 900 W Bonanza Rd.

The decade ended with the opening of the **Las Vegas Convention Center** (Map p265), which presaged the city's future as a major convention destination.

> ## VEGAS: IT'S DA BOMB
>
> The 1950s ushered in the era of nuclear weapons testing just 65 miles northwest of Las Vegas. Over the next four decades, nearly 1000 nuclear explosions were initiated at the Nevada Test Site. For the first 12 years, these tests were mostly above ground, at a rate of almost one a month, until after the 1963 Limited Test Ban Treaty pushed them below ground, where they continued until 1992.
>
> Initially unconcerned about radiation fallout, Las Vegans took the atomic bomb blasts in their stride – and even celebrated the publicity and notoriety they brought, not to mention the tourist boost, by selling atomburgers and crowning a Miss Atomic Bomb. One photo taken on downtown's Fremont St shows people casually going about their business while a mushroom cloud rises in the distance. Take a look for yourself at the **Atomic Testing Museum** (p87).

THE AVIATOR & THE AGE OF THE MEGARESORT

During a slowdown in casino construction during the first part of the '60s, federal and state regulators redoubled their efforts to 'clean up' the gambling industry. Scandal after scandal plagued the casinos, as charges of corruption, racketeering, influence peddling and tax evasion were investigated by federal agencies. Nevada's elected officials were finding it difficult to maintain the fiction that strict licensing standards and vigilant law enforcement were keeping the mob at bay. All the bad publicity was hurting tourism, too.

Then, after the opening of the **Aladdin** (p57) and **Caesars Palace** (p51) in 1966, into the picture stepped eccentric billionaire Howard Hughes. He arrived at the Desert Inn on

1980	1989
A fire sweeps through the MGM Grand, killing 87 guests and injuring more than 700	Steve Wynn's Mirage completed, accelerating the evolution of Stripside megaresorts

Thanksgiving night in the back of an ambulance, and didn't set foot outside the hotel for four years. He took over the high-roller suites on the 9th floor, and, when he'd worn out his welcome, rather than move, he simply bought the hotel for $13 million. Hughes, the subject of Scorsese's film *The Aviator*, eventually dropped $300 million in a Las Vegas buying spree that included the Sands, the Castaways, the **New Frontier** (p76) and the Landmark casino hotels.

It was a public relations boon for Nevada officials, as Hughes lent the casino business a much-needed patina of legitimacy. If gambling was a dirty business, local papers blustered, then an industrialist like Hughes wouldn't be getting into it. Legislation eventually made way for corporate ownership of casinos, which spurred a new round of construction in the late '60s and '70s. In the end, the only loser was crazy Hughes, who in record time had become Las Vegas' largest operator of casino hotels, but ultimately got the short end of the stick in many of his deals and left town several million dollars poorer.

The arrival of the $107-million MGM Grand in 1973 was the dawn of the megaresort. A slew of smaller hotels popped up along the Strip during the decade, while master illusionists **Siegfried and Roy** (p148) turned women into tigers at the Tropicana. A flash flood swept down a section of the Strip in 1975, and a few years later Atlantic City legalized gambling, causing Vegas tourism to dip dangerously.

The 1980s began tragically when a fire swept through the MGM, but Bally's (p49) quickly took over the property and reopened it. The decade ended the same way it began: with fire. But this time the fire was a triumphal not tragic – in the form of an erupting volcano in front of Steve Wynn's Mirage (p54), signaling another new age had begun.

2004	2005
The privately funded $654-million Las Vegas Monorail opens	Las Vegas celebrates its centennial; the Wynn megaresort opens

Gambling

Gambling

Gambling can be an exhilarating experience – every roll of the dice provides an electric rush of adrenaline – but when it comes to Vegas casinos, it's important to remember one thing: the house advantage. For every game except poker, the house has a statistical winning edge (the 'percentage') over the gambler, and for nearly every payout in nearly every game, the house 'holds' a small portion of the winnings. Amounts vary with the game and with individual bets, but over the long haul, you're guaranteed to lose everything you gamble. As such, think of gambling only as entertainment – for which you *do* pay a fee. Understand the games you're playing, don't bet more than you're prepared to lose, and learn to leave when you're ahead.

THE CASINO

You must be at least 21 years old to play. Traditional casino games include poker, black-jack, baccarat, craps, keno, roulette, slot machines and video poker. Each game has its own customs, traditions and strategies. Almost all casinos can provide guides that show you how to play the game and may offer free gaming lessons from professional instructors. Drop by the **Gambler's Book Shop** (p178) to browse literally hundreds of strategy books available for every game.

It's also acceptable to ask your dealer for help and advice. For instance, the dealer should gladly tell you the odds on a particular bet at craps, or what the strategy is for the blackjack hand you've just been dealt. It's polite to 'toke' (tip) your dealer if you're winning. Either place a chip on the layout (the area where you place your bet) for the dealer to collect, or place a side bet for the dealer to collect if it wins. Keno runners and slot-machine attendants also expect a small tip for any services rendered, especially if you hit the jackpot.

If you play table games seriously, ask the pit boss to rate your play, which he or she will do based on how much you bet and how many hours you play. Why? Because each year the city's casinos give out millions of dollars in 'comps' to rated players (un-rated players get nothing). Even if you're playing between $5 and $10 per hand, it's likely you can earn yourself a free meal.

POKER *Jonathan Grotenstein*

A decade ago, visitors to Las Vegas had a hard time finding a poker game. Many casinos, armed with profitability studies developed by MBAs, were replacing their card tables with high-limit slot machines.

Ten years later, it's still hard to get a game in Vegas, but for an entirely different reason: poker has become the hottest game in town. Fueled by seemingly endless TV coverage and the explosion of online games, players are flocking to the tables, ready to

Card table, New York–New York (p64)

TOP 10 POKER HANDS

You'll probably want to commit these rankings to memory before you sit down with the sharks:

Royal Flush A straight, ace through 10, all of the same suit. Eg A♣ K♣ Q♣ J♣ 10♣

Straight Flush Five consecutive cards of the same suit. The ace can be used for the high or the low end of the straight. Eg A♠ 2♠ 3♠ 4♠ 5♠. Note that 'wrapping around' is *not* permitted. Eg J♦ Q♥ K♦ A♠ 2♠

Four of a Kind Exactly what the name suggests. Also called a 'case.' Eg 7♣ 7♠ 7♥ 7♦ 9♣

Full House Three of a kind, plus a pair. Also called a 'boat.' Eg 5♣ 5♦ 5♥ J♥ J♠

Flush Any five cards of the same suit. Eg A♥ Q♥ 8♥ 5♥ 3♥. If two or more players both have a flush, ties are broken by the highest flush card (or cards).

Straight Five consecutive cards of any suit. Eg K♦ Q♣ J♦ 10♠ 9♠

Three of a Kind Also called 'trips,' or a 'set.' Eg 3♣ 3♦ 3♥ Q♥ 5♦

Two Pair If two or more players have the same two-pair, the fifth card, or 'kicker,' is used to decide the winner. Eg J♦ J♥ 5♣ 5♦ 7♣ beats J♣ J♥ 5♣ 5♦ 2♣

One Pair When your two hole cards match, you are said to have a pocket or wired pair. Eg Q♥ Q♠ A♥ 10♠ 8♥

High Cards If no one has a pair or better, the player with the highest cards wins. Eg A♦ K♣ 7♥ 6♥ 2♠ beats A♦ 10♥ 7♦ 3♦ 2♠

test their grit and cunning against other would-be legends and of course the 'locals.' Hit the **Bellagio** (p51) at the wrong time on a Friday night, and you may be in for a three-hour wait just to sit down. The same casinos that eliminated their poker rooms are tripping over themselves to reopen them. You'll run into queues, but some of the newer rooms, like **Wynn** (p59), have come up with innovative methods of ameliorating the pain, including letting you check the waiting list from your hotel room, and pagers to let you know when your seat is available.

The even better news is that poker is a 'beatable' game. Most card rooms take only a small percentage of each pot – the rake – leaving the vast majority of the money to be won and lost by the players themselves. Luck still plays a major role in determining success, but a shrewd poker player who waits for the right opportunities can, over the long haul, be a winner.

Texas Hold'em

If you're one of those people who grew up playing wild draw poker games where the deuces, treys, one-eyed jacks, suicide kings and the queen that's not looking at the flower are all wild, you're in for a bit of a shock. While it's not the only game in town, Texas hold'em is far and away the most common. Its origins are shrouded in mystery: one plausible explanation attributes its invention to a bunkhouse full of enterprising ranch hands with more money than decks of cards, because up to 23 players can participate at once.

Hold'em came to Las Vegas, where the game is typically dealt nine- or 10-handed, in 1963, when Texas native Felton 'Corky' McCorquodale introduced it at the long-departed California Club. It quickly became the game of choice among local professionals, as the structure of the game allowed a good player to risk a relatively small amount of money to win potentially enormous pots. When fellow Texan Benny Binion (p81) held the first World Series of Poker in 1971, Texas hold'em was chosen as the game that would decide the champion.

The rules of Texas hold'em are relatively simple. Each player is dealt two cards face down, known as hole cards. After a round of betting, three more cards – the 'flop' – are dealt face-up in the center of the table. These cards are community cards, shared by all the players still in the hand. After another round of betting, a fourth community card – the 'turn' – is dealt. After another round of betting, the fifth and final community card – the much-anticipated 'river' – is laid on the table. One last round of betting ensues, and the remaining players turn over their hole cards. The player who is able to make the strongest five-card hand (by combining his or her hole cards with the community cards) takes the pot.

UNDERSTANDING YOUR LIMITS

Poker comes in three basic flavors: limit, no-limit and pot limit.

Limit poker restricts the amount that you can bet at any given opportunity, usually comprising a small bet before and just after the flop, and a big bet on the turn and the river. For example, in a $4/8 limit hold'em game, you'd bet and raise in increments of $4 on the first two rounds of betting, $8 on the final two. In no-limit poker, players are allowed to bet as many chips as they have in front of them at any given time. If you don't have enough chips to match a bet, you can declare yourself all-in, putting all your chips on the line – just remember you're only eligible to win as much of your opponent's bet as you're able to cover. It is not a game for the fainthearted. Keep in mind that there is a world of difference between a $2/4 limit game – where a huge pot might contain $40 – and a $2/4 no-limit game, where pots may be worth hundreds of dollars.

Pot-limit is a hybrid, allowing you to bet an amount up to what's already in the pot at any given time. It may require the most sophistication to play, too, so approach with caution.

When sitting down to play a limit game, you'll generally want to buy in for at least 20 big bets (eg $120 in a $3/6 game). No-limit and pot-limit poker require substantially larger bankrolls.

ESSENTIAL READING

- *Hold'Em Poker for Advanced Players* (1996) The erratic structure and dense prose can make it an infuriating read, but this venerable book by David Sklansky and Mason Malmuth remains the closest Texas hold'em has to a Bible.
- *Poker: The Real Deal* (2004) For anyone new to the game, Phil Gordon and Jonathan Grotenstein entertainingly lay out nearly all that's necessary to become a winning player.
- *Winning Low-Limit Hold'Em* (2005) A solid set of strategies from Lee Jones for beating the loose and wild games you're likely to run into at poker's lower limits.

BASIC PLAY

Each time a hand is dealt, players act in an order dictated by their position at the table. A white button moves around the table with each hand; the player who has the button is said to be the dealer. The player/dealer doesn't really have to deal – there's a professional on hand for that – but he or she does have the advantage of being last to act during all of the post-flop betting.

Before the hand is dealt, the two players seated to the left of the dealer – the 'small blind' and the 'big blind' – post a mandatory bet. In limit games, the big blind is generally the size of the small bet, and the small blind some fraction – usually half – of the big blind. Even the blinds in no-limit and pot-limit games are set (eg a $1/2 no-limit game has a $1 small blind and a $2 big blind).

The initial betting begins with the player to the left of the big blind, the seat called 'under the gun.' As the big blind has already posted a bet, you aren't allowed to 'check' – that is, pass to the next player – before the flop. You must 'call' the bet (matching the big blind), raise the bet or fold your hand. If no one has raised, the player in the small blind can 'complete' the bet (adding enough to match the big blind), while the big blind is given the option to let his or her bet stand.

For all subsequent rounds of betting, the small blind (or the player closest on the left) is first to act.

BASIC STRATEGY

Hold'em is a relatively easy game to learn, but is remarkably difficult to play well. Novices are best served by reading a book or two on strategy. If you're hell-bent on sitting down at a table right this very minute, here are a few basic considerations to keep in mind.

Hand Strength. While any two cards can win, some will win a lot more often than others. Two aces are the strongest possible starting hand, while an unsuited 7-2 is the absolute worst. High pairs and high cards are best, especially if you can narrow the field to only a few players with a raise before the flop. Smaller pairs and suited connectors – like 9♥ 8♥ – work well when a lot of players are entering each pot; you won't make a big hand too often, but when you do, you can win a lot of money. Try to limit the total number of hands that you play, as most solid players will only pay to see one out of every four or five flops.

Position. The ability to act after everyone else is a huge advantage in poker. Most skilled players will tighten up when seated 'under the gun' or thereabouts (close to the left hand of the dealer). In these instances they play only the strongest starting hands, gradually increasing the range of hands they will play as they near the button (dealer position).

Know the Odds. While you'll occasionally 'flop the nuts,' connecting with the first three cards to make an unbeatable hand, you'll far more often have an incomplete hand, forcing you to decide whether or not you want to call a bet or two in the hopes of drawing to a stronger hand. Good poker players add up their outs – the number of cards that will improve their hand – and compare their chances with the size of the pot to decide if it's worth pursuing. Flop four cards to a flush, for example, and you've got about a 40% chance of landing a fifth suited card by the river to complete your hand, good enough odds (in most low-limit games) to call a bet or two. On the other hand, the odds of completing a 'gut-shot' – a situation where you are drawing to, say, a 7 to make a straight – are only about 16%, and there generally has to be a lot of money in the middle to make it worthwhile to chase that miracle card.

Aggression. The best poker players prefer to control the action, looking to bet and raise when they've got something, folding when they don't. Players who frequently check or call bets – calling stations, in the parlance of the pros – are generally losers at the table.

Bluffing is overrated. Bluffing only works against players who are sophisticated enough to fold a decent hand. Bluffing against most low-limit players – who will call all the way to the river with even the most speculative hands – is a good way to lose money.

TABLE ETIQUETTE

Poker is a community game and, like any community, has its own set of customs. When playing in a casino, you'll want to abide by a few basic principles.

Don't splash the pot. Don't throw chips haphazardly into the middle of the table, making it difficult for the dealer and other players to see how much you've wagered. Place your bets directly in front of you, and let the dealer add them to the pot.

Protect your cards. When involved in a hand, place some small object – a chip or, if you prefer, some lucky talisman – on top of your hole cards. Unprotected hands are often accidentally swept away by efficient dealers.

No 'string bets.' Unless you verbally declare your intention to raise, once you've pushed some chips forward, you are not allowed to reach back into your stack for more. Either announce your raises out loud, or make sure that you've got enough chips in your hand to cover whatever amount you want to bet.

Act in turn. Nothing generates more ire among locals than a player who acts out of turn. Don't be that player.

Don't abuse the dealers. It's not their fault. Really.

Other Poker Games

While Texas hold'em is the most popular game, it's not the only game.

Omaha is a lot like hold'em, except that each player starts with four hole cards instead of two. The trick is remembering that you must use two – and only two – of your hole cards to make your hand. There is no joy in looking down to find four aces, as you can only use two of them, and have virtually no chance of improving your hand.

Omaha is often played hi-lo, splitting the pot between the player with the highest hand

TOP 5 POKER ROOMS

- **Wynn** (p59) Fanciest poker room in Vegas.
- **Bellagio** (p51) Home to the World Poker Tour finals.
- **Mirage** (p54) The Strip's first great poker room.
- **Binion's** (p81) Formerly the Horseshoe, home to the World Series of Poker for the first 35 years.
- **Rio** (p91) The new and future home to the World Series of Poker.

and the player with the lowest. To qualify as a low hand, all of the cards usually have to be 8 or lower; if no low hand exists, the player with the high hand takes all the money. The Holy Grail of any hi-lo game is the bicycle straight – ace through five – which is not only the best possible low hand, but generally has a very good chance at turning out to be the high hand as well.

Seven-card stud is disappearing fast, but can still be found in some casinos. Each player starts with two hole cards and one up card, followed by three more up cards and one last down card. You've got to have a good memory to play, as it's extremely important to remember what up cards each of your opponents have received just to evaluate the strength of your own hand.

BLACKJACK *Jonathan Grotenstein*

The French, generally credited with its invention, called it *vignt-et-un*. In Las Vegas, it's 21, or blackjack, likely a historic reference to rewarding a player for being on the receiving end of an ace and a jack of spades. While poker may be grabbing the headlines, blackjack remains far and away the most popular table game Vegas has to offer.

Players love blackjack for many reasons. It's fairly easy to master its basic strategies. There are free drinks, smokes and easy camaraderie with sociable dealers. Casinos offer comps – freebies like meals, shows, even luxury suites – to those willing to gamble a lot of money. Most importantly, almost every player has had the experience of making an absolute killing at the table, leading them to feel blackjack is, in fact, a 'beatable' game.

Are they right? We'll get back to that. First, here's a brief primer on how to play.

BASIC PLAY

The rules are fairly simple: you're going to get some cards, the dealer is going to get some cards, and each of you is going to add them up. 'Number' cards (2 through 10) are worth their face value, 'picture' cards (jacks, queens and kings) are worth 10, and aces are worth 1 or 11, whichever works out to be more advantageous. The hand that comes closest to 21 – without going over – wins.

Play begins when you place a bet on the table. The players and the dealer are each dealt two cards, generally from a stack of cards called 'the shoe.' All cards are usually dealt face up, except for one of the dealer's cards – the 'hole card' – which is laid face-down on the table. If you're dealt a 'natural' 21 – an ace plus a picture card or a ten – you are immediately declared the winner (unless the dealer also has a natural 21, resulting in a tie, called a 'push'). In this case you're usually paid three dollars for every two you've wagered. If the dealer, who gets to peek at his or her hole card before play begins, discovers a natural 21, the hand immediately comes to an end and your (losing) wager is raked in by the house.

In most cases, however, neither you nor the dealer will have a natural 21, and it's up to you to decide how to play your hand. You can 'hit' – request an additional card in the hopes of getting closer to 21 – as many times as you want, but the moment you go over 21, or 'bust,' you've lost the hand. If you decide that you don't want any additional cards, you can 'stand' on your current cards.

Once every player has busted or decided to stand, the dealer turns over his or her hole card and, for the first time, you get to see what you are up against. Unlike you, dealers don't have a choice: if they've got a 16 or lower, they have to hit; a 17 or higher, and they have to stand. (Each casino has its own rules about what a dealer has to do with a 'soft' 17 that incorporates an ace, which can be valued at 1 or 11.) You have to hope that your hand, after the dealer has finished, is closer to 21 than anyone else's, or that the dealer busts in the process.

SPECIAL RULES

In addition to hitting and standing, many casinos offer options that can be invoked by players when special circumstances permit.

Splitting is allowed when you are dealt two of the same card, like 8-8. You simply place an additional bet – equal to the bet you started with – and your single hand is divided into two separate hands. One more card is added to each hand, and both hands are played according to the usual rules. Some casinos have special rules about splitting two aces – ask your dealer before you play.

Doubling down lets you double the amount of your initial bet; the downside is that you receive one – and only one – more card.

If the dealer's face-up card is an ace, many casinos allow you to make a separate 'insurance' bet against the possibility that the dealer already has a natural 21. The insurance bet favors the insurer, or in this case, the house, and is generally a bad idea.

Some casinos allow you to surrender a bad hand before it is completed, recouping half of your initial bet. This is actually good play in certain situations.

BASIC STRATEGY

Nearly all blackjack strategies revolve around one basic fact: because so many cards have a value of 10 – the tens, jacks, queens and kings make up nearly a third of the deck – it's usually good practice to assume that any unknown card, ie the dealer's hole card or the card you are thinking about hitting for, is going to be worth 10. By extension, it's very dangerous to hit on a 15 – where a 10 will cause you to bust – but you'll happily take another card when you've got an 11 (often a good time to double down), as a 10 will give you 21.

Keep in mind that the dealer doesn't act until you've finished making decisions about your hand. It might not seem like a big deal, but this positional advantage is what gives the house its statistical edge: if you bust, it doesn't matter what the dealer's two cards are – the house wins.

CARD COUNTING

When most people think of beating the house at blackjack, they're thinking about card counters. Based on mathematical studies showing that a deck loaded with high cards can shift the odds into the player's favor, many thinkers have developed systems for keeping track of which cards have already been played and adjusting their bets accordingly.

Card counters have waged – and continue to wage – a war against the casinos, each side constantly evolving their strategies. Savvy counters often work in teams, using hand signals and even disguises to elude detection, while nearly every card room employs professionals whose only job is to seek them out, in certain notorious cases exacting 'backroom justice' with a baseball bat to the knees.

What does this mean for you? Probably nothing, unless you're part of a professional card-counting team. There are still a few places in Vegas where you can find a single-deck blackjack game and can shift the odds in your favor by incorporating a simple system. A word of caution, however: card counting still has its dangers. While you're unlikely to incur the wrath of a baseball bat–wielding goon, a bad card counter – one who makes even one or two mistakes an hour – will lose more money than a 'normal' player.

'PERFECT' STRATEGY

Even if you're not counting cards, there's still an important piece of information available for every hand: the dealer's 'up' card. Since the dealer's hole card will often be worth 10, you can make an educated guess as to the value of his or her hand. You're only going to be right about a third of the time, but that turns out to be more than enough to put a substantial dent into the house's advantage.

There is, in every situation, an 'optimal' way to play your hand, one that maximizes the amount you stand to win, or at least minimizes whatever you are going to lose. A player who always makes optimal decisions – or employs what blackjack aficionados call 'perfect strategy' – can greatly improve his or her odds at the table, in many cases reducing the house's advantage to a mere half of a percentage point. While that provides plenty of profits for the casino over the long haul, it leaves the door open for someone playing 'by the book' to wind up a short-term winner, assuming you have enough intuition or discipline to recognize when that 'short term' ends.

As these small wins do little to affect the casinos' bottom line, they are more than happy to allow you to play with perfect strategy. Many Vegas gift shops sell little plastic cards telling you what your most advantageous play is in each situation, and friendly dealers are happy to offer the same advice. We've included a table for an 'average' game, that is, one involving multiple decks and a dealer who is forced to stand on 'soft' 17s.

You	What the dealer is showing									
	2	3	4	5	6	7	8	9	10	A
17-21	S	S	S	S	S	S	S	S	S	S
16	S	S	S	S	S	H	H	SR	SR	SR
15	S	S	S	S	S	H	H	H	SR	H
14	S	S	S	S	S	H	H	H	H	H
13	S	S	S	S	S	H	H	H	H	H
12	H	H	S	S	S	H	H	H	H	H
11	DD	DD	DD	DD	DD	DD	DD	DD	DD	H
10	DD	DD	DD	DD	DD	DD	DD	DD	H	H
9	H	DD	DD	DD	DD	H	H	H	H	H
5-8	H	H	H	H	H	H	H	H	H	H
2,2	H	H	SP	SP	SP	SP	H	H	H	H
3,3	H	H	SP	SP	SP	SP	H	H	H	H
4,4	H	H	H	H	H	H	H	H	H	H
5,5	DD	DD	DD	DD	DD	DD	DD	DD	H	H
6,6	SP	SP	SP	SP	H	H	H	H	H	H
7,7	SP	SP	SP	SP	SP	SP	H	H	H	H
8,8	SP	SP	SP	SP	SP	SP	SP	SP	SP	SP
9,9	SP	SP	SP	SP	SP	S	SP	SP	S	S
10,10	S	S	S	S	S	S	S	S	S	S
A,A	SP	SP	SP	SP	SP	SP	SP	SP	SP	SP
A,2	H	H	H	DD	DD	H	H	H	H	H
A,3	H	H	H	DD	DD	H	H	H	H	H
A,4	H	H	DD	DD	DD	H	H	H	H	H
A,5	H	H	DD	DD	DD	H	H	H	H	H
A,6	H	DD	DD	DD	DD	H	H	H	H	H
A,7	S	DD	DD	DD	DD	S	S	H	H	H
A,8	S	S	S	S	S	S	S	S	S	S
A,9	S	S	S	S	S	S	S	S	S	S
A,10	Blackjack!									

H=Hit, S=Stand, SP=Split, DD=Double Down, SR=Surrender (if allowed, otherwise Hit)

FINAL THOUGHTS

Not all blackjack games are created equal.

Every casino has its own set of rules and procedures. Some of these variations help the player. Most create a greater advantage for the house. Be on the lookout for games that won't allow you to split aces or that pay 6:5 instead of the usual 3:2 – you'll be playing at a greater than usual disadvantage. The same can be said for games that sound deceptively appealing such as 'No-Bust Blackjack' and 'Superfun 21,' whose rules ultimately favor the casino.

Where are the best places to play? Unfortunately, the answer is always changing. Casinos are constantly making adjustments to house rules. Take the Mirage, for example, where recently we found tables where the dealer was forced to stand on a soft 17 – which is better for the player – alongside tables where the opposite was true.

If you're serious about finding the best game in town, there's no more valuable resource than the *Current Blackjack News* (www.bj21.com). This monthly newsletter, published by long-time pro Stanford Wong, details the current rules and procedures used by just about every casino in North America, alongside an analysis of how each affects your odds of beating the game.

BACCARAT

Nothing conjures the image of high stakes, black tuxedoes and James Bond like baccarat, and yet, of the card games, it possesses the least strategy – none, in fact. The rules are fixed, and there are no decisions for the player except for how to bet. There are only three bets: on the bank, the player or a tie. High minimum bets ensure that most players have large bankrolls. However, you can now often find minibaccarat tables with $5 minimum bets.

One player and the banker are each dealt two cards from a 'shoe.' The hand closest to nine points wins. Aces through 9s count at face value; 10s and face cards are worth zero. If the cards exceed 10 points, only the second digit is counted (eg a 7 plus a 6 is worth 3, not 13). The dealer follows specific rules to determine whether to 'hit' the bank or the player with a third card. If there's a tie, the hands are redealt, but it's the least likely result.

The 'bank' is often passed around among the players. When the player's hand wins, the shoe is then passed to the next player, who then becomes the banker. A player can choose not to deal, but must then pass the shoe. If you bet on the bank and the bank wins, the house takes a 5% commission.

CRAPS

A lively, fast-paced craps table has players shouting, crowds gathering and everyone hoping for a 'hot' streak of the dice. The odds are exactly the same on every roll, but that doesn't stop people from betting their 'hunches' and believing that certain numbers are 'due.'

Since the betting possibilities are complicated, and shift as play continues, it's important to spend some time studying a betting guide and to begin playing with the simplest wager (on the pass/don't pass line), which also happens to be one of the better bets in the casino.

To begin, the 'stickman' hands the dice to a player, who becomes the 'shooter' for that round. A 'pass line' bet means that on the first roll (the 'come-out' roll) the dice will total 7 or 11. If the dice total 2, 3 or 12 (called 'craps'), the player loses. Any other number becomes the 'point,' and the dice are rolled again until either a 7 or the point number comes up – if a 7 comes up first, the player loses; if the point turns up, the player wins.

A 'don't pass' bet is basically the reverse – if the come-out roll totals 7 or 11, the player loses; if it's 2 or 3, the player wins; 12 is a push. If a point is established, the don't-pass bettor wins on a 7 and loses if the point is rolled again. All these bets pay even money.

'Come' bets are placed after a point is established; 7 and 11 win, while 2, 3 or 12 lose. If none of these come up, the dice are thrown again until the point is thrown, and the player wins, or a 7 is thrown and the player loses. The don't-come bet is the reverse, except that 12 is a push. Come and don't-come bets also pay even money.

If you've already made a pass or come bet, and a point has been established, you can bet that the point will come up before a 7 is thrown. Depending on the point being rolled, your odds of winning are just shy of 50%, which is about the best odds you'll get in a casino.

There are more betting options with even bigger payoffs, but most have very long odds and the house advantage is sky-high, and thus are avoided by most serious craps players.

KENO

This game is a lot like lotto. There are 80 numbered squares on a card. A player picks from 1 to 15 or 20 numbers and bets $1 or so per number or combination of numbers. You can bet straight, split, 'way' or combination. At the draw, the casino randomly selects 20 numbers. Winners are paid off according to how many of those numbers they chose, as shown on a 'payoff chart.' The amount paid off is distinctly less than the probability of selecting the numbers by chance, so the abysmal odds favor the house by 25% or more. Avoid it.

RACE & SPORTS BOOKS

The bigger casinos usually have a 'race and sports book,' a room where major sports events from around the country are televised. Players can bet on just about any game, boxing match or horse race in the country, except for any taking place in Nevada. Race and sports books are best during major events, when everyone is captivated by, betting on, and yelling about the same thing. The **Hilton** (p87) has the most high-tech race and sports book, while those at the **Bellagio** (p51) and **Caesars Palace** (p51) are impressive, but for old-school bettors, nothing beats the **Stardust** (p78), which has a sports handicappers' library. The stadium-like race and sports books that's hidden underground at **Bally's** (p49) is convenient to the monorail.

ROULETTE

This game is easy to understand and often hypnotic to play. Roulette provides the most clear demonstration of the house edge. The roulette wheel has 38 numbers – from 1 to 36, plus 0 and 00. (European roulette wheels typically do not have '00,' which makes the American version much harder.) Half the numbers are red, the other half are black. Zeros are green.

The table is marked with the numbers and various betting combinations. You can use either casino chips or special 'wheel chips,' which are dispensed at the roulette table and are a different color for each player. You can bet that a result will be odd or even, red or black, high (19 to 36) or low (1 to 18). All of these bets pay off at even money, but the chances of a win are less than 50%, because the 0 and 00 don't count as odd or even, red or black, high or low.

A bet on a single number (including the 0 and 00) pays out at 35 to 1, though true odds would be 37 to 1. These aren't the best odds in the casino, but they're far from the worst.

SLOT MACHINES

The slot are wildly popular and simplest of all – you put in money and pull the handle (or push a button). The player has no effect on the outcome. The probabilities are programmed into the machine, and the chances of winning are the same on every pull.

The only important decisions are which machine to play and when to stop. Some machines pay back a higher proportion of the money deposited than others. Those that return a lot to the player, as much as 97%, are called 'loose.' Some say loose slots are more likely in the highly visible areas of big casinos, such as doorways.

'Progressive slots' offer a jackpot that accumulates, and many slots are now linked in networks to generate bigger jackpots. Often these pay off in the form of a new car, which is prominently displayed in the casino. The jackpots are factored into the payout percentage, so there's no extra statistical advantage to the player.

Penny slots offer superior time-on value (the amount of time a player is able to stay on a machine with a small amount of money). But if you want to win a jackpot, you must bet the maximum amount on every pull to ensure that when you win, you'll get the maximum payout possible. If you do get lucky, always wait by the slot machine until an attendant arrives.

VIDEO POKER

Video poker games deal five electronic cards. Hold the cards you want, then draw again to complete a five-card hand. Quarter machines are common, though they can range from a nickel to $5 per bet. By employing correct strategy and finding machines with the best payout schedules, it's possible to improve your chances of winning and reduce the house advantage to nothing. Make sure the machine you play pays back your bet for a pair of jacks or better, and has a payout of nine coins for every coin that you bet on a full house and a payout of six coins for every coin bet on a flush (a 9/6 machine). Much has been written recently about video poker strategy (since there is a modicum of player control), and it's worth reading up on.

JOIN THE CLUB!

All the megaresorts and some of the smaller casinos have slot clubs – just go to the main change cage inside the casino where you'll be doing your gambling and ask to join their players' club. Membership is free, but you must be at least 21 years old and have photo ID. You'll have your slot-club card within minutes. Just remember to insert your plastic membership card into a slot machine before you begin playing. You are awarded points by how much money you put into the machine, and those points are in turn redeemable for cash, merchandise or 'comps' (complimentary meals, rooms etc) at the casino hotel or sometimes also at its sister properties.

Sights ■

Sights

If you haven't visited Vegas recently, you can't claim to know America's fastest-growing metropolis. In a real sense, Las Vegas is two cities: the Strip and the older downtown area, which attracts far fewer onlookers. During the 1990s, the Fremont Street Experience converted downtown Las Vegas from an eyesore into a vibrant, open-air pedestrian mall with nightly light shows to stop visitors in their tracks. The area has been upgraded still further by remarkable improvements to many of the casino hotels along Fremont St.

The Strip has likewise undergone a transformation in recent years. The themed megaresorts that opened on Las Vegas Blvd at the end of the 20th century emphasized a belief that bigger is better. That trend started in 1989 at the opening of the Mirage, with its erupting volcano, glass-enclosed atrium filled with jungle plants, white tigers, a 20,000-gallon aquarium and spectacular shows. Next up was the Excalibur, a gleaming white castle with a medieval interior to match.

In 1993, the architecturally stunning Luxor and the daily pirate battles at Treasure Island debuted. In the following years, the Hard Rock casino hotel just east of the Strip established Las Vegas as a major player with rock 'n' rollers, the Stratosphere took the city to new heights, and New York–New York transformed the Strip's skyline. Other themed megaresorts that arose during the late 1990s were the Venetian, Paris–Las Vegas, Bellagio and Mandalay Bay.

Today's adolescent Las Vegas is a self-assured brat with no idea what it wants to be when it grows up, but certain it's going to be fabulously rich and famous some day. The newest player on the Strip, Wynn casino hotel and megaresort, embodies this new, maturing trend par excellence. However, at the end of the day, Vegas is still whatever you want it to be.

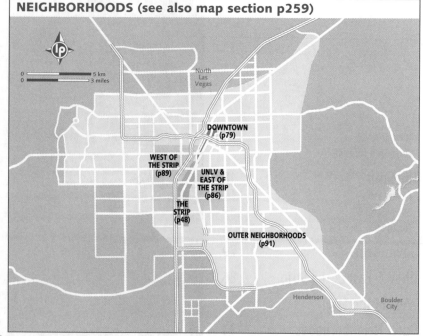

NEIGHBORHOODS (see also map section p259)

0 — 5 km
0 — 3 miles

North Las Vegas

DOWNTOWN (p79)

WEST OF THE STRIP (p89)

UNLV & EAST OF THE STRIP (p86)

THE STRIP (p48)

OUTER NEIGHBORHOODS (p91)

Henderson

Boulder City

TRANSPORTATION – THE STRIP

Bus CAT (p234) buses 301 (Strip) and 302 (Strip Express) travel Las Vegas Blvd S in both directions.

Car Traffic can be heavy on the Strip, especially stop-and-go Friday and Saturday nights. Unless you want to be part of the action, use one of the parallel surface roads (such as Industrial Rd on the west side or Paradise Rd to the east). I-15 can turn into a parking lot at any time of day. Tune into 970AM for traffic reports every 10 minutes.

Monorail The Las Vegas monorail (p235) is a speedy, almost stress-free way to get around – except that most monorail stations on the Strip are located at the far back of casinos on the east side of Las Vegas Blvd S. Count on walking the equivalent of a block east of the Strip just to reach the station, then another block back west from wherever you decide to get off. It's only really worth it if you're going to travel more than one stop.

Parking All casino hotels offer free self-parking garages (write down where you've parked, as finding your car again is harder than you'd think) and free valet parking (tip at least $2 when your keys are returned to you).

Shuttle Some off-Strip casinos provide free public shuttle service to/from the Strip. See p236 for details.

Taxi Don't expect to flag down a taxi (p236) on the Strip. Instead, taxi stands are found at major casino hotels and shopping malls.

Trolley The slowest form of Strip transportation are private air-con trolleys (p236), which stop at almost every casino hotel on Las Vegas Blvd S, as well as the Las Vegas Hilton near the convention center.

Walking Strolling along the Strip isn't as easy as it sounds. Distances are greater than they appear, so pack good walking shoes. Some intersections can only be crossed by elevated pedestrian skyways. Lonelier stretches of the Strip that are not fun to walk: Planet Hollywood (Aladdin) to the MGM Grand; the Bellagio to the Monte Carlo; and north of Circus Circus past the Sahara to the Stratosphere.

There's no shortage of things to see and do. That's particularly true of the Strip, where the vast majority of Las Vegas' casino hotels can be found and the choice of attractions day and night is overwhelming. When you grow weary of the glitz, it's worth checking out the vintage vibe downtown or in more off-beat locals' areas. Remember to factor in the substantial time it takes to get around, whether for trips along the Strip or to outer neighborhoods.

Not every casino hotel in Las Vegas is mentioned here, especially if they appeal only to locals. There are other places that should – and eventually will – be replaced, but so far are hanging on, buoyed by the success of the bright lights around them. This chapter focuses on attractions that we can recommend, though it also includes places so popular we couldn't avoid mentioning them, if only to warn you against wasting your time there.

Most attractions keep the same hours year-round, including on holidays (except Christmas). While entry to casino hotels is free, many of the big attractions inside them cost money. See the Sleeping chapter (p186) for more information on the casino hotels listed here.

ITINERARIES
One Day
Speed from the airport to the Strip in a limo (p233). Check in at your hotel, or just drop off your bags, and start gambling. Sample the Strip's fabulous free attractions (p56) and shopping (p172) as you stroll through its most opulent megaresorts, such as the **Bellagio** (p51), **Caesars Palace** (p51), the **Venetian** (p58) and **MGM Grand** (p63). Use the monorail (p235) as you bounce along Las Vegas Blvd. Dine at one of Vegas' top tables (p104), then do some more gambling before partying at one of Sin City's hottest nightclubs (p150). Don't stop till the sun comes up, then hit one of the buffets (p108) for brunch before catching your flight out.

One Weekend
Fly into Vegas on Friday afternoon and follow the itinerary above. Not feeling quite so rushed, you can make time for the **Stratosphere** (p79) tower and its sky-high thrill rides. Fire

up your first evening at one of the Strip's ultra lounges (p131) and wind it down before dawn at the Peppermill's **Fireside Lounge** (p136) or **Mr Lucky's** (p124) at the hip Hard Rock.

The next morning after breakfast, laze by your hotel pool (p196), take a gambling lesson (p36) or visit one of the Strip's primo **spas** (p164). After all, it's going to be another late night. Spend the afternoon visiting one of Vegas' more off-beat attractions, such as the **Atomic Testing Museum** (p87), or driving and walking in **Red Rock Canyon** (p213). Venture off-Strip for dinner at **Rosemary's Restaurant** (p128), as long as you've made reservations.

Start off your second night of gambling by heading downtown. The **Golden Nugget** (p83) is the classiest carpet joint facing the **Fremont Street Experience** (p82), best viewed from **Center Stage** (p137). Don't miss the vintage signs at the **Neonopolis** (p84) or playing poker in the back room at **Binion's** (p81). When midnight rolls around, it's time to head back to the Strip for clubbing (p150) until the break of dawn.

Rise and shine for the Sunday gospel brunch at House of Blues or another casino hotel's champagne buffet (p108), then gamble like crazy until the last minute (even the airport has slot machines, you know!).

One Week

In *Fear and Loathing in Las Vegas*, Hunter S Thompson wrote, 'After five days in Vegas you feel like you've been here for five years.' It's true. So break up your sojourn in Sin City by heading out of town to explore the desert. Can't bear to leave the poker rooms for more than a day? Make a quick loop via **Hoover Dam** (p209), **Lake Mead** (p211) and the **Valley of Fire** (p212), or spend just one glorious afternoon in **Red Rock Canyon** (p213). You can take more of a breather on a day trip to the **Mojave National Preserve** (p227) or an overnight excursion to the **Grand Canyon** (p215) or **Zion** (p220) and **Bryce Canyon National Parks** (p223) or **Death Valley** (p224). Fully rejuvenated, zoom back to Vegas for another couple of fun-filled days, maybe exploring the city's outer neighborhoods (p91) and letting it ride on the Strip one last time.

ORGANIZED TOURS

There are only a few organized tours of Sin City itself. Most tour operators focus on day trips outside the city limits (p208). For further tours, see p94.

GRAY LINE

☎ 702-384-1234, 800-634-6579; www.grayline .com; tours from $30; ✆ call for schedules & reservations

The granddaddy of group sightseeing runs the most popular night-time city tour, 'Neon & Lights' ($40), which combines bus rides and short walks and lasts six hours; stops include the Bellagio's fountains and the Fremont Street Experience. The daytime tour ($30) visits the **Clark County Museum** (p91).

HAUNTED VEGAS TOURS Map p265

☎ 702-737-5540; www.hauntedvegastours.com; Greek Isles, 305 Convention Center Dr; 30 min show & 2hr bus tour $47-58; ✆ 9pm Fri-Mon; monorail Convention Center

Most folks are disappointed by the campy sideshow that starts off the tour, but the bus trip around Sin City keeps you awake,

thanks to an energetic guide who spins yarns about Liberace creeping around the Tivoli Gardens, Bugsy haunting the Flamingo and even the spirit of Tupac Shakur. It's all over the top, and you've got to have an active imagination to enjoy it. Children under 16 aren't allowed. Half-price ticket booths (p143) may have same-day tickets.

VEGAS WALKS

☎ 702-376-1054, 800-313-6080; www.vegaswalks .com; adult/senior $22/20, child under 12 free; ✆ call for schedules

Historical walking tours of the Strip led by professional guides don't cover much ground, but they do delve into what you're seeing (and also what's sadly no longer there, like the Sands casino hotel). The ticket price includes a sun visor and a bottle of water. Cash or traveler's checks only.

THE STRIP

Eating p106; Shopping p172; Sleeping p188

Baby, this is where it's at. The Strip has the lion's share of hulking casino hotels and megaresorts. A few smaller hotels are slotted in between the high-rises, awaiting a grander fate while they squat on real estate guaranteed to rise in value. Interspersed between the glitz are garish parking structures, shopping malls and fast-food outlets.

Few visitors venture beyond the Strip. Indeed, many never even make it beyond the comfy confines of their hotel. That's fine, if you're staying at an all-inclusive megaresort like the Bellagio or MGM Grand. But you'll want to escape the smokier, smaller casinos and stretch your legs (and lungs), if only for a quick monorail ride or a longer walking tour (p94).

Orientation

The Strip is a 4.5-mile stretch of Las Vegas Boulevard. The Wynn megaresort and the Fashion Show Mall stand guard at the northern edge of the **Center Strip**, which runs south all the way to Planet Hollywood's Aladdin. Nicknamed the 'Four Corners,' the busiest intersection at Las Vegas Blvd S and Flamingo Rd is where you'll find the biggest crowds around the Bellagio, Caesars Palace and the legendary Flamingo.

Further south toward the airport, the Strip action picks back up again at Tropicana Ave. The MGM Grand marks the beginning of the **South Strip**, and the bright lights peter out a block past spectacular Mandalay Bay. Some of the oldest casino hotels still standing are on the **North Strip**, mostly on one long block from Desert Inn Rd up to Riviera Blvd and Circus Circus Dr. The Sahara and the Stratosphere straggle even further north at the terminus of the Strip, from where Las Vegas Blvd continues north through the Naked City and into downtown.

Disorientation is a constant risk, whether it be while searching for your hotel room, wending your way through a deliberately confusing casino or trying to remember where you parked. Outside, you can always look up, though: the colossal, three-legged Stratosphere Tower marks the north end of the Strip; to the south is the Luxor's 40-billion-candlepower beacon, which is visible even to astronauts, so you can't miss it.

I-15 parallels the entire length of the Strip. Work out in advance which cross street will bring you closest to your destination. If it's your first time in Vegas and you're driving, make sure you do a few things. First, arrive at night. Next, pull over and admire everything from afar before you hit the city limits. Finally, take the Frank Sinatra Dr exit off the interstate and cruise the length of the Strip.

CENTER STRIP

BALLY'S Map pp262-3

☎ 702-739-4111; www.ballyslasvegas.com; 3645 Las Vegas Blvd S; monorail Bally's & Paris
Unless it's 'bigger is better,' there's no real theme at the Strip's most staid megaresort. Everything inside seems oversize – the twinkling chandeliers, velvet chairs and the **casino** itself, which features 70-plus table games

---

TRANSPORTATION – CENTER STRIP

Bus CAT (p234) bus 301 runs along Las Vegas Blvd S in both directions. Bus 302 (Strip Express) stops at Spring Mountain Rd (Fashion Show Mall) and Flamingo Rd.

Car Although all major casino hotels have free parking, getting to the garage can be annoying. Either go for valet parking at TI (Treasure Island) or turn off Harmon Ave, one block east of the Strip, and take Audrie Lane north to the self-parking garage entrance for Paris–Las Vegas, which gives you easy access to the monorail. On weekends, consider parking off-Strip at one of the smaller casino hotels near the intersection of Koval Lane and E Flamingo Rd or park on the South Strip and ride the monorail up to the Flamingo.

Monorail There are three monorail stations on the Center Strip: Bally's & Paris, located all the way at the back of Bally's basement; Flamingo/Caesars Palace, behind the Flamingo (on the opposite side of the road from Caesars Palace); and Harrah's/Imperial Palace, just before the monorail turns east toward the convention center and the Las Vegas Hilton.

Shuttle You can catch free shuttles to the Rio (p91) from Harrah's, to the Orleans (p90) and Gold Coast (p90) from Barbary Coast, and from several Strip locations to Sam's Town (p203) on the Boulder Hwy. See p236 for shuttle details.

Tram There's a free tram service between the Mirage and TI (Treasure Island).

Walking The intersection of Las Vegas Blvd and Flamingo Rd has elevated pedestrian skyways, as do the Fashion Show Mall, TI (Treasure Island) and Wynn.

Clown face, Circus Circus (p75)

(the poker room hands out electronic beepers so you can gamble while you wait for a seat) and 1500 electronic slot and video poker machines. Bally's Sunday **Sterling Brunch** (p108) is an epic event, with French champagne and cracked crab legs galore.

'Big' also describes Bally's long-running production show, **Jubilee!** (p145), which is the largest of the last two remaining showgirl extravaganzas in town (the other is the Tropicana's *Folies Bergére*, p145). Just how big is it, you ask? More than 1000 costumes are worn during the $50-million show; almost 70 stagehands are required to operate the stage, sets, lights and sound equipment; and no less than 4200 pounds of dry ice are used each week to create the production's fog effects. Be astounded by such technical trivia on the **Backstage Tour** (☎ 800-237-7469; 1hr tour $15, with show ticket $10; 🕑 2pm Mon, Wed & Sat), where your escort is a real performer. After the tour, showgirls pose with their fiftysomething admirers at the **Indigo lounge** (🕑 appearances at approximately 9:10pm & 12:10am Sat-Thu).

Bally's originally opened in 1973 as the MGM Grand built by Kirk Kekorian, who was the driving force behind the International Hotel (now the **Las Vegas Hilton**, p87). In 1980, this was the site of a fire that killed 87 people and injured more than 700. Quickly rebuilt, the Bally's resort opened the following year. It has undergone several renovations since then. Rumors abound that Bally's may be redeveloped or even demolished in the near future by Harrah's, its new owners.

There used to be a 100-yard walk from the roadside into Bally's. Now a series of movable walkways under a brashly lit neon canopy carry you inside from Las Vegas Blvd. An interior walkway connects Bally's to Paris–Las Vegas.

SIZE MATTERS

In Vegas, size matters. Here are some records the city stakes a claim on:

Biggest slot machine payout Nearly $40 million to a single lucky guy at Excalibur (p61).

Fastest elevator in the United States Stratosphere Tower (p79).

Largest bronze statue in the United States MGM Grand's lion (p63) .

Tallest building in the western United States Stratosphere Tower (p79).

Tallest chocolate fountain in the world At Bellagio's Jean-Philippe Patisserie (p117).

World's biggest gold nugget Hand of Faith at the Golden Nugget (p83).

World's biggest hotel MGM Grand (p63).

World's first 'heartline' twist-and-dive roller coaster Manhattan Express at New York–New York (p64).

World's highest roller coaster High Roller atop the Stratosphere Tower (p79).

World's largest atrium Luxor (p61).

World's largest glass sculpture Bellagio (opposite).

World's largest public wine collection The Rio's Wine Cellar (p182).

World's largest race and sports book Las Vegas Hilton's SuperBook (p87).

World's largest stained-glass mural Barbary Coast (opposite).

World's most powerful beam of light Luxor (p61).

BARBARY COAST Map pp262-3

☎ 702-737-7111; www.barbarycoastcasino.com;
3595 Las Vegas Blvd S; monorail Bally's & Paris
Lavish Tiffany-styled stained glass (more
than $2 million worth), stately chandeliers
and polished dark wood dominate this
Victorian gem – only downtown's **Main Street
Station** (p84) evokes turn-of-the-20th-century
Nevada better. Don't miss the showpiece
Garden of Earthly Delights, a 28ft-long allegorical
stained-glass mural on the casino's west
wall; adorned with antique and handblown
glass, it took more than 8000 hours to complete. Opened in 1979, Barbary Coast has a
petite **casino** with a mere 680 slot and video
poker machines, precious few table games,
and only 200 rooms. Downstairs **Drai's restaurant** (p106) and after-hours club (p150) draw
a hip crowd, while old-school lounge acts
play to veteran gamblers upstairs. Parking is
nearly impossible.

BELLAGIO Map pp262-3

☎ 702-693-7111; www.bellagio.com; 3600 Las
Vegas Blvd S; monorail Bally's & Paris
Inspired by the beauty of a lakeside Italian
village and built by Steve Wynn on the site
of the legendary Dunes, the $1.6 billion Bel-
lagio is Vegas' original opulent, if parvenu,
pleasure palazzo. Its Tuscan architecture
and 8-acre artificial lake – the antithesis of
what most people expect of Las Vegas – is,
in a word, elegant. The view from the Strip
is of a green-blue lake from which spring a
thousand dancing **fountains** (☑ shows every
15min 8pm-midnight, every 30min 3-8pm
Mon-Fri & noon-8pm Sat & Sun). While the
recorded soundtrack varies, if you're lucky,
it'll be Italian opera or ol' Blue Eyes croon-
ing 'Luck Be a Lady.'

At the water's edge, a cluster of but-
ter-yellow buildings seem to have been
plucked from the Tuscan Lake District.
Beyond the glass and metal **porte cochere**,
inside the 36-floor resort that starred in
the remake of *Ocean's Eleven,* is a stable
of world-class gourmet **restaurants** (p106),
a swish **shopping concourse** (p175) and a
European-style **casino**. Nightlife heats up
at swanky **Light** (p152), luscious **Caramel**
(p131) and **Fix** (p131) for people-watching.
Although the nouveau-riche stink of the
Bellagio is that romance is always in the air, and
natural light swathes plenty of quiet nooks,
where you can sit and soak it all up.

The highlight of the hotel's stunning
lobby is the 18ft ceiling, which is adorned
with a backlit glass sculpture composed of
2000 hand-blown flowers in vibrant colors.
Real flowers, cultivated in a gigantic, on-
site greenhouse, brighten countless vases
throughout the property, including on the
Via Fiore leading to the new spa tower. Adjacent to the lobby, the conservatory and bo-
tanical gardens host ostentatious seasonal
floral arrangements, which are installed by
crane through the soaring 50ft ceiling. The
effect is unnatural, but that doesn't stop
gawking crowds from gathering here or not
far away in front of the chocolate fountain
at **Jean-Philippe Patisserie** (p117).

Since Steve Wynn sold his baby to the
MGM Grand group for $6.4 billion, the
Bellagio hasn't been blessed with the same
world-class art. Still, it does host unique
traveling shows at the **Bellagio Gallery of Fine Art**
(☎ 702-693-7871, 877-957-9777; adult/stu-
dent & senior $15/12; ☑ 9am-9pm) such as
*Claude Monet: Masterworks from the Museum
of Fine Arts, Boston*. Don't miss the original
artwork inside **Picasso restaurant** (p107).

Outside in the Bellagio's **courtyard**, the
distinctive pool area is surrounded by private cabanas and accented by carved Italian
columns and artfully formed citrus and par-
terre-style gardens. The Mediterranean villa
setting makes for a pleasant stroll, but use of
the facilities by nonguests is strictly limited.

Baby strollers and children under 18 are
not allowed inside the Bellagio. Exceptions
are made for children aged five and up
accompanying an adult to see Cirque du Soleil's **O** (p146), to visit the art gallery or with
reservations to dine at the restaurants. The
casino, like all gaming areas in Las Vegas, is
strictly off-limits to those under 21 years old.

CAESARS PALACE Map pp262-3

☎ 702-731-7110; www.caesars.com; 3570 Las
Vegas Blvd S; monorail Flamingo/Caesars Palace
Vegas' first fully realized megaresort upped
the luxury ante for the gaming industry
when it debuted in 1966. The Greco-Roman
fantasyland captured the world's attention
with its full-size marble reproductions of
classical statuary such as Michelangelo's
David, towering Stripside fountains and
cocktail waitresses costumed as goddesses.
Thanks to ongoing megabucks renovations,
Caesars is as impressive as ever, which you
already know if you've seen *Rain Man*.

BELLAGIO

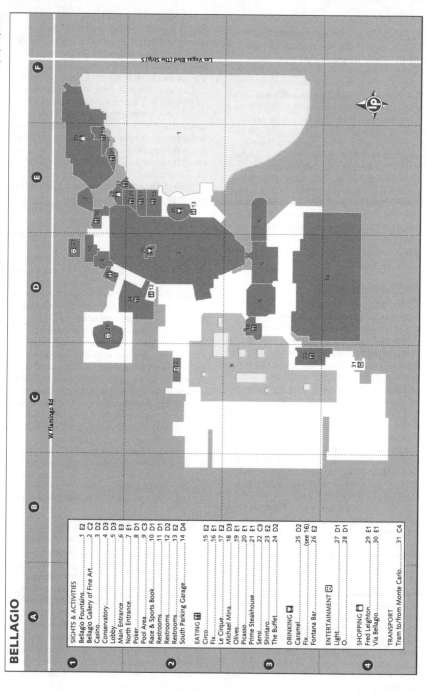

W Flamingo Rd

Las Vegas Blvd (The Strip) S

SIGHTS & ACTIVITIES
Bellagio Fountains...................1 E2
Bellagio Gallery of Fine Art.....2 C2
Casino......................................3 D2
Conservatory...........................4 D3
Lobby.......................................5 D3
Main Entrance.........................6 E3
North Entrance........................7 E1
Poker.......................................8 D1
Pool Area.................................9 C3
Race & Sports Book................10 D1
Restrooms..............................11 D1
Restrooms..............................12 D2
Restrooms..............................13 E2
South Parking Garage............14 D4

EATING
Circo......................................15 E2
Fix..16 E1
Le Cirque...............................17 E2
Michael Mina.........................18 D3
Olives.....................................19 E1
Picasso...................................20 E1
Prime Steakhouse..................21 E1
Sensi......................................22 C3
Shintaro.................................23 E2
The Buffet..............................24 D2

DRINKING
Caramel.................................25 D2
Fix.................................(see 16)
Fontana Bar............................26 E2

ENTERTAINMENT
Light......................................27 D1
O..28 D1

SHOPPING
Fred Leighton.........................29 E1
Via Bellagio...........................30 E1

TRANSPORT
Tram to/from Monte Carlo.....31 C4

Despite the upgrades, however, the kitschy Palace remains for many quintessentially Vegas. Bar girls continue to roam the gaming areas in skimpy togas, and the fountains out front are the same ones that daredevil Evil Knievel failed to jump on his motorcycle on December 31, 1967. The stuntman ended up with a shattered pelvis and a fractured skull, but also a helluva lotta fame for his pains. More than two decades later, his son Robby repeated the attempt – but successfully that time.

With the expansion of the stately pool complex, **Garden of the Gods Oasis** (p196), the spiffed-up outdoor **Roman Plaza** and four-ton Brahma shrine, plus the completion of a new luxury tower, Caesars appears poised to rule the empire once again. Inside, neon and cheesy mirrors have been replaced with hand-painted murals. Two central **casinos** proffer more than 100 card tables and thousands of slots, some of which will accept chips of up to $500. Caesars' state-of-the-art **race and sports book** has giant TV screens.

The **Colosseum**, a new 4000-seat showroom modeled after its Roman namesake, debuted in 2003 with the theatrical spectacle **Céline Dion: A New Day** (p144), conceived by former Cirque du Soleil director Franco Dragone. Nearby you'll find sexy silhouettes at the **Shadow: A Bar** (p133) and live entertainment in the equally laughable **Cleopatra's Barge** (p131). Walk past the Colosseum and through the casino to the upscale **Forum Shops** (p174), which harbors an **aquarium** (🕙 free

behind-the-scenes tour 3:15pm Mon-Fri), animatronic **fountain shows** (🕙 hourly 11am-11pm Sun-Thu, 11am-midnight Fri & Sat) and the **Exotic Cars showroom** (p173).

The nearest monorail station is more than a block away, tucked away inside the Flamingo.

FLAMINGO Map pp262-3
☎ 702-733-3111; www.flamingolasvegas.com; 3555 Las Vegas Blvd S; monorail Flamingo/Caesars Palace

In 1946 the Flamingo was the talk of the town. Its original owners – all members of the New York mafia – shelled out an unprecedented $6 million to build this tropical gaming oasis in the desert. Billy Wilkerson, owner of the *Hollywood Reporter* and a string of sizzling hot LA nightclubs, broke ground here first. He had grand visions of re-creating the Sunset Strip in the Silver State. But he ran out of money fast, so the mob stepped in.

It was prime gangster Americana, initially managed by the infamous mobster Ben 'Bugsy' Siegel, who named it after his girlfriend, a dancer named Virginia Hill who earned the nickname 'The Flamingo' for her red hair and long legs. Siegel died in a hail of bullets at her Beverly Hills home soon after the Flamingo opened, the victim of a contract killing ordered by the casino's investors; the Flamingo had got off to a slow start and the investors believed it would fail, so they 'took care of business.' They

Lied Discovery Children's Museum (p84)

had made a big mistake: the Flamingo not only survived, but has continued to thrive.

Today, the Flamingo isn't quite what it was back when its janitorial staff wore tuxedos. In 1970, Hilton purchased the casino hotel and has expanded it over the years. It no longer resembles the elegant original (think more *Miami Vice,* less *Bugsy*), nor does the casino try to evoke images of a tropical paradise or theme other than a cluster of pink-and-orange neon lights that vaguely resemble flamingo feathers.

Step away from the gaming area into the Flamingo's gardens, which, with 15 acres of pools, waterfalls and waterways, are still a sight to behold. The walk-through Wildlife Habitat (admission free) is filled with swans, exotic birds and ornamental koi; Chilean flamingos wander around; and palm trees and jungle plants are everywhere you look.

Today the Flamingo, where Judy Garland once sang on stage with her daughter Liza Minnelli, is still entertaining. Big laughs resound at Second City (p150), a comedy club. A prime place to observe the passing sea of humanity is from the balcony of Margaritaville (p132). Otherwise, drop by the casino for a madhouse happy hour, when you can often watch women of questionable repute stroll by the glitzy revolving doors, just like in *Leaving Las Vegas.* Bugsy would've loved it.

HARRAH'S Map pp262-3
☎ 702-369-5000, 800-392-9002; www.harrahs .com/our_casinos/las/; 3475 Las Vegas Blvd S; monorail Harrah's/Imperial Palace
Vacationing middle-aged Midwesterners know Harrah's casino chain for its riverboat theme, but that was thrown overboard in Vegas. Everywhere you look there's something suggestive of carnaval or Mardi Gras, although it's not nearly as racy as Harrah's sister property, Rio (p91).

Inside, what may be the brightest and most playful casino on the Strip is usually swimming with gamblers. A minor attraction is an enormous backlit mural over the front desk depicting the greatest Vegas entertainers of all time. At the northwest entrance off Las Vegas Blvd, you can take your own photo with a showgirl for free.

Entertainment is the name of the game here, with an Improv comedy club (p148), Toby Keith's country-and-western-themed

I Love This Bar & Grill, and nightly karaoke at the Piano Bar by the outdoor Carnaval Court (p131), where flair bartenders juggle fire and live-music acts get your booty shakin'.

IMPERIAL PALACE Map pp262-3
☎ 702-731-3311; www.imperialpalace.com; 3535 Las Vegas Blvd S; monorail Harrah's/Imperial Palace
The blue-roofed pagoda facade is hokey, but the faux–Far East theme at what was once the Flamingo Capri is quite alright. The popular 75,000-sq-ft low-limit casino is decked out in bamboo and rattan under a dragon-motif ceiling. Many 'dealertainers' do double-duty as celebrity impersonators, jumping up to show off their skills on the casino's small stage from noon into the wee hours. At the souvenir photo booth out front (⏰ 11am-10pm), in front of the casino, you can get your photo taken with an Elvis impersonator.

Apart from the coin-operated breathalyzer outside the liquor shop, other quirky attractions at the Palace include the Strip's best celebrity impersonator show, Legends in Concert (p146), the walk-in Stripside karaoke club at Tequila Joe's (p138), a summer poolside luau (p145), and an impressive auto collection (p174). There's even a drive-through sports book located behind the hotel, off Audrie Lane.

Incidentally, the Imperial Palace has made a point of hiring people with disabilities, who make up 13% of its staff. This initiative came from Ralph Engelstad, the sole owner of this major Las Vegas casino hotel until his death in 2002. A controversial man, Engelstad was once fined $1 million by the Nevada Gaming Commission for 'embarrassing the industry' by allegedly throwing parties in a secret Nazi memorabilia room hidden inside the Imperial Palace. He was also a lifelong philanthropist who refused to lay off employees after 9/11 gave the travel industry a beat-down. Recently sold by his widow to Harrah's corporation, the Imperial Palace may not be long for this world, so come see the kitsch while you still can.

MIRAGE Map pp262-3
☎ 702-791-7111; www.mirage.com; 3400 Las Vegas Blvd S; tram to TI (Treasure Island)
When the Mirage opened in 1989, then-owner Steve Wynn boasted that his goal was to create a property 'so overriding in

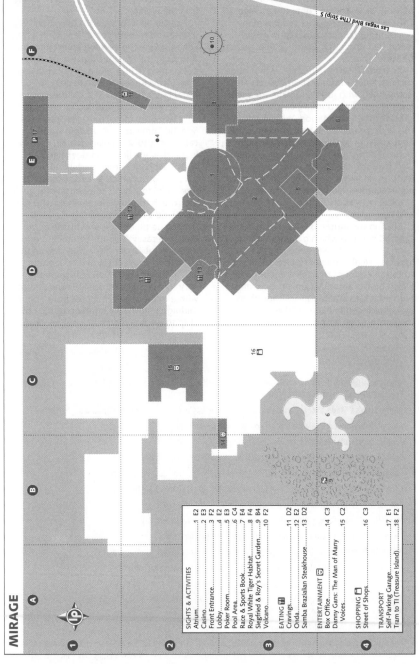

MIRAGE

Las Vegas Blvd (The Strip) S

SIGHTS & ACTIVITIES
Atrium	1 E2
Casino	2 E3
Front Entrance	3 F2
Lobby	4 E2
Pool Area	5 E3
Poker Room	6 C4
Race & Sports Book	7 E4
Royal White Tiger Habitat	8 F4
Siegfried & Roy's Secret Garden	9 B4
Volcano	10 F2

EATING 🍴
Cravings	11 D2
Onda	12 E2
Samba Braziilian Steakhouse	13 D2

ENTERTAINMENT 🎭
Box Office	14 C3
Danny Gans: The Man of Many Voices	15 C2

SHOPPING 🛍
Street of Shops	16 C3

TRANSPORT
Self-Parking Garage	17 E1
Tram to TI (Treasure Island)	18 F2

its nature that it would be a reason in and of itself for visitors to come to Las Vegas.' This $630-million resort – costing many times more than any other Strip mega-resort had up to that point – could claim to be such a place.

Its tropical setting, replete with a huge **rainforest atrium** under a 100ft conservatory dome filled with jungle foliage, meandering streams and soothing cascades, captures the imagination. Woven into this waterscape are scores of bromeliads enveloped in sunlight and fed by a computerized misting system. Tropical scents waft through the registration area, which features an awesome 20,000-gallon saltwater **aquarium** filled with 60 species of tropical critters, including pufferfish, tangs and pygmy sharks.

Circling the atrium is a huge Polynesian-themed **casino**, in which gaming areas have been placed under separate roofs to invoke intimacy. Real and faux tropical plants add to the splendor of this still elegant casino, which boasts a popular poker room and high-limit baccarat lounge. Although its glory has recently been outshone by newer megaresorts, an ambitious overhaul of the Mirage's eating and entertainment venues is in the works.

Acclaimed impressionist **Danny Gans** (p144) and touring comedians such as Jay Leno provide the evening entertainment. Although the dynamic duo are no longer performing (p148), you can still visit **Siegfried & Roy's Secret Garden & Dolphin Habitat** (☎ 702-791-7188; admission $12, children under 10 free when accompanied by an adult; ☾ 11am-5pm Mon-Fri, 10am-5pm Sat & Sun, till 7pm summer, 3:30pm winter). You can expect to see a black jaguar, a snow leopard, white lions and tigers, and an Asian elephant named Gildah. All of the feats of conservation talked about on the free audio tour can't compensate for enclosures much too small for animals who roam the world's wildest places. The Atlantic bottlenose dolphin pools are missable, too.

By the casino's south entrance, a **royal white tiger habitat** permits a free view of the big cats; if you're lucky, it'll be feeding time. Out in front set in a 3-acre lagoon, the fiery trademark 100ft **artificial volcano** erupts with a roar every 15 minutes from 7pm till midnight, inevitably bringing traffic on the Strip to a screeching halt. Look for wisps of

---

IT'S FREE

When you're down to the felt (your last dime), don't despair. Some of Vegas' most amusing diversions don't cost a thing. Popular low-roller attractions include the following:

All the Strip's a Stage Acrobats, animals and clowns at Circus Circus (p75), court jesters at Excalibur (p61).

Animatronic Wonders Inside the Forum Shops at Caesars Palace (p51).

Aquatic Spectacular Bellagio's romantic fountains (p51).

Gold That's Not for Fools Golden Nugget (p83) has mega-nuggets on display.

Idolatrous Shrines Hard Rock casino (p87) is a temple to the gods and goddesses of rock 'n' roll.

Laser Light Show At the Fremont Street Experience (p82), all eyes look toward heaven.

Lounge Acts Every major casino has them, and most are entertaining (p135).

Mardi Gras Celebrations In Rio's Masquerade Village (p91) several times a day.

Mermaids At the Silverton's Mermaid Lounge (p140), south of the Strip.

Pink Is In Acres of gardens and the wildlife habitat at the Flamingo (p53).

Roar like a Lion With the MGM Grand's signature animal in its casino habitat (p63).

Sirens of TI Sexy high-seas hijinks have never been so hilarious (p58).

Tigers and a Volcano Mirage (p54) is a feast for the eyes and ears. Hear the rumbling of the volcano and the royal white tigers at feeding time.

Wait, Who Was That?! Celebrity impersonators at the Imperial Palace (p54).

Window Shopping Million-dollar necklaces in Bellagio's shops (p175), high fashion at Caesars' Forum Shops (p174), the Ferrari-Maserati dealership at Wynn (p175) and strolling minstrels in the Venetian's Grand Canal Shoppes (p174).

smoke escaping from the top that signal the inferno is about to begin.

The Mirage's palate-pleasing eating options include the classy **Cravings buffet** (p108). A collection of upscale boutiques lines the Mirage's **Street of Shops** (p175).

Few people leave the Mirage unimpressed, although its appeal is subtle. A free tram glides over to Treasure Island.

PARIS–LAS VEGAS Map pp262-3

☎ 702-946-7000; www.parislasvegas.com; 3655 Las Vegas Blvd S; monorail Bally's & Paris

Napoleon once said, 'Secrets travel fast in Paris.' The same can be said for Las Vegas, where Paris, which opened in 1999, was one secret that made the rounds here in record time. This $785-million Gallic caricature evokes the gaiety of the City of Light – right down to the wandering mimes and accordion players.

The casino hotel strives to capture the essence of the grand dame herself by recreating her landmarks, including a 34-story replica of the **Hotel de Ville**. Fine likenesses of the **Paris Opéra House**, the **Arc de Triomphe**, the **Louvre**, **Parc Monceau** and even the **River Seine** frame the property. Like the French capital, the signature attraction is the **Eiffel Tower** (adult/senior & child 6-12 $9/7, Fri & Sat $12/10; ☾ 10am-1am, weather permitting), where visitors can travel in a glass elevator to an **observation deck** for panoramic views of the valley and mountains and the fountains at the **Bellagio** (p51). How authentic is this half-scale tower? Gustave Eiffel's original drawings were consulted, but the 50-story steel replica is welded together rather than riveted. It's also fireproof and engineered to withstand a major earthquake. You can dine in the gourmet **Eiffel Tower Restaurant** (p112), overlooking the Strip.

Surrounded by street scenes from both banks of the Seine, the bustling 85,000-sq-ft, vault-ceilinged **casino** with replica Métropolitain arches is home to almost a hundred gaming tables; a couple thousand slot machines; a popular **race and sports book**, located conveniently next to Le Bar du Sport, and two of the USA's only authentic French roulette wheels (they have no '0' or '00,' which slightly improves your odds of winning) in the high-limit area. A dozen crème de la crème **French restaurants** (p111) dish out authentic gourmet fare, but you should snag an alfresco Stripside table

Neon Museum (p84)

at **Mon Ami Gabi** (p112). Check out **Napoleon's** (p132), a champagne bar; the free lounge entertainment at Parisian-styled **Le Cabaret**; the beautiful people ascending the grand staircase to **Risqué** (p153); and the caviar facials at the **Spa by Mandara** (p165).

Paris is connected to Bally's and its monorail station by an extension of the quaint cobblestone Le Boulevard (p174), a *petit* shopping arcade.

PLANET HOLLYWOOD (ALADDIN) Map pp262-3

☎ 702-785-5555; www.planethollywood.com; 3667 Las Vegas Blvd S; monorail Bally's & Paris

Dating from the 1950s, the original Aladdin, where Elvis and Priscilla Presley tied the knot, was dramatically imploded in 1998. Retooled to target the Asian and European jet set, the $1.4-billion new Aladdin megaresort threw open its doors just two years later. Only 13 months after the grand opening, the owners made the largest bankruptcy filing in Nevada history, with an outstanding debt of $700 million.

By the time you read this, it is quite possible that Planet Hollywood, Aladdin's *new* new owners, will have dramatically changed the megaresort, which has been losing money almost from the day it opened. Once the theme shifts from Istanbul to Hollywood, the Sahara will be the only Middle Eastern fantasy left on the Strip. Not coincidentally, it was the owners of the Sahara in the 1960s who magically created Aladdin from the Tally Ho casino hotel. Wayne Newton owned Aladdin for a while, Johnny Carson once tried to buy it, and, during the 1980s, before the economic bubble burst in the Land of the Rising Sun, a Japanese businessman controlled it. But no one has ever made a mint with this hexed property. Not yet, anyway.

For now, inside the appealing Moroccan facade is a multilevel 100,000-sq-ft casino. When compared to the classy Bellagio (p51) or Venetian (right), Planet Hollywood's Aladdin is clearly second tier. But it's also fun. Atop a two-story replica of Scheherazade's Palace sits a live-music lounge and a few restaurants. The resort's real strengths are entertainment, especially its history of risk-taking productions, and the impressive Moorish shopping arcade, Desert Passage (p173). Back inside the casino, a revamped nightspot called Club Paris, owned by the infamous Paris Hilton, is set to open soon.

TI (TREASURE ISLAND) Map pp262-3
☎ 702-894-7111; www.treasureisland.com; 3300 Las Vegas Blvd S; tram to Mirage
Yo, ho, whoa: though traces of Treasure Island's original swashbuckling skull-and-crossbones theme linger (if you look hard), the reimagined TI, a tonier, terra cotta–hued resort striving for an elegant Caribbean hideaway appeal, practically screams 'leave the kids at home.' TI's shift away from family-friendly to bawdy and oh so naughty epitomizes Vegas' strident efforts to put the 'sin' back in 'casino.'

Visitors approach the property via a wood-bottomed bridge with hemp rope–supporting sides that span the artificial Sirens' Cove, beside which is a vague replica of an 18th-century sea village. The spicy Sirens of TI (7pm, 8:30pm, 10pm & 11:30pm, weather permitting) mock sea battle, a clash of the sexes pitting sultry temptresses against renegade freebooters, takes place in the cove. The show's two ships – a Spanish privateer vessel and a British frigate – face off on schedule several times nightly. It's free, but hardly worth watching, except for the pyrotechnics.

Inside, the adults-only theme continues in the sprawling casino. One-armed Playboy bandits await where playful pirates, plastic doubloons and chests full-o-booty once reigned. Slot machines and gaming tables

are tightly grouped, but no one seems to mind – the place is relentlessly packed. Thankfully, the sirens' song is toned down in the four-diamond guestrooms.

The latest grown-up additions to the casino hotel are deluxe poolside cabanas, a huge party-friendly hot tub and the Strip-side tangerine (p153) burlesque lounge and nightclub. There's no excuse for starving or dying of thirst here, with Canter's Deli (p115), an LA import; the tequila goddesses at Isla Mexican Kitchen & Tequila Bar (p112), and inexhaustible Dishes (p108).

The real must-see is Cirque du Soleil's fantastic evening production, Mystère (p146). Easing the journey there or back is a tram ride to the Mirage (p54), which shares the 100-acre site. A new skybridge links TI and the Fashion Show Mall (p173), just to the north.

VENETIAN Map pp262-3
☎ 702-414-1000, 877-883-6423; www.venetian.com; 3355 Las Vegas Blvd S; monorail Harrah's/Imperial Palace
Impresario Sheldon Adelson broke ground on his replica of La Repubblica Serenissima ('Most Serene Republic') – reputed to be the home of the world's first casino – less than six months after the controversial and dramatic implosion of the 44-year-old Sands hotel in 1996.

Inspired by the splendor of Italy's most romantic city, the $1.5 billion megaresort is being developed in phases. Facing the Strip are reproductions of Venetian landmarks, including a doge's palace and campanile (bell tower). Inside is a 120,000-sq-ft casino, with marble floors, hand-painted ceiling frescoes and 120 table games.

Graceful bridges, flowing canals, and vibrant piazzas faithfully capture the Venetian spirit, especially inside the Grand Canal Shoppes (p174) where gondolas (indoor/outdoor ride adult $12.50/15, child 12 & under $5/7.50, private 2-passenger rides $50-60; 10am-10:45pm, to 11:45pm Fri & Sat) sail; same-day, in-person reservations are required. As you roam around, don't miss the classically trained minstrels in period costume, the living statues near St Mark's Square and a festive gondolier march (9:45am & 4:15pm), always more enjoyable with a scoop of rich gelato in hand. Stop by Las Vegas Preview Studios (☎ 702-732-2733; 11am-9pm), near the gondola turnaround, to give your opinions about new TV shows or slot machines.

The stunning **Guggenheim Hermitage** (☎ 702-414-2440; www.guggenheimlasvegas.org; lobby level; adults/students & children 6-12/seniors $19/14.50/16.50; ☯ 9:30am-8:30pm), designed by Pritzker Prize–winning architect Rem Koolhaas, houses an austere, bilevel gallery with a natural skylight, the underneath of which flaunts an homage to Michelangelo's Sistine Chapel. A partnership between New York's Guggenheim Museum and Russia's State Hermitage Museum in St Petersburg ensures the masterpieces keep on coming.

The Venetian is linked to the ever-expanding, state-of-the-art **Sands Expo** convention center. The newest addition to the hotel is the all-suite Venezia Tower, with its exclusive concierge level. Other amenities include the **Canyon Ranch SpaClub** (p164) and top-drawer gourmet **restaurants** (p112), some with star chefs at the helm.

Even if you've had the good fortune to stroll the cobblestones and navigate the romantic canals of the one-and-only Italian port, you won't want to miss the Vegas version. In a city filled with spectacles, the Venetian is surely one of the most spectacular. Outside by the moving walkway of the **Rialto Bridge** is the interactive **Madame Tussauds** (☎ 702-862-7800; www.madametussaudslv.com; adult/child 6-12/senior & student $23/13/18, discounts for AAA cardholders; ☯ 10am-10pm) wax museum, where you can strike a pose with Elvis, star alongside J Lo in a music video, or play Texas hold'em in a celebrity poker showdown with Ben Affleck and a live-action dealer.

WYNN Map pp262-3

☎ 702-770-7000; www.wynnlasvegas.com; 3145 Las Vegas Blvd S; bus 301, 302

Casino impresario Steve Wynn's eponymous resort turns the themed casino hotel concept inside out. Instead of an exploding volcano or mini–Eiffel Tower out front to lure people, Wynn Las Vegas is all about exclusivity – getting inside is the goal, so you can then voyeuristically gaze at the hoi polloi flooding Las Vegas Blvd, secure in your lavish retreat. Reserve a suite and you even get to use a private VIP side entrance.

This signature – literally, it has Wynn's name written in script across the top – copper-toned hotel is semi-shielded from the Strip by an artificial 'mountain' of greenery and waterfalls. Slack-jawed tourists stroll over the bridges into the resort, waltzing by the haute couture of the shops on **Wynn Esplanade** (p175). Wynn's fine-art collection – with a dozen original works by Cézanne, Van Gogh, Matisse, Gauguin, Picasso and Warhol – is displayed in an **art gallery** (admission $15; ☯ 10am-11pm Sun-Thu, 10am-midnight Fri & Sat). Inside the 110,000-sq-ft **casino** is a popular **poker room** that's attracting pros around the clock; slot machines from a penny up to $5K per pull; a cavernous **race and sports book**, and a spread of table games (mostly high-minimum), along with poolside blackjack for guests.

Perhaps the most remarkable thing about Wynn is the painstaking attention to detail, from an easy-access self-parking garage with electronic signboards directing you toward vacant spaces to comfy chaise

Elvis-A-Rama Museum (p89)

longues in the registration area. In fact, it's as if Mirage and Bellagio were only Wynn's rough drafts. Elements of both of the mogul's former projects peek through here. This new resort has the decor of the Bellagio, but with more joyously vibrant colors and inlaid flower mosaics. The water features (though the hokey statues are laughable) and lush greenery recall the Mirage, but without the Mirage's claustrophobia, thanks to panoramic windows, natural light and outdoor seating at every turn.

Wynn has also reunited with successful past partners, such as Franco Dragone, who has created a new megaproduction show, **La Reve** (p146), then takes it one step further by bringing honest-to-goodness Broadway shows to town such as **Avenue Q** (p143) and Spamalot, based on the movie *Monty Python and the Holy Grail*.

Wynn boasts a stable of star chefs. Stand-out restaurants include Allesandro Stratta's **Alex** (p114), **Daniel Boulud Brasserie** (p114) and Paul Bartolotta's **Ristorante Di Mare** (p114). Out back of the hotel, more than 800,000 cubic yards of earth were moved while redesigning the world-class **golf course** (available to hotel guests only).

Wynn has single-handedly transformed the energy of the North Strip, giving folks a good reason to venture north to the **Fashion Show Mall** (p173) and beyond to the North Strip (p75). An estimated 10,000 people stood in line for hours just to get in Wynn's front door on opening night in 2005. Although it's overhyped, the resort's finesse and overwhelming emphasis on personal service are likely to give it stamina. With luck, it'll last as long as the Desert Inn,

which was imploded on this site to make way for Wynn, which was five years in the making.

It doesn't stop there. Wynn will debut Encore, another billion-dollar-plus megaresort, next door in late 2008. Wynn also plans to operate a free shuttle service to and from the monorail; call for details.

SOUTH STRIP

BOARDWALK Map pp262-3
☎ 702-735-2400; www.boardwalklv.com; 3750 Las Vegas Blvd S; monorail MGM Grand

One of the Strip's most bizarre low-roller casinos (how can you account for the enormous fake roller coaster and Ferris wheel out front?), Boardwalk is owned by the MGM Grand Mandalay group, which plans to redevelop it into a mixed-use property, with a casino hotel, residential condos and three boutique hotels, plus dining, entertainment and shopping. For now, this ex–Holiday Inn calls itself the 'Coney Island of Las Vegas.' Inside the **casino** are a few table games, hundreds of slot and video poker games, and a full **race and sports book** heavy on clown *objets d'art*. The colossal New York–New York resort next door overwhelms the more mild attractions offered here, namely free lounge acts (such as a Prince tribute artist) in the **Lighthouse Showroom** every evening. Still, after spending time in the Strip's megaresort casinos, it's refreshing to wander into this bright, cheerful place to play a few nickel slots and dine on graveyard steak and eggs at the 24-hour **Surf Buffet**.

TRANSPORTATION – SOUTH STRIP

Bus CAT (p234) bus 301 (Strip) runs along Las Vegas Blvd S in both directions. Bus 302 (Strip Express) stops near the intersection with Tropicana Ave.

Car The self-parking garage at MGM Grand (enter off Tropicana Ave) puts you close to the monorail station. For handy valet parking, follow the signs off the Strip to THEHotel at Mandalay Bay, which is a short walk from the casino.

Monorail The South Strip's only monorail station is off the Studio Walk at MGM Grand.

Shuttle There's a free shuttle service from Sam's Town (p203) on the Boulder Hwy to Hooters (San Remo) casino hotel (p194) beside the Tropicana. See p236 for shuttle details.

Tram There's a free tram between the Excalibur, Mandalay Bay and Luxor. Going from Excalibur to Luxor, you usually have to change trams at Mandalay Bay; take the moving underground walkway instead.

Walking The intersection of Las Vegas Blvd S and Tropicana Ave is criss-crossed by elevated pedestrian skybridges. Other pedestrian crossings on the Strip are in front of the Monte Carlo and further north at Harmon Ave.

EXCALIBUR Map pp262-3

☎ 702-597-7777; www.excalibur.com; 3850 Las Vegas Blvd S; tram to Mandalay Bay & Luxor

Arthurian legends aside, this caricature of a castle – it's white with bright orange-, red- and blue-roofed towers and a faux draw-bridge – epitomizes gaudy Vegas. Excalibur could have resembled an elegant English castle, but its designers decided to go the kitschy route, which is just fine with most of the families with rambunctious young kids who stay here.

Inside the castle, the walls of the **casino** are hung with coats of arms and cheap stained-glass art depicting valiant knights. Down on the **Fantasy Faire Midway** are buried ye olde carnival games like skee-ball, with joystick joys in the Wizard's Arcade. **Merlin's Magic Motion Machine** film rides (per 10-minute ride $5) virtually hurl you down a haunted mine, let you fly on the 'ultimate roller coaster' or unlock the secrets of a temple that Indy Jones would've loved. Riders must be at least 42in tall. Upstairs, the **Court Jester's Stage** (Medieval Village Level; ⏰ 11am-7:30pm, 10-min shows every 45 min) is a free extravaganza with musicians playing period instruments, such as the mandolin, flute and harp; magicians performing feats that medieval alchemists never would have imagined; and jugglers and puppeteers doing their thing. The **Tournament of Kings** (p146) is more of a demolition derby with hooves and sticky fingers than a flashy Vegas production show.

Excalibur is connected to the luxurious Luxor by a covered people mover, making it easy to zip over, if only for the snicker factor. A free tram links Excalibur, Mandalay Bay and Luxor.

GAMEWORKS Map pp262-3

☎ 702-432-4263; www.gameworks.com; Showcase Mall, 3785 Las Vegas Blvd S; rock climbing $10, 1/2/3hr play $20/25/27; ⏰ 10am-midnight Sun-Thu, till 1am Fri & Sat; monorail MGM Grand

Originally conceived by film director Steven Spielberg and developed by DreamWorks SKG in conjunction with Sega and Universal Studios, this high-tech arcade attracts both teens and adults. Squeezed between the **Everything Coca-Cola** (p177) and **M&M's World** (p176), the large underground room contains a full bar and grill, a 75ft climbing wall, pool tables, air hockey, retro arcade games and loads of virtual-reality games.

TOP FIVE VIDEO-GAME ARCADES

Exchange your slot-machine quarters for video-game tokens at the following:

- **ESPN Zone & Coney Island Emporium** (New York–New York; p64)
- **Fantasy Faire Midway & Wizard's Arcade** (Excalibur; left)
- **GameWorks** (left)
- **Games of the Gods** (Luxor; below)
- **Midway & Adventure Zone** (Circus Circus; p75)

Honorable mentions go to the following: **MGM Grand** (p63), for having the loosest Ms Pacman joysticks in town; **Las Vegas Hilton** (p87) for its Dance Dance Revolution machines sans long queues; **Sahara** (p77) for having the Las Vegas Cyber Speedway and Pit Pass Arcade; and the **Silverton** (p166) for miniature arcade bowling inside an Airstream trailer (but, alas, no video games).

Note that most video arcades are only open from 10am until 10pm (later on Friday and Saturday nights).

It's only crowded – and fun – at night, but you must be over 21 to enter after 9pm. Bring buddies, because the best games involve several participants. Local bands perform here almost weekly.

LUXOR Map pp262-3

☎ 702-262-4000; www.luxor.com; 3900 Las Vegas Blvd S; tram to Excalibur & Mandalay Bay

Named after Egypt's splendid ancient city perched on the east bank of the Nile, the landmark Luxor has the biggest wow factor of the South Strip's megaresorts. The resort's designers chose a theme that easily could have produced a pyramid of gaudiness, but instead resulted in an elegant shrine to Egyptian art, architecture and antiquities. The pyramid houses the **world's largest atrium**, has 120,000 sq ft of smartly arranged gaming areas and hosts a diverse array of attractions.

Built in 1993, the 30-story **pyramid** is the focus, cloaked in black glass from base to apex; in all, there are 26,783 glass plates totaling 13 acres. The atrium is so voluminous it could accommodate nine Boeing 747s and still have room for 50 Cessnas. At its apex, a 40-billion-candlepower **beacon**, the world's most powerful, sends a shaft of blueish white light 10 miles out into space, where it's visible to astronauts.

Out in front of the pyramid is a 10-story crouching **sphinx** and a sandstone **obelisk** etched with hieroglyphics. The pyramid's interior is decorated with huge **Egyptian statues** of guards, lions and rams; sandstone walls adorned with hieroglyphic-inscribed tapestries and grand columns; a stunning **replica of the Great Temple of Ramses II** and a pharaoh's treasure of polished marble.

Exquisite reproductions of artifacts discovered by English archaeologist Howard Carter in 1922 during his descent into the fabled tomb of an obscure Egyptian dynasty are explained during a 15-minute, self-guided audio tour (available in English, French, German, Spanish or Japanese) of the **King Tut Museum** (admission $10; ☾9am-5pm). Dr Omar Mabreuck, a renowned Egyptologist, oversaw the production of the museum pieces, which may be hard to appreciate without snickering due to the casino setting. Among the exhibits are King Tut's innermost gold-leaf coffin, decorated with ornate hieroglyphics and simulated precious stones; the antechamber, which contains wooden and gold funerary beds carved in the form of animals; and the treasury, which contains several miniature wooden boats intended to carry Tutankhamen on his voyage to the afterworld.

There's a **casino**, of course, featuring a few thousand slot and video machines, more than a hundred gaming tables, and a cutting-edge **race and sports book**. Upstairs in the Pharaoh's Pavilion, thrills and chills await at the revved-up **Games of the Gods**

arcade, complete with a virtual-reality ride that lets you design your own roller coaster; an **IMAX theatre** (p159) and motion-simulator **ridefilms** (per ride $7.50); and the **Pirates 4D movie** (admission $7; ☾9am-6pm).

The Luxor is connected to Excalibur by a moving walkway. The fastest way to the Luxor from Mandalay Bay is aboard the free tram, but you can also walk between the two casino hotels via **Mandalay Place** (p176).

MANDALAY BAY Map pp262-3
☎ 702-632-7777, 877-632-7800; www.mandalay bay.com; 3950 Las Vegas Blvd S; tram to Luxor & Excalibur

The $950 million, vaguely tropically themed 'M-Bay' is no exception to the grandeur of Vegas' megaresorts, although it stands apart at the distant southern end of the Strip. Gamblers will appreciate the vast and classy **casino** and **race and sports book**.

Vegas has long sought to boost its appeal by inviting celebrities to perform on its stages. In 1999 legendary tenor Luciano Pavarotti played a grand opening concert at the **Mandalay Bay Events Center** (p157), which now hosts championship boxing. The resort carried this star-studded strategy a few steps further by adding an entertainment complex, **House of Blues** (p156), and the exclusive club **Foundation Room** (p151).

Everything at M-Bay is a spectacle, if you know where to look. It has folk art inside the **House of Blues** restaurant (p116), flights of firewater at **rumjungle** (p135), catsuit-clad

---

WELCOME TO FABULOUS LAS VEGAS

Straddling Las Vegas Blvd, south of the Strip proper, is the city's most iconic sign (Map p260), which announces in vintage mod style, 'Welcome to Fabulous Las Vegas Nevada.' Of course, when Betty Willis designed it in the late 1950s, it wasn't retro – it was cutting-edge, with an atomic-modern starburst at the top and, on the back, a friendly reminder to 'Drive Carefully' and 'Come Back Soon.' The sign was placed on the highway to LA, but it was beyond the reach of the city's fingers. Even today, the Strip hasn't managed to spread quite this far south.

The city's centennial in 2005 was a rare chance for Las Vegans to reflect on history, which is often anathema in a place where the next big thing is always thought of more highly than what came before. These days, the original sign that had fallen into disrepair in the '70s is a tourist attraction in its own right. It even made a cameo appearance on limited-edition license plates. The city went so far as to install a smaller version of the sign North of the Strip (Map p265) that announces 'Welcome to Fabulous Downtown Las Vegas.' Which may not be truth in advertising yet, but downtown *is* getting more fabulous all the time.

As you drive by the original welcome sign, you may see limos pulled up alongside the road and camera-happy tourists dashing out onto the median to get a souvenir photo of themselves by the icon. Now, you can even take home a 12.5in-tall working model of the sign (it lights up! it flashes!) for a mere $40, with some proceeds benefiting the Nevada Cancer Institute; order online at www.thewelcometolvsign.com or call ☎ 702-735-7446. Alternatively, pick one up at the **Welcome to Fabulous Las Vegas souvenir store** (p177).

Liberace Museum (p88)

'wine angels' scaling a four-story tower at **Aureole** (p115); and a headless Lenin statue and solid ice bar at **Red Square** (p135). The latest stylish additions are **Mandalay Place** (p176), a shopping promenade that connects M-Bay to Luxor, and the minimalist modern **THEhotel** (p193) with its spa, **bathhouse** (p164).

Despite billboards around town advertising an image of a great white shark looking oh-so menacing, you won't see any great whites at Mandalay Bay. Nevertheless, the standout attraction is the **Shark Reef** (☎ 702-632-4555; adult/child 5-12 $16/10, child under 4 free; ⏲ 10am-11pm, last admission 10pm), an educational conservation facility. This 1.6-million-gallon walk-through aquarium complex is home to more than a thousand submarine beasties, including large and small sharks, jellyfish, moray eels and stingrays. There's even a shallow petting pool. Other rare and endangered toothy reptiles on display include some of the world's last remaining golden crocodiles. Admission to the overpriced compound includes a free audio tour and wandering staff members include biologists, scuba-diver caretakers and naturalists.

Rather save your money for the slots? Check out the two free, but not nearly as impressive **aquariums** near the registration desk and at the Coral Reef Lounge. Outside the hotel on the lower level, an 11-acre garden includes sandy **Mandalay Beach** (where surfing competitions are sometimes held on 6ft waves), a lazy river ride, a variety of pools, and the Euro-style, clothing-optional **Moorea Beach Club** and ultra lounge (p152).

A free tram shuttles from Mandalay Bay to Luxor and Excalibur.

MGM GRAND Map pp262-3

☎ 702-891-7777, 877-880-0880; www.mgmgrand .com; 3799 Las Vegas Blvd S; monorail MGM Grand

With more than 5000 rooms, the $1 billion MGM retains the 'world's largest hotel' title, despite mounting competition from the Genting Highlands resort complex in Malaysia. When the MGM opened in 1993, $3.5 million in quarters was needed for its slot machines and to make change. Thirty-nine armored cars were used to transport the 14 million coins, which were delivered in 3600 sacks, each of which weighed 60lb. Today the MGM Grand has no fewer than 18,000 doors, 7778 beds and 93 elevators. Despite its size, the shimmering emerald-green 'City of Entertainment' strives to make its attractions seem intimate. Owned by movie company Metro Goldwyn Mayer, the MGM has co-opted Hollywood themes.

Equal in size to four football fields, the **casino** consists of one gigantic, circular room with an ornate domed ceiling and replicated 1930s glamour, right down to gorgeous restrooms worthy of a quick primp. The gaming areas offer a whopping selection of slots and the full spectrum of table games, plus the requisite **race and sports book**, and a brand new **poker room** beside the flashy **Centrifuge** bar (p131) and opposite **Studio 54** (p153). More high-voltage nightlife options include Vegas' first ultra lounge, **Tabú** (p136), and the throbbing global jukebox at Euro-style **Teatro** (p136).

The $9-million **lion habitat** (admission free; ⏲ 11am-10pm) showcases up to six adult animals daily. At times, the lions sleep atop the see-through walkway tunnel, separated from their admirers only by a sheet of protective glass and a couple of feet of air. The caretaker has been working with exotic animals for more than three decades and lives with the felines on a ranch outside town. Trainers can often be seen inside the habitat, engaged in tug-of-rope with the big cats, which seem rudely confined. Next door is a shop with loads of lion-related souvenirs and the family-friendly **Rainforest Café.**

Out front, it's hard to miss the USA's largest bronze statue, a 100,000lb lion that's 45ft tall, perched atop a 25ft pedestal and ringed by lush landscaping, spritzing fountains and Atlas-themed statues. Other 'Maximum Vegas' attractions include the gigantic **Grand Garden Arena** (p157), which often hosts championship boxing bouts and megaconcerts; the saucy **La Femme** (p145) topless revue; an impressive lineup of celebrity chefs' **restaurants** (p118), and a Cirque du Soleil show, **Kà** (p145). On the **Studio Walk** (p176) shopping concourse, **CBS Television City** (admission free; ⊙ 1hr screenings usually 10am-10pm) lets you preview new TV-program pilots and voice your opinions afterward. Opposite the preview sign-up booth is the subterranean entrance to the MGM's video arcade.

With so much to do here, many guests choose not to spend their time anywhere else, though the monorail station makes for quick escapes up the Strip.

MONTE CARLO Map pp262-3

☎ 702-730-7000; www.montecarlo.com; 3770 Las Vegas Blvd S; monorail MGM Grand

A joint venture between the owners of Bellagio and Mandalay Bay, the Monte Carlo aims for the European elegance of the former and the entertainment brilliance of the latter. The casino is bustling and spacious, but otherwise this is a poor person's Caesars Palace rather than an evocation of the grandeur of its namesake in Monaco.

The $344-million resort is fronted by Corinthian-style colonnades, triumphal arches, petite dancing fountains and allegorical statuary. A magnificent marble-floored, crystal-chandeliered **lobby** with Palladian windows overlooking the pool area is reminiscent of a European grand hotel. For entertainment, there's master magician **Lance Burton** (p148), many critics' pick for Vegas' best illusionist.

Other reasons for a quickie visit here are a spacious **casino** with table games, slot machines, a high-limit gaming area, and a **race and sports book;** classy **Houdini's Lounge** (p135); and the sporty **Monte Carlo Pub & Brewery** (p135).

The Monte Carlo is a half-block walk north of New York–New York.

NEW YORK–NEW YORK Map pp262-3

☎ 702-740-6969; www.nynyhotelcasino.com; 3790 Las Vegas Blvd S; monorail MGM Grand

Give me your tired, huddled (over a Wheel of Fortune slot machine) masses. Opened in 1997, this $485-million mini-megapolis features scaled-down replicas of the **Empire State Building** (47 stories, or 529ft); a 150ft replica of the **Statue of Liberty**, ringed by a 9/11 memorial; a miniature **Brooklyn Bridge**; renditions of the Chrysler, Ziggurat and Liberty Plaza buildings; and a Coney Island–style roller coaster wrapped around the exterior facade.

Design elements throughout the property reflect the history, color and diversity of 'Nu Yawk.' The attention to detail is remarkable, down to the whiffs of steam rising from faux manhole covers near the Chrysler elevator. Don't miss the ornate casino-level Rockefeller restrooms or the playful USA bas-relief map at **America** (p119) eatery. Claustrophobes, beware: this Disneyfied version of the Big Apple can get even more crowded than the real deal: around a million pedestrians stride NYC's Brooklyn Bridge each year, but an estimated 15 million traverse the Vegas version on an annual basis.

The crowded **casino** attracts a mélange of mostly college-aged, middle-American humanity. Slews of slots and gaming tables are set against a rich backdrop of famous landmarks, with high-limit **Gaming on the Green.** Down with off-track betting? The **race and sports book** offers electronic satellite wagering. Excellent **restaurants** (p119), **budget eats** (p119) and retail shops hide behind colorful facades stolen from Park Avenue, Greenwich Village and Times Square storefronts. Upstairs inside **ESPN Zone** (p134), a sports-themed bar and eatery, you can play state-of-the-art boxing, pro golfing and other virtual-reality arcade games, go duckpin bowling or scramble up a 30ft rock-climbing wall.

NEW YORK–NEW YORK

Las Vegas Blvd (The Strip) S

Tropicana Ave

SIGHTS & ACTIVITIES
Brooklyn Bridge..................1 F2
Casino..................................2 B
ESPN Zone..........................3 E1
Gaming on the Green........4 E4
Lobby..................................5 C3
Main Entrance....................6 D4
Manhattan Express Roller Coaster
  (upstairs)..........................7 D1
Pool Area............................8 C3
Race & Sports Book............9 E2
Statue of Liberty..............10 F4

EATING
America..............................11 C3
Chin Chin...........................12 D2
Fulton Fish Frye.................13 E1
Gallagher's.........................14 D2
Gonzalez y Gonzalez.........15 E1
Greenberg & Sons Deli......16 E1
Il Fornaio...........................17 D2
Schrafft's Ice Cream (upstairs)...18 E3
Tropicana Smoothies (upstairs)...(see 18)

DRINKING
Bar at Times Square..........19 E2
Big Apple Bar.....................20 D3
Coyote Ugly.......................(see 18)
ESPN Zone..........................(see 3)
Nine Fine Irishmen............21 E3

ENTERTAINMENT
Box Office...........................22 D1
Rita Rudner........................23 E2
Zumanity Theatre..............24 D1

65

LOST LEGENDS

The world's largest gambling museum, the **Casino Legends Hall of Fame**, stockpiles more than 150,000 pieces of gaming and celebrity memorabilia. It almost lives up to its billing, too, offering terrific value and a wonderful trip down memory lane for old-timers. It is a must-see for history buffs and Vegas lovers alike.

Don't miss the museum's video about famous hotel implosions – a quirky bit of local lore. You'll also marvel at the attention to detail paid to a re-creation of a showgirl's dressing room, hear rare interviews with Vegas notables, gaze upon some classic photographs of legendary Vegas performers, and linger over thousands of souvenirs from long-gone casinos whose ghosts still haunt Vegas' green felt jungle.

Sadly, the museum, which had for years been hidden away inside the Tropicana's basement, was homeless at press time. Owner Steven Cutler, a local resident since the 1950s, intends to find a new public space for his collection soon. With corporate sponsorship, he hopes to make the whole shebang a 21st-century experience. Until that happens, you can visit the smaller **Lost Vegas Historic Gambling Museum** (p84) on downtown's Fremont St, next to the vintage signs inside the Neonopolis.

What would a big bad city be without a few watering holes? The **Big Apple Bar** (p134) hosts live lounge acts; **Coyote Ugly** (p134) is a saloon that takes its cue from the movie of the same name; the **Bar at Times Square** (p134) is popular with the fortysomething crowd; and **Nine Fine Irishmen** (p135) is a pub featuring well-poured pints and live jig bands. Meanwhile, Cirque du Soleil's **Zumanity** (p147) titillates couples, comedienne **Rita Rudner** (p149) splits sides with her one-woman show, and **Houdini's Magic Shop** (p175) amazes onlookers.

Above the casino, **Coney Island Emporium** (☾ 8am-midnight, till 2am Fri & Sat), a 32,000-sq-ft entertainment center, features more than 200 video-arcade games and the **Manhattan Express** (single-ride ticket $12.50, re-ride $6; ☾ 10:30am-11pm, till midnight Fri & Sat). The highlight of this roller coaster is a heartline twist-and-dive maneuver, producing a sensation similar to that felt by a pilot during a barrel roll in a fighter plane. The rest of the three-minute trip includes stomach-dropping dipsy-dos, high banked turns, a 540-degree spiral and blink-and-you'll-miss-it views of the Strip. As the train nears the end of its 4777ft of track, the coaster disappears through the casino roof. Unfortunately, your head and shoulders will take a helluva beating on this ride; hold on tight and secure loose valuables in the lockers out front (50¢). Riders must be at least 54in tall.

A pedestrian skybridge links New York–New York with the MGM Grand, which has a monorail station. Another skybridge crosses to Excalibur, where you can catch a tram to Mandalay Bay and Luxor.

TROPICANA Map pp262-3

☎ 702-739-2222; www.tropicanalv.com; 3801 Las Vegas Blvd S; monorail MGM Grand

Built in 1957, the Tropicana has had nearly half a century to sully its shine, lose its crowds and go the way of the Dunes and the Sands – ashes to ashes, dust to dust. But thanks to a few lifts and tucks, the Trop is still hanging in there. There's still a festive Polynesian village feel to it all. A clutch of exotic birds, including a green-winged macaw, a Moluccan cockatoo and a Congo African grey parrot, show off in the **Wildlife Walk** (admission free; ☾ 20min shows 11:30am, 1:30pm & 2:30pm Fri-Wed), a wide, elevated hallway with views of the waterfall gardens and lagoon pools below.

The tropical-paradise theme virtually disappears in the casino, however, except for floral carpets and a few exotic plants here and there. Entertainment options include the long-running **Folies Bergére** (p145), yuk-yuks at the **Comedy Stop** (p148), and free **AirPlay** (☾ 15min shows at 11am, 1pm, 3pm, 5pm, 7pm & 9pm), with singers, aerialists, acrobats and dancers performing on a stage at eye level with the slot machines under the vibrant Tiffany glass ceiling of the main casino. Smoke a stogie at **Havana Hideaway** (p140) before you slip out the door – and before the casino goes the way of so many other classic haunts, and is demolished to make way for a new megaresort, as pundits say may happen soon.

Pedestrian skybridges over the Strip link the Tropicana with the Excalibur and the MGM Grand, where you can hop on the monorail.

(Continued on page 75)

1 *A Vegas wedding with the King in attendance (p85)* 2 *Shopping, Via Bellagio (p175)* 3 *Fountains, Bellagio (p51)* 4 *Sin City lives up to its name (p14)*

1 *The sphinx, Luxor (p61)* 2 *Rio (p91), west of the Strip* 3 *Big Apple skyline, New York–New York (p64)* 4 *TI, Treasure Island (p58)*

1 *Caesars Palace (p51)* **2** *Eiffel Tower, Paris–Las Vegas (p57)* **3** *Fremont Street Experience (p82)* **4** *Stratosphere Tower (p79)*

1 *American Superstars production show (p79)* **2** *The volcano outside the Mirage (p54)* **3** *Cirque du Soleil (p146)* **4** *Blue Man Group (p144)*

1 *Poolside, Four Seasons (p192)*
2 *Lion habitat, MGM Grand (p63)*
3 *Exotic Car Rentals (p173)*
4 *Slot machines (p44)*

1 *In Vegas you can party 24/7 (p150)* 2 *Image above the main entrance of Harrah's (p54)* 3 *Your liquor of choice, Bellagio (p51)* 4 *Little Buddha restaurant (p127)*

1 Mon Ami Gabi (p112) **2** Four-story wine tower, Aureole (p115) **3** Buffet, Main Street Station (p84) **4** There's no shortage of bars (p130) in Vegas

1 *Cyclists, Death Valley (p224)*
2 *Hoover Dam (p209)* **3** *Grand Canyon (p215)* **4** *Red Rock Canyon (p213)*

(Continued from page 66)

NORTH STRIP

Just south of the Sahara, **Wet 'n Wild** (www .wetnwild.com) theme park once offered kids and adults alike relief from the city's scorching heat waves with more than 1.5-million gallons of cold water. At press time the now closed site was, according to rumors, being redeveloped into a brand new megaresort, which should liven up the north Strip.

CIRCUS CIRCUS Map pp262-3

☎ 702-734-0410; www.circuscircus.com; 2880 Las Vegas Blvd S; bus 301, 302

Few people cruising the Strip overlook Circus Circus casino hotel. Granted, it's pretty hard to miss, what with the enormous clown-shaped marquee and tent-shaped casino under a gaudily striped big top. From the outside, this sprawling resort looks pretty cheesy – and it *is*.

Open since 1968, Circus Circus is still a grand place for kids and fun-loving adults. If you're a real wild child, you can relive scenes from *Fear and Loathing in Las Vegas* here, but, even without the drugs, it's hallucinogenic enough. Cacophonous **Slots A' Fun** (p78) is just a drunken stumble away, too.

In keeping with its name, the decor inside is a carnival of colors, mainly pinks and oranges, but these days it aims more for *commedia dell'arte* than Ringling Bros. Three full-sized **casinos** contain more than 2200 slot machines (keep an eye out for the ones with spinning carousels), plus single-deck blackjack tables and a **low-limit poker room** open around the clock. Directly above the casino are **circus acts** (☺ shows every 30min 11am-midnight) with trapeze artists, high-wire workers, jugglers and unicyclists. Just come on in and take a seat; there's no admission charge or reserved seating.

Wrapped around the upper-level stage is the **Midway** arcade, which has high-tech video games and old-fashioned carnival diversions, one of which involves striking a catapult with a wooden mallet, which in turn flings a rubber chicken in the direction of a dozen pots placed on a rotating platform; if the chicken lands in a pot, voila! You win. That is, if you can stop cracking up long enough to collect your prize.

Behind the hotel's West Tower is the **Adventuredome** (☎ 702-794-3939; www .adventuredome.com; per ride $4-6, day pass

TRANSPORTATION – NORTH STRIP

Bus CAT (p234) bus 301 (Strip) runs along Las Vegas Blvd S in both directions. Bus 302 (Strip Express) stops at the intersections with Sahara Ave, Circus Circus Dr (southbound) and Riviera Blvd (Northbound).

Car The most tangled intersection in all of Las Vegas may be at Sahara Ave and Las Vegas Blvd S, so avoid driving on the Strip there. Self-parking garages with more convenient back entrances are found at the Riviera (enter off Riviera Blvd) and Circus Circus (enter off Circus Circus Dr from Industrial Rd). If you're going to the Stratosphere, the self-parking entrance is off Baltimore Ave. At the Sahara, the valet and self-parking entrances are off Sahara Ave, which is convenient to the monorail station.

Monorail The sole North Strip monorail station is at the Sahara, although there are secondary stations at the Las Vegas Hilton and convention center.

Shuttle Free shuttles from Sam's Town stop at the Stardust; see p236 for details.

Walking The main cluster of casino hotels, from the New Frontier north to Circus Circus, are easy enough to walk between. But it's a dull walk up to the Sahara monorail station and even further to the Stratosphere Tower. From the monorail stations at the Las Vegas Hilton and convention center, it's a long walk west to the Strip (not recommended after dark).

over/under 48in tall $23/15, kids under 33in tall ride free with a paying adult; ☺ usually 10am-6pm Mon-Thu, 10am-midnight Fri & Sat, 10am-8pm Sun, seasonal variations), where clowns perform on the main stage (☺ 1, 3 & 4pm daily, also 6, 7, 8 & 9pm Fri & Sat). It's fully enclosed by 8615 panes of pinkish glass, each weighing more than 300lbs. Amid its desert-canyon setting are dozens of attractions. Must-rides include the double-loop, double-corkscrew Canyon Blaster; the open-sided Rim Runner toboggan water ride; and new Sling Shot tower ride that effects 4 Gs of acceleration. Tamer sideshow rides for wee ones include a carousel, bumper cars and a Ferris wheel. You'll find attractions for older kids, such as a four-story rock-climbing wall and a bungee-jumping area, and IMAX ridefilms, too.

Nearby is **AJ Hackett Bungy** (☎ 702-385-4321; www.ajhackett.com; 810 Circus Circus Dr; first jump $60, then per jump $25, every 4th jump free; ☺ 11am-8:30pm Sun-Thu, 11am-10:30pm Fri & Sat). It's basically bungee jumping from a 175ft-high crane over a teeny, tiny swimming pool, but don't worry – more than a million people have survived the trip so far. Minimum age for jumpers is 13, and everyone under age 18 must be accompanied by an adult. Call ahead, as there's no jumping during inclement weather.

GUARDIAN ANGEL CATHEDRAL Map pp262-3

☎ 702-735-5241; www.lasvegas-diocese.org; 336 Cathedral Way; ✆ worship services 8am & 12:10pm Mon-Fri, several times daily Sat & Sun, gift shop 7am-3:30pm Mon-Fri, 10am-6:30pm Sat, 7:30am-1:30pm & 4-6:30pm Sun; bus 301, 302

With stained glass showing long-departed Vegas icons, this Catholic church resembling a ski chalet looks rather alien for the Strip. But if you get the urge to save your soul Sunday morning after going to hell and back on Saturday night, you won't have to venture all that far off Las Vegas Blvd.

NEW FRONTIER Map pp262-3

☎ 702-794-8200; www.frontierlv.com; 3120 Las Vegas Blvd S; bus 301, 302

Much like the other casino hotels on the North Strip, you've got to be drunk – or at least love nickel slots – to understand the divey appeal of the 'new' New Frontier. In 1956, Elvis played his first (and not very successful) show in Las Vegas here, just one year after the 1940s-era Last Frontier casino changed its name.

Over the years, this place has seen almost as many ups and downs as the Aladdin (p57). These days what it's got going for it is its country-and-western flavor, which otherwise you'd have to go way out to the Boulder Hwy to get. When you stop to think about it, it's really odd that in a town founded on sawdust-covered gambling halls like Las Vegas, none of the Strip's megaresorts even pays lip service to their Old West origins.

Near the front entrance, check out the vintage one-armed bandit 'gunslinger' slot machines, then make your way to the back, where Gilley's (p151) exhibits voyeuristic appeal with its bikini mud wrestling and mechanical bull riding, just as advertised on the Stripside marquee. Stop by for a bit of two-stepping and what may be your only chance to meet a real cowboy on Las Vegas Blvd.

The New Frontier is a short walk north of the Fashion Show Mall (p173).

RIVIERA Map pp262-3

☎ 702-734-5110, 877-892-7469; www.rivierahotel .com; 2901 Las Vegas Blvd S; bus 301, 302

The Riviera was the first high-rise on the Strip, rising to a then-impressive nine floors when it opened in 1955. Liberace did the ribbon-cutting honors, with Joan Crawford

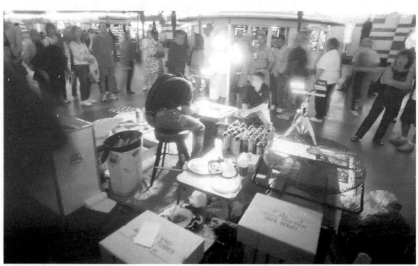

Artist at work

Sights

THE STRIP

LAS VEGAS FOR CHILDREN

Despite promoting itself as a family-friendly vacation destination, there are still many places that children legally cannot, or at least really shouldn't, be in Sin City. Our top 10 picks for places to keep the younger generation amused include the following:

- **Circus Circus** (p75) The original family casino hotel is still the most crowded with tots to teens.
- **Excalibur** (p61) Kids of all ages run amok here, with the Fantasy Faire Midway, free entertainment on the Court Jester's Stage and the rowdy Tournament of Kings dinner show.
- **Green Valley Ranch** (p202) Come here for bowling, movies and a pancake house, plus the nearby District shopping mall.
- **Luxor** (p61) This has video games fit for a Pharaoh, an IMAX cinema and ridefilms, and the quirky King Tut Museum.
- **MGM Grand** (p63) Visit the respectable video arcade, the irresistible lion habitat, and a mammoth guests-only pool complex with the longest 'lazy river' ride in town.
- **Neonopolis** (p84) Downtown's only kid-friendly haven, this is right on the electrifying Fremont Street Experience (p82).
- **New York–New York** (p64) Sample the Coney Island Emporium, Manhattan Express roller coaster, Houdini's Magic Shop, and eateries that won't break the bank.
- **Orleans** (p90) This is the best off-Strip casino hotel for families, with bowling, cinemas and on-site babysitting.
- **Planet Hollywood** (p57) Plans are still under wraps for Aladdin's grand reopening; no doubt it will appeal to families.
- **Stratosphere** (p79) Come for Vegas' best thrill rides, along with arcade games and Roxy's Diner.

Most of Vegas' outlying attractions (p91) are absolutely kid-friendly, and so are many excursions out of town (p207). For more advice on traveling with children, including accommodations, entertainment and babysitting, see p237.

Sights

THE STRIP

delivering the opening remarks. Surprisingly, film auteur Orson Welles appeared on stage the next year performing – of all things – magic acts.

A host of big-name entertainers have starred at the Riviera since then, including Louis Armstrong, George Burns and Tony Bennett. When Dean Martin became a 10% owner in 1969, he opened a lounge called Dino's Den and jump-started the serendipitous career of Engelbert Humperdinck, an Indian-born Briton named Arnold George Dorsey who stole his stage name from a classical German composer. Part of the original *Ocean's 11* was filmed here (so was Scorsese's *Casino*), although that Hollywood glamour has been lost almost entirely.

Designed by a Miami architect, the Riv has been renovated several times over the years. When it opened, it contained a mere 18 gaming tables and 116 slot machines. Today it boasts a 100,000-sq-ft **casino** (albeit a dimly lit and confusing one) that's among the Strip's largest, with more than a thousand slots and video poker machines, plus blackjack tables, craps tables, roulette wheels, a keno lounge, a wheel of fortune, baccarat, a **race and sports book**, and a rare three-dice game called *sic bo*. The low-roller slot havens of Penny Town and Nickel Town are faves with the old-as-the-hills clientele, who love the

hot slot tournies. If you're starving and it's after 10pm, hit the **World's Fare Buffet** (p108) for graveyard steak, eggs and cake.

In 1985, the Riviera's long-running female impersonator show, **An Evening at La Cage** (p145), began with a young Frank Marino, who still stars in it today. The Riv has spicy ads all over the place for its other tacky adult-themed shows, **Crazy Girls** (p144) and **Splash** (p147). In fact, it bronzed the behinds of its bawdy showgirls in a 1540lb statue (p11) outside the front entrance to honor Crazy Girls' 10th anniversary, an event that can only be explained by the proverb 'Sex sells.'

Despite not having lived a charmed life, the old-school Riviera is a survivor. It recently celebrated its 50th anniversary in style with a Liberace impersonator (of course), and with fireworks, cake and champagne for the masses.

SAHARA Map pp262-3
☎ 702-737-2111; www.saharavegas.com; 2535 Las Vegas Blvd S; monorail Sahara

Thanks to a $100-million face-lift, the Moroccan-themed Sahara is one of the few old-Vegas carpet joints (along with the Stardust and a few downtown casino hotels) to have survived the onslaught of the megaresorts. If you make it up here, check out who's performing in the **Conga Room**, which has showcased legendary entertainers from Ella Fitzgerald to the Beatles since the Sahara first opened its doors in 1952.

In the mid-'90s, the Sahara strengthened its Moroccan theme with a vastly improved Stripside entrance featuring several dozen royal palms and an arched marble dome. The *Arabian Nights* theme continues inside the 85,000-sq-ft **casino** guarded by a row of sultan statues. Elegant improvements include gold-painted ceilings, molded columns laced with colorful vines and more than two dozen golden chandeliers. Any gimmicks? The casino also hustles the Strip's largest variety of unique card games, including some you've never heard of (at which you will thus quickly be able to lose all your money). Outside is a lovely 5000-sq-ft heated **swimming pool** where Elvis Presley and Elizabeth Taylor once lounged, now adorned with Moroccan mosaic tiles, a gazebo-topped hot tub and a few private cabanas.

For many visitors, the most compelling reason to visit is the **Nascar Cafe**, where **Carzilla**, the world's largest stock car, is on display as a bar's centerpiece. Official racewear sells out when drivers make personal appearances during race week at the **Las Vegas Motor Speedway** (p162). But here the Indy car simulators of the **Las Vegas Cyber Speedway** (single-ride ticket $10, re-ride $6, combo ticket with Speed $15; ☷noon-9pm Mon-Thu, noon-10pm Fri & Sat, 11am-9pm Sun) are so real that they excite real Formula One drivers. Wannabe racers are bolted to hydraulic platforms fronting 20ft wraparound screens. After the computer-synchronized race, most drivers exit their virtual cars sweating and breathing heavily. A detailed souvenir printout shows individual lap record speeds, braking performances and more. Definitely pass if you have a heart condition or suffer from motion sickness. Upstairs, the **Pit Pass Arcade** has the latest and greatest video racing games. Finally, an electromagnetic roller coaster, **Speed – The Ride** (single-ride ticket $10, all-day roller coaster & speedway pass $20; ☷11am-midnight, till 1am Fri & Sat), slingshots riders to a top speed of 70mph as it loops up from underground through the Sahara's camel marquee sign and climbs a 200ft tower. Riders must be at least 54in tall.

SLOTS A' FUN Map pp262-3

☎ 702-734-0410; 2890 Las Vegas Blvd S; bus 301, 302

For cheap drinks, cheap eats and cheap thrills, it's tough to beat this low-brow dive. Park for free and grab a coupon book from neighboring **Circus Circus** (p75), a few 75¢ beers and $1 half-pound hot dogs. Then kick back, relax and enjoy the laughable lounge acts. Some visitors make lifelong friends with the bartenders and cocktail waitresses – it's just that kind of place. Look for the main entrance on the south side of Circus Circus.

STARDUST Map pp262-3

☎ 702-732-6441; www.stardustlv.com; 3000 Las Vegas Blvd S; bus 301, 302

In the no-man's-land of the North Strip, the old-school Stardust has stuck to its Rat Pack roots and continues to lure fans of bygone Vegas. You gotta love the landmark 188ft starry sign, which contains over two miles of neon tubing and is cast in nearly every Hollywood movie establishing shot of Vegas.

When it was completed in 1958 at a cost of $10 million, the Stardust was the most spectacular casino hotel in town. With 1065 guestrooms going for just $6 a night, it was also the world's largest resort complex. While the Dunes casino hotel had already brought bare-breasted showgirls to the Strip with its *Minsky Goes to Paris* revue, the day the Stardust opened, it imported actual French showgirls with its *Lido de Paris* revue, in a display of one-upmanship. No question about it, the Stardust was a 'real class joint' back then, as mobsters used to say. Even Howard Hughes once aspired to own it.

Today, *Lido de Paris* is gone. Until recently, the Stardust's entertainment consisted mainly of **Wayne Newton** (p147), a throwback to the Vegas of old, but he has since moved on. The Stardust often still has a stellar lineup of performers, including comedians like George Carlin and Joan Rivers. Live acts appear in the free **Starlight Lounge** (p156). Not so long ago the 'Dust expanded its **casino**, which was the first in Vegas to have a **race and sports book**, and now boasts a free **sports handicapper's library** full of the latest stats.

Now that **Wynn** (p59) towers just down the road, however, the Stardust is a likely implosion candidate. Compared to new beauties such as the Venetian, there's absolutely nothing spectacular about it. Nevertheless, it continues to see as much action as ever, thanks to its legendary status. For what it's worth, the Strip won't be the same when Stardust inevitably bites the dust. Maybe that's reason enough to see it while you can.

STRATOSPHERE Map pp262-3
☎ 702-380-7777; www.stratospherehotel.com; 2000 Las Vegas Blvd S; monorail Sahara

Las Vegas has many buildings exceeding 20 stories, but only one tops 100. At 1149ft, the three-legged, $550-million **Stratosphere Tower** is the tallest building in the USA west of the Mississippi River. At its base is a **casino** that has all the trappings of a sprawling gaming room, but little in the way of a theme (although it does have 1500 reputedly loose slots and video poker machines).

Atop the elegantly tapered tower is what people have been flocking to see for the last decade. Indoor and outdoor viewing decks afford the best 360-degree panoramas in town. You'll also find a **revolving restaurant** (p120) and **lounge** (p136). To get you up there, the Stratosphere boasts America's fastest elevators (round-trip ticket adult/ senior & hotel guest $10/6, child under 4 free) that ascend and descend at 20.5mph, or about three times the speed of regular elevators, lifting you 108 floors in a mere 37 ear-popping seconds.

TOP FIVE BIRD'S-EYE VIEWS
Rise far above the Strip at these faves:
- **Stratosphere Tower** (above) Altitude with attitude, especially during the Insanity or Big Shot thrill rides. Alternatively, sip a cocktail inside the Top of the World Lounge (p136).
- **Mix** (p135) Even the glass elevator ride up to this space-age lounge (no cover before 10pm) is jaw-dropping.
- **Eiffel Tower** (p57) Be sure to time your visit to coincide with Bellagio's fountain show (p51).
- **Mormon Temple** (Map p260; ☎ 702-452-5011; 827 N Temple Dr, off E Bonanza Dr; bus 208) Nonmembers can't go inside, but anyone can soak up the valley views.
- **McCarran International Airport** (p233) Park in the short-term garage near Terminal 1, then ride the elevator up to level 6 and walk over to the north side for free views of the Strip, including the Luxor, Eiffel Tower and the Stratosphere; bring quarters to feed the meters.

Once you've recovered, head for the newest thrill ride, **Insanity** (per ride $8), which swings riders 60ft out from the edge of the tower into thin air, then spins its huge claw arms that elevate to an angle of 70°. Rising further still above it all is the **Big Shot** ($8), which really gets the blood rushing by rocketing riders in outward-facing seats up and down a steel spire that forms the pinnacle of the tower itself. **High Roller** ($4), the world's highest roller coaster, is a dud. **X-Scream** ($8), which dangles riders teeter-totter style over the side of the tower, can be a letdown, too; try to grab a seat on the right-hand side. Try the **thrill rides** (incl round-trip elevator ticket $25, all-day ride pass $30; ☑ 10am-1am Sun-Thu, to 2am Fri & Sat) at night for maximum effect. Note, they don't operate when there's strong wind or rain.

Singing waitstaff serenade you inside **Roxy's Diner** (p120), tequila shots go like crazy at the **Crazy Armadillo** (p136) and hangover-beating breakfasts are dished up at **Lucky's Cafe** (p120). Entirely forgettable are the Stratosphere's cheesy production shows, like the celebrity impersonators of **American Superstars**, the obnoxious daytime cabaret **Viva Las Vegas** (p147) and late-night vampiric **Bite**. Occasionally, the Stratosphere's 3700-seat **outdoor events center** hosts boxing bouts and concerts.

DOWNTOWN
Eating p121; Shopping p177; Sleeping p196

Downtown sits at the north end of the tourist corridor, with the Fremont Street Experience streaking down its middle. The city's original quarter is often preferred by serious gamblers who feel that white tigers and faux volcanoes are beneath them. The smoky, low-ceilinged casinos have hardly changed over the years, and, as attractions, they've got little to offer nongamblers, not to mention kids.

Historically, the blocks around the intersection of Main and Fremont Sts were known as **Glitter Gulch**. Those neon icons, the 1950s cowboy **Vegas Vic** and latter-day cowgirl **Vegas Vickie** (aka Sassy Sally) atop the **Girls of Glitter Gulch** (p154) strip club, still beckon. Although casino hotels along Fremont St today aren't as swanky as Vegas' megaresorts, their proximity to one another is a real plus, and makes for a contrast to the challenges of navigating the Strip. You can easily stroll between half a dozen gaming joints here.

A more desolate area of Las Vegas Blvd links downtown with the **Stratosphere** (p79) back on the Strip. Locals refer to the 15-block-long neighborhood as 'Naked City' for its proclivity to prostitution. The streets here are mostly lined with tatty-looking buildings – cheap motels, strip clubs, quickie wedding chapels and so on.

A more artistic parallel universe is the **Gateway Arts District**, which has its locus at the **Arts Factory** (right). North of downtown, the ambitiously named **Cultural Corridor** has a handful of museums, an arts center, a historic site, a public library branch and the **Cashman Center Theatre** (p158).

Orientation

Situated at the historic town center, downtown is a compact grid. Its main artery, Fremont St, is a covered pedestrian mall lined with low-roller casinos and hotels for five city blocks east of Main St, where it's called the Fremont Street Experience. Fremont St gets seedier as you go further east of Las Vegas Blvd. Motels replace hotels and prostitution, not gambling, is the vice of choice.

Public buildings, such as the courthouse, are located a few blocks south of Fremont St, while a short walk to the north is the bus station and city hall. The 18-block Gateway Arts District hinges on the intersection of E Charleston Blvd and Main St, but

also stretches sporadically east to Casino Center Blvd, west to Commerce St, north to Bonneville St and south to Wyoming Ave. The Cultural Corridor runs along Las Vegas Blvd N, from Fremont St past the interstate overpass and all the way up to Washington Ave.

ARTS FACTORY Map p261

☎ 702-676-1111; www.theartsfactory.com; 101-109 E Charleston Blvd; ☽ most galleries noon-4pm Tue-Sat; bus 108, 206

Las Vegas' fractured art scene received an enormous boost in 1997 when commercial photographer Wes Isbutt somewhat by accident created the Arts Factory complex. Isbutt was looking for space for his own business, **Studio West Photography** (☎ 702-383-3133; www.studiowestphotography.com). Although he hadn't set out to establish an art colony in Vegas, that's what he did.

While some of the art is of debatable worth, talent is clearly in evidence. Most of the space inside the red-brick building is taken up by local artists and galleries exhibiting mostly southern Nevadan artworks, as well as architecture and graphic design firms and an experimental theater. The nonprofit **Contemporary Arts Collective** (CAC; ☎ 702-382-3886; www.cac-lasvegas.org) has high-quality, quirkily curated exhibits.

Warning: you may find the block-long complex nearly deserted, except on **First Fridays** (opposite. Check the online calendar for gallery openings and other events. Park in the back lot off E Boulder Ave.

TRANSPORTATION – DOWNTOWN

Bus Several local CAT bus lines (p234) stop at the Downtown Transportation Center (DTC), just two blocks north of Fremont St.

Car Two main highways come into Las Vegas: I-15 and US 95. For downtown, exit I-15 at Charleston Blvd or US 95 at Las Vegas Blvd (the Strip). Driving on Las Vegas Blvd from the Stratosphere at the northern terminus of the Strip all the way downtown takes at least 15 minutes. Most downtown casino hotels have self-parking garages just south or north of Fremont St. Parking up to four hours is usually free, as long as you validate the garage parking stub inside the casino (no purchase required). Valet parking is available at some casino hotels, including Golden Nugget.

Shuttle Sam's Town operates a free shuttle service between its casino hotel on the Boulder Hwy and downtown's California and Fremont casino hotels; see p236 for details.

Taxi You may be able to flag down a taxi (p236) on the side streets away from the Fremont Street Experience. Taxi stands are conveniently found at major casino hotels, such as the Plaza and the Golden Nugget.

Walking The covered canopy of Fremont St from Main St east to Las Vegas Blvd is a safe area for strolling. But venture off this five-block pedestrian strip at your own risk.

GALLERY HOPPING

Between 5pm and 10pm on the first Friday of each month, art lovers, hipsters and musicians wander the Gateway Arts District. **First Fridays** (www.firstfriday -lasvegas.org) are like a giant block party, with gallery openings accompanied by the sound of live music, performance art, fortune tellers and sidewalk chalk painting by kids.

After you stop by the **Arts Factory** (opposite), check out **Commerce Street Studios** (Map p261; www .commercestreetstudios.com; 1551 S Commerce St, at Wyoming Ave), also home to **Naked City Tattoo and Art**. For celebratory First Friday drinks, most people head to **Dino's Lounge** (p137).

North of downtown on the Cultural Corridor, but off the First Friday circuit, **Reed Whipple Cultural Center** (Map p261; ☎ 702-229-6211; 821 Las Vegas Blvd N; ☻ 1-9pm Mon & Thu, 10am-9pm Tue & Wed, 10am-6pm Fri, 9am-5pm Sat; bus 113) has an off-the-beaten-path gallery for temporary exhibitions of unusual works by local artists.

You can also venture further afield to **downtown Henderson** (Map p260; ☎ 702-568-6800; www .waterstreetdistrict.com; Water St & Pacific Ave) – its galleries fine art and photos throw open their doors on the third Thursday evening of every month.

BINION'S Map p261
☎ 702-382-1600, 800-937-6537; www.binions.com; 128 E Fremont St; bus 301, 302

In the grand Las Vegas tradition of one-up-manship, once upon a time Binion's Horseshoe casino hotel responded to the display of precious gems at the **Golden Nugget** (p83) by offering its visitors a chance to drool over $1 million in rare $10,000 gold certificates. There were 100 of 'em in all, kept under glass in a display case shaped, appropriately enough, like a lucky horseshoe.

But guess what? The $1 million in cash is gone now, sold by patriarch Benny Binion's daughter to a private collector, and so is the vintage neon horseshoe sign above the Fremont St entrance. The horseshoe now belongs to Harrah's, which temporarily took over the troubled downtown property in 2004, but just as quickly resold it, retaining rights to Binion's famous horseshoe.

However, you *can* still leave the casino with your own million dollars, at least in theory: a no-limit gambling policy has been a fixture at Binion's for years. That's one of the reasons the tables are usually filled day and night. Another is the casino's larger-than-life standing among Strip casino giants, despite being a diminutive downtown gambling hall. The Horseshoe was opened in 1951 by notorious Texan gambler Benny Binion, who wore gold coins for buttons on his cowboy shirts and oversaw the transformation of Fremont St from sawdust gambling halls to classy carpet joints with free drinks for slot-machine players and airport limousines for high rollers. In 1970, Binion lured the World Series of Poker (p10), which is now held at the **Rio** (p91), to his namesake casino, even though by that time he'd lost his gaming license for going to prison after being convicted of tax evasion in Texas.

Binion's has a real country-and-western flavor. It's the premier place downtown to stare at cowboys dressed up in their finest duds, especially during the **National Finals Rodeo** (p163), or winning big at the poker tables, after which they might head up the elevator for penthouse dining at **Binion's Ranch Steakhouse** (p121). Meanwhile, low rollers refuel downstairs at **Binion's Coffee Shop** (p123).

Don't neglect to pay your respects to Benny's **statue**, at the northeast corner of Ogden Ave and Casino Center Blvd, before you gallop out of downtown.

CALIFORNIA Map p261
☎ 702-385-1222; www.thecal.com; 12 E Ogden Ave; bus 301, 302

At many Vegas casino hotels, the lucky spin of a slot machine will earn you a brand spanking new BMW, a racy Jaguar or a red-hot convertible. At the 'just-call-me-Cal' California, one very lucky nickel player will someday ride home in a – drum roll please – a PT Cruiser! That simple fact tells you a lot about the Cal, 'the hotel with aloha spirit' built in 1975, where even the dealers wear Hawaiian shirts. (Over 80% of the Cal's guests hail from the Aloha state.)

The Cal's **casino**, though small by Strip standards, offers all the usual table games and has more than 1000 busy slots, video poker and video Keno machines. Few casino hotels can boast two $1-million-plus slot wins only a week apart; the Cal can. There's nothing spectacular about the Cal, but it does make cents. Lots of cents.

If hunger strikes, dine in style at the **Redwood Bar & Grill** (p122) steakhouse or just grab a scoop of rich Lappert's Hawaiian ice cream upstairs. Near the pedestrian

Sights

DOWNTOWN

skybridge to **Main Street Station** (p84), a more elegant Boyd Gaming property, look for photos of the Cal's Golden Arm Club, which immortalizes folks who luckily held the dice at the craps table for more than an hour.

EL CORTEZ Map p261

☎ 702-385-5200; www.elcortezhotelcasino.com; 600 E Fremont St; bus 107, 301, 302

A classic dive dating back to 1940, the El Cortez is choked with smoke, but also has vintage Vegas in spades. Jackie Gaughan, the man who once owned more downtown casino hotels than anyone, sold the El Cortez and other throwback properties, such as the **Plaza** (p86), to corporate Barrick Gaming in 2004, but he still resides in a penthouse suite here.

Downstairs in the **casino**, rough-edged local gamblers grudgingly allow accidental tourists to buy into the low-limit action on roulette, craps and other table games aimed at cheapskates and novices. It's almost impossible to lose your shirt at the El Cortez, but you'll need a few stiff drinks first.

FREMONT Map p261

☎ 702-385-3232; www.fremontcasino.com; 200 E Fremont St; bus 301, 302

The legendary Fremont casino hotel has been packing 'em in since 1956, when it opened as downtown's first high-rise. Separating it from the motley pack was its wall-to-wall carpeting – almost all of the nearby casinos had sawdust floors. It was here that famous lounge singer Wayne Newton (aka Mr Las Vegas) launched his career (p147).

Despite these firsts, the Fremont has since slipped into mediocrity in most regards. Like its sister casino hotel, the California, it welcomes planeloads of travelers from Hawaii. With its weak tropical motif, the 32,000-sq-ft **casino** is nothing special, but its location at the heart of the Fremont Street Experience has made it a favorite with many gamblers, not to mention film buffs for its covert role in the movie *Swingers*.

FREMONT STREET EXPERIENCE Map p261

☎ 702-678-5600; www.vegasexperience.com; admission free; ⏰ shows hourly 8pm-midnight; bus 301, 302

A decade ago, Vegas' downtrodden downtown had lost nearly all its tourists to the rapidly developing Strip. With the opening of each new megaresort on Las Vegas Blvd, the older casino hotels of Glitter Gulch, such as Fitzgerald's, Golden Nugget and Binion's Horseshoe, lost some of their luster. Downtown was headed downhill, fast. So, with no end in sight to development on the Strip, something had to be done – and fast.

Always ready for a gamble, city and business boosters came up with a plan, which was realized in December 1995: an $87-million, five-block **pedestrian mall** topped by an arched steel canopy filled with lights controlled by computers. Five times nightly, the 1400ft-long canopy over Fremont St

Madame Tussauds (p59)

between Main St and Las Vegas Blvd turns on a six-minute light-and-sound show enhanced by 550,000 watts of concert-hall-worthy sound. The latest addition is a super-big Viva Vision screen, featuring 12.5 million synchronized LEDs. When all the lights come on, the cheesy shows are awesome enough to hypnotize most people (especially if you're drunk).

Has the newfangled contraption helped business pick up downtown? Absolutely. What's more, the misting system built into the canopy provides welcome relief on hot days. Despite all its efforts to refashion itself into a bedazzling, family-friendly outdoor neon-lit amusement park, however, downtown remains the heart and soul of old Vegas, and Fremont St retains its happy-go-lucky feel as the origin of all the action. 'The Experience' is the eye-candy icing on the low-roller cake.

GOLDEN GATE Map p261
☎ 702-385-1906, 800-426-1906; www.goldengate casino.net; 1 E Fremont St; bus 301, 302
A gambling hall and hotel has stood on the corner of Fremont and Main Sts since 1906, one year after the whistle-stop railway town of Las Vegas was founded. But it didn't become the Golden Gate casino until the 1950s, when a troupe of Italian-Americans from San Francisco decamped and stayed on for four decades to manage what was at one time known as the 'Sal Sagev' (the city's name spelled backward, doncha know).

The Golden Gate's hypnotic mechanical sign is almost as irresistible as its famous 99¢ shrimp cocktails. You can get one in the deli (p122), which has already sold more than 25 million parfait glasses full of the cheapskates' crustacean delight to date. Other than the seafood, there's nothing much to draw you into this bowdlerized City by the Bay other than perhaps its snug casino, with lively craps tables and double-deck blackjack being dealt to the nostalgic sounds of live piano music.

GOLDEN NUGGET Map p261
☎ 702-385-7111; www.goldennugget.com; 129 E Fremont St; bus 301, 302
The Golden Nugget's claim to fame is the Hand of Faith. No, it's not the name of a religious relic. Rather, the Hand of Faith refers to the largest single gold nugget in the world, weighing a massive 61lb, 11oz. It's on display near the North Tower elevators, under glass along with another nugget weighing 13lbs and a treasury of smaller chunks of the most valuable yellow metallic element known to humankind. Although taking photos is not permitted in most casinos for security reasons, the Golden Nugget smiles benignly upon visitors who shoot the mighty rocks. And why not? It's not like any other casino in town (or the world) can claim to possess the heftiest hunk of gold ever found.

But that's not all this bejeweled casino is famous for. Opened in 1946 as the then largest casino in the world, the Nugget looked like a million bucks – and, in fact, cost exactly that much to build. It was transformed in the 1970s by Steve Wynn, the first casino impresario to bring vintage Vegas back into style when he invited Frank Sinatra to star at the opening of the Nugget's gorgeous Theatre Ballroom (p157). Wunderkinds Tim Poster and Thomas Breitling bought the casino hotel from MGM Mirage in 2004. The enterprising duo soon catapulted the Nugget into the national limelight on the Fox reality TV series *Casino*, but then sold it off right away to Landry's Restaurants.

At the moment, this swank joint rakes in a young, hip and moneyed crowd, proving that all that glitters is as good as gold. The 36,000-sq-ft casino has a spread of table games and an airy poker room that's as different from Binion's across the street as day and night. And here's a piece of trivia for you: when the Nugget first opened, poker players were allowed to deal their own cards!

From white-leather slot-machine seats to sizzlin' lounge acts to sophisticated steaks at Zax (p122), the Golden Nugget always shines.

LAS VEGAS CLUB Map p261
☎ 702-385-1664; www.vegasclubcasino.net; 18 E Fremont St; bus 301, 302
A sports-themed casino hotel with another aloha twist, the super-duper-friendly Club is notable for its prize-worthy collections of sports memorabilia, such as World Series autographed baseball bats. Naturally, there's a race and sports book inside the low-key casino, where dealers gamely don baseball-style uniforms. Upstairs, gigantic 9lb burgers

Sights

DOWNTOWN

are served inside the **Upper Deck Restaurant** (p121) and you may catch an impromptu Hawaiian hula performance at Friday night karaoke (p138). Get a taste of the islands back downstairs at **Mahalo Express** (p123).

LAS VEGAS NATURAL HISTORY MUSEUM Map p261

☎ 702-384-3466; www.lvnhm.org; 900 Las Vegas Blvd N; adult/child 3-11/senior & student 12-17 $6/3/5; ☼ 9am-4pm; bus 113

If you've ever been to a really good natural history museum you won't be wowed by this one, but youngsters might. A couple dozen or so stuffed exotic animals are rather weakly displayed, including in the Nevada *au naturel* room. The young scientists' center is a popular interactive area for kids, especially on Saturday mornings.

LIED DISCOVERY CHILDREN'S MUSEUM Map p261

☎ 702-382-3445; www.ldcm.org; 833 Las Vegas Blvd N; adult/child 1-17/senior $7/5/6; ☼ 10am-5pm Tue-Sun; bus 113

Attached to the public library, this award-winning museum is designed for much younger kids than the natural history museum across the street. However, most of the exhibits are either too complex for children to operate successfully without a lot of guidance or they are too simple and therefore boring. Check in advance about art activity schedules.

LOST VEGAS HISTORIC GAMBLING MUSUEM Map p261

☎ 702-385-1883; www.neonopolis.com; Neonopolis, 450 E Fremont St; adult/senior $2.50/1.50, children under 16 not admitted; ☼ 11am-9pm, till 10pm Fri & Sat; bus 107, 301, 302

Inside the **Neonopolis** (right), this nostalgic small museum holds pleasantly jumbled displays of Old Vegas memorabilia, including historic photographs, pulp tabloid clippings, and gaming chips from casinos that have been blown up. Entry to the attached souvenir shop (p178) is free.

MAIN STREET STATION Map p261

☎ 702-387-1896; www.mainstreetcasino.com; 200 N Main St; bus 301, 302

This gorgeous casino hotel re-creates Victorian opulence with its unique design,

detailed craftsmanship and extensive collection of antiques and architectural artifacts. The hotel **lobby** and beautifully lit **casino** have old-fashioned elegance everywhere you look. Pick up the hotel's free brochure guide at the registration desk.

Throughout the lovely establishment are notable *objets d'histoire,* most keeping to the turn-of-the-19th-century theme. Exquisite bronze chandeliers above the casino's central pit were originally installed in the 1890s Coca-Cola Building in Austin, Texas. Ornate mahogany woodwork now gracing the casino entry, hotel registration desk and players' club was lifted out of a 19th-century Kentucky drugstore. Peek inside the buffet at the Italianate statue of the goddess Fortuna holding a deck of cards. A graffiti-covered chunk of the Berlin Wall now serves as one of the supports for the urinals in the gentleman's restroom.

Over in the classy **Pullman Grille** (p122), the dining room is built around an ornate carved-oak fireplace and the wine storage cabinets were taken from a Scottish castle. A sideboard niche includes panels that depict characters and morals from *Aesop's Fables.* Also worth checking out is **Triple 7** brewpub (p137), where you can drink under the glow of big copper brewing vats.

A pedestrian skybridge connects Main Street Station to the **California** (p81). In the rotunda nearby is an art-nouveau chandelier from Paris' Figaro Opera House. Near the southeast street-level casino entrance is allegorical stained glass from movie star Lillian Russell's mansion. Outside on Main St, just to the south, stands the private rail car used by Buffalo Bill Cody to travel the USA with his Wild West Show from 1906 until his death in 1917.

NEONOPOLIS Map p261

http://neonopolis.com; 450 Fremont St; admission free; ☼ 11am-9pm, till 10pm Fri & Sat; bus 107, 301, 302

Anchoring the east side of the Fremont Street Experience, this almost empty multi-story mall has a multiplex **cinema** (p159), the **Lost Vegas Historic Gambling Museum & Store** (left) and bowling, billiards and arcade games at Jillian's (p137).

Where does the Neonopolis' name come from? Thank the folks at the brilliant **Neon Museum** (☎ 702-387-6366; www.neon museum.org), whose outdoor gallery of

MARRIAGES MADE IN SIN CITY

Heaven might not be the right word, and 'Marriages Made in Las Vegas' doesn't have the same magical ring to it. Then again, there must be something magical about it, since on average a couple ties the knot every five minutes in Sin City.

The reasons people cite for getting hitched here are countless, but the low licensing fee ($55) and the absence of waiting-period and blood-test requirements are often mentioned. The services themselves can range in quality from a 10-minute drive-through to a big 'do' at a casino hotel (more than a dozen resorts contain wedding chapels).

If you're thinking of 'making it official' in Las Vegas and want to know what's required, call Clark County's **Marriage Bureau** (Map p261; ☎ 702-455-4415; www.co.clark.nv.us/clerk/marriage_information.htm; 200 S 3rd St; ☽ 8am-midnight Mon-Thu, 8am Fri-midnight Sun, open 24hr on holidays). Civil ceremonies are performed at the courthouse from 9am till 10pm daily.

Be advised that New Year's Eve and Valentine's Day are crush times for Vegas wedding chapels; plan ahead if you want to say your vows on either of these days. You can apply for the license up to a year in advance online.

Among the scores of celebrity couples who have exchanged vows in Las Vegas are Elvis Presley and Priscilla Beaulieu, Dennis Rodman and Carmen Electra, Michael Jordan and Juanita Vanoy, and Clint Eastwood and Dina Ruiz. Not all marriages made in Vegas last, though. Short-lived promises like Britney Spears' have spurred the county to send follow-up letters, asking people if they really meant to get married or not.

There are many different ways to say 'I do'. You can hire an Elvis impersonator to serenade you, or dress up as the King yourself. Weddings are performed in gondolas at the **Venetian** (p58), inside the Stratosphere's Chapel in the Clouds, or atop the Eiffel Tower at **Paris–Las Vegas** (p57). Meanwhile, geeks proclaim their undying love to the galaxy at **Star Trek: The Experience** (p87). You can even get married on the floor of the Grand Canyon – or completely nekkid.

Of course, to be truthful, the more Vegas wedding chapels you see, the less you may be inclined to entrust them with the happiest day of your lives. Many are pretty tacky, full of plastic flowers, fake stained-glass windows and doll s house pews. You may feel rushed, too, as these places may crank out dozens of weddings every day. Expect to pay from $200 for a basic service, maybe including a limo ride to the chapel.

Popular places that get good reviews include the following:

A Special Memory Wedding Chapel (Map p261; ☎ 702-384-2211, 800-962-7798; www.aspecialmemory.com; 800 S 4th St) Has a drive-up window on Lovers Lane with a wedding menu board (breakfast packages from $55, but don't forget a tip for the minister).

Graceland Wedding Chapel (Map p261; ☎ 702-382-0091, 800-824-5732; www.gracelandchapel.com; 619 Las Vegas Blvd S) Operating for more then 50 years, this is the original Elvis wedding (from $200). If it's good enough for Jon Bon Jovi, then it's probably good enough for you, too.

Little Church of the West (Map p260; ☎ 702-739-7971, 800-821-2452; www.littlechurchlv.com; 4617 Las Vegas Blvd S) When we eventually get married in Vegas, this is where you'll find us: in a quaint, quiet little wooden chapel built in 1942, south of the Strip. As seen in *Viva Las Vegas*.

Maverick Helicopters (☎ 702-261-0007, 888-261-4414; www.maverickhelicopter.com) Grand Canyon, Valley of Fire and sunset yacht wedding packages.

Viva Las Vegas Wedding Chapel (Map p261; ☎ 800-574-4450; www.vivalasvegasweddings.com; 1205 Las Vegas Blvd S) As kitschy as all get-out, especially the themed villas (p198). Invite your family and friends to watch your ceremony broadcast live online.

Wee Kirk o' the Heather (Map p261; ☎ 702-382-9830, 800-843-5266; www.weekirk.com; 231 Las Vegas Blvd S) The oldest continuously operating wedding chapel in Las Vegas (since 1940). It's close to the county marriage bureau.

A few last practicalities before you run off with your sweetheart to do the deed: several shops around Las Vegas rent tuxedos and wedding gowns for the occasion; many spas (p164) offer beauty treatments and updos especially for brides; and vintage **Freed's Bakery** (☎ 702-456-7762, 866-933-5253; www.freedsbakery.com; 4780 South Eastern Ave; ☽ 9am-6:30pm Mon-Sat, 9am-3pm Sun) bakes same-day wedding cakes.

vintage signs from Vegas and across the USA adorns the Neonopolis's central courtyard. Smaller installations hide just off the Fremont Street Experience; click to the museum's website for self-guided walking tour directions, or poke around on your own. Tours of the museum's awesome **sign graveyard** (cnr Encanto Blvd & E McWilliams Ave) are by appointment only, although you can see tons just by driving past the gates.

OLD LAS VEGAS MORMON FORT STATE HISTORIC PARK Map p261

☎ 702-486-3511; http://parks.nv.gov/olvmf.htm; 500 E Washington Ave; adult/child 6-12 $3/2; ⏰ 8:30am-4:30pm; bus 113

The remains of the historic fort are unspectacular, but this religious mission is exactly where the area was first settled way back in 1855 (p30). An adobe quadrangle provided a refuge for travelers along the Mormon Trail between Salt Lake City and San Bernardino. Some of the original walls still stand, and a new visitor center showcases artifacts and photos from the early days. Outside are replicas of the first crops grown here by the wildly successful **Las Vegas Ranch** (p31), which took up residence after the Mormons abandoned the settlement. It's a dusty place, and engaging only for historians.

PLAZA Map p261

☎ 702-386-2110, 800-634-6575; www.plazahotel casino.com; 1 Main St; bus 108, 301, 302

Built on the site of the old Union Pacific Railroad Depot, Jackie Gaughan's Plaza doesn't look like it's changed much since it opened in 1971. The enormous 80,000-sq-ft **casino** is jammed with slot and video machines and thousands of tiny recessed lights and mirrors designed to give the illusion of space.

Like most downtown joints, the Plaza is for hardcore gamblers; it leaves the Parisian, Venetian and New York themes to others. Its tacky decor doesn't correspond to any known theme, unless the theme is *cheap*. Even the chandeliers – yes, there are chandeliers – look gaudy. And that's just fine with the Plaza's gamblers, many of whom are attracted to the casino for its penny slots and $1 blackjack tables with friendly dealers and cocktail waitresses.

Its prime location also goes a long way toward explaining why the down-and-out Plaza casino is perennially popular. Although it could find new life as a vintage Vegas showpiece à la the Golden Nugget, for now you have to slum it here with the package tourists and feisty blue-haired ladies who play for keeps in the 400-seat **bingo room**. Also upstairs is the bar at **Center Stage** (p137), which has cockpit views of the Fremont Street Experience.

The **Greyhound bus depot** (p234) is next door and the train station is actually inside the Plaza, though it's been dormant since Amtrak (p236) stopped service to Las Vegas years ago.

POST MODERN Map p261

☎ 702-229-6792; 300 E Stewart Ave; admission free; ⏰ call for hrs; bus 107, 301, 302

Inside downtown's historic post office, this new museum and cultural center is going to be a vivacious site for city-sponsored exhibitions on everything from Las Vegas in decades past to mock mob trials to postcard art. Watch this space.

UNLV & EAST OF THE STRIP

Eating p123; Shopping p179; Sleeping p199

The center of off-Strip gravity swings east toward Paradise Rd, where the dynamic Hard Rock anchors the after-dark action. During the day, it's all business north on Paradise Rd near the convention center and Las Vegas Hilton, while to the south is the University of Nevada at Las Vegas (UNLV) campus. A few idiosyncratic museums scattered around the area are worth a detour to see the truly outrageous sides of Sin City.

Everything Coca-Cola (p177)

TRANSPORTATION – UNLV & EAST OF THE STRIP

Bus Most CAT (p234) local buses run east–west and north–south on major surface streets. Bus 108 runs along Paradise Rd and Swenson St, buses 202 and 807 (Bronze Line Express) run along Flamingo Rd, and buses 201 and 804 (Gold Line Express) run along Tropicana Ave.

Car Parking is free at all casino hotels and attractions.

Monorail The monorail (p235) connects the Las Vegas Hilton and convention center to the Strip.

Check out the **Gun Store** (p181), too. For outlying attractions further east, see p91.

Orientation

Streets east of the Strip (Las Vegas Blvd S) follow a gridlike pattern, except around McCarran International Airport. The fastest north–south alternative to Las Vegas Blvd is Paradise Rd, which is one-way southbound of Harmon Ave. Northbound traffic takes Swenson St, one block east, which borders the UNLV campus. The busiest segment of Paradise Rd stretches from the Hard Rock north past Flamingo Rd. The landmark Las Vegas Convention Center stands on the northeast corner of Desert Inn Rd.

ATOMIC TESTING MUSEUM Map p265

☎ 702-794-5161; www.atomictestingmuseum.org; 1st fl, Frank H Rogers Bldg, Desert Research Institute, 755 E Flamingo Rd; adult/senior & youth 7-17 $10/7, child under 6 free; ☾ 9am-5pm Mon-Sat, 1-4pm Sun; bus 202

During the atomic heyday of the 1950s, gamblers and tourists downtown could see mushroom clouds rising behind Fremont St, and the city even crowned a Miss Atomic Bomb. Buy your tickets at the replica of a Nevada Test Site guard station, then spend an hour or two browsing this awesome 8000-sq-ft Smithsonian affiliate.

Exhibits focus heavily on the science, less on the social history, but do include lots of declassified documents. View historical footage from the 'Atomic Age,' which lasted from WWII until atmospheric bomb testing was driven underground in 1961 and a worldwide ban on nuclear testing

was declared in 1992. The **Ground Zero Theater** mimics a concrete test bunker.

Don't miss the free contemporary art exhibits beside the übercool museum shop, or the drive-through espresso bar inside a giant coffee cup at the strip mall on the opposite side of Flamingo Rd, just west of the museum.

HARD ROCK Map p265

☎ 702-693-5000; www.hardrockhotel.com; 4455 Paradise Rd; bus 108

Las Vegas' Hard Rock was the world's first rock 'n' roll casino. It embraces what may be the most impressive collection of **rock-star memorabilia** ever assembled under one roof. Among the priceless items being watched over by eagle-eyed security guards are concert attire worn by Elvis, Brittney Spears and Prince; a drum kit used by Alex Van Halen; a custom motorcycle that was originally owned by the Hell's Angels and donated by Nikki Sixx of Mötley Crüe; a huge display case filled with Beatles mementos; Jim Morrison's handwritten lyrics to one of the Doors' greatest hits, 'The Changeling'; and dozens of jackets and guitars formerly owned by the biggest names in rock 'n' roll.

The hip hotel itself opens on to a roomy circular **casino** with a state-of-the-art **race and sports book**. Raised above the main floor are the Hard Rock's hip **bars** (p138), a megaconcert venue called **The Joint** (p157), **Body English nightclub** (p150), ultra-trendy **restaurants** (p123) and a handful of priceless boutique **shops** (p181). There's seasonal swim-up blackjack out back in the guests-only **Beach Club** (p196).

All in all, this sexy, see-and-be-seen scene is perfect for entourage wannabes – it's always hot, hot, hot.

LAS VEGAS HILTON Map p265

☎ 702-732-5111; www.lvhilton.com; 3000 Paradise Rd; monorail Las Vegas Hilton

The Las Vegas Hilton does not attract nearly as many glassy-eyed slot jockeys as it does suited-up execs. Opened in 1969 by casino impresario Kirk Kekorian, the former International Hotel became famous when Elvis made his comeback in the late 1960s with a string of sold-out shows here. The hotel still books big-name performers like Wayne Newton and Barry Manilow into its **Hilton Theater** and **Shimmer Cabaret** (p157).

The casino hotel has starred in many films including James Bond's *Diamonds Are*

Forever. Off to the side of the **main casino**, where Demi Moore blew on the dice for Robert Redford in *Indecent Proposal*, is the Hilton's **Race & Sports SuperBook**, one of the largest of its kind in the world, with dozens of giant projection and plasma screens. No wonder so many guests view visiting the Hilton as mixing business with pleasure.

For out-of-this-world entertainment, head to the North Tower. That's where you'll find the $70-million interactive attraction **Star Trek: The Experience** (☎ 888-462-6535; www.star trekexp.com; museum & unlimited motion-simulator rides adult/senior & child under 12 $35/32; ⏰ open daily, call ahead to check hours). First, cruise by the museum-of-the-future exhibit, featuring authentic *Star Trek* costumes, weaponry, makeup, special effects and props used in the TV series and motion pictures. Then queue for the live-action, motion-simulation rides: the newer 'Borg Invasion 4-D,' which flashes special effects in a 3D theater after hustling you through a freaky skit; and the classic **Klingon Encounter**, a motion-simulated voyage through space at warp speed aboard – what else? – the starship *Enterprise*. So, is it worth the price of admission? You bet, even for curious Trekkies, not just hard-core Trekkers (some of whom get married here). Discount admission tickets may be available from half-price ticket booths (p143). Children must be 42in tall; under 13s must also be accompanied by an adult.

TOP 10 OUTRAGEOUS VEGAS EXPERIENCES

Siegfried and Roy may not be performing anymore (p148), but Vegas still has wild, wacky and way-out stuff:

- Elvis-A-Rama Museum (opposite) and all the King's impersonators (p156)
- Liberace's rhinestone-studded capes and fabulous furs (right)
- Strippin' off the Strip (p154) and topless showgirl revues (p49)
- Getting hitched at a moment's notice (p85)
- The trippy Fremont Street Experience (p82)
- Slots A' Fun (p78) – oh, yeah, baby
- Mechanical bull riding at the New Frontier (p76)
- Burlesque lives on at Forty Deuce (p134)
- Stripper apparel and out-of-this-world sex shops (p178)
- Chasing aliens outside Area 51 (p225)

Also at the attraction is a complete re-creation of the promenade from *Star Trek: Deep Space Nine,* where guests can dine in **Quark's Restaurant** (p125), down Klingon Ale at the **bar** (p139), browse the largest selection of *Star Trek* merchandise in the known universe (p180), and even converse with a variety of interplanetary visitors (where *do* they get those super-tall actors to portray Klingons anyway?!).

The gateway to *Star Trek: The Experience* is the 20,000-sq-ft, very futuristic **SpaceQuest Casino**, where guests are supposed to feel as if they're stepping aboard a simulated spaceship that's orbiting the Earth. The focal points are 'space windows' above the gaming area, which create the illusion of a genteel passage around our happy planet. It doesn't cost anything to enter the casino or the DS9 Promenade, where you'll be fleeced just like any other Earthling.

LIBERACE MUSEUM Map p265

☎ 702-798-5595; www.liberace.org; 1775 E Tropicana Ave, at Spencer Ave; adult/senior & student $12.50/8.50,/child under 10 free; ⏰ 10am-5pm Mon-Sat, noon-4pm Sun; bus 201

Known and loved throughout the world as 'Mr Showmanship,' Liberace was honored during his lifetime with two Emmy Awards, six gold records and two stars on the Hollywood Walk of Fame. Following his death in 1987, just a few months after his final performances at New York's Radio City Music Hall, the late great entertainer was posthumously honored with the creation of this outrageously cheesy off-Strip museum.

While audiences enjoyed listening to Liberace's exuberant keyboard artistry, they were also amazed and amused by his outlandish style. Liberace's favorite stage pianos are not to be missed in the first building, where a rhinestone-encrusted Baldwin and a concert grand covered in mirrors are a visual feast. Many rare pianos are also on display, among them a hand-painted Pleyel on which Chopin played and a Chickering grand once owned by Gershwin. The lineup of Liberace's cars includes a hand-painted red, white and blue Rolls-Royce convertible, a Rolls-Royce clad entirely in mirror tiles, and a roadster covered in Austrian rhinestones.

Many visitors are enamored of the second building, where Liberace's wardrobe and jewelry are exhibited. Elaborately feathered

FLYING HIGH

If you love to watch jetliners take off and land, then **McCarran International Airport** (p233) has just the place for you. Located on the north side of Sunset Rd between Paradise Rd and Eastern Ave, the **plane watchers' parking lot** (Map p265) was created specifically for plane watchers, and affords perfect views of McCarran's four parallel runways. Enjoy!

capes, sequined suits and million-dollar furs are as funny as they are frightening in their oddity. En route to these exhibits, you may pass the fur salon of Liberace's last costume designer, couturiere Anna Nateece, as it's in the same Strip mall as the museum. This museum's gift shop and café are next to the Italian restaurant, Tivoli Gardens, which Liberace originally opened in 1983.

Time your visit to join one of the free guided tours led by passionate, but self-censorious Liberace fans ('Red Hatters'). No mention will be made of the more creepily bizarre sides of Liberace, such as the rumors that he had a lover undergo plastic surgery in order to make him look more like Liberace himself. Call ahead for tour schedules.

Although expensive, the nonprofit museum supports a foundation that funds music scholarships for talented students. Discounted 2-for-1 entry coupons are often available in tourist publications or can be printed out from the website.

UNLV SPECIAL COLLECTIONS Map p265
☎ 702-895-2234; 3rd fl, Lied Library, 4505 S Maryland Pkwy; admission free; ⏱ 9am-5pm Mon, Wed & Fri, 9am-9pm Tue & Thu; bus 109

Lots of memorabilia gets cast off into this ahistorical town. Thankfully, some of it ends up here, where it's closely guarded by the university. The Lied Library holds a pit boss's ransom of books, photos, maps, posters, manuscripts and more from the city's early, hurly-burly days. Researchers must sign in to view the special collections, but the evolving online exhibits are free to all.

WEST OF THE STRIP

Eating p126; Shopping p181; Sleeping p201

West of the Strip, there are only two main destinations for tourists: the cluster of casino hotels on Flamingo Rd (where you'll find the Rio and Palms) and the Orleans casino hotel on Tropicana Ave. For outlying attractions further west, see p91.

Orientation

Surface streets west of the Strip (Las Vegas Blvd S) and I-15 mostly follow a gridlike pattern. The fastest alternative to the interstate is Industrial Rd, which snakes under I-15 just north of Flamingo Rd.

ELVIS-A-RAMA MUSEUM Map p264
☎ 702-309-7200; www.elvisarama.com; 3401 Industrial Rd; adult $13, child under 10 free, tribute show $18, with museum admission $27; ⏱ 10am-6pm, afternoon tribute shows 2pm & 4pm; free Strip shuttles

You would think a museum devoted to 'The King' would be simply too much, but acolytes can't help falling in love with this place. There are 2000 personal items that once belonged to that big hunk o' love, for which the museum's fanatical owner paid a whopping $5 million. On display are such nifty collectibles as Presley's army uniform, a scintillating love letter to a girlfriend, even some of his cars. Curation isn't high on the list here; it's a random assortment and the museum may not leave you all shook up. It's worth the price of admission only for the 15-minute impersonator show, which takes place several times daily in a spooky cabaret-style venue. You'll

TRANSPORTATION – WEST OF THE STRIP

Bus Most CAT (p234) local buses run east–west and north–south on major surface streets. Buses 201 and 804 (Gold Line Express) run along Tropicana Ave; buses 202 and 807 (Bronze Line Express) run along Flamingo Rd.

Car Parking is free at all casino hotels and attractions.

Shuttle The Rio, Orleans and Gold Coast casinos operate free shuttle services to/from the Strip, but they don't run around the clock. Shuttle buses connect the Rio and Harrah's (from 10am to 1am, every 20 to 30 minutes) and the Gold Coast, Orleans and Barbary Coast (from 9:30am to midnight, every 20 minutes).

Walking It's too far to walk here from the Strip, although you can hoof it between the Flamingo Rd casino hotels (Rio, Gold Coast and Palms).

see crowds here for the afternoon tribute shows, with multiple Kings in full regalia.

GOLD COAST Map p264

☎ 702-367-7111; www.goldcoastcasino.com; 4000 W Flamingo Rd; free shuttle to the Strip & Orleans

The chief selling points of the Gold Coast casino hotel are its bowling center (p166), busy bingo parlor and a plain but easily navigated casino with Spanish facades and – gasp! – windows, a feature found at none of the other big players in town. A hit with locals are the no-cost lounges, from which stream sounds such as Dixieland jazz on weekday afternoons. Catering to Asian package tourists is the restaurant Ping Pang Pong (p127).

Gold Coast combats its distance from the ever-popular Strip by offering a free shuttle service to and from Barbary Coast (p51) and also Orleans (below).

NEVADA STATE MUSEUM Map p264

☎ 702-486-5205; http://dmla.clan.lib.nv.us/docs/museums/lv/vegas.htm; Lorenzi Park, 700 Twin Lakes Dr, off Bonanza Rd, take US 95 exit Valley View Blvd; adult/senior $4/3, child under 18 free; ☽ 9am-5pm; bus 215

Unless you've got a hankering to see a stuffed Columbian mammoth or the Nevada state fossil, an ichthyosaur, you can safely skip this small historical society. It does have one room dedicated to Las Vegas Valley, with casino memorabilia, exhibits about the Hoover Dam project, 1950s atomic testing, and the like. Look for the museum's brand new location opening in 2007 at the Springs Preserve (opposite).

ORLEANS Map p264

☎ 702-365-7111; www.orleanscasino.com; 4500 W Tropicana Ave; free shuttle to Strip & Gold Coast

A mile west of the Strip, this New Orleans–themed casino hotel has done a so-so job of re-creating the Big Easy, but in many minds the Orleans' family-friendly attractions more than make up for its shortcomings. Among its most popular diversions are the 70-lane bowling alley (p167), Century 18 Orleans (p159) and numerous specialty bars, including Brendan's Irish Pub (p155), which has live music some nights. Entertainment legends like Willie Nelson and LeAnn Rimes have performed in the Orleans' showroom, while megaconcerts and sports events take place in the arena (p157) out back. The 112,000-sq-

ft, high-ceilinged casino is an airy, rectangular room; on the floor are more than 3000 slot, video poker and video keno machines, plus card tables, a 20-screen race and sports book, 35-table poker room and 60-seat keno lounge that's open 24 hours.

The Orleans offers shuttles to Gold Coast (left) and Barbary Coast (p51) on the Strip.

PALMS Map p264

☎ 702-942-7777; www.palms.com; 4321 W Flamingo Rd; bus 202, 807

The ultramodern Palms casino hotel, built in 2001, offers an eclectic mix of entertainment designed to seduce gen-Xers and -Yers. It's best known for its starring role in the MTV Real World: Las Vegas reality series and now Bravo's Celebrity Poker Showdown. The high-drama, neon-lit atmosphere is equal parts sexy and downright sleazy – just take a look at the pinup Palms Girls.

As for the theme – every casino hotel has to have a theme, right? – the Palms really doesn't have one. Instead, there's a somewhat Mediterranean feel to the place, which doesn't detour from the gaudiness so often found in Vegas.

What's special about the Palms is that almost everything is done right, due in part to visionary developers of the casino hotel's many venues, including Raymond Visan, creator of Paris' Buddha Bar; Andre Rochat, one of Las Vegas' most revered French restaurateurs; and Scott DeGraff and Michael Morton, nightlife innovators from Chicago. Fashionable places to dine include Alizé (p126), N9NE steakhouse (p127) and the restaurant and sushi bar, Little Buddha (p127). The Palms' first-rate cinema multiplex, Brenden Palms Casino (p159), hosts the CineVegas film festival (p10) and has the only off-Strip IMAX.

The 95,000-sq-ft casino has more than 2000 slot and video machines, table games, two poker rooms (one low-limit, one high-stakes), a keno lounge, and a race and sports book. Topping off its venues (literally) is ghost bar (p139), located on the roof of a 55-floor tower. It's a hip-hop and celebrity hangout that provides a fantastic view back to the Strip. But the real partying happens inside Rain nightclub (p152).

The Palms is upping the ante with a $600-million expansion project that will add a 50-story condo, hotel and spa complex, Palms Place (www.palmsplace.com), which will have a 2200-seat showroom, a sexy pool complex with private bungalows, an 8000-sq-ft recording studio and a Playboy lounge and shop. Construction starts in 2006.

RIO Map p264

☎ 702-777-7777; www.playrio.com; 3700 W Flamingo Rd; free Strip shuttle

The name of this wildly popular casino hotel says a lot about the all-suites Rio, which has a carnaval theme. When it opened in 1990, a lot of people thought it wouldn't survive. They were wrong. The festive **Masquerade Village**, now the center of the action, occupies the first two floors of Rio's towers and offers a hearty mix of food, shopping and gaming choices, as well as loads of entertainment, which all adds up to an ongoing party atmosphere. For the **Show in the Sky** (☉ 3pm, 4pm, 5pm, 6:30pm, 7:30pm, 8:30pm & 9:30pm), Mardi Gras floats suspended from tracks in the ceiling parade above the gaming tables while costumed performers dance, lip-synch to jazzy songs and toss out bead necklaces. The fun is infectious, and you can ride along and have your photo taken in one of the floats for $10.

Occupying most of the 'village' is a 100,000-sq-ft **casino** decked out with a colorful Rio-esque motif. It has more than 1200 slot machines, 80 table games, a keno lounge and a full-service **race and sports book**. Instead of just cocktail waitresses, 'BevErtainers' manage to bring your drinks in between doing 90-second song-and-dance numbers on the main floor. Ringed around the casino are specialty retail **shops** (p182), such as the museumlike **Wine Cellar** (p182) and two of the best **buffets** (p108) in town.

There's no Ipanema at Rio, but guests will find a beach beside one of the resort's five pools. Fifty floors above the village, atop one of Rio's towers (and reached by a glass elevator ride) is the **VooDoo Lounge** (p140). Rio also offers evening entertainment, some pretty good and some truly awful. At press time, your best bet was **Penn & Teller** (p149), though bachelorettes will want to head for the **Flirt Lounge** outside the **Chippendales theater** (p154). The ground-floor **Club Rio** (p150) spins some of the only Latin beats around the Strip.

Although Rio's not on the Strip, it's worth the trip, and free shuttle services to and from **Harrah's** (p54) make it easy to get to.

SPRINGS PRESERVE Map p264

☎ 702-258-3205; www.springspreserve.org; 3701 W Alta Dr; admission free; ☉ 8am-5pm; bus 207

These beautiful desert gardens have walking trails. By the end of 2006, the entire complex will have moved to the northeast corner of Alta Dr and S Valley View Blvd, where it'll have historic displays, a wildlife habitat with replanted gardens, panoramic movie theater and the **Nevada State Museum** (opposite). Call ahead to check new opening hours, admission prices, bus information and driving directions.

OUTER NEIGHBORHOODS

Eating p128; Shopping p182; Sleeping p202

Aside from the casino hotels downtown and on the Strip, most of Las Vegas consists of residential neighborhoods. Bordering the city to the southeast is Henderson, a satellite suburb. Summerlin, a planned community, is northwest of downtown off US 95. The Boulder Strip, where you'll find locals' casino hotels, runs along the Boulder Hwy, which heads east of downtown past Henderson to Boulder City and Hoover Dam (p209). Bordered by Nellis Air Force Base on its east side, North Las Vegas is a pretty tough area. South of the Strip, near Blue Diamond Rd, is an outlet shopping mall, a couple of casino hotels and other diversions.

Orientation

Most of the Las Vegas metro area is laid out on a grid of slow-moving surface streets. Traffic on the highways usually moves faster if you're driving longer distances, although the section of I-15 west of the Strip and the spaghetti bowl of freeways northwest of downtown can be incredibly congested day and night.

CLARK COUNTY MUSEUM Map p260

☎ 702-455-7955; www.co.clark.nv.us/parks/Clark _County_Museum.htm; 1830 S Boulder Hwy, Henderson; adult/senior & child $1.50/1; ☉ 9am-4:30pm; bus 107

Far off the beaten path, this humble but jam-packed museum makes for a sweet stop en route to Hoover Dam. Inside are

TRANSPORTATION – OUTER NEIGHBORHOODS

Bus Most CAT (p234) local buses run east–west and north–south on major surface streets, but these routes are designed for commuters, not tourists. From any of these attractions, the closest bus stop may be quite a walk.

Car Driving is the only feasible way of getting around. Parking is free.

Shuttle Some casino hotels offer free shuttle services (p236), including Sam's Town (to the Strip and downtown).

exhibits on the history of Las Vegas as an ancient desert, Native American settlement and frontier town. Even more interesting, though, is the outdoor railroad stock and vintage memorabilia on Heritage Street, where you can walk through historic houses from the turn of the 20th century through to the WWII era, listen to big band music, inspect a 1930s motor court and snap a photo next to the shiny Airstream trailer – go nuts. The germ of the museum was the artifact collection of pioneer Anna Robert Parks.

ETHEL M CHOCOLATES & CACTUS GARDEN Map p260

☎ 888-627-0990; www.ethelm.com; 2 Cactus Garden Dr, east of Mountain Vista Rd & Sunset Rd, Henderson; admission free; ⏰ 8:30am-7pm; bus 114, 212

This chocolatier's self-guided 'factory tour' won't take you more than five minutes, but you can still snap up a free fudge or truffle sample before exploring the pleasant, 2.5-acre desert garden outside with more than 350 species of succulents, such as teddy bear cholla, organ pipe, beavertail cacti, and crazy octotillo. It's not worth a special trip, but maybe just a quick stop on your way to Hoover Dam.

LAS VEGAS ART MUSEUM Map p260

☎ 702-360-8000; www.lasvegasartmuseum.org; Sahara West Library, 9600 W Sahara Ave; adults/student/senior $6/3/5, children under 12 free; ⏰ 10am-5pm Tue-Sat, 1-5pm Sun; bus 105, 204

Fans of contemporary art revel in this imposing white edifice, filled with light and

cutting-edge exhibitions from across the country and abroad, but focusing on the art of the Southwest. Soothing and well funded at a cool $20 million, the museum is a Smithsonian affiliate. It also offers art classes, and local artisans' works are sold inside the shop.

PLANETARIUM & OBSERVATORY Map p260

☎ 702-651-4759; www.ccsn.edu/planetarium; 3200 E Cheyenne Ave, east of I-15; adult/senior & child under 12 $5/3; ⏰ 6pm & 7:30pm Fri, 3:30pm & 7:30pm Sat, public observatory 8:30pm Fri & Sat (weather permitting), store 5-8pm Fri & 3-8pm Sat

On the south side of the Cheyenne campus of the Community College of Southern Nevada (CCSN), science geeks give popular seasonal multimedia presentations. You'd best show up early just to get a seat (no late admissions allowed). It's kid-friendly, too.

RICHARD PETTY DRIVING EXPERIENCE Map p260

☎ 702-643-4343, 800-237-3889; www.1800bepetty.com; Las Vegas Motor Speedway, 6975 Speedway Blvd; rides from $99; ⏰ varies, call for schedule

Curious about what it's like to be in high-speed pursuit? Here's your chance to ride shotgun during a Nascar-style qualifying run of three laps at the **Las Vegas Motor Speedway** (p162). The 600-horsepower stock cars can reach speeds of over 150mph. Also based at the Speedway, the **Mario Andretti Racing School** (☎ 877-263-7388; http://andrettiracing.com) offers ride-along opps from $70, plus the chance to drive for a mere $360, at least one weekend every month.

SOUTHERN NEVADA ZOOLOGICAL-BOTANICAL PARK Map p260

☎ 702-647-4685; www.lasvegaszoo.org; 1775 N Rancho Dr; adult/senior & child 2-12 $7/5; ⏰ 9am-5pm; bus 106, 210

This 3-acre zoo takes care of Canadian river otters, ostriches, swamp wallabies, Barbary Apes and more – including every poisonous snake found in the entire region. Kids get to feed some critters (not the snakes, of course), while you browse the rare bamboos, cycads and gem displays. Nonprofit educational programs are offered, too.

Walking & Driving Tours

Walking & Driving Tours

Vegas ain't made for walking. Distances along the Strip are always a lot further than they seem. Be sure to bring good walking shoes because you're going to end up walking *a lot*, whether you spend your entire trip in only one casino or wandering around a dozen. Entrances to Strip casino hotels on Las Vegas Blvd are designed to draw gamblers like moths to a flame, and inside confusing signs and odd layouts are meant to trap you there.

So, what's the good news? The tours in this chapter will help maximize your fun and minimize the distances you have to walk. They use public transport wherever feasible. Plus, you won't need to finish a tour to get your money's worth. For most of these tours, you can start anywhere along the route and follow the itinerary for only as long as you've got stamina, then quit or maybe pick up the route again after a few lucky pulls on the slot machines.

For organized tours of the city, see p48. Turn to p208 for group trips out of town.

AROUND THE WORLD IN A DAY

Las Vegas is itself a wonder of the postmodern world. One of the things that makes it so is its shameless re-creations of famous world wonders right here on the Strip. You can zoom from Italy to France to Egypt to Polynesia without changing time zones. All that jet-setting can be exhausting, so stop to refuel on the Strip whenever you feel like it; after all, taking the time to savor the whole world as you go is part of the fun. You can take this tour anytime, day or night, but it's best done in the early evening, when attractions are still open, free casino shows are going on and fabulous neon signs are lit up.

Start inside the **Venetian** 1 (p58), grab a gondola or stroll through the Grand Canal Shoppes (p174) by St Mark's Square. Outside the casino, cross over Las Vegas Blvd on the skybridge to **TI** 2 (p58), the artist formerly known as Treasure Island. Check out the free Sirens of TI show in Sirens' Cove. Walk south to the **Mirage** 3 (p54) and

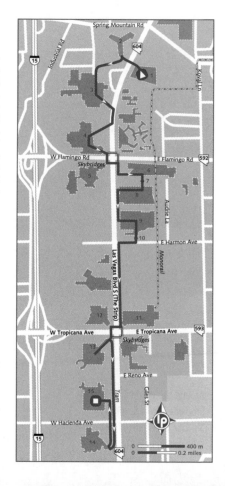

TOUR FACTS

Start Venetian (monorail Harrah's/Imperial Palace).

End Luxor (tram from Mandalay Bay & Excalibur).

Distance 2 miles.

Time 3 hours, up to a full day.

Fuel Stops Anywhere along the Strip (p106), especially at Mon Ami Gabi (p112).

Gondola on the canals of the Venetian (p58)

its faux volcano, then duck inside the tropically scented hotel lobby to view the 20,000-gallon aquarium and jungle atrium. You can give Siegfried & Roy's Secret Garden a miss, but look for the royal white tiger habitat as you exit the casino.

Back on Las Vegas Blvd, saunter south along the Strip to Caesars' Forum Shops (p174). Pace yourself as you walk through the mall – now would be a good time to stop for a bite to eat (p108) – and into the gargantuan casinos of **Caesars Palace** 4 (p51). Watch the cocktail waitresses dressed as ancient Greeks sashay by, and take a break to gamble on the giant slot machines. Stroll out of the casino and through the Roman Plaza. Cross Flamingo Rd via a skybridge south to **Bellagio** 5 (p51), where you'll be delighted by dancing fountains and floral displays.

Cross back over to the east side of the Strip, head all the way to the back of **Bally's** 6 (p49) and wend your way via the cobblestone Rue de la Paix shopping arcade, **Le Boulevard** 7 (p174), into **Paris–Las Vegas** 8 (p57) to soak up 'Le Atmosphere' and maybe take a romantic ride up the Eiffel Tower. Then amble south to gaze upon what's left of the Middle Eastern fantasy that was **Aladdin** 9 **(p57)**, now owned by Planet Hollywood. At the adjacent **Desert Passage** 10 (p173) shopping mall, you can hire a pedicab to whisk you through the 1.2-mile passageway of shops.

Walk one long block south to the imposing **MGM Grand** 11 (p63). Cross over the elevated pedestrian walkway to **New York–New York** 12 (p64). Be awed by its miniature skyline, complete with a Brooklyn Bridge and Stripside benches for resting. Wander inside to Greenwich Village. Consider taking a ride on the Manhattan Express coaster. Cross the skybridge south toward **Excalibur** 13 (p61) and top off your transglobal journey with a tram ride via **Mandalay Bay** 14 (p62) down to **Luxor** 15 (p61) with its pyramid and reconstructed King Tut's tomb.

STRIPSIDE THRILLS & SPILLS
This city is its own virtual-reality ride. Think of it all as one big, outdoor amusement park that never charges an admission fee. For an added adrenaline rush, jump on some (or all) of the Strip's best thrill rides. Most of the casino arcades shut down by midnight on weekends, or 10pm or 11pm on other nights. Elsewhere, lines for the most popular rides are often jam-packed, so get an early start if you want to experience it all. Bring loads of

TOUR FACTS

Start Stratosphere (monorail Sahara).

End Luxor (tram from Mandalay Bay & Excalibur).

Distance 4 miles.

Time 4 hours, up to a full day.

Fuel Stops Quark's Restaurant (p125), Slots-A'-Fun (p78), 'Wichcraft (p120), America (p119), Village Eateries (p119).

cash, or just pick and choose a few of these amusements.

This tour starts at the Stratosphere because, if you do nothing else in Las Vegas, you should experience the thrill rides at the top of the tower. But the advantage of starting at the opposite (south) end of the Strip and walking this tour in reverse is you can time your trip to end up at the Stratosphere after dark for beautiful night views of the Strip.

At the **Stratosphere Tower** 1 (p79) buy a combo ticket and ride the USA's fastest elevators past the Top of the World Lounge (p136) to the Big Shot and Insanity rides. Decompress with a southbound sprint along the Strip past **Bonanza Gifts** 2 (p177), allegedly the world's largest (and tackiest) gift shop. Cross over Las Vegas Blvd to the **Sahara** 3 (p77), where you can hop aboard the roller coaster Speed – The Ride, or race nearly full-sized, very realistic stock cars at the Las Vegas Cyber Speedway.

Once you're back on the west side of Las Vegas Blvd, catch a bus headed south down the Strip to **Circus Circus** 4 (p75) to check out the rides at the Adventuredome. Then take a taxi or walk a half mile east along Riviera Blvd to the **Las Vegas Hilton** 5 (p87) for Star Trek: The Experience. Near the Hilton's SpaceQuest Casino, board the monorail southbound to the **MGM Grand** 6 (p63). Pause to watch a free show at CBS Television City and to play the retro arcade games in the basement. Save some stamina to detour north for the virtual-reality rides at **GameWorks** 7 (p61).

Return to the corner of Las Vegas Blvd and Tropicana Ave, then cross the skybridge to **New York–New York** 8 (p64), where the Coney Island Emporium arcade and rickety Manhattan Express roller coaster await. Shoot some hoops or go duckpin

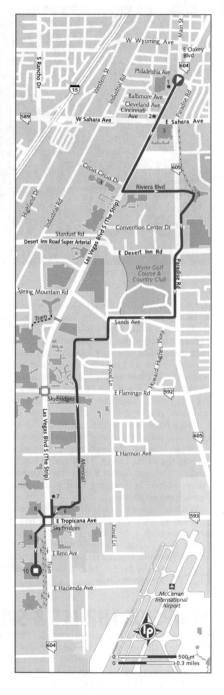

bowling at New York–New York's ESPN Zone before taking the skybridge to **Excalibur 9** (p61), which has all sorts of carnival games in its Fantasy Faire Midway. A moving walkway connects the castle to **Luxor 10** p61). Inside the pyramid, make a beeline for the Games of the Gods arcade to test-drive some of the latest and greatest interactive amusements.

SIN CITY AFTER DARK

Warning: this tour is adults-only, and you can't hold us responsible for any liver damage that might occur. But if booze, baccarat and bodacious bodies are what you've come to Vegas for, then a drunken crawl on the Strip is just what the witch doctor ordered. The beautiful thing about Sin City is you don't have to wait until the cocktail hour comes around to start carousing, though you *will* want to walk this way under the cover of darkness. We don't expect that you will actually stop everywhere on our tour, especially not while walking under the influence, but, if you do manage it, then consider yourself an honorary gonzo journalist – and know that you're our hero, too. (Or if you get too soused early on and miss a few watering holes along the way, it won't matter a whit.)

You could spend the whole evening in **Mandalay Bay 1** (p62), but tonight it's only the beginning. Strut into THEhotel and ride the glass elevator up 64 floors to Mix (p135) for a sunset cocktail in the sky-high lounge. Wander back down through the casino over to rumjungle (p135) or Red Square (p135) for a specialty shot of rum or vodka. Once you've done that, drop by House of Blues (p151) for 'rock star' karaoke early in the week or retro dance sounds on the weekends.

TOUR FACTS

Start Mandalay Bay (tram from Excalibur & Luxor).

End Peppermill (CAT bus 301).

Distance 3.5 miles.

Time Dusk till dawn.

Fuel Stop Anywhere along the way. See the Drinking (p130) and Entertainment (p150) chapters for recommendations.

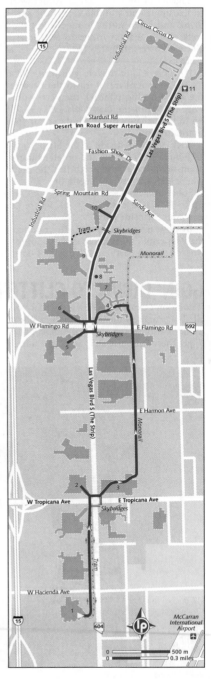

Take a ride on the free tram (don't worry, you won't be the only drunk one on it) north to Excalibur and stumble across the skybridge to **New York–New York** 2 (p64). Have another drink and listen to the lounge act at the Big Apple Bar (p134). When you're refreshed, walk across the skybridge to **MGM Grand** 3 (p63). Flirt at Centrifuge (p131), pierce the electric flower of Teatro (p136), lounge at Tabú (p136) and shake your booty at Studio 54 (p153).

If you're a club maven, you won't be anywhere near satisfied yet. So it's time to hop on the monorail travel up to the **Flamingo** 4 (p53). Tip your souvenir margarita glass to the ghost of Bugsy Siegel, then cross over the Strip to Light (p152) at **Bellagio** 5 (p51) or Pure (p152) inside **Caesars Palace** 6 (p51). If nightclubs aren't your thing, make your way on to the balcony of the Fontana Bar (p131), which overlooks the Bellagio's spectacular fountain show.

Back on the east side of the Strip, stagger north to the **Imperial Palace** 7 (p54) for karaoke at Tequila Joe's (p138) and amateur impersonators (called 'dealertainers') on the casino's main-floor stage. Just north lies the madness of Harrah's outdoor **Carnaval Court** 8 (p131), where 'flair bartenders' juggle fire.

Sober up with a stiff walk north up the Strip past the exploding volcano of **Mirage** 9 (p54) up to **TI (Treasure Island)** 10 (p58), where tangerine (p153) boasts burlesque dancers and a gorgeous Stripside patio.

By now, it's probably well after midnight, Cinderella. So finish off by hailing a cab up to the Peppermill's **Fireside Lounge** 11 (p136) for romantically retro drinks. For after-hours joints where you can party till the break of dawn, see p150.

GOIN' DOWN TO GLITTER GULCH

If you don't experience downtown for yourself, you can't really know what Old Vegas was all about, namely diehard gambling, cheap booze, lotsa food and free entertainment. Fremont St also happens to be the most pedestrian-friendly part of the city. The quickest way to get there from the Strip is to take a taxi; for the scenic route, catch CAT bus 301 or 302

Speed – The Ride (p78), Sahara

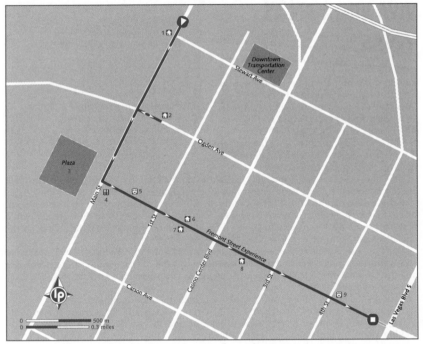

express up Main St through the downtrodden Naked City district. Downtown looks best after dark, so start walking in the early evening as all the neon starts to glow and watch the show.

Start at **Main Street Station** 1 (p84) and take a self-guided tour of its architectural and historical artifacts, then stop for a microbrew at Triple 7 (p137) and take a peek inside the Pullman Grille (p122). Cross the skybridge over Main St to the **California** 2 (p81) for a little aloha spirit, then walk down to the **Plaza** 3 (p86) and try to imagine what life was like in 1905 when the Union Pacific Railroad auctioned off dusty lots in what was then known as Ragtown.

TOUR FACTS

Start/End Downtown Transportation Center (CAT bus 301, 302).

Distance 1 mile.

Time 1 to 2 hours.

Fuel Stops Pullman Grille (p122), Center Stage (p137), Bay City Diner (p122), Binion's Coffee Shop (p123), Chicago Brewing Company (p137).

Escape the smoke and cross over to Fremont St to sidle into Vegas' oldest casino hotel, the **Golden Gate** 4 (p83), for a 99¢ shrimp cocktail. Walk east through the heart of Glitter Gulch, where Vegas' original Strip has been refashioned into the Fremont Street Experience (p82). The only remaining evidence of the former name is the **Girls of Glitter Gulch** 5 p154) strip club. Drop in to **Binion's** 6 (p121) and check out the action in the high-stakes poker room.

Across Fremont St, step inside the classy, vintage **Golden Nugget** 7 (p83) to have a drink in the Oasis Lounge (p137) and to ogle the gigantic Hand of Faith. Relax for a while – and if you're feeling lucky, gamble a bit – then duck into the **Four Queens** 8 p197) for a quick taste of beer at the Chicago Brewing Company (p137). Complete the tour by heading down to 3rd St and the Neon Museum, an alfresco assemblage of vintage signs, around the **Neonopolis** 9 (p84).

VIVA VINTAGE LAS VEGAS

You've already been dazzled by the Strip, gotten down and dirty downtown, but still haven't recaptured the old-school vibes you first felt when you drove by that famous Welcome to Fabulous Las Vegas sign (p62). In a town that moves as fast as this one, little pieces of history get lost every day. Devote some time to unraveling the past in the present. Go further and dig deeper to uncover Vegas behind the scenes.

This tour is probably too big and too bold to do it all. Unless you're intrepid, just pick and choose what sounds good – and that'll be enough to give you a taste of Old Vegas. The route darts on and off the Strip, eventually winding up downtown. You'll venture into places that even locals may never have seen. You'll really need a car to do it all, and you'd best start out bright and early in the day, because many of these attractions close in the late afternoon.

Start your sleuthing at the Strip's original casino hotel, the **Flamingo** 1 (p53). Jump in your car or hop a bus over to the **Atomic Testing Museum** 2 (p87). Drive south to Tropicana Ave and the **Liberace Museum** 3 (p88) to see the outlandish costumes once worn by this legendary Vegas entertainer.

Back on the Strip at Tropicana Ave, drive or take the monorail north to **Bally's** 4 (p49), standing on the ashes of the original MGM Grand, which suffered a tragic fire in 1980. Make sure you've made reservations for the behind-the-scenes tour of *Jubilee!* – still kicking after 25 years – led by a real showgirl or choir boy. After the tour, drive over or call for a shuttle to the **Elvis-a-Rama Museum** 5 (p89). The King has left the building, but you might be able to just catch the last afternoon Elvis impersonator show. Head back to the Strip when it's over.

The Starship Enterprise, Las Vegas Hilton (p87)

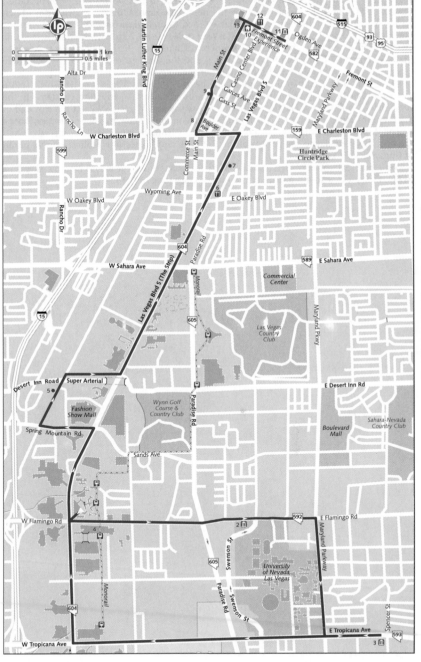

If you're riding the bus, board 301 or 302 straight to the Downtown Transportation Center (DTC), and then skip ahead to the next paragraph. Otherwise, drive downtown on Las Vegas Blvd, detouring east on Oakley Blvd to **Luv-It Frozen Custard 6** (p117). Continue north back on Las Vegas Blvd, past **Viva Las Vegas Wedding Chapel** 7 (p85), which broadcasts its kitschy theme weddings live online. Turn left at Charleston Blvd, then take a right on to Main St, stopping by **Rainbow Feathers** (8; p179) and the **Gamblers General Store** 9 (p178), where you can marvel at the slot machines and other casino goodies.

Follow Main St north to Fremont St, the heart of old Las Vegas' Glitter Gulch (p79). The **Golden Gate** 10 (p83) casino hotel has been around since the early 20th century. On the same block, look for the classic neon signs Vegas Vic and Vegas Vicky. At the east end of the Fremont Street Experience, duck inside the Neonopolis's **Lost Vegas Historic Gambling Museum** 11 (p84), peer at the display cases of knick-knacks from casinos that have already bitten the dust, tip your hat to the photos of the Rat Pack and inspect the replica morgue photo of Bugsy Siegel's corpse.

For a real taste of cowboy Nevada, walk back west to dine at **Binion's Ranch Steakhouse** 12 p121). Finish off with a nightcap at the Plaza's **Center Stage** 13 (p137).

Eating

Eating

Star-studded Sin City is a culinary adventure. Although the fabulous heyday of Vegas dinner shows may be over, showmanship is still the order of the day at any establishment worth its salt. Splashy casino restaurants all compete to dream up the next big thing, whether that's a peekaboo wine tower, a frosty caviar bar made of ice, or a live bamboo grove sprouting up by a sushi kitchen.

Wolfgang Puck brought Spago from Los Angeles to Caesars Palace in 1992. Since then celebrity chefs have set up shop at nearly every megaresort, with more famous names arriving each year. They don't always stick around. In fact, many of the most famous chefs have almost nothing to do with the day-to-day operations of their namesake Las Vegas kitchens, so *caveat diner*. With so many hyped-up tables to choose from, the stakes are high, but the payoffs can be huge.

Foodies can eat their way around the world here, with delights from Tuscany to Tokyo, Mexico to the Middle East, delivered straight to your table. Most of the Strip restaurants are nestled inside the huge casino hotels that flank both sides of Las Vegas Blvd from the Stratosphere south to Mandalay Bay. These places get the lion's share of the business, but some of the independents (both on and off the Strip) are crowd-pleasers, too, and the gourmet quotient stays higher. Cheap buffets and meal deals exist, mostly around downtown and at less glitzy Strip addresses.

We've recommended a mix of old standbys and fiery newcomers in this chapter, but in a mercurial city like Vegas, the eating scene can change literally overnight (for background, see p14). If the prospect of deciding on a meal becomes so daunting that you feel the need to toss back a few vodka martinis before committing yourself, you might like to know that many of the 400-plus bars and cocktail lounges in Las Vegas offer full dinners. Decisions, decisions.

Locals monitor foodie trends and the latest chef gossip in the *Las Vegas Review-Journal*'s Wednesday 'Appetizers' column. More reviews are also found in the *Review-Journal*'s Friday 'Neon' section and the city's free alternative weeklies, *Las Vegas Weekly* and *CityLife*, which focus their attention on off-beat, off-Strip eateries that won't empty your wallet.

Opening Hours

Las Vegas is on the go 24/7, so it's easy to get a meal anytime. Every major casino has a 24hr café, and breakfast is often served nonstop (otherwise it's available from about 7am). Weekend champagne brunch buffets (9am to 4pm) are a hot ticket. Lunch begins around 11am and runs until 2:30pm or so. Dinner starts promptly at 5:30pm (so you can catch an early show) and ends around 10pm weekdays, 11pm on weekends. If restaurants take a day off, it's Monday or Tuesday.

How Much?

Unlike most things in Vegas, what you spend is entirely under your control when it comes to food. After all, this is the city of $5 steak-and-eggs specials dished up around the clock. It's also the place where you'll pay more than $100 per person for a chef's tasting menu at a star eatery, plus another $50 for wine pairings with each fantastic dish. Both are likely to be memorable and worth their respective price tags. Where hungry diners are taken advantage of is at midrange establishments inside casino hotels, especially near the gaming areas – $20 for a bowl of noodles is never a bargain. Some top-end restaurants are grossly overrated, too.

At dinner, expect to pay around $35 per person (with a drink, taxes and tip) at a midrange establishment. The Cheap Eats category at the end of each neighborhood section includes places to get a meal for under $10. Stretch your budget further by eating well at lunch, when some restaurants charge about half as much for a meal as at dinner – often for almost the same menu. 'Fun books' given to hotel guests and players' club members contain 2-for-1 meal deals and other dining discounts, which you can also scout out in the free tourist magazines widely available around town.

Chef, Pink Taco (p124)

Reserving Tables & Dress Code

Book top-end restaurants a few days in advance. Many places now offer online booking. Reservations at the biggest names are essential on weekends – ask your concierge for help.

A few restaurants refuse to bother with reservations despite (or maybe because of) the crowds. Steel yourself to wait an hour or more unless you arrive pretty early or late for a meal. Sometimes there's immediate bar seating and you can order from the same menu.

Unless otherwise noted, the dress code at upscale restaurants is business casual. Athletic shoes, flip-flops and hats may be prohibited at finer places. At top-notch dining rooms, jackets are required for men. Inquire about the dress code when making reservations.

Taxes & Tipping

With such a feast of tables and cuisines to choose from, the one sour note is taxes. A meal priced at $7.95 on the menu will cost over $10 by the time you walk out the door. The standard tip is 15% to 20% before tax; that's double the 7.5% meal tax, plus an added 'toke' for exceptional service. Discreetly leave the tip behind on the table or add it onto the credit or debit card receipt. A service charge of 15% to 18% is often added for groups of six or more; no tip should be added in these cases. At buffets, it's standard to leave a tip of $1 per person. For a cheap (or even 'comped,' ie free) meal, some people advise leaving a tip proportional to the approximate real-world price for such a meal instead of what you actually paid. For room service, tip 15% minus any gratuity already charged.

GREEN GRAZING

At first glance, it may look like slim pickings for vegetarians in a city known for its steakhouses. But on almost any menu on the Strip you can stitch together a few creative appetizers or side dishes, often for much less than your fellow diners are paying. Think of dining in terms of themes: Italianate casino hotels, such as the **Bellagio** (p106) and the **Venetian** (p112), will have scores of pasta joints, for example. Even the most exclusive restaurants, such as **Fleur de Lys** (p116), take care to offer at minimum one stand-out option for vegetarians. Buffets (p108) everywhere are a good bet for salad fixings, fresh fruit and more. In fact, the only place vegetarians are likely to run into trouble is downtown on Fremont St, where meaty fare still rules the roost. Try Main Street Station's **Triple 7** (p137) brewpub, which has an oversized menu of salads and other light fare.

Groceries & Liquor Stores

Relying on snack bars and convenience shops in most casino hotels will quickly empty your wallet. Many shops in **New York–New York** (Map p65) sell above-average snacks, including bottled fruit smoothies and Cliff bars. The Hawaii-born **ABC Store** (Map p261; ☎ 702-380-3098; 23 E Fremont St; ☥ 7:30am-1am) sells discounted liquor and nonalcoholic drinks, snacks and even fresh fruit, with a handy branch downtown. On the Strip and elsewhere around the city, you can always stock up on drinks and snacks at branches of **Walgreens** or **CVS** (p242).

Most hotel rooms don't have refrigerators or coffee makers. To cook your own meals, you'll have to rent a motel room with a kitchenette, stay at a nongaming establishment with full amenities or book an extended-stay apartment suite. Supermarkets are found in residential neighborhoods off the Strip. A healthy alternative for groceries and meals to go is **Trader Joe's** (☎ 702-367-0227; 2101 S Decatur Blvd; ☥ 9am-9pm), which prices its beer, wine and liquor competitively, too. See offmap arrow Map p264.

THE STRIP

Casino hotels make up the backbone of the Vegas economy, so it's no surprise that most of the city's restaurants are inside them. Every one has a 24-hour café, a fast-food court, a buffet and at least a couple of restaurants. The Strip's eateries could be fodder for an entire guidebook; here are some favorites, but there are many, many more.

CENTER STRIP

Barbary Coast

Often overlooked, the Coast nevertheless has two top-flight dining rooms.

DRAI'S Map pp262-3   Californian Continental
☎ 702-737-0555; downstairs, Barbary Coast, 3595 Las Vegas Blvd S; mains $25-45; ☥ 5:30-11pm; monorail Bally's & Paris
LA style elevates this subterranean dining space, designed by ex-movie producer Victor Drai, into a paparazzi-worthy place, complete with its own private elevator. Contemporary updates of classic fare – such as seven-hour leg of lamb or a blackened ahi tuna steak – don't always fulfill the promise of the sexy lounge decor with bordello-red walls and leopard-skin prints. After hours, Drai's (p150) morphs into a DJ haunt.

MICHAEL'S Map pp262-3   Continental
☎ 702-737-7111; Barbary Coast, 3595 Las Vegas Blvd S; mains $45-90; ☥ seatings 6pm & 9pm; monorail Bally's & Paris
Lavished with the Barbary Coast's signature Tiffany-styled stained glass, this petite dining room is old Vegas at its most rococo – and

oh, will you ever pay for it (just cast an eye over the wine list). À la carte delicacies include chateaubriand, Maine lobster and rack of lamb. Reservations are essential; jackets are required for men.

Bellagio

A culinary stable of haute cuisine features several James Beard Award winners. Click to www.bellagio.com or call ☎ 877-234-6358 for table bookings; reservations are required. Note children aged five to 18 are allowed at only some of the Bellagio's restaurants.

A more casual option for light meals is **Jean-Philippe Patisserie** (p117), or pig out at **The Buffet** (p108).

CIRCO Map pp262-3   Tuscan
☎ 702-693-8150; casino level, Bellagio, 3600 Las Vegas Blvd S; lunch mains $12-29, dinner mains $28-50; ☥ lunch Wed-Sun, dinner daily; monorail Bally's & Paris
From the people who brought you Le Cirque, this whimsical, big top–inspired *osteria* overlooks the dancing fountains of Lake Como. Rustic yet complex handmade pasta and *secondi*, such as Tuscan stew or honey-glazed duck with semolina gnocchi, perform well alongside an international cellar of 500 wines.

FIX Map pp262-3   Fusion
☎ 702-693-8400; www.fixlasvegas.com; casino level, Bellagio, 3600 Las Vegas Blvd S; mains $20-30; ☥ 5pm-midnight Sun-Thu, 5pm-2am Fri & Sat; monorail Bally's & Paris
A vibrant and warm – no, make that cutting-edge and *hot* – space for watching celebs and the casino floor. A three-course

Pre 'O' Fix menu ($40) might bring forth such goodies as roasted tomato soup with a grilled-cheese sandwich, chicken with smoked mash, and choco-java 'shake & cake' for dessert. Or just have a quick cocktail and gourmet Kobe beef sliders topped with aged cheddar and some spicy fries.

LE CIRQUE Map pp262-3   Contemporary French
☎ 702-693-8100; casino level, Bellagio, 3600 Las Vegas Blvd S; 3-course prix fixe menu $95; ☾ dinner; monorail Bally's & Paris
A legendary name from NYC, Le Cirque pairs artful haute cuisine with world-class wines in a joyous, intimate lakeside setting, all under a silk-tented ceiling. Among the signature dishes are foie gras terrine, roasted truffle-skin chicken and roasted duck with Tasmanian honey. Jacket and tie are preferred for men.

MICHAEL MINA Map pp262-3   Seafood
☎ 702-693-8100; near the conservatory, Bellagio, 3600 Las Vegas Blvd S; mains $36-72, 6-course tasting menu $110 (veg $85); ☾ dinner; monorail Bally's & Paris
For impeccably fresh seafood, don't miss Michael Mina, the new incarnation of Aqua. An adventurous fusion menu whispers of *hamachi* parfait or Maine lobster pot pie with black truffles. Sadly, nothing could ever measure up to the sky-high prices, and the crowded room is too close to the crushing conservatory crowds. Mina's **Seablue** (p118) at the MGM Grand is a more value-conscious choice.

OLIVES Map pp262-3   Mediterranean
☎ 702-693-8181; www.toddenglish.com; Via Bellagio, Bellagio, 3600 Las Vegas Blvd S; lunch $16-23, dinner mains $25-46; ☾ 11am-10:30pm; monorail Bally's & Paris
East Coast chef Todd English dishes up homage to the life-giving fruit. Flatbread pizzas, house-made pastas and flame-licked meats get top billing. The chef's trademark farm table faces the open kitchen while patio tables overlook the fountains of Lake Como. With a good wine list and flamboyant desserts, it's always packed – come for lunch, but even then, you'll need reservations.

PICASSO Map pp262-3   French/Mediterranean
☎ 702-693-7223; Via Bellagio, Bellagio, 3600 Las Vegas Blvd S; 4-course prix fixe $90-100; ☾ 6-9:30pm Wed-Mon; monorail Bally's & Paris
Five-star chef Julian Serrano delivers artistic Franco-Iberian fusion in a museum-like setting. Original masterpieces by Picasso don't overshadow indulgent entrées like the signature sautéed fallow deer medallions or seafood boudin. Vaulted ceilings and exposed wood beams create an impressive feel. Linger on the patio over a digestif. Reservations are essential but difficult; jacket and tie are suggested for men.

PRIME STEAKHOUSE
Map pp262-3   Steakhouse
☎ 702-693-7223; Via Bellagio, Bellagio, 3600 Las Vegas Blvd S; dishes $25-50; ☾ dinner; monorail Bally's & Paris
Downstairs by **Picasso** (above), this luxurious chop house has a few precious stylistic nods to 1930s speakeasies, with gilt chandeliers and plush velvet curtains. Indulgent dishes reveal ginger sweet potatoes, veal chops with kumquat-pineapple chutney and Maine lobster with braised artichokes. A bold wine list is dominated by Californian and French reds. Jackets for men are preferred.

SENSI Map pp262-3   Global Fusion
☎ 702-693-7223; past Via Fiore shops, Spa Tower, Bellagio, 3600 Las Vegas Blvd S; lunch $16-25, dinner mains $23-40; ☾ lunch & dinner; monorail Bally's & Paris
A beautiful spot tucked away back by the Bellagio's new spa tower, here the minimalist architecture complements a harmonious

TOP 10 RABELAISIAN FEASTS

When it comes to buffets, the old adage 'You get what you pay for' was never truer. Among the starring entrées (mains) at the upscale megaresorts: shrimp, lobster claws, carved-to-order roast meats, fresh fruit, various soups and lots of salad fixings. Some buffets feature live-action stations specializing in sushi, seafood, pasta, stir-fries, omelettes and so on. Buffet prices, like hotel room rates, fluctuate. Generally, expect to pay $7 to $15 for breakfast, $10 to $20 for lunch and $15 to $25 or more for dinner or a weekend champagne brunch. Leave a tip of at least $1 per person on the table.

Timing is everything at buffets, too. These places never take reservations. Lines can be excruciatingly long, although you can rely on being seated – eventually. Typically there are separate lines for VIPs and hotel guests. Otherwise, showing up before noon for Sunday brunch is essential if you want to leave town before the sun starts to set.

Bally's Sterling Brunch (Map pp262–3; ☎ 702-967-7999; upstairs, Bally's, 3645 Las Vegas Blvd S; $58; 🕙 9:30am-2:30pm Sun; monorail Bally's & Paris) Indulge in the best – and most expensive – Sunday brunch in town. Ice sculptures and lavish flower arrangements add to the rich ambience, while selections like broiled lobster, beef tenderloin, caviar and seafood on ice accompany a dessert bar and French champagne (or sake, if you prefer) that never stops flowing.

Carnival World Buffet (Map p264; ☎ 702-252-7777; Rio, 3700 W Flamingo Rd; breakfast $13, lunch $15, dinner & weekend champagne brunch $23, discounts for children; 🕙 7am-10pm Mon-Fri, 7:30am-10pm Sat & Sun; free Strip shuttle) With dishes from China, Brazil, Mexico and Italy on offer, as well as loads of fresh seafood, some say this is the best all-around buffet in town. It's pretty darn hard to dispute that claim, especially with award-winning homemade desserts and Italian gelato. Also at the Rio, **Village Seafood Buffet** (Map p264; ☎ 702-252-7777; Masquerade Village; $35, discounts for children; 🕙 4pm-10pm Sun-Thu, 3pm-11pm Fri & Sat) is for those who just can't get enough crab legs, baby lobster tails and oysters, plus salads, pasta and fresh-baked breads.

Cravings (Map pp262–3; ☎ 702-791-7111; casino level, Mirage, 3400 Las Vegas Blvd S; breakfast $13, lunch $18, dinner & weekend brunch $23; 🕙 7am-10pm Mon-Fri, 8am-10pm Sat & Sun; tram to TI [Treasure Island]) What sets this buffet apart is good crowd control and an architect-designed space. Fresh fruit, salads and seafood here could be called healthy. Stand-out Asian cooking, including dim sum, round out the features.

Dishes (Map pp262–3; ☎ 702-894-7111; casino level, TI [Treasure Island], 3300 Las Vegas Blvd S; breakfast $12, lunch $15, dinner $20-26; 🕙 7am-10:30pm; tram to Mirage) A traditional American buffet, with regional tastes of the South, plus a soup cart wheeled to your table. Sleek Californian-style decor adds to the appeal, but plan on doing time standing in line just to fill your plate. Top it all off with cotton candy and fresh doughnuts.

menu of seafood and pastas with Asian and Italian influences. After dinner, the fantastic sorbets, gelatos and chocolate confections of **Jean-Philippe Patisserie** (p117) are just around the corner.

SHINTARO Map pp262-3   Japanese

☎ 702-693-7223; casino level, Bellagio, 3600 Las Vegas Blvd S; mains $25-50, teppanyaki $35-85; 🕙 5:30-10pm; monorail Bally's & Paris

There's a bit of everything here: premium sake and Japanese beer, sublime sushi, teppanyaki (tabletop live-action BBQ grills) and tea ceremony–influenced *kaiseki* tasting menus, all artfully presented. Don't miss the kaleidoscopic jellyfish aquarium banks behind the sushi bar.

Caesars Palace

Make dining reservations at www.caesars palace.com or by calling ☎ 877-346-4642. For a quick, tasty bite, swing by **Cypress Street Marketplace** (p115).

808 Map pp262-3   Pacific Rim

☎ 877-346-4642; Caesars Palace, 3570 Las Vegas Blvd S; mains $27-39, chef's tasting menu $79; 🕙 5-11pm; monorail Flamingo/Caesars Palace

Chef Jean-Marie Josselin dials Hawaii (area code 'eight-oh-eight') daily on the coconut wireless to procure the raw goods that fuel this tropical-island delight. In a creative mingling of French, Mediterranean, Indian and Pacific Rim elements, the new-wave bento box of trademark appetizers is revered, but don't neglect the 'deconstructed' ahi roll with avocado, crab ceviche and white truffle dressing. Tastes of the tropics appear in desserts such as *lilikoi* (passion fruit) cheesecake and lemongrass ice cream.

BERTOLINI'S Map pp262-3   Northern Italian

☎ 702-735-4663; Fountain of the Gods, Forum Shops, Caesars Palace, 3570 Las Vegas Blvd S; mains $10-20; 🕙 11am-11pm Sun-Thu, 11am-midnight Fri & Sat; monorail Flamingo/Caesars Palace

Garden Court Buffet (Map p261; ☎ 702-387-1896; casino level, Main Street Station, 200 N Main St; breakfast, lunch & brunch $6-10, dinner $11-16; ⏰ 7am-10:30am & 11am-3pm Mon-Fri, 7am-3pm Sat & Sun, 4-10pm daily; bus 301, 302) The elegance of Main Street Station infuses the airy central courtyard buffet, which is mostly memorable for its soul food, Hawaiian specialities and meringue pies. If you're staying downtown, this is your best buffet bargain.

House of Blues' Gospel Brunch (☎ 702-632-7600; casino level, Mandalay Bay, 3950 Las Vegas Blvd S; $39, discounts for children; ⏰ seatings 10am & 1pm Sun) Church might be a foreign concept in Sin City, but you can find holy redemption at House of Blues' Sunday gospel brunch. It comes with unlimited champagne, down-home Southern favorites like jambalaya, turnip greens and jalapeño cornbread, and warm banana-bread pudding and fruit cobbler for dessert.

Le Village Buffet (Map pp262–3; ☎ 702-946-7000; Le Boulevard, Paris, 3655 Las Vegas Blvd S; breakfast $13, lunch $18, dinner & Sunday brunch $25; ⏰ 7am-10pm Sun-Thu, 7am-11pm Fri & Sat; monorail Bally's & Paris) Selections from France's various regions are dished up at distinct cooking stations, with an emphasis on seafood. Fresh fruit and cheeses, cracked crab legs and a range of pastries make the Village arguably the best value buffet on the Strip, plus the low-lit faux sky ceiling above is appealing. Breakfasts are *magnifique*, including the champagne brunch (⏰ 11:30am-4:30pm Sun).

Spice Market Buffet (Map pp262–3; ☎ 702-785-9005; downstairs, Planet Hollywood [Aladdin], 3667 Las Vegas Blvd S; breakfast $13, lunch $16, weekend champagne brunch $21, dinner $24; ⏰ 8-10:30am, 11am-2:30pm & 4-9:30pm Mon-Fri, 8:30am-2:30am Sat & Sun; monorail Bally's & Paris) The Spice Market is the Aladdin's five-star buffet, although once Planet Hollywood takes over the resort, this jewel may disappear. Middle Eastern specialties are now thrown into the global mix, with delectable desserts.

The Buffet (Map pp262–3; ☎ 702-693-7111; casino level, Bellagio, 3600 Las Vegas Blvd S; breakfast $14, lunch $18, brunch $22-28, dinner $26-36; ⏰ 8-10:30am & 11am-3pm Mon-Fri, 8am-3:30pm Sat & Sun, 4-10pm Mon-Thu, 4-11pm Fri & Sat, 4:30-10:30pm Sun; monorail Bally's & Paris) The Bellagio competes for honors among Vegas' best live-action buffets, though it fails to live up to the hype. The sumptuous spread includes crowd-pleasers such as smoked salmon, duck and innumerable creative dishes from around the world. Go for lunch.

World's Fare Buffet (Map pp262–3; ☎ 702-734-5110; 2nd fl, Riviera, 2901 Las Vegas Blvd S; $10; ⏰ 10pm-6am Sat-Thu; bus 301, 302) Surprisingly, for a city that's permanently sleep-deprived, Vegas doesn't have many graveyard buffets, and many are sore sights for epicureans to behold. You can rely on the World's Fare Buffet for sizzling NY Strip steak and eggs, plus a full array of velvety desserts.

Eating

THE STRIP

A fave with locals and tourists, this fountain-side trattoria races ahead of the pack with fresh pastas, wood-fired pizzas, and gelato and sorbet. The friendly atmosphere and attentive service makes all the difference in the world.

BRADLEY OGDEN Map pp262-3 New American
☎ 877-346-4642; opposite Colosseum, Caesars Palace, 3570 Las Vegas Blvd S; dinner mains $41-52; ⏰ 5-11pm; monorail Flamingo/Caesars Palace
With gourmet farm-fresh fare, this kitchen excels. This San Francisco Bay area chef's eponymous restaurant is one of the few in Las Vegas where the famous name actually slaves over the stoves, instead of governing his restaurant from afar. Cascading water-falls and torch lights demarcate a soothing space away from the casino buzz. Almost all of the nouveau takes on classics, like market-fresh salads, blue-cheese soufflés, Florida red snapper and fried frog legs, are available on the more sensibly priced lunch menu. Service is sometimes unpolished.

CHINOIS Map pp262-3 Eurasian Fusion
☎ 702-737-9700; www.wolfgangpuck.com; opposite FAO Schwarz, Forum Shops, Caesars Palace, 3570 Las Vegas Blvd S; lunch $9-15, dinner mains $30-40; ⏰ 11:30am-10pm Sun-Thu, 11:30am-11pm Fri & Sat; monorail Flamingo/Caesars Palace
Peripatetic chef Wolfgang Puck scores again, this time with signature Eurasian fusion served in a chic Far East setting. Pair the fire-cracker shrimp with a premium glass of cold sake. It's a better deal at lunch. Happy hour is 5pm to 7pm daily, except Saturday.

MESA GRILL Map pp262-3 Southwestern
☎ 877-346-4642; opposite the Colosseum, Caesars Palace, 3570 Las Vegas Blvd S; lunch mains $13-20, dinner mains $25-45; ⏰ lunch Mon-Fri, brunch 10:30am-3pm Sat & Sun, dinner daily; monorail Flamingo/Caesars Palace
Bobby Flay's bold new endeavor lives up to the hype. While the star New York chef doesn't cook on the premises, his signature menu of Southwestern fusion fare is

spicy and satisfying. Whether it's a sweet potato tamale with crushed pecan butter, blue corn pancakes or spice-rubbed pork tenderloin, this Iron Chef's Vegas grill is an iron-clad value.

TERRAZZA Map pp262-3   Italian

☎ 877-346-4642; Caesars Palace, 3570 Las Vegas Blvd S; mains $20-30; ☽ dinner Tue-Sat; monorail Flamingo/Caesars Palace

Rustic, well-prepared northern Italian fare, such as rigatoni carbonara, wood-fired pizzas and winter-squash ravioli with roasted walnuts, are all served in a delicious poolside setting. The plush lounge usually has live jazz Tuesday to Thursday nights.

Desert Passage

At press time, dining faves still inside the Aladdin casino hotel, now owned by Planet Hollywood (p108), included the **Spice Market Buffet** (p108). But the hottest culinary action is inside the adjacent shopping mall, **Desert Passage** (p173).

COMMANDER'S PALACE

Map pp262-3   Creole

☎ 702-892-8272; Desert Passage, 3663 Las Vegas Blvd S; breakfast $6-12, 3-course brunch $36, dinner mains $25-40; ☽ 9-11am & 11:30am-2pm Mon-Fri, 10:30am-2:30pm Sat & Sun, dinner from 5:30pm daily; monorail Bally's & Paris

Not quite the same as the 19th-century N'awlins original, but, knowing that more than three dozen original staff moved

---

TOP FIVE CENTER STRIP EATERIES

When nothing but the best will do, these high-roller spots are aces:

- **Delmonico Steakhouse** (Venetian; p113) Creole cooking with undeniable class.
- **Eiffel Tower Restaurant** (Paris–Las Vegas; p112) Impeccable French cuisine that's as good as the sky-high views.
- **Lutèce** (Venetian; p113) Elegantly reinterpreting French classics and seafood, above the romantic canal.
- **Picasso** (Bellagio; p107) Namesake artwork on the walls – what more could you possibly need?
- **Alex** (Wynn; p114) Crazy lobster, crazy prices. Modern French cuisine has never flown so high.

---

across the Mississippi expressly to work here, you can rest assured that the Brennan family, which owns both restaurants, takes food seriously. Turtle soup au sherry, pecan-crusted catfish and shrimp *rémoulade* are on the divine menu, and a live dixieland jazz band turns up for Sunday brunch. Breakfast beignets and weekday lunch specials are unbeatable.

TODAI JAPANESE SEAFOOD BUFFET

Map pp262-3   Asian Seafood

☎ 702-892-0021; enter off Harmon Ave, Desert Passage, 3663 Las Vegas Blvd S; lunch $15, dinner $26, discounts for children; ☽ 11:30am-2:30pm, 5:30-9:30pm Sun-Thu, 5:30-10pm Fri-Sun; monorail Bally's & Paris

Patronize this all-you-can-gorge 160ft spread of Japanese, Chinese and Korean fare featuring dozens of sushi selections and Asian salads. Lobster, shellfish and crab legs are added to the mix at dinnertime. The desserts rock.

Fashion Show Mall

At the north end of the Center Strip, the off-the-beaten-path restaurants at this spruced-up shopping mall are sitting pretty now that Wynn has finally opened across the way.

CAFE BA-BA-REEBA!

Map pp262-3   Spanish Tapas

☎ 702-258-1211; street level, Fashion Show Mall, 3200 Las Vegas Blvd S; tapas $5-8, paella $8-15; ☽ 11:30am-11pm Sun-Thu, 11:30pm-midnight Fri & Sat; bus 301, 302

An outpost of the renowned Chicago restaurant, this alluring Spanish tapas bar and bistro has attentive servers who present paellas for two, *brochetas* (meat and seafood skewers) and a parade of authentic hot and cold tapas like *patatas aioli* (garlic potatoes), spicy *gambas* (shrimp) and imported artisan cheeses. Uniquely flavored sangrias and bite-sized dessert tapas tempt you to linger.

CAPITAL GRILLE Map pp262-3   Steakhouse

☎ 702-932-6631; 3rd level, Fashion Show Mall, 3200 Las Vegas Blvd S; mains $30-40; ☽ lunch Mon-Fri, dinner daily; bus 301, 302

What sets this clubby chain steakhouse apart is hand-cut, dry-aged beef, carved chops and succulent seafood. For a kicky power lunch, fork into a tenderloin Caesar salad or lobster-crab burger. Two-dozen wines are available by the glass, with more than 400 new- and old-world vintages stocking the shelves, which garnered a nod from *Wine Spectator*.

NM CAFÉ Map pp262-3 — Contemporary
☎ 702-697-7340; 2nd level, Nieman Marcus, Fashion Show Mall, 3200 Las Vegas Blvd S; dishes $12-16; ☽ 11am-6pm Mon-Sat, noon-5pm Sun; bus 301, 302

This contemporary café at Neiman Marcus department store, which has outdoor terrace tables above the Strip. A menu of light fare tastes bicoastal, with club sandwiches and calamari salad, but the Middle Eastern and Asian fusion appetizers are far tastier.

RA SUSHI Map pp262-3 — Japanese Fusion
☎ 702-696-0008; www.rasushi.com; street level, Fashion Show Mall, 3200 Las Vegas Blvd S; sushi $1.50-14, lunch $6.50-9.50, dinner mains $9-18; ☽ 11am-midnight, bar to 2am; bus 301, 302

A raucous, sceney spot with Stripside seating and ambient DJ music. Come for the creative taste concoctions, such as wasabi mash or apple-teriyaki salmon; all sound fun, but few are notable. It's not for raw-fish connoisseurs, though the short sake list hits happy notes. Bento boxed lunches are served until 3pm.

Harrah's
Buffalo wings, quesadillas, salads and sandwiches cost $10 or less in the alfresco **Carnaval Court** (p131), on the south side of the casino.

RANGE STEAKHOUSE
Map pp262-3 — Steakhouse
☎ 702-369-5084, 800-392-9002; 2nd fl, Harrah's, 3475 Las Vegas Blvd S; mains $25-55, sides $6; ☽ dinner; monorail Harrah's/Imperial Palace

A standby favorite with an older gamblers crowd, this chophouse has wraparound windows overlooking the sea of humanity on the Strip below. Design your own surf-and-turf specials with seafood surprises including Kumamoto oysters and lobster strudel in ginger-citrus-butter sauce. Live lounge acts croon on weekends.

Mirage
Make reservations for the Mirage's top-end restaurants online at www.mirage.com or by calling ☎ 866-339-4566. **Cravings** (p108), a buffet, is noteworthy. Also, look for Stack, a high-concept restaurant by the team behind **Fix** (p106).

ONDA Map pp262-3 — Italian
☎ 702-791-7111; casino level, Mirage, 3400 Las Vegas Blvd S; mains $27-48; ☽ 5:30-11pm; tram to TI (Treasure Island)

Chef Todd English's powerhouse dining room shares almost none of the signature items from his more popular **Olives** (p107) over at the Bellagio. Onda emphasizes elegant renditions of Italian American classics, like osso bucco, lasagna and cioppino, which have never tasted quite so fresh before.

SAMBA BRAZILIAN STEAKHOUSE
Map pp262-3 — Steakhouse
☎ 702-791-7111; casino level, Mirage, 3400 Las Vegas Blvd S; mains $28-36, buffet $36; ☽ dinner; tram to TI (Treasure Island)

The spit-roasted meats, poultry and seafood just keep on coming at this tropical-themed *rodizio* tableside buffet, where a bottomless salad, sweet fried plantains and black beans with rice contribute to the ravenous appeal. À la carte options like chicken and brazil nut soup are also on offer, with wild cocktails like *batidas* (sugarcane liquor infused with fruit).

Paris–Las Vegas
On **Le Boulevard** (p174) shopping arcade, good options also run by the hotel's topnotch culinary staff of 500 include **Le Village**

Eating THE STRIP

Buffet (p108), sweet and savory crepes at **La Creperie** and pastries at **JJ's Boulangerie** and Parisian export **Lenôtre**. For a divine nosh with a little bubbly, **Napoleon's** (p132) champagne bar has a complimentary carving station for those imbibing during its happy hour (⏰ 4-7pm).

EIFFEL TOWER RESTAURANT
Map pp262-3   French
☎ 702-948-6937; www.eiffeltowerrestaurant.com; 11th fl, Eiffel Tower, Paris, 3655 Las Vegas Blvd S; mains $24-51; ⏰ dinner; monorail Bally's & Paris
The adage about the better the view, the worse the food doesn't apply here. Views of the Strip and Bellagio's fountains are as breathtaking as master chef J Joho's near-perfect contemporary renditions of haute classics like foie gras at this French masterpiece. The tasting menu ($90) is recommended, and so is the vast wine list. Reservations are required; dress is business casual.

MON AMI GABI Map pp262-3   French Bistro
☎ 702-944-4224; www.monamigabilasvegas.com; casino level, Paris–Las Vegas, 3655 Las Vegas Blvd S; dishes $10-29; ⏰ lunch Sun-Thu, dinner 5-11pm Sun-Thu, 5pm-midnight Fri & Sat; monorail Bally's & Paris
Think of a *três* charming Champs Élysées bistro. The elevated patio seating in the shadow of the Eiffel Tower – just about

the only Stripside alfresco dining – is great for people-watching. The steak frites are *parfait*, or take your pick at the raw seafood bar, grand salads, vegetarian crepes and quiches. A good, reasonable French wine list. No reservations.

TI (Treasure Island)
At the artist formerly known as Treasure Island, even the eating options have had a makeover. When only an endless buffet will sate you, there's **Dishes** (p108).

ISLA MEXICAN KITCHEN & TEQUILA
BAR Map pp262-3   Mexican/Southwestern
☎ 702-894-7111; TI (Treasure Island), 3300 Las Vegas Blvd S; mains $12-30; ⏰ 4pm-11am, bar 11am-2am; tram to Mirage
Modern art enlivens the walls at Isla, invented by Mexican-born chef Richard Sandoval, who serves a fusion of south-of-the-border tastes. You might taste guacamole tweaked with citrus and mint or *huitlacoche* (corn 'truffles') in his mashed potatoes. Be forewarned: the food is apportioned for giants. Calling on Isla's tequila goddess to help decipher the bounteous menu of agave elixirs is a must.

Venetian
This mid-Strip bite of Italy is a world-class dining destination. Reservations (☎ 702-

Wine-tasting room, Venetian (above)

414-1000; www.venetian.com) and more formal dress are musts for the fancier places.

Casual dining spots include **Canyon Ranch Café** (☎ 702-414-3600; 4th fl, Grand Canal Shoppes; items $3-18; ⌚ 7am-6pm) for healthy spa cuisine and **Noodle Asia** (☎ 702-414-1000; casino level, Venetian; mains $10-15; ⌚ 11am-3am) with its steaming late-night bowls of noodles and rice.

BOUCHON Map pp262-3 *French Bistro*

☎ 702-414-6200; Venezia Tower, Venetian, 3355 Las Vegas Blvd S; breakfast $8.50-16, lunch & dinner mains $17-32; ⌚ breakfast 7am-10:30am daily, lunch 11:30am-2:30pm Sat & Sun, dinner 5-11pm daily, oyster bar & cocktail lounge 3pm-midnight; monorail Harrah's/Imperial Palace

From Napa Valley's French Laundry wunderkind, Thomas Keller, comes this rendition of a Lyonnaise bistro, featuring an award-winning menu of seasonal classics. An elegant poolside garden setting complements the oyster bar, the extensive selection of seafood, a super wine list and the classic desserts. It's the Strip's most popular breakfast spot *du jour*.

CANALETTO Map pp262-3 *Northern Italian*

☎ 702-733-0070; St Mark's Square, Grand Canal Shoppes, Venetian, 3355 Las Vegas Blvd S; mains $12-32; ⌚ 11:30am-10pm, to 11pm Fri & Sat; monorail Harrah's/Imperial Palace

A showy exhibition kitchen and sky-high ceilings emphasize the solid northern Italian cooking, especially fresh-baked breads from Il Fornaio bakery. To be safe, stick with signature dishes like porcini risotto and roasted chicken. Aim for a table with a gondola view.

DELMONICO STEAKHOUSE

Map pp262-3 *Steakhouse*

☎ 702-414-3737; www.emerils.com; casino level, Venetian, 3355 Las Vegas Blvd S; mains $30-50; ⌚ lunch & dinner; monorail Harrah's/Imperial Palace

Bam! It's celeb chef Emeril Lagasse's greatest gourmet hits, as seen on TV. The cuts are ready for prime time and the influences are Creole, as seen in the grilled pork chops with bourbon smashed potatoes. Desserts seem endless, from country peach pie to whiskey crème brûlée and beyond. Big oak doors open into a vault-ceilinged space.

TOP FIVE BREAKFAST SPOTS

Everyone sleeps in late in Sin City. On the weekends, brunch buffets (p108) are the places to be. Otherwise, the following are fave places to rise and shine:

- **America** (New York–New York; p119)
- **Bouchon** (Venetian; left)
- **Grand Lux Cafe** (Venetian; below)
- **Mr Lucky's** (Hard Rock; p124)
- **Verandah** (Mandalay Bay; p117)

GRAND LUX CAFE Map pp262-3 *Global Eclectic*

☎ 702-414-3888; casino level, Venetian, 3355 Las Vegas Blvd S; mains $9-30; ⌚ 24hr; monorail Harrah's/Imperial Palace

A sophisticated quick bite for those who are reluctant to stray too far from the gaming tables. Plates of global comfort food (salads, sandwiches, seafood, pastas) are piled high. Even nit-picky eaters will find something toothsome here, and the desserts are fabulous. The ambience is elegant yet casual.

LUTÈCE Map pp262-3 *French*

☎ 702-414-2220; Venetian, 3355 Las Vegas Blvd S; mains $28-42; ⌚ 5:30-10:30pm, last reservation 9:30pm; monorail Harrah's/Imperial Palace

Impeccable modern renditions of classic gourmet French fare (sautéed foie gras with huckleberry compote) are presented in a sophisticated, austere black-and-white setting. The French and American wine cellar is top-notch, the superb seafood dishes are as sought after as canalside seats with Strip views. Reservations are required.

PINOT BRASSERIE

Map pp262-3 *Californian French*

☎ 702-414-8888; casino level, Venetian, 3355 Las Vegas Blvd S; lunch $11-18, dinner mains $28-35, tasting menu $65, with wine $90; ⌚ 7-10am & 11:30am-3pm Mon-Fri, 7am-3pm Sat & Sun, dinner daily; monorail Harrah's/Imperial Palace

The architectural accents and the kitchen's copper pots are authentic French imports. Traditionally, a brasserie (derived from the Alsatian word for 'brewery') was for beer and the sustenance was cheap. At this star LA eatery, the spotlight shines on gourmet fare. Don't miss the fresh-shucked shellfish and wine-tasting flights.

Eating | THE STRIP

POSTRIO Map pp262-3 *Californian Italian*

☎ 702-796-1110; St Mark's Square, Grand Canal Shoppes, Venetian, 3355 Las Vegas Blvd S; café: lunch & dinner $11-32, dining room: dinner $28-50; ✆ 11:30am-10pm; monorail Harrah's/Imperial Palace

This offshoot of Wolfgang Puck's San Francisco original features playful original dishes like the lobster club sandwich. Devotees can't get enough of the creative pizzas and pastas (under $20), rich desserts and a selective, yet reasonable wine list. The umbrella-covered patio tables are designed for people-watching, so skip the interior dining room and sit outside instead.

TAO Map pp262-3 *Asian Bistro*

☎ 702-414-1000; Grand Canal Shoppes, Venetian, 3355 S Las Vegas Blvd; most mains $20-45; ✆ call for hrs; monorail Harrah's/Imperial Palace

Feng shui principles must have guided the architectural design of this exquisitely appointed Hong Kong–style eatery. Tableside dim sum service utilizes traditional carts, and features Cantonese delicacies like roast duck and 'drunken crab.' The full bar even stocks sake.

ZEFFIRINO Map pp262-3 *Italian*

☎ 702-414-3500; Grand Canal Shoppes, Venetian, 3355 Las Vegas Blvd S; mains $26-42; ✆ 11:30am-midnight; monorail Harrah's/Imperial Palace

Housemade pasta and seafood specialities prepared with Venetian techniques, such as risotto with lobster and saffron, are highlights. *Maestro di cucina* Gian Paulo Belloni imports the most authentic ingredients straight from Italy, and his executive chef is Sardinian-born. Handcrafted furnishings accent the dining room. Next door, **Tintoretto Bakery** (✆ 7am-midnight Mon-Thu, 7am-1am Fri & Sat) has rich espresso and biscotti.

Wynn

For reservations at the Strip's newest mega-resort, click to www.wynnlasvegas.com or call ☎ 702-770-3463 or ☎ 888-320-7110. The elegant **Terrace Point Café** (mains $8-20; ✆ 24hr) and **Sugar and Ice** (✆ 7am-11pm Sun-Thu, 7am-midnight Fri & Sat) are perfect for coffee and pastries, and both are by cool patios.

ALEX Map pp262-3 *Mediterranean French*

☎ 702-770-3300; 3131 Las Vegas Blvd S; prix fixe menu $110-135, with wine pairings $235; ✆ dinner; bus 301, 302

James Beard Award–winning chef Alessandro Stratta stretches his wings at this haute French restaurant, with high-concept dishes like foie gras ravioli and giant clams with caramelized fennel, sour orange and mint. Some of the most decadent items show Asian influences. No casual attire; jackets are required for men.

BARTOLOTTA RISTORANTE DI MARE
Map pp262-3 *Italian Seafood*

☎ 702-770-3305; 3131 Las Vegas Blvd S; mains $30-55; ✆ lunch & dinner; bus 301, 302

Another James Beard Award winner, chef Paul Bartolotta interprets seafood in a Mediterranean style, along with fresh-made pastas, rabbit loin and beef tartar with white truffles. The spiny lobster *all'acqua pazza* (literally, 'crazy water') is a signature dish.

DANIEL BOULUD BRASSERIE
Map pp262-3 *French*

☎ 702-770-3310; 3131 Las Vegas Blvd S; mains $27-39; ✆ lunch & dinner; bus 301, 302

From the chef who birthed Manhattan's Daniel restaurant, all the brasserie classics such as pâté and brochettes are cooked up here, but also some palate-tinging choices like gourmet burgers topped with black truffles and foie gras or pulled pork and jalapeños. At lunch, casual attire is allowed.

OKADA Map pp262-3 *Japanese/Fusion*

☎ 702-770-3320; 3131 Las Vegas Blvd S; mains $16-29; ✆ dinner; bus 301, 302

This combination sushi bar, robatayaki and teppanyaki grill overlooks a lagoon. Chicago star chef Takashi Yagahashi has mastered Eurasian twists on Japanese classics, like red miso bouillabaisse or tea-smoked Maine lobster with marinated beets. Go for the daily bento box ($29). Dress is elegant casual.

RED 8 ASIAN BISTRO
Map pp262-3 *Cantonese/Pan-Asian*

☎ 702-770-3380; www.wynnlasvegas.com; 3131 Las Vegas Blvd S; mains $13-30; ✆ 11am-10:30pm; bus 301, 302

A bustling spot just off the main casino floor where the action never stops. People

Red Square (p117)

line up for dishes of roast chicken and pork, bowls of steaming hot noodles or dim sum, all from the vivid mind of Malaysian chef Hisham Johari.

Cheap Eats

More spots for quick, cheap meals are mentioned under the individual headings for each major casino hotel introduced earlier.

CANTER'S DELI Map pp262-3   Jewish Deli
☎ 702-894-7111; next to race & sports book, TI (Treasure Island), 3300 Las Vegas Blvd S; meals $8-15; ⏰ 11am-midnight; tram to Mirage

What did Canter's bring over the state line from its landmark LA delicatessen? You guessed it: the infamously gruff service, proving that West Coast Jews have attitude, too (take *that*, NYC). Shoving aside all considerations of politeness, steal one of the seats at the stainless-steel counter or a mod booth for authentic deli fare that's as good as it gets.

CYPRESS STREET MARKETPLACE
Map pp262-3   Food Court
☎ 702-731-7110; opposite the Colosseum, Caesars Palace, 3570 Las Vegas Blvd S; most mains $5-10; ⏰ 11am-11pm Sun-Thu, 11am-midnight Fri & Sat; monorail Flamingo/Caesars Palace

Only New York–New York can claim to have a food court that's better than Caesars.

Charge made-to-order salads, global wraps, Asian stir-fries, southern barbecue and pizza, plus beer, wine and healthier drinks, to your 'smart' card, then pay as you exit. Courtyard tables perch right over the casino floor.

STAGE DELI Map pp262-3   Deli
☎ 702-893-4045; near Festival Fountain, Forum Shops, Caesars Palace, 3570 Las Vegas Blvd S; meals $5-15; ⏰ 8am-11pm Sun-Thu, 8am-midnight Fri & Sat; monorail Flamingo/Caesars Palace

Sky-high sandwiches, named after celebs like Wayne Newton (triple-decker turkey with Swiss) and a huge selection of heaping sides, make this New York import cheap and filling. Dr Brown's sodas, egg creams and the cheesecake are pure Big Apple bliss.

SOUTH STRIP
Monte Carlo

The Monte Carlo is blessed by **Andre's Monte Carlo** (Map pp262-3; ☎ 702-798-7151; casino level; mains $24-58; ⏰ dinner), a branch of the highly esteemed **Andre's** (p121). Seek out commoners' grub at the **Monte Carlo Pub & Brewery** (p135).

Mandalay Bay

For reservations at M-Bay's upscale dining rooms (but not at THEhotel, the Four Seasons or in Mandalay Place), click to www .mandalaybay.com/dining or call ☎ 877-632-7800.

The chichi **THEhotel** (p193) puts a SoHo twist on Vegas coffee shops at **THEcafé** (lobby level; meals $15-30; ⏰ 24hr), a chocolate-brown minimalist lounge for people-watching and ravenous night owls.

AUREOLE Map pp262-3   New American
☎ 702-632-7401; www.charliepalmer.com/aure ole_lv/; near west valet, Mandalay Bay, 3950 Las Vegas Blvd S; prix-fixe menu $75-95; ⏰ 6-10:30pm, wine tower lounge till midnight; tram to Luxor & Excalibur

Executive chef Charlie Palmer's inspired seasonal American dishes like oven-roasted pheasant with sweet-potato gnocchi soar to new heights here. The prix-fixe tasting menu is pure art and it's worth ordering from the extensive wine list (using a handheld electronic sommelier, no less) just to watch catsuit-clad 'wine angels' ascend the four-story tower of vintages. Reservations are essential, but just as difficult to get as good service. Dress is formal.

BORDER GRILL Map pp262-3 Mexican
☎ 702-632-7403; www.bordergrill.com; beach level, Mandalay Bay, 3950 Las Vegas Blvd S; lunch $12-18, dinner mains $13-29; 11am-10pm Mon-Thu, 10am-11pm Fri & Sat, 11:30am-10pm Sun; tram to Luxor & Excalibur
Overlooking Mandalay Beach, this festive restaurant with colorful modern murals features fare by Mary Sue Milliken and Susan Feniger, as seen on the Food Network's *Too Hot Tamales*. The tortilla soup, green corn tamales and pork in molé negro sauce pass for authentic Latin American. Show up for lunch, or just order tasty *bocaditos* and fine margaritas at the bar during dinner. This subterranean spot is hidden back by the Shark Reef (p62).

BURGER BAR Map pp262-3 American
☎ 702-632-9364; Mandalay Place, 3930 Las Vegas Blvd S; meals $10-60; 10:30am-11pm Sun-Thu, 10am-1am Fri & Sat; tram to Mandalay Bay or Luxor
Since when can a hamburger claim to be worth $60? When it's built with Kobe beef, sautéed foie gras, shaved truffles and Madeira sauce (sounds shamefully messy, and it is). Chef Hubert Keller of M-Bay's Fleur de Lys serves up his signature Rossini burger, or you can select all of your own toppings for a meat- or veggie-burger base. Whimsical desserts and other gourmet comfort food are served daily until late.

CHARLIE PALMER STEAK
Map pp262-3 Steakhouse
☎ 702-632-5120; www.charliepalmer.com/steak_lv/; lower level, Four Seasons, Mandalay Bay, 3950 Las Vegas Blvd S; mains from $35; dinner, lounge till midnight; tram to Luxor & Excalibur
Artisan-aged beef is grilled to perfection at this classy, Spanish-influenced hideaway with flawless service and a famous name. Starring on the regional American menu are a Kansas City rib eye and Hudson Valley foie gras. Peruse the wine list with its 500 choices as you sink into the overstuffed chairs of the cigar-friendly lounge. Reservations are essential.

TOP FIVE TABLES ON THE SOUTH STRIP
- **Aureole** (p115) Come here for showy, seasonal cuisine and a famous wine tower.
- **Charlie Palmer Steak** (left) Hands down, this is the South Strip's most solid steakhouse.
- **Fleur de Lys** (below) Hubert Keller reinvents a famous name.
- **Burger Bar** (left) Sample another Keller establishment.
- **RM** (opposite) Savor the democratically priced seafood from Michael Mina.

CHINA GRILL Map pp262-3 Chinese
☎ 702-632-7404; www.chinagrillmanagement.com/chinaLV/; near west valet, Mandalay Bay, 3950 Las Vegas Blvd S; mains $29-50; 5-11pm Sun-Thu, 5pm-midnight Fri & Sat; tram to Luxor & Excalibur
Ambitious, oversized Marco Polo–inspired takes on traditional themes result in neo-Asian dishes like garlic shrimp with black fettuccine and red coconut curry. The demeanor is too cool for school and the overpriced menu is meant for groups. But at least pop in to have a look at the famously indiscreet unisex 'restroom garden' bathrooms designed by Jeffrey Beer.

FLEUR DE LYS Map pp262-3 French
☎ 702-632-9400; www.fleurdelyssf.com; near west valet, Mandalay Bay, 3950 Las Vegas Blvd S; 3-/4-/5-course menu $74/82/94; 5:30-10pm; tram from Excalibur & to Luxor
French chef Hubert Keller has a Vegas outpost of San Francisco's famed Fleur de Lys. A soaring, dramatic space accompanied by European linens and flower-patterned china enhances the thoughtful, seasonal tasting menus. Expect selections like roasted sea bass with pine nut–pesto crust and Colorado lamb with rustic potato stew (imaginative vegetarian options are offered, too).

HOUSE OF BLUES
Map pp262-3 Southern American
☎ 702-632-7600; casino level, Mandalay Bay, 3950 Las Vegas Blvd S; mains $10-20; 7:30am-midnight Sun-Thu, 7:30am-2am Fri & Sat; tram to Luxor & Excalibur
This swampy bayou roadhouse serving down-home Southern cuisine such as

blackened seafood and barbecue is a good pit stop before a show, especially since a dinner receipt whisks you past the concert line. Skip church for HOB's uplifting **Sunday gospel brunch** (p108).

MIX Map pp262-3
Eurasian

☎ 702-632-9500; www.alain-ducasse.com; 64th fl, THEhotel, 3950 Las Vegas Blvd S; mains $37-55; ☽ 6-10:30pm, lounge from 5pm; tram to Excalibur & Luxor

A glorious glass elevator ride sets the stage for Mix's sophisticated, space-age decor. A haute dining room reproduces classic dishes from star chef Alain Ducasse's Paris and Monaco restaurants, like the inimitable elbow pasta with black truffle, ham and Gruyere cheese. Service can be spotty, but at these prices, it really shouldn't be. The sky-high lounge (p135) has better views.

RED SQUARE Map pp262-3
Russian

☎ 702-632-7407; near west valet, Mandalay Bay, 3950 Las Vegas Blvd S; caviar from $35, mains $22-38; ☽ dinner; tram to Luxor & Excalibur

Prices here, next to **rumjungle** (p135), will keep most comrades away unless they've got roubles to spare for chicken Kiev, salmon *kulebyaka* or clams topped with caviar. Propaganda art hangs on the walls and the velvety Russian tea-room atmos-

phere is intoxicating. Top-shelf vodka and more than two dozen types of martini are poured at the sensational ice bar (p135).

RM Map pp262-3
Seafood

☎ 702-632-9300; www.rmseafood.com; Mandalay Place, 3930 Las Vegas Blvd S; restaurant mains $32-52, café mains $19-32; ☽ restaurant 5-10:30pm daily, café 11am-3pm, 5-11pm Sun-Thu, 5pm-midnight Fri & Sat; tram to Mandalay Bay or Luxor

Steps away from M-Bay's casino, New York chef Rick Moonen takes a dual approach to the catch of the day. Upstairs in the restaurant, American seafood dishes, such as Cajun popcorn and Maine lobster, come with suggested beer pairings and comfort-food sides like gourmet mac and cheese. The downstairs café, with rich mahogany tables and shopping promenade tables, offers a stripped-down menu, a raw bar and a 'biscuit bar' serving seafood salads.

VERANDAH Map pp262-3
American

☎ 702-632-5000; lower level, Four Seasons, Mandalay Bay, 3950 Las Vegas Blvd S; breakfast $6-20, dinner mains $27-36, afternoon tea $30-38; ☽ 6:30am-10pm Mon-Fri, 7am-10pm Sat & Sun, weekend brunch buffet 8am-1pm Sat & Sun, afternoon tea 2-5pm Mon-Thu; tram to Luxor & Excalibur

This upper-crust oasis is just about as far away from the ding-ding-ding of the slot

TOP FIVE SWEET SPOTS

- **Chocolate Swan** (Map pp262–3; ☎ 702-632-7777; upper level, Mandalay Place, 3930 Las Vegas Blvd S; items $3-8; ☽ 10am-11pm, to midnight Fri & Sat; tram to Mandalay Bay or Luxor) Truffles, chocolate éclairs, hand-dipped fruits and cherry and chocolate-chip cookies with pecans are just a few of the sweet temptations.
- **Ghiradelli Soda Fountain & Chocolate Shop** (Map pp262–3; ☎ 702-892-8442; Carnaval Court, outside Harrah's, 3475 Las Vegas Blvd S; items $3-7; ☽ soda fountain 11:30am-7pm, store 10am-midnight; monorail Harrah's/Imperial Palace) Dive into the most magnificent hot fudge sundae of your life at San Francisco's traditional Italian chocolate maker (since 1852).
- **Jean-Philippe Patisserie** (Map pp262–3; ☎ 702-693-7111; Bellagio, 3600 Las Vegas Blvd S; most items $5-10; ☽ 7am-11pm Sun-Thu, 7am-midnight Fri & Sat; monorail Bally's & Paris) Stop by if only to see the world's largest chocolate fountain cascading inside this champion pastrymaker's shop. The sorbet and gelato bar scoops more than a dozen different flavors, and the sugar-free sweets won't disappoint.
- **Luv-It Frozen Custard** (Map p261; ☎ 702-384-6452; www.luvitfrozencustard.com; 505 E Oakey Blvd; items $3-6; ☽ 1-10pm Tue-Thu, 1-11pm Fri & Sat; bus 301) A mecca for locals since 1973, Luv-It's handmade concoctions are creamier than ice cream. Flavors change daily (they're posted online), so you'll be tempted to go back. Try a 'Luv Stick' custard bar, thick milkshake or sundae piled higher than Everest.
- **Mermaids** (Map p261; ☎ 702-382-5777; 32 E Fremont St; items from 99¢; ☽ 24hr; bus 301, 302) Grab a strand of Mardi Gras beads at the door, then weave your way back past the bleary-eyed slot jockeys and belly up to the back counter for outrageous 99¢ deep-fried Twinkies and Oreos snowed under by powdered sugar. So sinful, but tasty.
- An honorable mention goes to **Vosges Haute Chocolate** in Caesars' Forum Shops (p174) for superb truffles.

Eating

THE STRIP

machines as you can get. Classic and contemporary American breakfasts, afternoon tea and the poolside patio seating justify a detour.

MGM Grand

For reservations, click to www.mgmgrand.com or call ☎ 877-880-0880. Good, quick bites include 'wichcraft (p120) and Stage Deli (p115; ☒ 7am-9pm), near the MGM's race and sports book.

CRAFTSTEAK Map pp262-3 Steakhouse
☎ 702-891-7318; Studio Walk, MGM Grand, 3799 Las Vegas Blvd S; mains $26-78, 3-course tasting menu $80-125; ☒ dinner; monorail MGM Grand
From James Beard Award–winning chef Tom Colicchio, this contemporary, richly wood-laden space may lack exclusivity, but makes up for that with an intriguing menu of grass- vs grain-fed strip steaks, braised lamb shanks and bounty from the sea like regional American oysters, Beluga caviar and Australian lobster tail.

EMERIL'S Map pp262-3 Creole/Cajun Seafood
☎ 702-891-7374; www.emerils.com; Studio Walk, MGM Grand, 3799 Las Vegas Blvd S; lunch mains $21-27, dinner mains $25-60; ☒ lunch & dinner, seafood bar & café 11:30am-10:30pm; monorail MGM Grand
Emeril Lagasse cranks the creativity up a notch at his New Orleans–style fish house (you can't help but smile at the spouting fish sculptures over the entryway), which boasts delicacies such as barbecued shrimp, rosemary biscuits and a sumptuous lobster cheesecake appetizer. The wine list is first class. Reservations are required only for the dining room.

SEABLUE Map pp262-3 Seafood
☎ 702-891-3486; Studio Walk, MGM Grand, 3799 Las Vegas Blvd S; dishes from $5, mains $33-72; ☒ dinner; monorail MGM Grand
The newest creation of Michael Mina (p106) flies in gourmet seafood from around the world, anything from Nantucket Bay scallops to Kumamoto oysters. Raw, fried, steamed or roasted, nothing that the two exhibition kitchens turn out disappoints. Mix-and-match salads ($13) will fit your every culinary whim. The ambience is elegant, yet laid-back; bar seating is available.

SHIBUYA Map pp262-3 Modern Japanese
☎ 702-891-7777; Studio Walk, MGM Grand, 3799 Las Vegas Blvd S; mains $29-50; ☒ dinner; monorail MGM Grand
Come for the stellar sake cellar, dramatic art behind the spreading sushi bar and tastebud-awakening hot and cold appetizers, like seaweed dressed up in orange ponzu sauce, Kumamoto oysters spiked with green apple tang or snapper ceviche with lemon-lime and white soy. Teppanyaki grill set menus come with a choice of lobster miso or Kyoto mushroom soup, plus a sampling of desserts (gingered mint sorbet, anyone?).

WOLFGANG PUCK BAR & GRILL
Map pp262-3 Californian Italian
☎ 702-891-3000; www.wolfgangpuck.com; casino level, MGM Grand, 3799 Las Vegas Blvd S; mains $9-38; ☒ 11:30am-10:30pm Sun-Thu, 11:30am-11:30pm Fri & Sat; monorail MGM Grand
Californian flair pervades this beach-styled bistro glowing just off the casino floor. Truffled potato chips with blue cheese, skirt steak skewers, wood-fired pizzas and

Pastries for sale

ricotta gnocchi in an ultra-contemporary setting are a thrill, and so is the New World wine list.

New York–New York

This casino hotel has the best midrange eats on the South Strip, including at **Nine Fine Irishmen** (p135). Sports fans head for the **ESPN Zone** (p64), while pennypinchers hit up the mock-storefront joints in **Greenwich Village** (right).

AMERICA Map pp262-3   American
☎ 702-740-6451; near lobby, New York–New York, 3790 Las Vegas Blvd S; mains $5-23; ⏰ 24hr; monorail MGM Grand
A fanciful, 18,000-sq-ft bas-relief US map hangs over this reliable, patriotic all-hours eatery. Many go red-white-and-blue in the face trying to pick something from the far-reaching menu, which offers regional fare that ranges from Philly cheesesteaks to San Antonio skillets to Hollywood Cobb salads. There's an extensive bi-coastal beer and wine selection, too. Look for all-you-can-eat pancake specials from 5am until 11:30am.

CHIN CHIN CAFÉ Map pp262-3   Chinese
☎ 702-740-6300; Greenwich Village, New York–New York, 3790 Las Vegas Blvd S; mains $7-13, breakfast buffet $11; ⏰ 7:30am-11pm Mon-Fri, 8am-11pm Sat & Sun; monorail MGM Grand
Another import from the City of Angels, this kitchen's name roughly translates as 'To your health!' Shredded chicken salad topped with toasted almonds and red ginger dressing is satisfying, while unusual tofu dishes provide some variety for vegetarians. Groups should go for the handmade dim sum.

GALLAGHER'S Map pp262-3   Steakhouse
☎ 702-740-6450; Greenwich Village, New York–New York, 3790 Las Vegas Blvd S; mains $27-38; ⏰ dinner daily; monorail MGM Grand
You can't ignore the house speciality, dry-aged sirloin, hanging in the stomach-turning meat lockers out front. The rest of the surf-and-turf offerings from this USDA-choice menu are justifiably famous. To whet your appetite, try the baked oysters with crab, baby spinach, smoked bacon and hollandaise sauce.

IL FORNAIO Map pp262-3   Northern Italian
☎ 702-740-6403; casino level, New York–New York, 3790 Las Vegas Blvd S; breakfast $5-9, dinner mains $12-25; ⏰ 7:30am-midnight; monorail MGM Grand
At dinner, feast on wood-fired pizzas, seasonal salads and pastas, or make a meal of the antipasto platter with scallops wrapped in pancetta, baked eggplant, truffled cheeses and more (per person $12). Delectable, fresh-baked breakfast goodies like lemon-pecan scones, cinnamon coffee cake and hazelnut pastries are also available at **Il Fornaio Paneterria** (⏰ 6am-7:30pm), near the hotel lobby.

Tropicana
Avoid the Island Buffet.

MIZUNO'S Map pp262-3   Japanese
☎ 702-739-2222; Tropicana, 3801 Las Vegas Blvd S; dinners $17-34; ⏰ dinner; monorail MGM Grand
Your personal chef prepares tempura, shrimp, lobster, chicken and steak tableside on hibachi grills courtesy of swordsmenlike moves under strobe lights. Piña coladas are ace. Despite the cheesy overtones, the restaurant itself is a work of art, with gorgeous marble floors and many Japanese antiques. Early bird dinners are a steal ($13).

Cheap Eats
There's a take-out tacqueria upstairs from the **Border Grill** (p116), which is handy for conventioneers. By the upper-level Strip entrance to New York–New York, a cluster of fast-food stands vend Nathan's Famous hot dogs, Schrafft's ice cream, hot pretzels and Tropicana smoothies. See the casino hotel introductions earlier for more budget options.

VILLAGE EATERIES Map pp262-3   Fast Food
☎ 702-740-6969; casino level, New York–New York, 3790 Las Vegas Blvd S; meals $6-12; ⏰ hrs vary; monorail MGM Grand
The cobblestoned streets of NY–NY's ersatz Greenwich Village are bursting with incredibly tasty, wallet-saving options: **Greenberg & Sons Deli**, authentic down to the egg cream sodas; **Fulton's Fish Frye** for fresh fish and chips; and gourmet **Jodi Maroni's Sausage Kingdom** from Venice Beach. **Gonzalez Y Gonzlez** (mains $10-18) is a tequila-soaked Tex-Mex cantina.

'WICHCRAFT Map pp262-3   Deli
☎ 702-891-3166; Studio Walk, MGM Grand, 3799 Las Vegas Blvd S; sandwiches $4-9, half-sandwich combo with soup or salad $9; ☽ 10am-6pm; monorail MGM Grand

This airy, bewitching kitchen has belly-warming sandwiches such as grilled cheddar with smoked ham and baked apples, Sicilian tuna with black olives on a baguette, or plain ol' peanut butter and jelly. Perfect side salads of chick peas, mustard potato salad or fresh fruit are uplifting additions, as are the s'more desserts and wakey-wakey breakfast specialities.

NORTH STRIP

You can get a little south-of-the-border flair along with fajitas, seafood gumbo and fried cheesecake at the Stratosphere's **Crazy Armadillo** (p136), where the restaurant and oyster bar stay open till midnight. There's a 24-hour coffee shop at the Peppermill's **Fireside Lounge** (p136; mains $8-23), where you can eavesdrop on Nevada cowboys and old-school politicos over a late-night bite or early (and gigantic!) breakfast.

STEAKHOUSE Map pp262-3   Steakhouse
☎ 702-794-3767; Circus Circus, 2880 Las Vegas Blvd S; mains $28-38, brunch $39; ☽ dinner daily, brunch seatings 9:30am, 11:30am & 1:30pm Sun; bus 301, 302

In a town filled with meat mongers, the one under the big top is top drawer. All clowning aside, this revered establishment takes itself very seriously, resembling a British hunting lodge with dark wood and an elegant bar. Aged mesquite-grilled steaks are always cooked to perfection and include sides. The Sunday champagne brunch is also well regarded.

TOP OF THE WORLD
Map pp262-3   American/Continental
☎ 702-380-7711; www.stratospherehotel.com; 106th fl, Stratosphere, 2000 Las Vegas Blvd S; lunch $7-21, dinner mains $30-60; ☽ 10am-3pm & dinner; monorail Sahara

While taking in the cloud-level views at this revolving romantic roost perched atop the **Stratosphere Tower** (p79), patrons dressed to the nines enjoy impeccable service and delicious (if overpriced) Colorado rack of lamb

and Cajun prime rib. Dinner reservations are required, or just pop by for a casual lunch or brunch. The award-winning wine list is also available in the gorgeous **lounge** (p136).

Cheap Eats
Just so you know, the **Stratosphere Tower** (p79) has the world's highest Starbuck's.

LUCKY'S CAFÉ Map pp262-3   Coffee Shop
☎ 702-380-7777; www.stratospherehotel.com; casino level, Stratosphere, 2000 Las Vegas Blvd S; mains $5-12; ☽ 10pm-noon Sun-Thu, 10pm-1pm Fri & Sat; monorail Sahara

With opening hours made for night owls, this coffee shop reinvents vintage Vegas with tribute photography and art-deco style. Of course, the food isn't quite so fabulous, but it's still serviceable. A 'midnight madness' menu (served till 5am) has cheapie meal deals.

ROXY'S DINER Map pp262-3   Diner
☎ 702-380-7777; www.stratospherehotel.com; casino level, Stratosphere, 2000 Las Vegas Blvd S; most mains $6-10; ☽ 11am-10pm Sun-Thu, 11am-11pm Fri & Sat; monorail Sahara

Every place in Vegas has a gimmick. At this '50s-style diner, every 15 minutes servers drop everything to do a song-and-dance

---

TOP VEGAS STEAKHOUSES

Vegas has hundreds of places to get a hunka burnin' red meat. Props go to the following:

Binion's Ranch Steakhouse (opposite) Where all the real cowboys eat, plus killer views.

Charlie Palmer Steak (Mandalay Bay; p116) Mediterranean decor and impeccable service.

Pullman Grille (p122) The city's clubbiest and most cigar-friendly steakhouse.

Delmonico Steakhouse (Venetian; p113) Classy and classic steaks with a Cajun twist.

Envy (p124) A cutting-edge bistro that shifts red-meat gravity east of the Strip.

Steakhouse (left) Be lord of the manor.

N9NE (p127) The Windy City's steakhouse almost blows the rest away.

Prime Steakhouse (p107) Where you'll feel like a million bucks.

Redwood Bar & Grill (p122) A favorite with many Hawaiians; great apple dumplings.

AJ's Steakhouse (p123) Where all the swingers eat.

number straight out of *Grease*. It's hilarious fun, but it sure does slow service down. The copiously apportioned comfort food tastes just about right for the prices; big plates won't leave you hungry. The super-thick milkshakes with silver sidecars are just like when you were a kid.

DOWNTOWN

Fremont Street is no culinary mecca, but downtown can claim a few fine-dining spots for steaks and more. In the Naked City, which stretches between the north end of the Strip and downtown, are a few holes-in-the-wall worth a detour.

ANDRE'S Map p261　　　　　French
☎ 702-385-5016; www.andrelv.com; 401 S 6th St; mains $30-55; ⏱ dinner Mon-Sat; bus 301
Chef André Rochat's Provençal-decorated 1930s home is proof that casino hotels don't hold a monopoly on haute cuisine. Seasonal menu highlights might include roasted sautéed duck breast with duck confit and peach cobbler. Sommelier-led wine flights from the world-class cellar start at $30. Reservations are essential; try for patio seating instead of one of the many small interior dining rooms. Dress to impress.

BINION'S RANCH STEAKHOUSE
Map p261　　　　　Steakhouse
☎ 702-382-1600; 24th fl, Binion's, 128 E Fremont St; mains $21-45; ⏱ 6-10:30pm; bus 301, 302
When high rollers finish up in Binion's poker room, they tip back their Stetsons and ride the glass elevator up to this classy old Vegas penthouse meatery for views par excellence and fine feasts of juicy chops with all of the venerable old-school fixin's.

CARSON STREET CAFÉ
Map p261　　　　　Coffee Shop
☎ 702-385-7111; Golden Nugget, 129 E Fremont St; mains $6-15; ⏱ 24hr, closed 3rd Wed 11pm-6am Thu; bus 301, 302
Downtown's appealing around-the-clock eatery has surprisingly pricey grub. The chintzy Euro-flavored café dishes up an endless selection of sandwiches, Mexican standards, filet mignon and prime rib, all rating above average for Fremont St. For dessert, try one of the delectable sundaes. Full bar.

TOP FIVE DOWNTOWN TABLES
- Andre's (left)
- Binion's Ranch Steakhouse (Binion's; left)
- Pullman Grille (Main Street Station; p122)
- Redwood Bar & Grill (California; p122)
- Second Street Grill (Fremont; p122)

CHICAGO JOE'S Map p261　　　　　Italian/American
☎ 702-382-5637; www.chicagojoesrestaurant.com; 820 S 4th St; mains $15-35; ⏱ 11am-10pm Mon-Fri, 5-10pm Sat; bus 301
An old-school Italian eatery stranded on a lonely block south of downtown, this draws devotees of traditional 'red sauce' faves from all over. Judges, lawyers and other movers-and-shakers crowd the tables inside this quaint, cozy house (be prepared to chat with your neighbors), which is just about as far away from the Bellagio as you can get.

FLORIDA CAFÉ Map p261　　　　　Cuban
☎ 702-385-3013; www.floridacafecuban.com; next to Howard Johnson's, 1401 Las Vegas Blvd S; breakfast $5-16; ⏱ 7am-10pm; bus 301
This hub of Naked City's Cuban community is advertised on bus stops all over town, but don't let that dissuade you. Island artworks hang on the walls and a Cuban chef reigns over the kitchen, cooking up American breakfasts and Cuban-style shredded steak, hearty fried pork and seasoned chicken with yellow rice. The café con leche, flan and *batidos* (tropical shakes) are superb.

HUGO'S CELLAR Map p261　　　　　Continental
☎ 702-385-4011; Four Queens, 202 E Fremont St; mains $25-50; ⏱ dinner; bus 301, 302
Ladies get roses on arrival at this cheesy, romantic and retro institution, a classic Vegas gourmet room. Meals begin with a superb tableside salad cart and end with chocolate-dipped fruit for dessert. In-between, it's pure martinis and surf-and-turf.

ICEHOUSE LOUNGE
Map p261　　　　　Contemporary American
☎ 702-315-2570; www.icehouselounge.com; 650 S Main St; mains $5-15; ⏱ 10am-11pm Mon-Thu, 11am-midnight Mon-Sat; bus 108, 207
From the stainless-steel and neon exterior to the mod furnishings inside, this beautiful

but struggling downtown eatery has a swanky Old Vegas feel. Here coffee shop fare meets upmarket grill, with items like filet mignon sliders and steak au poivre with candied shallots and red-pepper coulis. Once the sun sets, DJs may appear as the after-work crowds come for happy hour.

PULLMAN GRILLE Map p261 Steakhouse

☎ 702-387-1896; Main Street Station, 200 N Main St; mains $20-40; ☽ dinner Wed-Sat; bus 207, 301, 302

A well-kept secret, the clubby Pullman features the finest Black Angus beef and Pacific Rim seafood specialities, plus a good wine list amid gorgeous carved wood paneling and a fortune's worth of antiques. The centerpiece namesake is a 1926 Pullman train car, now a cigar lounge where you can quaff port or brandy after dinner. Enter the restaurant through the impressive mansion doors.

REDWOOD BAR & GRILL

Map p261 Steakhouse

☎ 702-385-1222; www.thecal.com; California, 12 E Ogden Ave; mains $18-30; ☽ 5:30-11pm Fri-Tue; bus 301, 302

Next to the Pasta Pirate, this is the Cal's friendly steakhouse, infused with aloha spirit. The porterhouse special (just $15) isn't on the menu, but it's available to anyone who asks for it, which you should do, especially since the grand finale is apple dumpling à la mode in cinnamon-rum sauce.

Buffet chef, Venetian (p112)

SECOND STREET GRILL

Map p261 Pacific Rim/Steakhouse

☎ 702-385-3232; Fremont, 200 E Fremont St; mains $22-35; ☽ dinner Thu-Mon; bus 301, 302

At this downtown gem, which thankfully not too many tourists know about, chef Rachel Bern flies in seafood fresh from Hawaii. You can also get a 16oz T-bone steak with all the trimmings for less than 20 bucks, or try the Mongolian rack of lamb. Bring the love of your life, and dine regally among the art-deco fixtures.

ZAX Map p261 Steakhouse

☎ 702-385-7111, 800-634-3403; off the lobby, Golden Nugget, 129 E Fremont St; mains $21-40; ☽ 5-11pm; bus 301, 302

A faux-retro steakhouse inside the glittering Golden Nugget, with tender steaks, lobster tostadas and sushi appealing to the multi-ethnic downtown crowd. When it's not busy, servers make you feel like royalty, but at other times they may be neglectful. The mod design is classy, perfect for swilling cocktails.

Cheap Eats

On Fremont St, the low roller's surf-and-turf would be a 99¢ shrimp cocktail from the Golden Gate's deli, followed by an old-fashioned burger from Binion's **East Side Snack Bar** (☽ 10am-10pm).

The Las Vegas Club's **Upper Deck restaurant** (☽ 24hr, closed 11pm-6am Wed & Thu) has made a name for itself with its 9lb 'Big Daddy Barrick Burger' ($50); if one person can polish it off, it's free. Good luck, partner.

Triple 7 (p137) brewpub at Main Street Station has a menu with global reach (it's even got a sushi bar). You can get decent, if not Chicago-style pizza and handcrafted beers at **Chicago Brewing Company** (p137).

BAY CITY DINER Map p261 American

☎ 702-385-1906; Golden Gate, 1 E Fremont St; dishes $3-13; ☽ 7am-2am; bus 301, 302

Dirt-cheap breakfasts, graveyard steak and eggs, and roast chicken are the draws at this quaint, cheap eatery inside Fremont Street's most historic hotel. Way on the other side of the main casino floor at the **San Francisco Shrimp Bar & Deli** (☽ 11am-2:30am), you can order the best 99¢

TOP TABLES FOR EATING WITH CHILDREN

It's an Olympic challenge to dine well on the Strip when you've got kids in tow. At high-end restaurants, young children are often simply not allowed. Off-strip casino hotels and neighborhood restaurants are a safer bet. A few faves:

Carnival World Buffet (Rio; p108) One of the few buffets offering discounts for kids.
In-n-Out Burger (p127) Treat your kid to a burger, 'animal-style'.
Lucille's Smokehouse Bar-B-Que (District; p128) Be messy here, and no one will mind.
Luv-It Frozen Custard (p117) For the kid in all of us.
Metro Pizza (p125) Oh so ooey-gooey.
Quark's Restaurant (Las Vegas Hilton; p125) The Klingon will take your order now.
Original Pancake House (Green Valley Ranch; p128) Plates of cakes.
Roxy's Diner (Stratosphere; p120) Free song-and-dance numbers while you wait.
Sazio (Orleans; p127) Kids eat free on Wednesdays.
Village Eateries (New York–New York; p119) Variety is the spice of family life.

shrimp cocktail in town (or super-size it for $2.99).

BINION'S COFFEE SHOP

Map p261   American
☎ 702-382-1600; basement level, Binion's, 128 E Fremont St; meals $8-12; ⊗ 24hr; bus 301, 302
This vintage 24-hour coffee shop is the real deal. Stuff yourself silly with the oversized portions, then choke on the roughed-up coffee, which lets you know you've really arrived downtown. The waitresses are as friendly as your mom; ask 'em about the specials, day or night.

MAHALO EXPRESS Map p261   Hawaiian
☎ 702-385-1664; casino level, Las Vegas Club, 18 E Fremont S; meals $5-8; ⊗ 11am-1am; bus 301, 302
The truest *kine* tastes of the islands are found at this unprepossessing cafeteria inside the Las Vegas Club. Your fellow diners are likely to be homesick Hawaiian families or bleary-eyed, degenerate gamblers who know there's nothing like a mixed-plate lunch of two-scoop rice, macaroni salad and succulent meat to stave off a hangover.

RINCON CRIOLLO Map p261   Cuban
☎ 702-388-1906; 1145 Las Vegas Blvd S; meals $7-10; ⊗ 11am-10pm Tue-Sun; bus 301
A few doors down from an adult video store, this storefront café sports checked tablecloths and an unfailingly cheerful waitress. Daily '(e)specials' include succulent pork chops. Other tasty, authentic offerings are the Cuban sandwich, fried green plantains, *chorizo frito* and extra-strong *cafécitos*.

UNLV & EAST OF THE STRIP

Most of the action east of the Strip is along Paradise Rd. You can get a good taste of Munich at **Hofbräuhaus** (p138). Across the street is the queer-friendly **Hamburger Mary's** (p151).

AJ'S STEAKHOUSE Map p265   Steakhouse
☎ 702-693-5500; www.hardrockhotel.com; Hard Rock, 4455 Paradise Rd; mains $35-50, 4-course prix-fixe menu $60; ⊗ 6-11pm Tue-Sat; bus 108
The Rat Pack would feel right at home in this clubby steakhouse. The superb steak fillets and smooth martinis are almost overshadowed by the 1950s-style decor. There's live piano jazz. Make reservations.

BATTISTA'S HOLE IN THE WALL

Map p265   Italian/American
☎ 702-732-1424; 4041 Audrie Lane; meals $20-35; ⊗ dinner; monorail Flamingo/Caesars Palace
Behind the Flamingo is this kitschy Old Vegas hideaway. For more than 30 years, the Battista family has been dishing up the likes of steak Caruso, manicotti and veal parmegiana all with complimentary sides, including house wine and cappuccinos. It's just a block from the Strip, but decades away in feel, thanks to a strolling accordion player.

CAFE HEIDELBERG Map p265   German Deli
☎ 702-731-5310; 601 E Sahara Ave; lunch $7-14, dinner mains $18-25; ⊗ 11am-10pm; bus 204
At an authentic German deli and market, a half dozen or so modest tables are filled

by loyal expats and locals looking for a fix of strudels and schnitzels of all types. A unique list of German beers and wines, plus live music on many weekend evenings.

ENVY Map p265 — Steakhouse
☎ 702-784-5716; Renaissance Las Vegas, 3400 Paradise Rd; mains $25-40; ⏱ lunch & dinner; monorail Convention Center

Competitors may indeed envy this eatery, one of the hottest new steakhouses in town. A dramatic entrance leads to an interior that won't disappoint, with plush high-backed chairs and hanging lanterns. Both the steak and seafood get high marks, along with inventive side dishes like bourbon creamed corn. Its wine list has 1500 choices.

FIREFLY Map p265 — Fusion Tapas
☎ 702-369-3971; www.fireflylv.com; Citibank Plaza, 3900 Paradise Rd; dishes $3-10, mains $10-20; ⏱ lunch Mon-Fri, dinner 5pm-2am Sun-Thu, 5pm-3am Fri & Sat; bus 108

Firefly is always packed with fine young thangs and cigar-smoking Mr Bigs, especially on weekends. But folks are showing up not just for the late-night patio scene; it's also for the food. Spain shakes hands with Asia, as chorizo clams jostle alongside shrimp potstickers in a mustard-sesame glaze. A backlit bar dispenses sangria and lychee-infused vodka. On some enchanted nights, hot turntablists or live Brazilian bands perform.

MISTRAL Map p265 — French
☎ 702-792-6373; www.mistrallv.com; Las Vegas Hilton, 3000 Paradise Rd; mains $24-58, tasting menu $95; ⏱ dinner; monorail Las Vegas Hilton

The latest culinary creation of chef André Rochat (p121) is named after a Provençal poet. Wraparound murals of French countryside complement the flawless cuisine, by turns classic and contemporary. Like at the chef's other dining rooms, the wine collection is phenomenal. Though it lacks the views of the Palms' Alizé (p126), it's still romantic. Reservations suggested.

MR LUCKY'S Map p265 — Diner
☎ 702-693-5000; Hard Rock, 4455 Paradise Rd; mains $5-15; ⏱ 24hr; bus 108

Babe-a-licious waitresses dish up the best around-the-clock coffee-shop fare in Vegas.

Become hypnotized by the rock 'n' roll art posters on the walls or tune into the big-screen TVs. The Hard Rock's full, late-night comfort-food menu doesn't list the $7.77 surf-and-turf special: a juicy 8oz steak, three jumbo shrimp and your choice of starchy sides. In a hurry? Bypass the wait for a table and head for the back counter stools.

NOBU Map p265 — Japanese Fusion
☎ 702-693-5090; Hard Rock, 4455 Paradise Rd; sushi from $2, mains $22-55, omakase dinner from $100; ⏱ 6-11pm; bus 108

At chef Matsuhisa's sequel to his NYC establishment, not every bite is quite as good as at the original. The beats are downtempo, the setting pure Zen. The menu is uneven, so stick to Nobu's classics, such as black cod with miso. Andean influences surface in spicy offerings like the Peruvian chicken skewers. The cocktails are creative. Feeling flush? Try the chef's special *omakase* dinner. Reservations are essential.

PINK TACO Map p265 — Mexican
☎ 702-693-5000; Hard Rock, 4455 Paradise Rd; meals $8-15; ⏱ 11am-10pm Sun-Thu, 11am-11pm Fri & Sat, bar open till 3am daily; bus 108

The food is Californiafied but tasty at this lowriders' Baja fish taco shack criss-crossed with a Sunset Strip tequila bar. Appetizers are half price and house beers and margaritas are two-for-one during the happening happy hour (from 4pm to 7pm).

Chinois (p109)

QUARK'S RESTAURANT

Map p265   American

☎ 702-697-8725; DS9 Promenade, Las
Vegas Hilton, 3000 Paradise Rd; mains $9-18;
☺ 11:30am-11pm; monorail Las Vegas Hilton
Star Trek fans should beam right into this
surprisingly cool and palatable eatery.
Amid a futuristic setting, fork into 'Little
Green Salads,' 'Hamborgers' and other
amusingly named dishes, which your server
may straight-facedly force you to pro-
nounce. Chat with a Guinan lookalike at the
bar (p139).

SIMON KITCHEN & BAR

Map p265   Eclectic American

☎ 702-693-4440; www.simonkitchen.com; Hard
Rock, 4455 Paradise Rd; mains $22-42; ☺ reserva-
tions accepted 6-10:30pm Sun-Thu, 6-11:30pm Fri
& Sat; bus 108
The newest buzz at the Hard Rock is all
about Kerry Simon. Eclectic takes on American classics, such as 'topless' apple pie,
colossal crab cakes with papaya slaw, and
macaroni and cheese gratin, is a foodie fad
you've seen before, but the hot scene puts
it over the top. The dress code is 'denim to
diamonds.'

SWEET GEORGIA BROWN'S

Map p265   Southern American

☎ 702-369-0245; 2600 E Flamingo Rd; mains
$9-19; ☺ 11am-10pm; bus 202
Limos pulling up right outside the front
door are not an unusual sight at this classy
soul-food joint. If you're not a high roller or
a famous face, you may not get star treatment. But if you crave fried chicken, corn-
bread and peach cobbler, then it's worth
the trek.

TILLERMAN Map p265   Seafood

☎ 702-731-4036; www.tillerman.com; 2245 E
Flamingo Rd, at Channel 10 Dr; mains $24-55;
☺ 5-11pm; bus 202
Among the best seafood restaurants in Las
Vegas, with prices to match, Tillerman has
an ornately dated atmosphere yet breathes
with green foliage. Specialities include
Alaskan halibut, Florida red snapper, Australian whole lobster, and blackened yel-
lowfin tuna served almost rare in a tangy
mustard sauce, plus a boutique wine list.
Sadly, service can be lackadaisical.

RED MEAT, AFTER HOURS

Late-night meal deals come and go, but the following
are hard to beat:

- **Binion's Coffee Shop** (p123) Tender 10oz New
  York strip steaks ($5.95) are available from 11pm
  to 7am.
- **Mr Lucky's** (opposite) At the Hard Rock, does an
  unlisted 24/7 surf-and-turf special ($7.77).
- **Ellis Island Casino & Brewery** (p201) Attached
  to the Super 8 motel, this offers a full 10oz steak
  dinner ($5) around the clock.
- **Terrible's** (p201) Sink your teeth into a T-bone
  steak dinner with a beer ($7.95).
- **Redwood Bar & Grill** (p122) and **Bay City Diner**
  (p122) Both offer porterhouse steak specials
  ($15).
- **Fresh Harvest Cafe** (p128) For a generous steak-
  and-eggs special ($3.99) drop in on this eatery at
  Sam's Town.
- **World's Fare Buffet** (p108) Last but not least,
  here you'll find all-you-can-eat graveyard steak
  and eggs.

Cheap Eats

Stop by **Rainbow's End** (Map p265; ☎ 702-
737-1338; 1100 E Sahara Ave; ☺ 9am-8pm
Mon-Sat), a natural foods store, for healthy
vegan and vegetarian take-out.

LOTUS OF SIAM Map p265   Thai

☎ 702-735-3033; Commercial Center, 953 E Sahara
Ave; dishes $5-15; ☺ lunch Mon-Fri, dinner daily;
bus 204
The most authentic Thai kitchen this side
of Chiang Mai, the Lotus of Siam boasts a
super-fresh menu with Isaan and Northern
Thai specialties like savory larb salads with
sticky rice. Just ignore the strip mall location while you concentrate on the fresh
flavors bursting out of your bowl. Skip the
lunch buffet, though. Excellent German and
American wine list.

METRO PIZZA Map p265   Pizza/Take-Out

☎ 702-736-1955; 1395 E Tropicana Ave; pizzas
$6.50-23.50; ☺ 11am-10pm Sun-Thu, till 11pm Fri
& Sat; bus 201
If you don't make it all the way out here
to taste Vegas' best thin-crust pie, you can
still devour a cheesy slice at Metro's smaller
kitchen inside **Ellis Island Casino & Brewery** (Map
p265; ☎ 702-733-8901; 4178 Koval Lane,

cnr Flamingo Rd; 🕑 24hr; bus 105, 202), just about within walking distance of the Strip.

PAYMON'S MEDITERRANEAN CAFÉ

Map p265   Deli & Market

☎ 702-731-6030; www.paymons.com; 4147 S Maryland Pkwy; dishes $6-10; 🕑 restaurant 11am-1am Mon-Thu, 11am-3am Fri & Sat, 11am-5pm Sun, market open 9am-8pm Mon-Fri, 10am-5pm Sat; bus 109, 202, 213, 807

One of the city's few veggie spots serves Middle Eastern specialities like baked eggplant with fresh garlic, baba ganoush, tabouli and hummus, plus kebab sandwiches, gyros and savory rotisserie lamb for carnivores. The adjacent **Hookah Lounge** (p138) is a tranquil spot to chill out and digest.

WEST OF THE STRIP

There are few reasons to venture west of the Strip just to dine. But if you're staying at the Rio or Palms, you do have some choices, including **Carnival World Buffet** (p108).

ALIZÉ Map p264   French

☎ 702-951-7000; www.alizelv.com; 56th fl, Palms, 4321 W Flamingo Rd; mains $28-55; 🕑 dinner; bus 202

Chef André Rochat's (p121) top-shelf gourmet room at the Palms is named after a gentle Mediterranean trade wind. The panoramic floor-to-ceiling views enjoyed by nearly every table are as stunning as the haute cuisine. A tower of wine bottles dominates the center of the room. Make reservations; dress to the nines.

ALL-AMERICAN BAR & GRILLE

Map p264   American

☎ 702-252-7767; opposite front desk, Rio, 3700 W Flamingo Rd; mains $10-50; 🕑 11am-6am Sun-Thu, 11am-11pm Fri & Sat; free Strip shuttle

This casual tavern specializes in thick dry-aged steaks, seafood and pork ribs, all cooked to order on a mesquite grill at the entrance to the dining room, which has been redesigned with water, rock and fire elements. Sports games play on plasma-screen TVs. Burgers, seafood and entrée-sized salads, plus regional beer, wine and spirits are on the menu.

GARDUÑO'S Map p264   Mexican

☎ 702-942-7777; casino level, Palms, 4321 W Flamingo Rd; mains $10-25; 🕑 11am-10pm Sun-Thu, 11am-midnight Fri & Sat; bus 202

Voted the top Mexican joint in Vegas by locals, but take that with a large grain of margarita-glass salt. While the menu of combos *tradicional* plays more to the frat-boy palate, there are a few authentic tastes, like the pork posole. Belly up to the Blue Agave Oyster & Chile Bar for a coconut margarita.

Restaurants, New York–New York (p119)

GOLDEN STEER Map p264   Steakhouse

☎ 702-384-4470; www.goldensteerlv.com; 308 W Sahara Ave; mains $22-49; ☯ lunch Mon-Fri, dinner 4-11pm daily; bus 204

No, it's not the best steak in town. But that's not why you're coming to this un-abashedly tacky steakhouse with the steer's head out front. This is the same place where the Rat Pack and Elvis dined, so you're here to soak up the vibes and pre-tend it's 1958 all over again.

LITTLE BUDDHA Map p264   Eurasian

☎ 702-942-7778; Palms, 4321 W Flamingo Rd; mains $15-35; ☯ 5:30-11pm Sun-Thu, 5:30pm-midnight Fri & Sat; bus 202

An offshoot of Paris' terribly popular Bud-dha Bar, this dishes super-fresh sushi and French-Chinese fusion at reasonable prices. The duck confit, tempura pizza and spicy tuna tartar are recommended. The music and interior will sweep you away.

N9NE Map p264   Steakhouse

☎ 702-933-9900; Palms, 4321 W Flamingo Rd; mains $28-42; ☯ 5-11pm Sun-Thu, 5-11:30pm Fri & Sat; bus 202

A sizzlin' hot steakhouse that skews toward twenty/thirtysomethings and is packed with celebs, all courtesy of the people who brought you **ghost bar** (p139) and **Rain** (p152). A dramatically lit room centers on the champagne caviar bar, while at tables and booths the Chicago-style aged steaks and chops keep coming, along with everything from oysters Rockefeller to sashimi.

PING PANG PONG Map p264   Chinese

☎ 702-367-7111; Gold Coast, 4000 W Flamingo Rd; mains $7-30; ☯ 5pm-3am; free Strip shuttle

Asian package tourists vote with their feet, and it's always crowded here. Designed by chef Kevin Wu, a wok-tossed menu ranges across the regions of China, from Canton-ese roast chicken to Beijing seafood stew. Slurping the black peppered beef noodles after midnight is a pleasure. Service is fast.

SAM WOO BBQ Map p264   Cantonese

☎ 702-368-7628; Chinatown Plaza, 4215 W Spring Mountain Rd; meals $8-15; ☯ 10am-11pm Sun-Thu, 10am-midnight Fri & Sat; bus 203

Betcha didn't know Las Vegas has a Chinatown! There's a lively Asian immigrant community west of the Strip, just past the ornate Chinese gate on Spring Mountain Rd. And if the barbecued fowl hanging in the windows doesn't tempt you, there are plenty of pan-Asian bubble tea dis-pensaries, Vietnamese phở shops, Korean barbecue houses and Japanese sushi bars nearby.

SAZIO Map p264   Italian American

☎ 702-948-9500; www.saziolasvegas.com; Orleans, 4500 W Tropicana Ave; lunch $6-10, dinner $8-20, kids menu $5; ☯ lunch 11am-4pm daily, dinner 4-10pm Sun-Thu, 4-10:30pm Fri & Sat; free Strip shuttle

With whimsical portraits of Vegas show-girls and stand-up comics on colorful walls, Sazio (which translates as 'to be satisfied') is a family-friendly eatery by chef Gustave Mahler. Traditional pastas, pizzas and creative salads are respectable, but don't neglect the flavored cheese-cakes either.

TASTE OF INDONESIA   Indonesian

☎ 702-365-0888; www.atasteofindonesia.com; 5700 W Spring Mountain Rd; mains $5-15, tasting menu $23; ☯ 11am-10pm Mon-Sat; bus 203

A half dozen kinds of satay, plus *laksa* (noodle soup), seasoned beef in coconut curry and even frog legs in black-bean sauce, mark this light-hearted café in a strip mall as adventurous territory. An avo-cado or durian shake, anyone? The *rijsttafel* tasting menu is available in a vegetarian version. See offmap arrow Map p264.

Cheap Eats

At California's famous **In-N-Out Burger** (Map p264; ☎ 800-786-1000; 4888 Industrial Rd; meal $5; ☯ 10:30am-1am Sun-Thu, 10:30am-1:30am Fri & Sat), where the patties are never frozen and the fries are hand-diced every day, ask for your burger 'animal style' (with a mustard and onion-grilled bun, plus extra special sauce). **Sonic Drive-In** (Map p264; ☎ 702-873-4328; 4260 W Flamingo Rd; items $1-5; ☯ 7am-2am) is a guilty fast-food pleasure, from pancake-wrapped sausages on a stick to blue coconut slushies. Elsewhere, homesick Londoners flock to **British Foods** ☎ 702-579-7777; 3375 S Decatur Blvd; ☯ 10am-6pm; bus 103). See offmap arrow on Map p264.

OUTER NEIGHBORHOODS

Out on the Boulder Strip, Sam's Town (p203) has tasty eats, including at **Billy Bob's Steak House & Saloon** (mains $16-45; 🕓 dinner), which boasts leather chairs, gigantic rib eye steaks, draft beers and a foot-long Grand Canyon chocolate cake. Also at Sam's Town, **Fresh Harvest Cafe** (meals under $10; 🕓 24hr, closed 11pm Tue-6am Wed) is a casino coffee shop that's way above average.

If you somehow end up in North Las Vegas, head to **Austins Steakhouse** (Map p260; ☎ 702-631-1033; Texas Station, 2101 Texas Star Lane; mains $20-40; 🕓 dinner; bus 106), where the steaks are aged, hand-cut, marinated and mesquite-broiled to perfection, or just stop by for one of the gourmet fillet sliders topped with roasted garlic and chipotle mayo. If you have to wait, have a few drinks at the casino's Martini Ranch first.

South of the Strip, the Silverton's **Mermaid Lounge** (p140) has an appealing menu of seafood and free aquatic shows if you show up at the right time (call ahead to check schedules).

TOP FIVE TABLES OFF THE STRIP

- Alizé (Palms; p126)
- Envy (Renaissance Las Vegas; p124)
- Firefly (p124)
- N9NE (p127)
- Rosemary's Restaurant (right)

BOOTLEGGER BISTRO

Map p260   Italian American

☎ 702-736-4939, take-out 702-736-7080; www
.bootleggerlasvegas.com; 7700 Las Vegas Blvd S;
breakfast $4-9, lunch $7-15, dinner mains $10-25,
kids menu $5-6; 🕓 24hr; bus 117, 303

If you're doing some outlet shopping or killing time before a red-eye flight, try this classy 24-hour joint, which hand-tosses the best thin-crust pizzas in town and features live nightly entertainment (p155). Classic fare includes the likes of seafood del Diavolo, with good graveyard specials (from 11pm to 6am).

LUCILLE'S SMOKEHOUSE BAR-B-QUE

Map p260   Southern Barbecue

☎ 702-257-7427; www.lucillesbbq.com; District at
Green Valley Ranch, 2245 Village Walk Dr, off I-215
exit Green Valley Pkwy, Henderson; sandwiches &
burgers $9.50-12.50, meals $16-25, kids menu $4-7;
🕓 11am-11pm Sun-Thu, 11am-midnight Fri & Sat;
bus 111, 114

In the upscale **District** (p183) mall, this pricey chain 'cue joint gets the thumbs-up from locals for its hickory-smoked ribs and chicken with sides like sweet potatoes, garlic mashed potatoes and mac 'n cheese. Come for lunch (it's cheaper) or live blues on some Friday and Saturday nights. Takeout is available, too.

ROSEMARY'S RESTAURANT

Map p260   New American

☎ 702-869-2251; www.rosemarysrestaurant.com;
suite 110, 8125 W Sahara Ave; 3-course prix-fixe
lunch/dinner $21/40; 🕓 lunch Mon-Fri, dinner
5:30-10pm daily; bus 204

Words fail to describe the epicurean ecstasy you'll encounter at Rosemary's. Yes, it's in a strip mall, and it's also a long drive from the Strip. But once you bite into heavenly offerings like Texas BBQ shrimp with Maytag blue cheese slaw, roasted chestnut soup and creole honey mustard-glazed salmon, you'll forget about everything you endured just to get here. Wine and beer pairings make each course sublime. Beware that lunch is far less creative than dinner. Artworks enhance the upscale atmosphere. Always make reservations.

Cheap Eats

ORIGINAL PANCAKE HOUSE

Map p260   American

☎ 702-614-7200; casino level, Green Valley Ranch,
2300 Paseo Verde Pkwy, off I-215 exit Green Valley
Pkwy, Henderson; meals $6-10; 🕓 6am-10pm;
bus 111

This chain has been flippin' griddlecakes since 1953, and now it's Henderson's heartiest breakfast spot. A kid-friendly menu includes at least a half dozen styles of waffles and pancakes, from smothered apple to southern-style Georgia pecan. Special '49er flapjacks are made from a sourdough starter. Skip the bacon and eggs, though.

Drinking

Drinking

Much of the drinking in Vegas takes place while staring down slot machines and gaming tables. But the casinos and a few other watering holes offer plenty of diversity – from the trendy celebrity ultra lounge that could just as well be in Los Angeles or New York to quiet, low-lit romantic hideaways – so you'll never be left out to dry in Vegas.

The 'ultra lounge' fad landed in Vegas first at Tabú (p136), and it has since stolen the scene. What is an ultra lounge? Basically, a bar that has lofty aspirations, often with a DJ-driven atmosphere, sexy staff and sofas instead of a dance floor. Dance divas favor them as places to jumpstart their evening before moving on to the clubs. Theme nights and experimental DJs can make these lounges a destination in their own right. Some you pay to get in, while others minimize the hassle with no cover and no line. Turn up early if you want a seat.

The vast majority of Sin City's bars are smoke-filled; the antismoking laws in neighboring California banning cigarette, pipe and cigar smoking in all public facilities are viewed with disgust, disdain and indignation in Las Vegas. Many bars are open until the wee hours, and some are open around the clock. Many offer two-for-one drinks and food during happy hour, typically starting after 4pm and ending before 7pm, though exact times vary from one place to another. 'Graveyard' happy hours start after midnight.

Free alternative newspapers like *Las Vegas Weekly* and *City Life* can tip you off to the latest and greatest boozing grounds, although their target audience is locals, so some of their recommendations are the opposite of the glam places you're probably looking for, almost all of which are on the Strip.

This chapter includes a wide-open range of reviews, everything from sexy cabarets to kitschy karaoke clubs to dive bars for postmodern punks. Keep in mind that many of these places aren't worth a major detour; almost every casino hotel has a place to imbibe in style, so pick one that's close to where you are now. If there's no cover charge listed here, admission is usually free. For more after-dark entertainment venues, see p150. For Sin City's gay and lesbian bars, turn to p151.

AIN'T NOTHING TO GETTIN' FREE DRINKS

'A gin and tonic, please.'

If you're 21 years or older and can say those words, or words like them, while shoving coins into a slot machine or otherwise distributing wealth in a Vegas casino, you've mastered the fine art of obtaining complimentary beverages. It's that easy. Really.

Simply saddle up to a one-armed bandit, get the attention of a cocktail waitress and order a drink. Unless you're asking for fine champagne at El Cheapo Casino, nine times out of 10 the cocktail waitress will quickly return with your drink.

The key to endless bar service in Vegas casinos resides in the answer to this question: 'Are you playing?' If you're putting your child's college fund into dollar slots, or wowing a poker dealer with your deadpan face, you are playing and have met the not-so-rigid requirements for free booze.

If you're just walking through a casino and ask a cocktail waitress for a drink, expect her to ask you where you're sitting. Replying that you're just wandering aimlessly around and would prefer to do it with a drink in each hand isn't going to get you fistfuls of hooch.

If you've holed yourself up with a slot machine that doesn't appear on the radar screen of a cocktail waitress, feel free to hunt one down, tell her where you're sitting and ask her to bring you a drink. In fact, feel free to order two drinks. Unless you're falling-down drunk or being obnoxious, the casino couldn't care less how much swill you swallow.

Remember, the gears of Las Vegas are greased by tips. The smiling, short-skirted cocktail waitress who descended on you like an angel and brought you a Cuba Libre in record time might vanish forever if you don't favor her with a tip. The drink is free, but the cocktail waitress lives on tips. At least a buck per drink will keep her coming.

Napoleon's (p132)

THE STRIP

High-action bars and lounges run the length of the Strip, from Mandalay Bay all the way north to Wynn. You'll find more old-school and eclectic spots isolated on the North Strip.

CENTER STRIP

CARAMEL Map pp262-3

☎ 702-693-8300; casino level, Bellagio, 3600 Las Vegas Blvd S; ☯ 5pm-4am; monorail Bally's & Paris
A launching pad for those headed to Light (p152) afterward, this buttery-yellow and rich chocolate-brown lounge shakes a mean martini and spins retro lounge tunes to 21st-century hip-hop. Velvet curtains, leather couches, hand-blown glass sculptures and plasma TVs will keep your eyes mesmerized. No line, no hassles.

CARNAVAL COURT Map pp262-3

☎ 702-369-5000; outside Harrah's, 3475 Las Vegas Blvd S; ☯ 11:30am-2am Sun-Thu, 11:30am-3am Fri & Sat; monorail Harrah's/Imperial Palace
Flair bartenders juggle fire as they keep Harrah's outdoor bar packed with the kind of people for whom spring break never ends. Free live music, from beach pop to rock 'n' roll, burns up the stage at night, but all eyes are usually on the hot bods at the bar. Party on, dudes.

CENTRIFUGE Map pp262-3

☎ 702-891-7777; next to poker room, MGM Grand, 3799 Las Vegas Blvd S; ☯ 4pm-4am; monorail MGM Grand
The MGM's nightlife just keeps getting bolder, with this flashy, extraordinary circular space. The neon glowstick spiked through

its center is like a giant mood ring. It's a movie-worthy backdrop for the bartenders and cocktail waitresses who dance up an electronica storm on the bartop. Best of all, the MGM stole the specialty drinks from all its phenomenal restaurants to serve here.

CLEOPATRA'S BARGE Map pp262-3

☎ 702-731-7110; Caesars Palace, 3570 Las Vegas Blvd S; ☯ 8:30pm-3am; monorail Flamingo/ Caesars Palace
A kitschy floating cocktail lounge that's a replica of one of the majestic ships that sailed the Nile in ancient Egypt. A hydraulics system raises and lowers the boat to mimic sailing. Due to its small size, there are almost no places to sit, although there are a few more tables set on terra firma. DJs spin after 10pm early in the week, with live bands from 9:30pm Wednesday to Sunday.

FIX Map pp262-3

☯ 877-234-6358; casino level, Bellagio, 3600 Las Vegas Blvd S; ☯ 5pm-midnight Sun-Thu, 5pm-2am Fri & Sat; monorail Bally's & Paris
Although it's primarily a restaurant (p106), Fix's lounge, furnished in Costa Rican hardwood, is to die for. Even Leonardo DiCaprio has sampled the scene and cuisine here. It stands open to the casino, yet the people-watching is focused heavily inside.

FONTANA BAR Map pp262-3

☯ 702-693-7111; casino level, Bellagio, 3600 Las Vegas Blvd S; ☯ 5pm-1am Sun-Thu, 5pm-2am Fri & Sat; monorail Bally's & Paris
An older, well-heeled crowd unwinds at this polished lounge with live jazz and a lakeview patio that's far removed from the hoi polloi on the Strip, but perfect for watching the Bellagio's fountain shows.

KAHUNAVILLE Map pp262-3

702-894-7390; TI (Treasure Island), 3300 Las Vegas Blvd S; 8am-3am; tram to Mirage
Dueling pianos on some nights, karaoke others, but it's always a rowdy party. Sip a mai tai under a fake palm tree and watch the flair bartenders work the crowd while you soak up the beach-party atmosphere, especially when the poolside patio is open in summer. Give the tropically styled food a miss, though.

LURE Map pp262-3

702-770-3633; 3145 Las Vegas Blvd S; cover $10-20; 10pm-4am; bus 301, 302
At press time, the jury was still out on Wynn's ultra lounge, a long, narrow room with gauzy drapery, candlelit tables, a fiery patio and premium VIP bottle service. A cheaper, yet still chic place for a quiet, smoochy drink is **Parasol Down**, the counterpoint to which is hectic **Parasol Up** on the casino level.

MARGARITAVILLE Map pp262-3

702-733-3302; outside the Flamingo, 3555 Las Vegas Blvd S; 11am-2am Sun-Thu, 11am-3am Fri & Sat; monorail Flamingo/Caesars Palace
Parrot Heads, you've found your very own paradise on the Strip, with three floors, five bars and hundreds of fortysomething couples spilling onto the sidewalk every night. As the lead singer of the house cover band says, 'Yes, we do play Skynnard.' Inside, a faux volcano explodes hourly, overflowing margaritas with names like 'Last Mango in Paris' into big blenders. Full restaurant menu.

MIST Map pp262-3

702-894-7330; www.caramelbar.com; casino level, TI (Treasure Island), 3300 Las Vegas Blvd S; 5pm-4am; tram to Mirage
Before hitting up **tangerine** (p153), heat up the night at this plush, intimate lounge with a hideaway feel and late-night DJs. The 'Vegas Vixen' (vodka with Peach schnapps, OJ and a splash of cranberry) should be enough to get your baby all warm and tingly.

NAPOLEON'S Map pp262-3

702-946-7000; Le Boulevard, Paris–Las Vegas, 3645 Las Vegas Blvd S; 4pm-2am; monorail Bally's & Paris
Whisk yourself off to a never-never land of 19th-century France, with overstuffed sofas as luxurious as the menu of 100 types of bubbly, including vintage Dom Perignon. Ask the staff for help with a handy 'champagne flight.' A cigar humidor, dueling pianos and a happy-hour carving station doling out meat sandwiches make it worth making your way down Le Boulevard.

PUSSYCAT DOLLS LOUNGE Map pp262-3

702-731-7873; casino level, Caesars Palace, 3570 Las Vegas Blvd S; cover $10; 6pm-4am Tue-Sat; monorail Flamingo/Caesars Palace
Lingerie-clad ladies do a little aerial swinging, rub-a-dub-dub in a tub or sexy song-and-dance numbers every half-hour starting at 9:30pm. Busta Rhymes jumped on stage during the grand opening, which was also attended by Eva Longoria of *Desperate Housewives*. Look for celebs to make surprise appearances at this SoCal import.

CAFFEINE FIXES

Apart from the machines vending energy drinks on the monorail platforms, it's hard to know where to get a buzz in Vegas for less than $5.

For cheap java on the run, the food stands upstairs at New York–New York (p119) charge just 99¢ a cup. **Starbucks** outlets are ubiquitous, including the world's highest-elevation barista bar at the Stratosphere Tower (p79). Other chains have made inroads onto the Strip, including **Seattle's Best Coffee**, which has a sidewalk branch inside the Barbary Coast (p51), and **Peet's Coffee & Tea**, served at restaurants and cafés inside the casinos and shopping malls at the Venetian (p58) and Caesars Palace (p51).

Where can you go for a little more personality and less assembly-line latte? For an honest-to-goodness indie coffee shop, you're out of luck unless you're willing to drive for miles off-Strip. Assuming you're not, the lobby of THEhotel (p193) has a **SoHo-style coffee bar** where you can glimpse artworks by Richard Serra. Small bakery-cafés hidden inside the Strip's high-class megaresorts, like **Tintoretto Bakery** (p114), beside the Grand Lux Cafe (p113), **Il Fornaio Panetteria** (p119) next to **America**, and **Sugar & Ice** (which has the bonus of outdoor seats) at Wynn (p59), also brew rich espresso coffee.

SPIN THE BOTTLE

Without a wet bar in your lavish suite, you've got to shop around for a bottle that's worthy of tonight's assignation.

At Mandalay Place, **55° Wine + Design** (p175) is as beautiful and intimidating as a supermodel. West of the Strip at the Rio's multi-floor **Wine Cellar** (p182), you'll also need to know what you're choosing, because the mark-up on bottles can be extreme. Both of these specialty shops have small wine bars where you can pay for a tipple first.

A much more modest, though again overpriced, selection of Californian and European wines is stashed inside **La Cave**, on Paris–Las Vegas's quaint Le Boulevard (p174) shopping arcade. East of the Strip near **Firefly** (p124) is the **International Vintage Wine Cellar** (Map p265; ☎ 702-892-9424; Citibank Plaza, 3900 Paradise Rd; ☽ 9am-10:30pm Mon-Thu, 9am-11:30pm Fri, 10am-11:30pm Sat, 2-10pm Sun; bus 108). Downtown, the low-cost, chain **ABC Store** (Map p261; ☎ 702-380-3098; 23 E Fremont St; ☽ 7:30am-1am) is a cheap stop for liquor, wine and Hawaiian macadamia nuts.

Don't forget to buy a corkscrew or bottle opener, too. Having one sent up from your hotel's front desk might otherwise cost you a ten-spot. Or just simplify things by going all the way: order up a bucket of champagne from room service instead. Ice ice, baby.

SHADOW: A BAR Map pp262-3
☎ 702-731-7110; casino level, Caesars Palace, 3570 Las Vegas Blvd S; ☽ till 2am; monorail Flamingo/Caesars Palace
Perhaps it's only a gimmick that will keep you distracted just long enough to down a single beverage, but you can't help but stare at the screened silhouettes of go-go dancers shimmying to house music beats. The effect is as retro '70s as a bad James Bond flick.

SPANISH STEPS Map pp262-3
☎ 702-731-7110; outside Caesars Palace, 3570 Las Vegas Blvd S; ☽ noon-midnight Sun-Thu, noon-2am Fri & Sat; monorail Flamingo/Caesars Palace
Worthy of your notice only because the Strip has so few places to sit outside and watch the world pass by. Outside Caesars, you can pick up a fruity, frozen concoction to stave off the heat. Try a 'Colosseum Lemonade' spiked with Smirnoff vodka or an 'Et tu, JD?' (lemon ice with good ol' Jack Daniels).

TEQUILA BAR Map pp262-3
☎ 702-739-4111; casino level, Bally's, 3645 Las Vegas Blvd S; ☽ 11am-2am; monorail Bally's & Paris
A blink-and-you-miss-it sidewalk bar shoved to the side of the main casino, it nevertheless serves more than 50 types of tequila and Mexican appetizers. It's not any kind of a scene, but if you're in the area and are jonesing for agave, they've got silver and gold, plus sangria, here.

V BAR Map pp262-3
☎ 702-414-3200; casino level, Venetian, 3355 Las Vegas Blvd S; ☽ 5pm-2am Sun-Thu, 6pm-4am Fri & Sat; monorail Harrah's/Imperial Palace
Celebrities, agents and glamorous young thangs meet and greet in this beautiful minimalist lounge. The acid jazz and low-key house music are mere accoutrements since low lighting and secluded sitting areas (and sturdy martinis) encourage intimate behavior. Service can be iffy, though. For less attitude, walk upstairs to **Vivid** (below).

VIVID Map pp262-3
☎ 702-414-4870; 2nd fl, outside Grand Canal Shoppes, Venetian, 3355 Las Vegas Blvd S; cover $10-20, women often free; ☽ lounge 10:30pm-4am Wed-Sat; monorail Harrah's/Imperial Palace
Svelte cocktails, wines by the glass and close proximity to balconies overlooking the Strip make this mod bar/lounge combo with exotic backlighting a favorite hangout for locals. Because this cool space is often empty, there's room to spread out with your entire entourage.

The Joint (p157)

SOUTH STRIP

BAR AT TIMES SQUARE Map pp262-3

☎ 702-740-6969; Greenwich Village, New York–New York, 3790 Las Vegas Blvd S; $10 after 8pm Fri & Sat; ☾ live music 8pm-2am Sun-Thu, 3-7pm & 8pm-3am Fri & Sat; monorail MGM Grand

Baby boomers dig the sing-along vibe at this packed dueling piano bar. Show up early on weekends or risk waiting out in Greenwich Village, where latecomers can still catch a glimpse of the festivities taking place inside. If you can't stand the queue (or the tunes), grab a pint at Nine Fine Irishmen (opposite) instead.

BIG APPLE BAR Map pp262-3

☎ 702-740-6969; casino level, New York–New York, 3790 Las Vegas Blvd S; ☾ 11am-2am, live music from 9pm Wed-Mon, 11am-6am Fri & Sat

Raising torch singers on a stage above the bar, this high-impact lounge flung wide open to the casino really jumps. Red velvet curtains and gold filigree make it as tempting as the Garden of Eden, especially for after hours. Even better, it's not at all claustrophobic.

COYOTE UGLY Map pp262-3

☎ 702-740-6969; near Strip skybridge, New York–New York, 3790 Las Vegas Blvd S; after 8pm $10; ☾ 6pm-4am; monorail MGM Grand

If you've seen the movie, you know all about what's goes down here. The antics at this serial Southern saloon are contrived, but fun nonetheless. A rowdy mix of conventioneers and frat boys worship gyrating babes in crop tops pouring free shots from the bartop. If you don't wake up with a hangover, then they haven't done their job.

ESPN ZONE Map pp262-3

☎ 702-933-3766; casino level, New York–New York, 3790 Las Vegas Blvd S; ☾ 11:30am-midnight Mon-Thu, 11:30am-1am Fri, 11am-1am Sat, 11am-midnight Sun; monorail MGM Grand

This chain bar and eatery is a high-tech sports fan's wildest dream come true. 'Zone Throne' viewing stations (reclining chairs with headsets) are installed in front of giant screens. Alternatively, you can slide into a booth to surf sports online or flip the TV channel to any televised game. Memora-

SHAKEN, NOT STIRRED

You know exactly what you like to drink, just like 007. And sometimes you need a bar that stocks your favorite top-shelf hooch. In that case, here's a thumbnail guide to Vegas' specialty bars:

Rum

Head to none other than **rumjungle** (opposite), where bartenders climb a two-story tower of rum bottles.

Tequila

The tequila goddess at **Isla Mexican Kitchen & Tequila Bar** (p112) will bring out your shot in a three-story tower, complete with a Bloody Mary-style chaser. More off-the-cuff are Bally's sidewalk **Tequila Bar** (p133) and the Stratosphere's **Crazy Armadillo** (p136).

Vodka

M-Bay's **Red Square** (opposite) wins; look for the headless statue of Lenin outside.

Whiskey

Naturally, there's a decent selection at most Irish-themed bars, including **Nine Fine Irishmen** (opposite) and **McMullan's Irish Pub** (p139).

Wine

The most famous wine tower is at **Aureole** (p115), but many top-end restaurants have amazing wine lists, including some more reasonable vintages available by the glass at **Mon Ami Gabi** (p112), **Wolfgang Puck Bar & Grill** (p118) or **Rosemary's** (p128).

bilia hangs on the walls, and upstairs is an innovative arcade.

FORTY DEUCE Map pp262-3

☎ 702-632-9442; near Mandalay Bay casino entrance, lower level, Mandalay Place, 3930 Las Vegas Blvd S; cover $10-25; ☾ 10pm-4am Wed & Sun, 10pm-6am Thu-Sat; tram to Mandalay Bay

A speakeasy vibe invades this opulent bilevel club, where you should ignore the bachelorette parties and instead feast your eyes on the smoking-hot traditional burlesque acts backed up by a brassy three-piece band. It's all the vision of Ivan Kane, a New Yorker married to burlesque queen Champagne Suzy. Acts appear on stage every 90 minutes, starting before midnight. Near the club entrance, vintage mannequins make it look like just another store, until you see the tell-tale velvet rope.

HOUDINI'S LOUNGE Map pp262-3

☎ 702-730-7000; casino level, Monte Carlo, 3770 Las Vegas Blvd S; ☯ live music 10pm-1am Thu-Sun; monorail MGM Grand

Almost like an illusion, it has the class appeal of a private club, though it's open to the casino and free to all. Piano jazz, magic tricks and other entertainment may take place here, but even if they don't, this luxe lounge is still ideal for a soothing drink and tête-à-tête.

MIX Map pp262-3

☎ 702-632-9500; 64th fl, THEhotel, 3950 Las Vegas Blvd S; after 10pm $20-25; ☯ 5pm-1am, later on weekends; tram to Luxor & Excalibur

At THEhotel, this is THE place to grab sunset cocktails. A free, glassed-in elevator rides up to the lounge and restaurant (p117) entrances with one of the best views in town, and that's before you even glimpse the wall-to-wall leather and champagne bar. When you come back down to earth, the ground-floor lobby of THEhotel has a more laidback lounge with billiard tables and a coffee bar.

MONTE CARLO PUB & BREWERY Map pp262-3

☎ 702-730-7777; off Street of Dreams, Monte Carlo, 3770 Las Vegas Blvd S; ☯ 11am-3am Sun-Thu, till 4am Fri & Sat, kitchen closes 10pm Sun-Thu, 11pm Fri & Sat; monorail MGM Grand

An industrial-sized microbrewery with big copper brewing vats, this fills up after sundown. Kick back with a High Roller Red or a Silver State Stout and do your best imitation of a couch potato while you watch any of the three-dozen TV monitors, often tuned to sports. The oversized menu has some of the best-value pub grub anywhere around, including pizzas. Service is lackluster.

TOP FIVE CASINO LOUNGES

For a little libation break from the poker room, sniff out these stylish spaces:
- **Big Apple Bar** (opposite)
- **Fontana Bar** (p131)
- **Centrifuge** (p131)
- **Fix** (p131)
- **Zuri** (p136)

TOP FIVE DRINKS WITH VA-VA-VA VOOM

Looking for a little eye candy with your cocktail?
- **Forty Deuce** (opposite)
- **Pussycat Dolls Lounge** (p132)
- **Coyote Ugly** (opposite)
- **Teatro** (p136)
- **Tabú** (p136)

NINE FINE IRISHMEN Map pp262-3

☎ 702-740-6969; casino level, New York–New York, 3790 Las Vegas Blvd S; ☯ 11am-11pm Mon-Fri, 9am-11pm Sat & Sun; monorail MGM Grand

Built in Ireland and then shipped over piece by piece to America, this pubby establishment has semi-private booths inside and open-air patio tables next to the faux Brooklyn Bridge. Live entertainment includes a mix of traditional country Irish tunes, sing-alongs and occasionally dancing.

RED SQUARE Map pp262-3

☎ 702-632-7407; near west valet, Mandalay Bay, 3950 Las Vegas Blvd S; ☯ usually 5pm-2am Sun-Thu, 5pm-4am Fri & Sat; tram to Luxor & Excalibur

This place is very post-*perestroika*. A headless Lenin invites you to join your comrades for a tipple behind the blood-red curtains of this modern Russian restaurant (p117). Vodka is the house specialty. There are heaps of caviar, a solid ice bar and a huge selection of frozen vodkas and infusions. There are also loaner sable fur coats for when you step into the locker! Note that the bar may close early, depending on the crowd.

RUMJUNGLE Map pp262-3

☎ 702-632-7408; near west valet, Mandalay Bay, 3950 Las Vegas Blvd S; no cover before 11pm; ☯ till 2am Sun, Tue & Wed, till 4am Mon & Thu-Sat; tram to Luxor & Excalibur

Wannabe pirates get a whole lot more than just their bottle of rum here when the restaurant transforms into a theatrical nightclub (p153). For those who take their firewater seriously, you can take a seat at the bar and sample a dark, light or spicy rum flight from the towering selection of more than 100 bottles.

Drinking · THE STRIP

TOP FIVE ULTRA LOUNGES

Every new place that opens will top the last, but for now these are the hot properties:

- **ghost bar** (p139)
- **Mix** (p135)
- **Tabú** (below)
- **tangerine** (p153)
- **V Bar** (p133)

SKY LOUNGE Map pp262-3

☎ 702-261-1000; 19th fl, Polo Towers, 3745 Las Vegas Blvd S; late-night cover varies; ⊗ 9am-1am Sun-Thu, 9am-3am Fri & Sat; monorail MGM Grand

High atop a timeshare condo complex, this lounge is best known to for its 180° Strip view. The rooftop pool, private Moroccan cabanas and oversized elevated beds open up for down tempo DJ nights. Friday and Saturday feature live hip-hop and a twenty-something crowd. Call to check hours for special events.

TABÚ Map pp262-3

☎ 702-891-7183; casino level, MGM Grand, 3799 Las Vegas Blvd S; cover $15-20; ⊗ 10pm-dawn Tue-Sun; monorail MGM Grand

Stylish indulgence and sensual sophistication rule at MGM's original ultra lounge. Above-par DJs spin Euro-style house to an interactive backdrop while stunning model/hostesses mix cocktails tableside. A monthly 'Boutique' night brings local fashion designers' stuff strutting out on the catwalk.

TEATRO Map pp262-3

☎ 702-891-1111; casino level, MGM Grand, 3799 Las Vegas Blvd S; ⊗ 6pm-4am Thu-Tue; monorail MGM Grand

Like a glowing lotus blossom, Teatro has a peekaboo entrance to tease folks outside. Inside this wall-hugging ultra lounge, go-go girls dance on the bar every half hour. Celebrity sightings, risk-taking DJs and a champagne bar enhance the sexy vibe.

ZURI Map pp262-3

☎ 702-891-1111; casino level, MGM Grand, 3799 Las Vegas Blvd S; ⊗ 24hr; monorail MGM Grand

Off the main lobby, this plush, 100-seat gilt and velvet bar serves up new twists on old martinis, plus fruit- and spice-infused liquors, unusual beers and a cigar humidor. The menu for 'the morning after the night before' mixes up liquid brunch options, though the crowd here is more sophisticated than that might suggest.

NORTH STRIP

CRAZY ARMADILLO Map pp262-3

☎ 702-380-7777; casino level, Stratosphere, 2000 Las Vegas Blvd S; ⊗ 5pm-5am; monorail Sahara

Another casino glomming onto that flair bartender trend, it's the closest you can get to Tijuana without leaving the state. Come just for the dozens of tequilas, maybe a five-shot sampler, and get some oyster shooters, too. Karaoke happens earlier in the week, with DJs and live bands after midnight other nights.

FIRESIDE LOUNGE Map pp262-3

☎ 702-735-4177; Peppermill, 2985 Las Vegas Blvd S; ⊗ 24hr; bus 301

The Strip's most unlikely hideaway shares its outlandishly bright neon with a coffee shop. Courting couples flock here for the sunken fire pit and blue velvet booths. It's a spellbinding scene after a couple of mai tais, blue Hawaiians or piña coladas. Skip the food, but sup a bowl-sized Scorpion.

TOP OF THE WORLD LOUNGE Map pp262-3

☎ 702-380-7711; 107th fl, Stratosphere, 2000 Las Vegas Blvd S; no cover most nights, elevator ride $10; ⊗ 10am-12:30am Sun-Thu, 10am-1:30am Fri & Sat; monorail Sahara

There's no place to get any higher in Las Vegas without the approval of an air traffic controller. Every night, beginning about 8:30pm, a trio or pianist plays popular tunes in the 220-seat cocktail lounge that overlooks the revolving restaurant (p120) on the 106th floor.

DOWNTOWN

Every casino hotel around downtown has a bar or two (or a dozen) handily near the main gaming areas. Generally, there isn't much more to them, though.

Special events at the Icehouse Lounge (p121) are worth showing up for.

ATOMIC LIQUOR STORE Map p261
☎ 702-384-7371; 917 Fremont St; ⊗ 11am-11pm; bus 107

East of the Fremont Street Experience, quite a few down-and-out bars offer cheap booze, cheap company and little or nothing else. Loyal locals call this the best dive bar around.

BEAUTY BAR Map p261
☎ 702-598-1965; 517 E Fremont St; cover $5-15; ⊗ 5pm-4am Wed-Fri, 9pm-4am Tue & Sat-Sun; bus 301, 302

Expect all the downtown hipsters to latch on to the fad that started in New York, then spread to San Francisco and LA. Swill a cocktail, watch the manicure demonstrations or just chill. It's actually the salvaged innards of a 1950s New Jersey beauty salon. Martini happy hour happens from 6pm to 9pm daily, with wacky drink specials and DJs nightly.

BUNKHOUSE SALOON Map p261
☎ 702-384-4536; 124 S 11th St; ⊗ 24hr; bus 107

Owned by a judge, the out-of-the-way Bunkhouse Saloon is beloved by downtown's legal community. As you might have guessed, it's got a cowboy theme, with Old West art and saddles lying about. Gamewise, there's video poker, pool tables and darts, and occasionally live music or barbecues.

CENTER STAGE Map p261
☎ 702-386-2512; 2nd fl, Plaza, 1 Main St; ⊗ 4pm-midnight; bus 108, 301, 302

With its glass dome hovering at the west end of the Fremont Street Experience, you may have seen it in *Casino* and *Pay It Forward*. Can't vouch for the food, but the view is amazing, plus it has a nightly lounge singer and piano player. Dress up so you don't feel out of place.

TOP FIVE DRINKS WITH VIP VIEWS

- Center Stage (above)
- Fontana Bar (p131)
- Sky Lounge (opposite)
- Mix (p135)
- Top of the World Lounge (opposite)

CHICAGO BREWING COMPANY Map p261
☎ 702-385-4011; 2nd fl, Four Queens, 202 E Fremont St; ⊗ 11:30am-1:30am; bus 301, 302

With just a dozen bar stools set up in front of video poker machines, this brewpub outlet also has a few cigar lounge chairs overlooking the casino floor. The beer sampler ($5) should be enough to satisfy you, with Ultimate Weiss, Black Star, Red Rocker and Old Town Brown. Very friendly service.

DINO'S LOUNGE Map p261
☎ 702-382-3894; 1516 Las Vegas Blvd S; ⊗ 24hr; bus 301

A true dive bar and proud of it, this spot, where you may end up doing shots with the owner, calls itself 'the last neighborhood bar in Vegas' (surely, that's an exaggeration). Local bands, midnight movies, Monday Night Football, karaoke and after parties on First Fridays (p81) keep things cooking.

JILLIAN'S Map p261
☎ 702-759-0450; Neonopolis, 450 E Fremont St; ⊗ 11am-2am; bus 301, 302

Aimed at an all-ages family crowd, with its video games, pool tables downstairs and bowling alley upstairs, all just around the corner from a cinema, Jillian's is still a decent place downtown to grab a beer while you listen to local bands in the over-21 area.

OASIS LOUNGE Map p261
☎ 702-385-7111; casino level, Golden Nugget, 129 E Fremont St; ⊗ till midnight; bus 301, 302

Granted, it's too near the race and sports book. Still, downtown's swankiest lounge has a hot lineup of live bands, and occasionally comedy or magic acts, performing from 9pm Tuesday to Saturday. Also hidden inside the casino, you'll find an international beer bar, with above-average brews.

TRIPLE 7 Map p261
☎ 702-387-1896; Main Street Station, 200 N Main St; ⊗ 24hr; bus 301, 302

A lot of locals and older gamblers frequent this huge downtown brewpub. Come for Monday Night Football, happy hours and graveyard specials ($1 beers from midnight to 7am), a sushi and oyster bar, and five microbrews on tap, including award-winning fruit beers. Don't expect snappy service.

Drinking

DOWNTOWN

LAS VEGAS IDOL

If you want to be a pop star:

House of Blues (p151) 'Rock Star Karaoke' is the place to be, usually on Monday and Tuesday nights. After signing up, you'll wait a really long time before you get to hop on stage and front your own live band (they even sing helpful back-up). Everyone in the party-hardy crowd acts like your groupie.

Tequila Joe's (☎ 702-731-3311; Imperial Palace, 3535 Las Vegas Blvd S; ✿ karaoke from 8pm; monorail Harrah's/ Imperial Palace) Just walk on in and join the party at the karaoke club inside this tiny Stripside bar. If you're lucky, amateur impressionists will be doing their thing (usually on the third Thursday of the month); if not, you can always walk inside the casino to see the Imperial Palace's 'dealertainers.'

Piano Bar On the north side of Harrah's Carnaval Court (p131), the all-star karaoke party with plasma screens, impressionists and stand-up comedy interspersed with amateur lounge lizards typically goes on from 6pm to 9pm.

Gilley's (p151; ✿ from 8pm Sun) If you can sing like LeAnn Rimes, you can make all of the urban cowboys swoon at this country-and-western themed dance hall and saloon on the North Strip.

Las Vegas Club (p83; ✿ 8pm-midnight Fri) Loyal downtowners and visiting Hawaiians belt out easy listening and super-'70s classics upstairs from the casino. The aunties usually get up to a do little impromptu hula, too. Fun!

Ellis Island (p201; ✿ 9pm-3am) At this place, attached to Super 8 Motel, the drinks are stiff, the microbrews pretty cheap and the nightly karaoke a big hit with locals. The lounge, with its red high-backed booths, feels like Old Vegas.

Bootlegger Bistro (p155) On Monday nights, the Bootlegger hosts celebrity karaoke, where Strip performers like Clint Holmes might drop by to sing a duet or backing vocals for little ol' you.

UNLV & EAST OF THE STRIP

Near the university campus are dime-a-dozen dive bars. The following are some places that aren't quite so run of the mill.

DOUBLE DOWN SALOON Map p265
☎ 702-791-5775; 4640 Paradise Rd, enter off Swenson St; ✿ 24hr, shows at 10pm; bus 108
You've gotta love a gin joint whose tangy, blood-red house drink is named 'Ass Juice.' For one thing, it has a behavior code: 'You puke, you clean.' For another, it's dark, psychedelic and appeals to the lunatic fringe. The jukebox vibrates with New Orleans jazz, British punk, Chicago blues and surf-guitar king Dick Dale. There's never a cover charge, it doesn't accept credit cards, and it claims to be 'the happiest place on Earth.' Monday is the Bargain DJ Collective night, with lotsa local bands other nights.

HARD ROCK Map p265
☎ 702-693-5000; 4455 Paradise Rd; ✿ 24hr; bus 108
Some of Vegas' most dynamic places to hook up are at the Hard Rock. The circular **Center Bar** is the place to be seen mid-casino,

while off to the side you can seat yourself at the **Sports Deluxe** bar to watch its plasma TVs. Off the shopping arcade, **Cuba Libre** has a cigar humidor. During summer, Sunday 'Rehab' pool parties open up the **Beach Club** (p196). All this, and we haven't even mentioned **Body English** (p150) and **The Joint** (p157).

HOFBRÄUHAUS Map p265
☎ 702-853-2337; 4510 Paradise Rd; ✿ 11am-11pm Sun-Thu, 11am-midnight Fri & Sat; bus 108, call for free group shuttle
Diagonally opposite the Hard Rock, this new $12-million beer hall and garden is a replica of the original in Munich. Celebrate Oktoberfest year-round with premium imported suds, big Bavarian pretzels, fair *frauleins,* oom-pah bands and trademark *gemütlichkeit* (congeniality). It has an outdoor beer garden and a main dining hall.

HOOKAH LOUNGE Map p265
☎ 702-731-6030; www.hookahlounge.com; 4147 S Maryland Pkwy; ✿ 5pm-1am Sun-Thu, 5pm-3am Fri & Sat; bus 109, 202, 213, 807
Next to **Paymon's Mediterranean Café** (p126), here you can recline with a water pipe stuffed with one of 20 premium flavored Egyptian tobaccos. Fig-flavored cocktails are pricier than the off-Strip norm, but for pasha-style

quarters and calm ambience, why not? Half-off happy hour is 5pm to 7pm daily.

QUARK'S BAR Map p265
☎ 702-697-8725; Deep Space Nine Promenade, Las Vegas Hilton, 3000 Paradise Rd; ☺ 11am-11pm; monorail Las Vegas Hilton
The Hilton's *Star Trek*–themed bar is a wacky place. Eavesdrop on sci-fi geeks debating the strategies of the Romulan Empire or the virtues of the Prime Directive as you take on a Warp Core Breach ($25), basically loads of shots in a big bowl steaming with dry ice. For the food, see p125.

WEST OF THE STRIP

The Uscene at the Palms is hottest, with the Rio rapidly atrophying and the Orleans already quite sedate.

GHOST BAR Map p264
☎ 702-942-7777; 55th fl, Palms, 4321 W Flamingo Rd; cover $10-20; ☺ 8pm-4am; bus 202, 807
A clubby crowd, often thick with celebs, packs the Palms' sky-high watering hole with 360° panoramas. DJs spin hip-hop and house while the hoochie mamas and wannabe gangsters sip overpriced cocktails amid sci-fi decor. Dress to kill.

I-BAR Map p264
☎ 702-777-6869; casino level, Rio, 3700 W Flamingo Rd; ☺ 9pm-2am Sun-Thu, 9pm-4am Fri & Sat; free Strip shuttle
This chic ultra lounge, which boasts some soulful grooves, is sexier than the beach

TOP FIVE NON-CASINO WATERING HOLES
If you're tired of the casino hotel scene, even downtown, off-Strip faves include the following:
- **Beauty Bar** (p137)
- **Double Down Saloon** (opposite)
- **Hofbräuhaus** (opposite)
- **Hookah Lounge** (opposite)
- **McMullan's Irish Pub** (below)

blanket bingo happening inside the Rio's Bikinis bar. Without any walls and open to the casino, it may lack exclusivity but in part makes up for it by bathing you in an ice-blue glow while modelesque ladies shake it on a miniature circular stage.

LITTLE BUDDHA Map p264
☎ 702-942-7778; casino level, Palms, 4321 W Flamingo Rd; ☺ 5:30-11pm Sun-Thu, 5:30pm-midnight Fri & Sat; bus 202, 807
At this dark fusion restaurant (p127) imported straight from Paris, you can hole up with your paramour under the watchful eyes of a bodhisattva, then let your desires be enflamed. It's not a very Buddhist thought, but it is oh-so sexy, with a chilled-out ambient French soundtrack.

MCMULLAN'S IRISH PUB Map p264
☎ 702-247-7000; 4650 W Tropicana Ave; ☺ 24hr; bus 104, 201
'Purveyors of the perfect pint,' McMullan's is the friendliest pub in Vegas. Thursday is all-you-can-eat fish and chips, Tuesday is quiz

Drinking

WEST OF THE STRIP

A ROOM WITH A BREW
Believe it or not, you don't even need to venture off the Strip to find a microbrew. North of New York–New York, there's the **Monte Carlo Pub & Brewery** (p135). Downtown is Main Street Station's enormously popular **Triple 7** (p137) or the cozy **Chicago Brewing Company** (p137) outpost upstairs at the Four Queens.

East of the Strip, more fine brews await, including at the **Hofbräuhaus** (opposite); national chain **Gordon Biersch** (Map p265; ☎ 702-312-5247; www.gordonbiersch.com; 3987 Paradise Rd; ☺ 11:30am-midnight Sun & Mon, 11:30am-2am Tue-Sat; bus 108), handy for conventioneers; the Brit-style pub **Crown & Anchor** (Map p265; ☎ 702-739-8676; 1350 E Tropicana Ave; ☺ 24hr; bus 109, 201, 804); and little **Ellis Island** next to the Super 8 (p201).

Further afield, brewmeisters will want to make the drive out to **Barley's Casino & Brewing Company** (Map p260; ☎ 702-458-2739; www.barleys.com; 4500 E Sunset Rd; ☺ 24hr; bus 114, 212), for lagers and gold-medal Heffeweizen; **Big Dog's** (Map p260; ☎ 702-876-3647; 6390 W Sahara Ave; ☺ 24hr; bus 204), for its corny fire hydrants and award-winning Holy Cow beers; and posh **Tenaya Creek Brewery** (Map p260; ☎ 702-362-7335; www.tenayacreekbrewery.com; 3101 N Tenaya Way; ☺ 24hr) for pilsner, nut-brown ale and unusual barley wine.

TOP FIVE CIGAR HUMIDORS

Las Vegas is a paradise on earth for smokers. Get your premium stogies, light 'em up and even down a cocktail at the following:

Casa Fuente (Map pp262–3; ☎ 702-893-4800; Caesars Palace, 3500 Las Vegas Blvd S; ✆ 10am-11pm Sun-Thu, 10am-midnight Fri & Sat; monorail Flamingo/Caesars Palace) A million-dollar cigar shop with a Cuban-themed bar.

Cuba Libre (Hard Rock; p138) So hip it hurts.

Don Pablo Cigar Company (Map pp262–3; ☎ 702-369-1818; 3049 Las Vegas Blvd S; ✆ 9am-6pm Mon-Sat, 10am-4pm Sun; bus 301, 302) No drinks, sorry. But the Stardust is right across the street.

Havana Cigar Co (Map p265; ☎ 702-892-9555; Citibank Plaza, 3900 Paradise Rd; ✆ 9am-10:30pm Mon-Thu, 9am-11:30pm Fri, 10am-11:30pm Sat, 2-10pm Sun; bus 108) At the International Vintage Wine Cellar (p133).

Havana Hideaway (Map pp262–3; ☎ 702-739-5414; Tropicana, 3801 Las Vegas Blvd S; ✆ noon-10pm Sun-Thu, noon-midnight Fri & Sat; monorail MGM Grand) Upstairs at the vintage Trop, with showgirl-style service.

night (from 8pm), and Irish musicians perform most weekends around 9pm. Ask about the free wi-fi and gambling happy hour.

VOODOO LOUNGE Map p264

☎ 702-247-7923; 51st fl, Masquerade Tower, Rio, 3700 W Flamingo Rd; cover after 8pm $5-20, waived with dinner reservations; ✆ 5pm-2:30am, dancing from 9pm; free Strip shuttle

The views from the patio are fab, but the Day-Glo decor and lounge tunes are just for laughs. A middle-aged crowd orders exotic drinks, like the 'Witchy Woman,' which comes in a bowl steaming with dry ice. It's not worth much of a wait to get in, let alone a cover charge. Quasi-strict dress code.

WINE CELLAR Map p264

☎ 702-247-7923; Masquerade Village, Rio, 3700 W Flamingo Rd; ✆ 3-11pm Mon-Thu, 3pm-midnight Fri, noon-midnight Sat & Sun; free Strip shuttle

Admittedly overpriced, but if you're at the Rio, duck over to this multilevel tasting room just to gawk or try one of the wine flights (priced from $10 to the sky's the limit) with cheese pairings. It's rarely busy, making it a sweet spot for cooing oenophilic couples.

OUTER NEIGHBORHOODS

If you find yourself south of the Strip or in Henderson, these places have some unique scenery and will do for a quick swill.

DROP Map p260

☎ 702-617-7704; casino level, Green Valley Ranch, 2300 Paseo Verde Dr, Henderson; ✆ 24hr; bus 111

Before you head for **Whiskey** (p154), linger at this gorgeous casino bar at least long enough to appreciate its snowflake-style chandeliers, ambient chill-out tunes and white leather chairs.

GAUDI BAR Map p260

☎ 702-547-7777; casino level, Sunset Station, Sunset Rd, west off I-515/US 93 & 95, Henderson; ✆ 24hr; bus 212

A casino bar that goes above and beyond, although the local crowd doesn't seem to appreciate the Barcelona architectural touches, with a ceiling that appears to melt, colorful stained glass and leather chairs. It's not worth a special trip, but if you're on the Boulder Hwy, it's a casual place to detour on your way back from Hoover Dam.

MERMAID LOUNGE Map p260

☎ 702-263-7777; Silverton, casino level, 3333 Blue Diamond Rd, off I-15; ✆ 11am-3am Sun-Thu, 24hr Fri & Sat, mermaid shows Wed-Mon, call for schedules; bus 117

Situated out at the Silverton casino resort, near the entrance to **Bass Pro Shops Outdoor World** (p183), this watery lounge puts on choreographed mermaid shows almost daily in its adjacent aquarium. The redneck crowd in attendance will be just as incredulous about it as you are, but still, it's diverting.

Drinking

OUTER NEIGHBORHOODS

Entertainment

Entertainment

Las Vegas doesn't call itself the entertainment capital of the world for nothing. The city is famous for its showgirls, lounge acts, illusionists, championship fights, headliner shows by some of today's biggest stars and, of course, for its casino gambling (p36).

A person can go broke seeing and doing all there is to see and do in Las Vegas, but you can also be entertained in Sin City for little or nothing. The choices are almost infinite, with new shows, new venues and new attractions opening all the time. There's no excuse for being bored with all the concerts, amusement rides, nightclubs, magic shows, virtual-reality arcades, circus acts and jaw-dropping outdoor spectacles such as the erupting volcano at the Mirage, the light shows over Fremont St and the fountains at the Bellagio.

In the Sights chapter (p46), you'll find reviews of casinos, thrill rides, arcades, outdoor attractions, museums, galleries and other daytime activities. Here you'll find recommendations for after-dark entertainment: clubbing, production shows, live-music venues, the performing arts and cinema. Check out the Drinking chapter (p130) for the lowdown on Vegas' bars, pubs and ultra lounges. For spectator sports, turn to p162.

PRODUCTION SHOWS

It's surely some kind of crime to leave town without having seen a big-deal production show. But don't see just any show. Las Vegas has some great ones, some terrible ones and many that fall somewhere in between. Old-school production shows feature a variety of song, dance and magic numbers that don't follow a story line. Comedians, impersonators, contortionists and topless showgirls still all appear on stages here, but these can be unbelievably kitschy experiences that aren't worth your money. Capitalizing on Sin City's reputation are a grab-bag of erotically themed shows, from rock musicals to late-night vampire revues. The most in-demand tickets are for big-name performers like Céline Dion and Cirque du Soleil shows, which have spawned legions of less-talented imitations. The new Wynn resort upped the cultural ante by importing *Avenue Q* from New York, the only Broadway show to run simultaneously only in New York and Vegas. Watch for the debut of a new special-effects rendition of Andrew Lloyd Webber's *Phantom of the Opera* – complete with an onstage lake and an exploding replica of the Paris Opera House chandelier – in a purpose-built $25-million theater at the Venetian in spring 2006.

By the time you read this, some of these productions may have changed venues or

---

DUDE, WHERE'S MY SEAT?

When you buy your tickets, be sure to ask if seating is reserved or general admission. With reserved box-office seating, you're in luck. In that case, you'll only need to show up 30 minutes or so before curtain time because your seats are guaranteed. In most theaters, the best advice is to ask to be seated in the center of the house, but not so close to the stage that you miss out on some of the action while you're craning your neck.

All bets are off with general admission seats. VIP admission costs a bit more, but it lets you bypass the regular lines and walk right into the theater. Otherwise, you should show up at least an hour before the show starts and queue up while the captains (ushers) seat everyone. Another way into the VIP line marked for 'invited guests' is if the casino 'comps' you with a line pass, usually given out to members of players' clubs or serious gamblers who request one from the pit boss or the floor personnel in the casino gaming area.

Tipping the maître d' might help get you a better seat, but you need to do it subtly (for example, with a folded bill ready to place in the person's hand when you reach the front of the line and request your seats). Tip about 5-10% of the total ticket price, rounded up to $10 or $20. Or you can wait until the captain seats you, then if you're not happy with where you've been seated, discreetly tip the captain as you politely ask for a better seat. Your chances of this strategy working are better on weekdays at less popular shows.

closed entirely. But most stick around for a few months, some for years, and a very few for decades. Whether or not you get your money's worth is always debatable. Prices to all shows on the Strip are inflated (so think of them in 'Vegas dollars'). You'll probably only attend one production per trip, so choose carefully. Once you purchase tickets, try your darnedest to enjoy yourself and forget about how much money you've spent.

If you see a show advertised around town that's not reviewed here, remember that, much like the buffets in Las Vegas, the quality of production shows generally corresponds to the star level of the casino where the theater is located (ie budget hotels put on low-budget productions, megaresorts have higher-quality shows) – that's a fairly reliable formula. Most shows run for about 90 minutes, some only an hour.

Tickets & Reservations

Always call ahead to check showtimes, which are highly subject to change. Tickets are usually sold direct from the venue, the casino hotel's box office, and sometimes over the phone and Web. For low-budget shows, same-day tickets are often available. But tickets for in-demand shows like Cirque du Soleil can sell out months ahead of time.

The best way to get a taste of what Vegas has to offer, as long as you're not picky about seeing a particular production show, is to stop by a half-price ticket booth around noon. Like discount ticket outlets in NYC and other major cities, they'll never have cheap seats for the most popular show in town. But sometimes they have surprisingly good deals on tickets for magic, comedy troupes and dinner theater, as well as afternoon and late-night variety shows. The specific shows being discounted don't vary much on a daily basis, so you can stop by the night before to see what may be available. Lines are longest just before the ticket booths open, yet many shows don't sell out immediately, so swing by later in the afternoon when there's no line. Try the following:

Tickets 4 Less (Map pp262–3; ☎ 888-484-9264; Showcase Mall, 3769 Las Vegas Blvd S; ☽ noon-9pm; monorail MGM Grand) Located on the South Strip in front of the giant Coca-Cola bottle. Charges a $4 service fee plus tax for each ticket sold.

THAT'S THE TICKET!

ShowTickets.com (☎ 702-597-5970, 800-838-9383; www.showtickets.com) Twenty-one pick-up locations around town, including McCarran Airport.

Vegas.com (☎ 702-992-7970, 866-807-4697; www.vegas.com) Tickets to a variety of high-profile and low-budget shows, plus sporting events.

Las Vegas Ticketing (☎ 888-777-7664; www.las vegasticketing.com) Mostly smaller casino shows, but a few big-name productions, too.

TicketsGuaranteed.com (☎ 702-597-1588, 800-597-7469; www.ticketsguaranteed.com, www .lasvegastickets.com) Sold-out tickets source.

Tickets 4 Less (☎ 888-484-9264) Same-day, half-price tickets; see left.

Tix 4 Tonight (☎ 877-849-4868; www.tix4tonight .com) Same-day, half-price tickets; see left.

Ticketmaster (☎ 702-474-4000; www.ticket master.com) Broker for mainstream music and sporting events.

UNLVtickets (☎ 702-739-3267, 866-388-3267; www.unlvtickets.com) Source for all university events.

Tix 4 Tonight (☎ 877-849-4868; www.tix4tonight. com; ☽ noon-9pm) Has three sites: Center Strip (Map pp262–3; Fashion Show Mall, 3200 Las Vegas Blvd S; bus 301, 302) ; South Strip (Map pp262–3; 3729 Las Vegas Blvd S; monorail MGM Grand), next to the Harley-Davidson Cafe; and North Strip (Map pp262–3; 2955 Las Vegas Blvd S; bus 301, 302), across from the Stardust. Charges a $4 service fee plus tax for each ticket sold.

Many of the freely available tourist magazines, such as *Showbiz Weekly, Today in Las Vegas* and *What's On,* have comprehensive listings of shows and offer discount coupons in the ads. Sometimes you can get into a show for the price of a drink (or two), or buy one ticket and get the second one free. The bottom line is: you should almost never have to pay full price to see a show, except for headliners and long-running spectaculars.

AVENUE Q Map pp262-3

☎ 702-770-7100; www.wynnlasvegas.com; Wynn, 3201 Las Vegas Blvd S; tickets from $75; ☽ shows Tue-Sat; bus 301, 302

An anything-goes puppet show for adults, with a racy soundtrack. Laugh along with the humanly flawed characters all struggling

Clown, Circus Circus (p75)

to make it in the Big Apple, from a kindergarten teacher looking for true love to Trekkie Monster, who believes 'the Internet is for porn' (that's what the song says!).

BEACHER'S MADHOUSE Map p265

☎ 702-693-5066; www.beachersmadhouse.com; Hard Rock, 4455 Paradise Rd; tickets $25; ☺ some Saturday nights, call for schedules; bus 108

Spotting celebs in the VIP box may steal your attention from this interactive comedy show, where you might get pulled up on stage to sing your heart out like the next *American Idol* or boogie along with the red-hot Beacher's Babies. Expect frenetic frat-boy antics, sick stand-up and a little magic in this bawdy, short-attention-span theater effort.

BLUE MAN GROUP Map pp262-3

☎ 702-414-7469, 866-641-7469; www.blueman .com; Venetian, 3355 Las Vegas Blvd S; tickets $75-110; ☺ 7pm daily, 10pm Sat; monorail Harrah's/Imperial Palace

Three blue-headed, non-speaking, comedic percussionists mix mind-bending audiovisual displays with some juvenile behavior in an extraordinarily bizarre show. Sit in the front rows to be the recipient of catapulted Jell-O tubs, hurled marshmallows and paint splattered off the tops of snare drums. The show may be a crowd-pleaser, but the talent actually leaves a lot to be desired.

CÉLINE DION: A NEW DAY Map pp262-3

☎ 702-731-7110, 877-423-5463; www.celinedion .com; Caesars Palace, 3570 Las Vegas Blvd S; tickets $88-225; ☺ 8:30pm Wed-Sun; monorail Flamingo/ Caesars Palace

Cirque du Soleil maestro Franco Dragone pushed Céline to expand her limits for her new spectacular, which routinely fills Caesars' purpose-built, $95-million, 4000-seat Colosseum to capacity. She rips through new ballads and greatest hits during 100 minutes, with plenty of backup from North America's biggest LED screen – and lots of buff male dancers. Whenever the diva is indisposed, Elton John sells out the stage with his biographical retro-'70s pop fantasia, *The Red Piano* (tickets $100-250).

CLINT HOLMES Map pp262-3

☎ 702-369-5000, 800-392-2002 ext 5222; www .showtickets.com; Harrah's, 3475 Las Vegas Blvd S; tickets $60; ☺ 7:30pm Mon-Sat; monorail Harrah's/Imperial Palace

A headliner that harks back to the Vegas showmen of yesteryear, this former Entertainer of the Year in Atlantic City is the son of a British opera singer and an African American jazz musician. His little-known songs don't always draw the crowds, but the 12-piece band really gives it their all.

CRAZY GIRLS Map pp262-3

☎ 702-794-9433, 800-634-3420; www.lasvegas ticketing.com; Riviera, 2901 Las Vegas Blvd S; tickets $35; ☺ 9:30pm Wed-Mon; bus 301, 302

It could be called nothing but a titty show gussied up with costumes, props and sets, but that would be wrong. Between the lip-synched tits-and-ass numbers, there *is* a stand-up comedian who comes out and tells X-rated jokes, after all.

DANNY GANS: THE MAN OF MANY VOICES Map pp262-3

☎ 702-792-7777; www.themirage.com; Mirage, 3400 Las Vegas Blvd S; tickets $100; ☺ 8pm Tue-Thu, Sat & Sun; tram to TI (Treasure Island)

Gans is an impressionist, perhaps the best one alive. Of course, you have to be fluent in Americanisms to enjoy it. Otherwise the voices of Clint Eastwood, Ray Charles, Frank Sinatra and Marge Simpson (among others) won't translate in this fast-paced show in desperate need of some updating.

FOLIES BERGÉRE Map pp262-3

☎ 702-739-2222, 800-829-9034; www.tropicanalv
.com; Tropicana, 3801 Las Vegas Blvd S; table/booth
seating $45/55; ☯ 7:30pm (covered) & 10pm
(topless) Mon, Wed, Thu & Sat, 8:30pm (topless) Tue
& Fri; monorail MGM Grand

A tribute to the Parisian Music Hall, Vegas'
longest-running production includes some
of the most beautiful showgirls in town.
The straight-up formulaic theme and song-
and-dance numbers include the inevitable
can-can routine, plus a comedic juggler to
lighten it up.

IMPERIAL HAWAIIAN LUAU Map pp262-3

☎ 702-794-3261, 888-777-7664; www.lasvegas
ticketing.com; Imperial Palace, 3535 Las Vegas
Blvd S; dinner & show adult/child under 13 $35/18;
☯ doors open 6:30pm Tue & Thu (weather permitting), Apr-Oct; monorail Harrah's/Imperial Palace

This kitschy but fun and high-energy
Polynesian revue happens poolside at the
Imperial Palace. Get lei'd at the door, pick
up your piña coladas, then sit back and
enjoy the hula dancing, Hawaiian songs
performed by a musical trio and tricks
played with fire.

JUBILEE! Map pp262-3

☎ 702-967-4567, 800-237-7469; www.ticketmaster
.com; Bally's, 3645 Las Vegas Blvd S; tickets $55-75;
☯ 7:30pm & 10:30pm Sat-Thu; monorail Bally's &
Paris

Girls, girls, girls! It's a showgirl production
that Vegas wouldn't be Vegas without.
Jubilee! has dancers in flashy costumes
and enormous headdresses, and some less
exciting filler acts. And as it started so does
it end: with lots of knockers and twinkling
rhinestones on display. If you can forgive
the cheesy undertones, you will have a
riot, especially if you take the backstage
tour beforehand, then strike a pose with
the girls after the show at Bally's lounge,
Indigo (p49).

KÀ Map pp262-3

☎ 702-891-7777, 877-264-1844; www.ka.com;
MGM Grand, 3799 Las Vegas Blvd S; tickets $99-150;
☯ 7:30pm & 10:30pm Fri-Tue; monorail MGM Grand

Cirque du Soleil's winning streak makes this
sensuous story of imperial twins, mysteri-
ous destinies, love and conflict the hottest
ticket in town. Instead of a stage, there's

WHEN THE CURTAIN COMES DOWN

Stars losing their stages is an everyday event in
Vegas, especially for small but critically acclaimed
shows.

At press time, **Forbidden Vegas** (www.forbid
denvegas.com) – at last, a show that makes fun of
Vegas itself – was without a showroom to call home,
but look for them to pop up again soon. This entertaining music and comedy revue parodies more than
two-dozen famous acts, skewering anyone from the
Blue Man Group to Céline Dion to Elvis. Think *Saturday
Night Live* live from Las Vegas.

At Desert Passage, the **Fashionistas** (www
.fashionistastheshow.com) may not be long for
the Strip. Currently, this imaginative erotic show is
staged inside the gay nightclub **Kräve** (p151). But
once Planet Hollywood takes the reins of the Aladdin
casino hotel in 2006, it's hard to imagine anything
this racy will be allowed to stay. The Aladdin's other
popular shows, such as **V: The Ultimate Variety
Show**, may get the axe, too.

just a grid of moving platforms elevating
a frenzy of martial arts–inspired performances. Weak storytelling gets in the way,
though. Premium seats at the back are best
positioned to take it all in.

LA CAGE Map pp262-3

☎ 702-794-9433, 800-634-3420; www.lasvegas
ticketing.com; Riviera, 2901 Las Vegas Blvd S;
tickets $55; ☯ 7:30pm Wed-Mon; bus 301, 302

In this mainstream female-impersonator
revue, the award-winning Frank Marino
(who cameoed in *Miss Congeniality 2*) acts
as a catty Joan Rivers, dispensing naughty
jokes and remarks between mostly lip-
synched impersonations of Diana Ross,
Cher, Liza Minnelli and others. It could flop
big-time, but most of the middled-aged
straight couples from Iowa leave with
smiles on their faces.

LA FEMME Map pp262-3

☎ 702-891-7777, 800-929-1111; http://mgm
.admission.com; MGM Grand, 3799 Las Vegas Blvd S;
tickets $59; ☯ 8pm & 10:30pm Wed-Mon;
monorail MGM Grand

Za, za, zoom. It's the artiest topless show in
town. The red room's intimate bordello feel
oozes *amour*. Onstage, ballet-trained dancers straight from Paris' Crazy Horse Saloon
perform provocative cabaret numbers

Entertainment

PRODUCTION SHOWS

interspersed with voyeuristic and humorous *l'art du nu* vignettes. *Zut alors* – it's a classy peep show par excellence.

LA REVE Map pp262-3

☎ 702-770-7100; www.wynnlasvegas.com; Wynn, 3131 Las Vegas Blvd S; tickets $120; ☯ 7:30pm Thu-Mon; bus 301, 302

The newest creation from former Cirque du Soleil director Franco Dragone is rumored to have cost Steve Wynn at least $90 million. Aquatic acrobatic feats flow through a fanciful series of vignettes. The centerpiece of the theater, which brings the audience close to the performers, is a one-million-gallon swimming pool.

LEGENDS IN CONCERT Map pp262-3

☎ 702-794-3261, 877-777-7664; www.lasvegas ticketing.com; Imperial Palace, 3535 Las Vegas Blvd S; adult/child 2-12 $40/25; ☯ 7:30pm & 10pm Mon-Sat; monorail Harrah's/Imperial Palace

It's been around since the early '80s, and it will likely be around for years to come. Vegas' top pop-star impersonator show features talent who must not only look like famous vocalists, such as Gloria Estefan, Elton John and Dolly Parton, but must sound like them, too; no lip-synching is allowed. The acts frequently change. Video screens beside the stage show clips of the

real performers in concert, while the back-up dancers shimmy up a *Saturday Night Fever* storm. Admission includes one drink.

MIDNIGHT FANTASY Map pp262-3

☎ 702-262-4400, 800-557-7428; www.luxor .com; Luxor, 3900 Las Vegas Blvd S; tickets $44; ☯ 8:30pm & 10:30pm Tue, Thu & Sat, 10:30pm Wed & Fri, 8:30pm Sun; tram to Excalibur & Mandalay Bay

A tame topless revue set by the Nile a long, long time ago features gorgeous women (and, oddly, a male tap dancer). Most of the music is lip-synched, with more emphasis on speed than sex appeal. More than a few of the numbers resemble middle-school cheerleading routines. Hats off to the comedienne, if she's still in the show.

MYSTÈRE Map pp262-3

☎ 702-796-9999, 800-392-1999; www.cirquedu soleil.com; TI (Treasure Island), 3300 Las Vegas Blvd S; tickets $60-95; ☯ 7:30pm & 10:30pm Wed-Sat, 4:30pm & 7:30pm Sun; tram to Mirage

Cirque du Soleil director Franco Dragone imitates what Dali did for painting. His evocative celebration of life begins with a pair of babies making their way in a world filled with strange creatures. A misguided clown's humorous antics are interwoven with acrobats, aerialists and dancers performing one spectacular feat of strength and agility after another. If you see just one Cirque du Soleil performance, make sure it's this one.

O Map pp262-3

☎ 702-693-7722, 877-488-7111; www.cirquedu soleil.com; Bellagio, 3600 Las Vegas Blvd S; tickets $99-150; ☯ 7:30pm & 10:30pm Wed-Sun monorail Bally's & Paris

Phonetically speaking, it's the French word for water (*eau*). After searching the globe for likely candidates, casino impresario Steve Wynn approached Montréal-based Cirque du Soleil about producing a totally original show that would be among the most expensive on earth. This is the result. With an international cast performing in, on and above water, *O* tells the tale of theater through the ages. It's a spectacular feat of imagination and engineering, but even true Cirque fanatics may come away feeling they overpaid for what is essentially a one-trick-pony show.

JUST FOR KIDS

Most production shows are adults-only, with no under-18s allowed. Family-friendly shows like **Legends in Concert** (above), the **Imperial Palace Hawaiian Luau** (p145) and the **Blue Man Group** (p144) are the exception, not the rule. Of the Cirque du Soleil shows, **Mystère** (right) is a parent's best bet. **Mac King** (p148) offers families clean comedy and a little magic. For straight-up magic, try the **World's Greatest Magic Show** (p150) for younger kids or take teens to see the masterful **Lance Burton** (p148).

At Excalibur's **Tournament of Kings** (Map pp262–3; ☎ 702-597-7600, 877-750-5464; www.excalibur .com; King Arthur's Arena, Excalibur, 3850 Las Vegas Blvd S; dinner & show $50; ☯ 6pm & 8:30pm; monorail MGM Grand), guests are expected to eat the medieval way – with their fingers. Armor-clad Arthurian knights joust and battle with swords in the arena as Merlin makes the pyrotechnics fly. It's popular with kids, but most adults will quickly tire of the RenFair routines.

SCINTAS Map p264

☎ 702-777-7776, 888-746-7784; www.showtickets
.com; Rio, 3700 W Flamingo Rd; tickets $60;
🕙 7:30pm Fri-Wed; free Strip shuttle

This musical-comedy act consists of three
Italian family members and an 'adopted'
Scinta, Peter O'Donnell. Avoid this truly
awful family affair with bad singing, worse
impersonations and lots of corny jokes,
most of them tediously offensive. Move on.

SKINTIGHT Map pp262-3

☎ 702-369-5111, 800-392-9002; Harrah's, 3475
Las Vegas Blvd S; tickets $50; 🕙 10:30pm Mon-
Wed & Sat, 10pm & midnight Fri, 7:30pm & 10pm
Sun; monorail Harrah's/Imperial Palace

A medley of near-naked showgirls and
male hard-bodies sing and dance, bump
and grind, and slither around the stage. It's
currently rounded out by an appearance
by *Playboy*'s Shannon O'Keefe. For a girlie
show, it could be worse, and a lucky guy
might get a pseudo–lap dance out of it.

SPLASH Map pp262-3

☎ 702-794-9433, 800-634-3420; www.lasvegas
ticketing.com; Riviera, 2901 Las Vegas Blvd S;
tickets $65-80; 🕙 7pm Tue-Sun, also 9:30pm Sat;
bus 301, 302

A variety show of wildly unrelated production numbers – some better than others,
but most not very good – and a constantly
changing lineup of acts throw together ice
skaters, topless showgirls, contortionists
and the show-stopping finale of motor-
cycles racing around a domed cage.

TRIBUTE TO FRANK, SAMMY, JOEY & DEAN Map p265

☎ 702-737-5540, 800-633-1777; www.greekisles
vegas.com; Greek Isles, 305 Convention Center Dr;
show $45, dinner & show $55; 🕙 dinner 6pm,
show 8:15pm Sat-Thu; monorail Convention Center

Capitalizing on Rat Pack nostalgia, the Greek
Isles tries to return the old Sands hotel's
Copa Room to what it was in 1960. The
show faithfully replicates the gang's routines, with the same songs, politically incor-
rect jokes and some embarrassing behavior
by Marilyn Monroe. Ol' Blue Eyes may not
be convincing, but you'll fall in love with
Dino and the fantastic live big band. If only
the crowd had more young hipsters and
fewer cranky senior citizens, it'd be aces.

VIVA LAS VEGAS Map pp262-3

☎ 702-380-7711; www.stratospherehotel.com;
Stratosphere, 2000 Las Vegas Blvd S; tickets $17;
🕙 2pm & 4pm Mon-Sat; bus 301, 302

What's in a name? Everything, we guess.
Otherwise there's no excuse for this tacky
production being the longest-running afternoon variety show in Las Vegas. Expect
low-brow comedy, showgirls dressed like
Hooters waitresses, and a magician with a
poodle impersonating Elvis. Avoid it at all
costs.

WAYNE NEWTON

http://waynenewton.com

This celebrated lounge singer isn't widely
regarded as 'Mr Las Vegas' for nothing.
Wayne Newton has taken a lot of criticism
for not repeatedly reinventing himself. But
he's old school, one of the last of a dying
breed, just like the Stardust casino hotel
where he used to perform. He was last seen
at the Las Vegas Hilton, performing alongside the winner of *The Entertainer,* a reality-
TV series he starred in. Check the website
for upcoming shows.

ZUMANITY Map pp262-3

☎ 702-740-6815, 866-606-7111; www.zumanity
.com; New York–New York, 3790 Las Vegas Blvd
S; tickets $65-95, love seats per couple $250;
🕙 7:30pm & 10:30pm Fri-Tue; monorail MGM Grand

Billed as 'another side of Cirque du Soleil,'
this human zoo amps up the energy, con-
torted acrobatics and flirtatious eroticism
of the troupe's other risk-taking resident
Strip shows. It won't take your breath away,
though. So what's the hook? Maybe it's the
curvilinear thrust stage, uninhibited costumes or – shh, don't tell your mother –
sadomasochistic scenes.

Entertainment

PRODUCTION SHOWS

SIEGFRIED & ROY'S STORY

Prior to the near-fatal mauling of Roy Horn by one of his trained white tigers in October 2003, the legendary illusionists had been wowing audiences for decades. After debuting at the Tropicana in 1967, the Germans made a name for themselves with their charm, illusions and white tigers, and, despite more than 5000 performances, their show was always a sellout. The pair mixed illusions and dance with fairytale, fueling a series of spectacles with so many special effects, showgirls and wonderful props – well, it was totally over the top. Las Vegans loved the act so much that the city declared February 17 Siegfried & Roy Day.

So, what happened? Everyone has a different theory, but the official publicity angle on it is that the disobedient tiger was attempting to save Roy from falling, and that in so doing the animal merely misjudged its own strength. But reports from observers at the time of the incident suggest something quite different may have happened. Given the restrictive living conditions that many showcase animals endure, perhaps the astonishing fact is that this tragedy was a first for Vegas. In a bizarre twist of fate, less than a year after the mauling, the house of the two magicians was shot at in a drive-by shooting by a former pro-football player who had some wildly homophobic and paranoid reasons for committing that randomly violent act. Thankfully, no one was hurt.

At press time, Roy was undergoing rehabilitation after the tiger mauling and had made a remarkable partial recovery. There are no plans for the duo's show to return, but you can still get a glimpse of their white tigers at the **Mirage** (p54) and imagine what being in the audience was once like by surfing to www.siegfriedandroy.com.

COMEDY & MAGIC

Big-name comedians often headline at the Las Vegas Hilton, MGM Grand, Flamingo, Stardust and Riviera; see p157 for more info on casino showrooms and major-events arenas. You'll find street-level comedy and magic bargains downtown – warning: they're a crapshoot, but you might get lucky – at the Plaza, Binion's and other small casinos on and off Fremont St. Look for discount admission coupons in the free tourist glossies (p242).

COMEDY STOP Map pp262-3

☎ 702-739-2714, 800-829-9034; www.comedystop .com; mezzanine level, Tropicana, 3801 Las Vegas Blvd S; admission incl 1 drink $20; ☾ nonsmoking show 8pm, smoking 10:30pm; monorail MGM Grand
A-list funny men and women crack up the Trop's 400-seat cabaret for two nightly shows. Because the Comedy Stop is an Atlantic City export, you can catch touring acts, including up-and-comers as seen on the 'Late Show with David Letterman.'

IMPROV Map pp262-3

☎ 702-369-5223, 800-392-9002 ext 2522; Harrah's, 3475 Las Vegas Blvd S; cover $25; ☾ 8:30pm & 10:30pm Tue-Sun; monorail Harrah's/Imperial Palace
Harrah's established showcase spotlights stand-up headliners, often on week-long engagements off TV appearances on *The Tonight Show* etc. The Vegas franchise of

this New York–based chain has that signature Big Apple red-brick backdrop, too.

LANCE BURTON: MASTER MAGICIAN
Map pp262-3

☎ 702-730-7160, 877-386-8224; www.lanceburton .com; Monte Carlo, 3770 Las Vegas Blvd S; tickets $67-73; ☾ 7pm Tue-Sat, 10pm Tue & Sat; monorail MGM Grand
There are lots of illusionists in Las Vegas, but few are as engaging and talented as Lance Burton. He has several grand illusions, including his signature 'flying' white Corvette, but he stands out from the rest of the illusionist pack by emphasizing sleight-of-hand tricks and other close-up magic. The juxtaposition of his mellow manner with mind-boggling feats makes tickets a good value, plus the 1275-seat theater built for the master doesn't contain a bad seat.

MAC KING Map p264

☎ 702-369-5111, 800-392-9002 ext 2522; www .mackingshow.com; Harrah's, 3475 Las Vegas Blvd S; tickets $25; ☾ 1pm & 3pm Tue-Sat; monorail Harrah's/Imperial Palace
This guy has the front-running afternoon comedy show, with lots of laughs and a little bit of magic thrown in. A former four-star chef, he's really riding the crazy train with his bag of tricks, which includes baiting a live goldfish with a Fig Newton cookie.

PENN & TELLER Map p264

☎ 702-252-7777, 888-746-7784; www.playrio.com; Rio, 3700 W Flamingo Rd; tickets $75; ⏰ 9pm Wed-Mon; free Strip shuttle

A duo (one talks, the other doesn't) that has been creating illusions for more than two decades spellbinds the audience with wit, charm and some amazing stunts like catching bullets in their teeth. The gimmick is that they actually explain some of their tricks to you, but not others. If you don't like talkative acts, this is not the show for you.

RICK THOMAS Map pp262-3

☎ 702-732-6325, 866-888-3427; www.rickthomas.com; Stardust, 3000 Las Vegas Blvd S; tickets from $25; ⏰ 2pm & 4pm Thu-Tue; bus 301, 302

It's flawless magic in the afternoons in a small but state-of-the-art showroom. Incidentally, the magician keeps the endangered Bengal tigers he uses in his shows at his own home in northwest Las Vegas, where he also gives educational tours to school groups.

RITA RUDNER Map pp262-3

☎ 702-740-6815, 866-606-7111; www.nynyhotelcasino.com; New York–New York, 3790 Las Vegas Blvd S; tickets $55; ⏰ 8pm Sun-Thu, 9pm Fri & Sat; monorail MGM Grand

The comedienne, whose trademark is telling stories and delivering one-liners with soft-spoken naiveté, delivers a PG-rated kick in the pants. Her shrewd, but borderline cliché observations about life can be a hoot. Besides, the intimate theater lends itself well to her shtick.

TOP FIVE VINTAGE VEGAS ENTERTAINMENT PICKS

- **Celebrity impersonators** Variety show at the Imperial Palace (p146), just Elvis (p156) or the Rat Pack (p147)
- **Lounge acts** Wayne Newton (p147), aka Mr Las Vegas, or whoever is playing at the Golden Nugget's Theatre Ballroom (p157)
- **Magic** Lance Burton's the king (opposite)
- **Showgirls** Bally's Jubilee (p145), the Trop's Folies Bergére (p145) and MGM Grand's La Femme (p145)
- **Strippers** Everywhere you look, just not on the Strip (for club reviews, see p154)

RIVIERA COMEDY CLUB Map pp262-3

⏰ 702-794-9433; www.rivierahotel.com; Riviera, 2901 Las Vegas Blvd S; tickets $18; ⏰ 8:30pm & 10:30pm; bus 301, 302

If sick and twisted comedy is your style, where no holds are barred, then sit yo' ass down here, mother 'effer. The Riv's 350-seat neon cabaret showcases shock-style comedians, ventriloquists, hypnotists – the whole X-rated, low-brow tradition.

RONN LUCAS Map p264

☎ 702-252-7777, 888-746-7784; www.ronnlucas.com; Rio, 3700 W Flamingo Rd; tickets $30; ⏰ 3pm Sat-Thu; free Strip shuttle

A crowd-pleasing ventriloquist keeps it at the PG-13 level. Fast-talkin' cowboys, a scorching dragon and other routines haven't changed much over the years, but if vocal stunts throw your switch, then this guy's the best in town.

Lance Burton: Master Magician (left) performs at this theatre

SECOND CITY Map pp262-3

☎ 702-733-3333, 800-221-7299; www.secondcity
.com; Flamingo, 3555 Las Vegas Blvd S; tickets
$33; ⊙ 8pm nightly, 10:30pm Fri & Sat; monorail
Flamingo/Caesars Palace

For the most reliable, best-value sketch
comedy acts in the city, come here. This national chain of comedy theatres has moved
into Sin City, where it's quickly climbed
to the top of the scene. Wednesday goes
totally 'scriptless,' with an all-improv show
that draws in audiences.

WORLD'S GREATEST MAGIC SHOW
Map pp262-3

⊙ 702-737-2111; www.saharavegas.com; Sahara,
2535 Las Vegas Blvd S; tickets $56-66, children free;
⊙ 7pm & 9:30pm Sat-Thu; monorail Sahara

Two big advantages here are that you're not
stuck with one performer for the whole 90-
minute show, and it's family-friendly. What
you get is a fast-paced merry-go-round of
magicians (up to a dozen). Also in Sahara
(p77), stand-up comics play the free Casbar
Theatre Lounge some nights.

CLUBBING & AFTER HOURS

No expense has been spared to bring clubs
at the Strip's megaresorts on par with New
York and Los Angeles. Wildly extravagant
dance floors on and off Las Vegas Blvd
are a Hollywood set designer's dream. DJs
tend to play it safe, though, spinning mostly
mainstream grooves guaranteed to appeal
to the tourist masses.

To see a different side of the scene, show
up for 'industry night,' when locals often
get in free. It's when the clubs seem least
like Vegas. If something less artificial appeals, go for it – at least you usually won't
have to fight your way in past the bouncers
on those nights.

Opening hours for the clubs vary, with
most closed early in the week. Ladies may
get in free before midnight, especially on
weeknights. Surf www.vegasafter10.com
and www.vegas.com for pics, VIP tips and
passes, and current listings. Free alternative newspapers like *City Life* and *Las Vegas
Weekly* have extensive club, after-hours and
DJ event calendars.

TOP FIVE DANCE CLUBS

Hot spots lighting up Las Vegas:
- Ice (p152)
- Body English (below)
- Light (p152)
- Pure (p152)
- Rain (p152)

An honorable mention goes to tangerine (p153).

Nothing stays the same for long in Las
Vegas. A club featuring hip-hop may have
turned to rock 'n' roll or something else
entirely by the time you read this. At press
time, Paris Hilton was set to open a new
club inside Planet Hollywood (Aladdin).

BODY ENGLISH Map p265

☎ 702-693-4000; www.bodyenglish.com; Hard
Rock, 4455 Paradise Rd; cover women/men $20/30;
⊙ 10:30pm-4am Fri-Sun; bus 108

The Hard Rock's dance floor may change
names, but it's always voted most hip.
Body English, an elegant new rock
star–style club, emphasizes posh pampering. Leather booth reservations require
one bottle ($300 minimum) per foursome.
Famous faces hang out in VIP rooms, while
lesser knowns dance to mainstream house,
hip-hop and rock tunes below a crystal
chandelier.

CLUB RIO Map p264

☎ 702-777-7977; www.playrio.com; Rio, 3700 W
Flamingo Rd; cover $10-20; ⊙ 11pm-dawn Thu,
11:30pm-dawn Fri & Sat; free Strip shuttle

This sweaty club lures a mixed, local crowd
of twenty- to fortysomethings with its laser
lights, thumpin' sound system and sunken
circular dance floor. Thursday's a hot Latin
Libido frenzy while other nights feature
hip-hop and high-energy dance music. It's
no longer nearly as exclusive as the long
lineup out front would have you believe,
so relax: there's always room to move here.

DRAI'S Map pp262-3

☎ 702-737-0555; Barbary Coast, 3595 Las Vegas
Blvd S; cover $10-20; ⊙ midnight-dawn Wed-Sun;
monorail Flamingo/Caesars Palace

Ready for an after-hours scene straight
outta Hollywood? Drai is an LA producer
and gourmet restaurateur (p106) to the

starlets. Things don't really get going until 3am, when DJs start spinning progressive discs to keep the fashion plates content. Dress to kill.

DYLAN'S DANCE HALL & SALOON
Map p260

☎ 702-451-4006; 4660 Boulder Hwy; ⏰ 7pm-dawn Fri & Sat; bus 107, 202, 213
A real-live honky-tonk, with line dancing and two-stepping that are more Nashville than Sin City. Show up early for free country dance lessons from 7:30pm till 9pm. There's never a cover charge.

FOUNDATION ROOM Map pp262-3
☎ 702-632-7631; http://hob.com; 43rd fl, Mandalay Bay, 3950 Las Vegas Blvd S; admission by invitation only; tram to Luxor & Excalibur
House of Blues' exclusive club room hosts after parties in a luxurious dining room. Celebs like Andre Agassi hold court here, where DJ entertainment and special events liven up the vibe. Call for the scoop on public access events, such as the after-hours **Godspeed** (cover $30; ⏰ 11pm-5am Mon).

GILLEY'S Map pp262-3
☎ 702-794-8434; www.gilleyslv.com; New Frontier, 3120 Las Vegas Blvd S; cover after 10pm Thu-Sat $5-10; ⏰ 4pm-dawn; bus 301, 302
Yeehaw! The Strip's only country-and-western dance hall and saloon, with a lusty crowd coming for the bikini mud wrestling and mechanical bull riding on special nights. With a wide-open dance floor, and DJs almost every night, plus live music on Thursday, Friday and Saturday nights, it's a rowdy place to kick up your cowboy-booted heels.

HOUSE OF BLUES Map pp262-3
☎ 702-632-7600; http://hob.com; Mandalay Bay, 3950 Las Vegas Blvd S; cover $5-15; ⏰ 11pm-4am Thu-Sat; monorail MGM Grand
On the casino side of **House of Blues restaurant** (p116), HOB ramps up the weekends with retro dance-club theme events such as Thursday's Metal Shop, Flashback Fridays, Boogie Nights on Saturday when you can get your *Solid Gold* groove thang back. Live bands, hip-hop and R&B, and 'rock star' karaoke (p138) happen other nights. **OBA Lounge** (☎ 702-221-2583; ⏰ 2am-8am Tue-Sun) is an after-hours party with DJs.

GAY & LESBIAN LAS VEGAS

East of the Strip and just west of the UNLV campus, the Fruit Loop triangle is an island of flamboyance in a sea of straightness and home to Vegas' queer community.

For the moment, **Kräve** (Map pp262–3; ☎ 702-836-0830; www.kravelasvegas.com; enter off Harmon Ave outside Desert Passage, 3663 Las Vegas Blvd S; cover $10-20; ⏰ 10pm-6am Fri & Sat, 6pm-4am Sun; monorail Bally's & Paris) is the hottest nightclub, and the only one on the Strip. It's a glam place packed wall-to-wall with bodies, booth seating and VIP cabanas. The lounge has karaoke, salsa and girls-only nights, plus after-hours events revving up past 3am on weekends.

Find fuel in the Fruit Loop at friendly **Hamburger Mary's** (Map p265; ☎ 702-735-4400; www.hamburgermaryslv .com; 4503 Paradise Rd; ⏰ 11am-1am; bus 108), which has a coffee and desserts corner, pool tables, lip-synching contests and trivia, karaoke, TV and bingo nights. **Gipsy** (Map p265; ☎ 702-731-1919; 4605 Paradise Rd; cover $5-10; ⏰ 9pm-late; bus 108) was once the premier gay dance club in town; look for Illusions Cabaret drag shows on Sunday night. Every night is a party inside **FreeZone** (Map p265; ☎ 702-794-2300; 610 E Naples Dr, off Paradise Rd; ⏰ 24hr; bus 108), where Tuesday is ladies' night, Thursday is boyz' night and Friday and Saturday nights feature drag cabaret. Levi's- and leather-clad boyz hang out at **Buffalo** (Map p265; ☎ 702-733-8355; 4640 Paradise Rd; ⏰ 24hr; bus 108), a cruisy biker bar with pool tables, beer busts and plenty of tough-looking, but laid-back fellows out for a good time.

Apollo Spa (Map p265; ☎ 702-650-9191; www.apollospa.com; Commercial Center, Suite A-19, 953 E Sahara Ave; ⏰ 24hr; bus 204) is a steamy men's health club. In the same strip mall are a couple of neighborhood gay bars and the **Pride Factory** (p239) café and bookshop.

Next to the Liberace Museum, **Goodtimes** (Map p265; ☎ 702-736-9494; 1775 E Tropicana Ave; ⏰ 24hr; bus 201) is a men's neighborhood bar where conversation rules, though there's a stainless-steel dance floor, video poker and pool tables, and a legendary Monday liquor bust (happy hour) from 11pm to 4am. The **Backdoor Lounge** (Map p261; ☎ 702-385-2018; 1415 E Charleston Blvd; cover Fri & Sat $5; ⏰ 24hr; bus 206) is a hole-in-the-wall with Latin dance nights on Fridays and drag shows on Saturdays.

Stop by **Get Booked** (p239), in the Fruit Loop, for more party invites. See p239 for more info on Sin City's queer scene.

ICE Map p265

☎ 702-699-9888; www.icelasvegas.com; 200 E Harmon Ave; cover $5-20; ⏰ 10pm-6am Fri & Sat; bus 105

It's no contest. The most stellar DJs spin at this off-Strip jewel box, home to internationally renowned 'Godskitchen' on Saturday nights. Resident and guest-star DJs are always on fire. Deep house, trance and techno play in the main multistoried dance hall, while the sidecar lounge heaves with hip-hop, retro '80s and mash-ups. Shortish lines outside the door help you get inside to see the honeys quick. Look out for special midweek events.

LIGHT Map pp262-3

☎ 702-693-8300; www.lightlv.com; Bellagio, 3600 Las Vegas Blvd S; cover $25; ⏰ 10:30pm-4am Thu-Sun; monorail Bally's & Paris

Intimate, sophisticated Light emphasizes socializing in plush surrounds. High-NRG pop and hip-hop dance mixes dominate the dance floor, while professional hosts push the top-shelf bottle service. If you want to chill, book a VIP booth. A celeb hangout, reservations are recommended.

MOOREA ULTRA BEACH LOUNGE
Map pp262-3

☎ 702-632-7997; Mandalay Bay, 3950 Las Vegas Blvd S; cover women/men $10/20; ⏰ 10pm-dawn Fri & Sat summer only; tram to Luxor & Excalibur

This laid-back, yet stylish, after-hours poolside ultra lounge at Mandalay Bay is open only during summer. Chill out here on red chaise longues by flickering candles while DJs spin house and hip-hop tunes under the stars. Park in the south lot, off Russell Rd.

OPM Map pp262-3

☎ 702- 387-3840; www.o-pm.com; Forum Shops, Caesars Palace, 3570 Las Vegas Blvd S; cover $10-20; ⏰ 10pm-dawn Thu-Mon; monorail Flamingo/Caesars Palace

The pounding beats at this modest dance room peak earlier than at other clubs, and there's rarely a long line. At the moment, Latin rules Wednesday but hip-hop takes you straight through the weekend, including old-skool Sunday nights. Asian-inspired bites from Chinois (p109) downstairs are served until 3am.

PLUSH Map p260

☎ 702-869-2335; www.plushvegas.com; JW Marriott, 211 N Rampart Blvd; usually no cover charge, except for special events; ⏰ 7pm-12am Wed, 7pm-2am Thu, 6pm-4am Fri, 7pm-4am Sat

Toast the return of Vegas' sexy summer pool season at this terraced lagoon lounge in Summerlin, where DJs rev up two dance floors after 10pm. It's too far to go from the Strip, but may be perfect for Friday night tequila sunset happy hours (6pm to 10pm) on the way back from Red Rock Canyon.

PURE Map pp262-3

☎ 702-731-7873; Caesars Palace, 3570 Las Vegas Blvd S; cover $10-30; ⏰ 10pm-dawn Fri-Tue; monorail Flamingo/Caesars Palace

With the most immovable bouncers in Vegas, this modern-chic space is the hottest club on the Strip: electric blues, whites and silvers, gorgeous female DJs much of the time and a patio overlooking the Strip. Crowds of fine young thangs lounge inside on couches inside a labyrinth of rooms that make it feel a lot like LA, especially now that the Pussycat Dolls Lounge (p132) has arrived. Dress code is strictly enforced.

RA Map pp262-3

☎ 702-262-4949; www.ralv.com; Luxor, 3900 Las Vegas Blvd S; cover $10-20; ⏰ 10pm-5am Wed-Sat; tram to Excalibur & Mandalay Bay

Vegas' most spectacular club is fit for the ancient Egyptian god of the sun, who inhabited the heavens by day and raged in the underworld at night. Wednesday's Pleasuredome brings deep house; other nights feature big-name house and hip-hop DJs. The dress code is fashionable and the crowd is young and sybaritic. Rumor has it this place may be redeveloped, so call to check.

RAIN Map p264

☎ 702-942-6832; Palms, 4321 W Flamingo Rd; cover $10-25; ⏰ 11pm-5am Thu, 10pm-5am Fri & Sat; bus 202

Britney Spears once threw an impromptu concert while partying at this hot, hot club. You enter through a bright futuristic tunnel and are immediately immersed in color and motion. The bamboo dance floor appears to float on a layer of fountains. Fog and pyrotechnics set the outrageous mood, as seen on MTV's *Real World: Las Vegas*.

Music showcase, House of Blues (p116)

RISQUÉ Map pp262-3
☎ 702-946-4589; www.risquelv.com; Paris–Las Vegas, 3655 Las Vegas Blvd S; cover women/men $10/20; ⏱ 10pm-4am Thu-Sun; monorail Bally's & Paris

Flounce up the spiral staircase up from the casino to reach a small dance floor that doesn't quite fly. It's like a version of what French people might call an American club. At least there are sofas to pose on, room to move and small balconies overlooking the Strip. Sunday's 'Red Light District' has a vamped-up girlie revue after midnight.

RUMJUNGLE Map pp262-3
☎ 702-632-7408, 877-632-7800; Mandalay Bay, 3950 Las Vegas Blvd S; cover $20-25; ⏱ 11pm-2am, to 4am Fri, Sat & Mon; tram to Luxor & Excalibur

Aglow with go-go dancers, aerialists and percussionists, rumjungle has been around forever and is still worthy of note for the entryway wall of fire, tumbling ceiling-to-floor cascades of water inside and a dance floor that really heats up on weekends. Not to mention the unisex bathrooms!

SEVEN Map pp262-3
☎ 702-739-7744; http://sevenlasvegas.com; 3724 Las Vegas Blvd S; cover $10-20; ⏱ 11pm-8am Fri-Sun; monorail Bally's & Paris

The vibe at this spacious club is DJ driven, although there are occasional live sounds on the Stripside patio in summer. Bonuses include a fine dance floor and oversized beds with bottle service in the lounge. After hours, it morphs into a primo spot to watch the sunrise while drinking a Red Bull.

STUDIO 54 Map pp262-3
☎ 702-891-7254; MGM Grand, 3799 Las Vegas Blvd S; ladies free, weekday/weekend cover for men $10/20; ⏱ 10pm-dawn Tue-Sat; monorail MGM Grand

Like a flawed remake of a great film, this huge three-story club fails to capture the magic that existed at the New York nightspot of the same name. The decor is black, silver and industrial and the grooves are always chart toppers. Inside are mostly tourists wondering where all the glamorous people went. Thursday's Dollhouse fashion night is your best bet. Tuesday's three-play (cover $15) gets you into Tabú (p136) and Teatro (p136), too.

TANGERINE Map pp262-3
☎ 702-894-7580; TI (Treasure Island), 3300 Las Vegas Blvd S; cover after 10pm women/men $10/20; ⏱ patio open 5:30pm-4am Tue-Sat, 5:30pm-midnight Sun & Mon, club open 6pm-4am Tue-Sat, burlesque shows hourly 10:45pm-1:45am; tram to Mirage

TI redefines sexy with its orange-flavored lounge and nightclub. DJs spin pop, house and hip-hop, and burlesque dancers scorch the bartop with 15-minute quickies. The outdoor patio overlooking Sirens' Cove

GIRLS JUST WANNA HAVE FUN

Why should the boys have all the fun? Girls, if you're hot for a night of sexy male bods, Vegas is your town.

The famous **Chippendales** (Map p264; ☎ 702-382-9347, 888-746-7784; Rio, 3700 W Flamingo Rd; tickets $35-40; ☻ 8pm nightly, 10:30pm Fri & Sat; free Strip shuttle) seem more concerned with basking in the spotlight than giving the girls a good time. Private sky boxes, a plush bathroom complete with a 'gossip pit,' and a spacious cocktail lounge called Flirt, where you can buy a drink served by chivalrous boys before the show, add icing to the hunky cake.

Or head to where you can touch the lovely Australian lads of **Thunder Down Under** (Map pp262–3; ☎ 702-597-7600, 800-933-1334; Excalibur, 3850 Las Vegas Blvd S; tickets $44; ☻ 8:30pm nightly, also 10:30pm Fri & Sat; tram to Mandalay Bay & Luxor), who provide nonstop flirting and fun, as along as you can look past their hilarious costumes.

At any of these mainstream shows, you can get a photo with the boys afterward. But we mustn't forget the down-and-dirty **Men of Olympus** (☻ 9pm-2am Wed & Thu, 8pm-4am Fri & Sat), who strut their stuff upstairs at the **Olympic Garden** (opposite). You can get a little more one-on-one action when Playgirl presents the **Men of Sapphire** (www.menofsapphire.com; tickets $25; ☻ 10pm-2:30am Fri & Sat) at **Sapphire** (opposite).

For a different bachelorette-party twist, check out the all-female burlesque at **Forty Deuce** (p134).

is a place to sit and sip while ships cruise by during the battle royale. 'Moonshine' Wednesday is service industry night.

THE BEACH Map p265

☎ 702-731-1925; www.beachlv.com; 365 Convention Center Dr; ladies free, cover for men $5-15; ☻ bar open 24hr, dance club open 10pm; monorail Las Vegas Convention Center

Spring break never ends, less is more and skin is in at this casual, surf-themed meat market that's popular with college kids and conventioneers. Bikini-clad women roam the club with shot belts, trying to keep up with the demand for their body shots. Music is mostly Top 40 and ladies often drink free early in the night.

WHISKEY Map p260

☎ 702-617-7560; www.midnightoilbars.com; Green Valley Ranch, 2300 Paseo Verde Pkwy; cover from $10; ☻ 5pm-2am Sun-Thu, 6pm-3am Fri & Sat; bus 111

Where postmod meets disco, the recently rejigged Whiskey is a locals' lounge with opium beds for lounging by the pool and views back over the Strip. DJs spin from 9pm Wednesday to Saturday (from 11pm Sunday), and the microscopic dance floor gets jammed mostly on the weekends.

STRIP CLUBS

Vegas is the original adult Disneyland. Prostitution is illegal, but there are plenty of places offering the illusion of sex on demand. All strip clubs are, ironically enough, found off the Strip. You'll need plenty of dollar bills for tips, especially if you're seated near the stage. Lap dances cost $20. Unescorted women are welcome at some clubs, but not on super-busy nights.

CHEETAHS Map p264

☎ 702-384-0074; 2112 Western Ave; cover $10; ☻ 24hr; bus 204

The movie *Showgirls* was filmed here, but real life is nothing like that, folks. Some call it classy, some call it frat-boy; you can afford to judge for yourself, with cover charges this low.

CLUB PARADISE Map p265

☎ 702-734-7990; 4416 Paradise Rd, north of Harmon Ave; cover $10-20; ☻ 5pm-6am Sun-Thu, 6pm-6am Fri & Sat; bus 108

Choreographed showgirls perform Wednesday to Saturday nights, with specialty acts thrown into the mix (you might see former Cirque du Soleil acrobats here, or women in evening wear seemingly out of a Miss USA pageant). Stripteases are tame, but they've got show-biz appeal.

GIRLS OF GLITTER GULCH Map p261

☎ 702-385-4774; 20 E Fremont St; admission free, two-drink minimum; ☻ 24hr; bus 301, 302

As you 'experience' Fremont Street, you can't help but notice this topless joint, which downtown boosters wish would just go away. Inside you will usually find friendly dancers and a crowd of mostly tourists.

OLYMPIC GARDEN Map p261

☎ 702-385-9361; www.ogvegas.com; 1531 Las Vegas Blvd S; cover $20; ⏰ 24hr; bus 301

The unpretentious OG wins high marks from topless club aficionados – and the nickname 'Silicone Valley' from the competition. Up to 50 dancers work the rooms at any given time, so there's something to please everyone. That's why it's been going strong for over a decade.

SAPPHIRE Map p264

☎ 702-796-6000; www.sapphirelasvegas.com; 3025 Industrial Rd; cover $20; ⏰ 24hr; bus 105

Everything is larger-than-life at Vegas' biggest adult entertainment complex, which features a massive multilevel main stage and a story-high martini-glass display. Celebrities often appear at Sapphire, but you probably won't catch a glimpse of 'em – they have a private entrance and VIP skybox seating.

SPEARMINT RHINO Map p264

☎ 702-796-3600; 3344 Highland Dr; cover $20; ⏰ 24hr; bus 105

The glam factor is high at this topless club chain. The women are beautiful, but the place has a laid-back air. A smallish place with an intimate vibe, Spearmint fills up fast, so arrive early for the best seating.

LIVE MUSIC

Check the free tourist magazines, such as *Showbiz Weekly*, *Today in Las Vegas* and *What's On*, for comprehensive listings of upcoming shows. See p142 for megaproduction shows, such as Céline Dion. Tickets are sold at the venues' box offices and often through Ticketmaster (☎ 702-474-4000; www.ticketmaster.com).

Many of the bars, pubs and lounges reviewed in the Drinking chapter (p130) have live music, too. You can catch traditional Irish tunes at Nine Fine Irishmen (p135). There are inexplicably popular dueling piano bars on the Strip at the Bar at Times Square (p134), Napoleon's (p132), Kahunaville (p132) and Carnaval Court (p131). Pop and retro swing bands perform outdoors on many nights at the Fremont Street Experience (p82).

On Wednesday night, you'll usually find a local blues band at the Double Down Saloon (p138). For mostly all-ages shows by local rock bands go downtown to Jillian's (p137)

and to the South Strip at GameWorks (p61). Surf to www.sincitysounds.com and www.yourlocalscene.com for complete local music listings and featured artists.

BRENDAN'S IRISH PUB Map p264

☎ 702-365-7075; Orleans, 4500 W Tropicana Ave; ⏰ 11am-1:30am, live music from 8pm Sun, 9:30pm Mon-Sat; free Strip shuttle

Blue-collar Brendan's in the Orleans casino hosts a variety of live music like rip-roarin' Zydeco Wednesday nights and Sunday evening acoustic sing-alongs. It's nothing fancy, takes all comers and isn't worth going too far out of your way for, but it's got Irish whiskeys, ales and more.

BOOTLEGGER BISTRO Map p260

☎ 702-736-4939; www.bootleggerlasvegas.com; 7700 Las Vegas Blvd S; ⏰ 24hr; bus 117, 303

Run into local stars who perform on the Strip unwinding here with quiet drinks. Weekend lounge sets are by amazing people you've never heard of, but who've backed up everyone you *have* heard of. Come earlier in the evening, as the entertainment usually finishes well before midnight. Vocalists and pianists perform during the week; karaoke is on Monday night.

CASBAR THEATRE LOUNGE Map pp262-3

☎ 702-737-2111; www.saharavegas.com; Sahara, 2535 Las Vegas Blvd S; ⏰ shows nightly; monorail Sahara

There's never a cover charge for this classic lounge. Don't expect high-class acts, but if you're in the neighborhood, drop by most evenings or some afternoons to catch an up-and-coming torch singer, Elvis impersonator, vintage swingin' cover band or stand-up comedy acts. Post-midnight shows go on occasionally, too.

COOLER LOUNGE Map p260

☎ 702-646-30009; www.coolerlounge.com; 1905 N Decatur Blvd; cover $3-5; ⏰ most shows from 10pm

The motto of this lounge, in an unprepossessing strip mall far off the Strip, is 'live and loud since 1981.' And that's the way locals like it. Lots of local bands with intimidating names like Bare Knuckle and the Apocalyptics are center stage here. Nearby Pogo's Tavern (Map p260; ☎ 702-646-9735; 2103 N Decatur Blvd) has legendary big-band sounds from 9pm to midnight on Friday.

HOUSE OF BLUES Map pp262-3

☎ 702-632-7600; www.hob.com; Mandalay Bay, 3950 Las Vegas Blvd S; tickets $15-100; ☾ schedule varies; tram to Luxor & Excalibur

Blues is just the tip of the hog at this Mississippi Delta juke joint, which opened in 1999 with performances by Bob Dylan and the Blues Brothers. HOB features a variety of big-name live music including soul, pop and rock. Capacity is 1900, but seating is limited, so show up early if you want to take a load off. The sight lines are good and the outsider folk-art decor is übercool. Acts range from living legends like Al Green and BB King to new rockers Jimmy Eat World and Lenny Kravitz. For the dance club, see p151.

HURRICANE BAR & GRILL Map p260

☎ 702-407-8976; www.hurricanelv.com; 10420 S Bermuda Rd, south of Pyle Rd, off I-15 exit Silverado Ranch Blvd; cover Sat only $5

Way off the beaten track, this spot is a welcoming, locals' fave for seeing live local and national touring bands. Country twangs, hard rock guitar and fusion sounds – anything goes here. The Sunday night jazz sessions starting around 9:30pm are another draw for experimental minds.

MATTEO'S UNDERGROUND LOUNGE

☎ 702-293-0098; downstairs, Boulder Dam Hotel, 1305 Arizona St, Boulder City; ☾ most shows 9:30pm Fri & Sat

Not as much of a drive from the Strip as you might think, this hangout near Hoover Dam is made for indie-music lovers. Some of the best bands Sin City has to offer play intimate shows here. Always call ahead to check schedules; sometimes there are jazz- and open-mic nights midweek.

SAND DOLLAR BLUES LOUNGE Map p264

☎ 702-871-6651; 3355 Spring Mountain Rd, off Polaris Ave; cover $5-10; ☾ 24hr; bus 203

A few doors down from a Harley repair shop, this unpretentious club is the only one in town featuring live jazz and blues almost nightly after 10pm. It's smoky, casual and nautical-themed with video poker and pool tables and draws a mixed mostly local crowd.

STARLIGHT LOUNGE Map pp262-3

☎ 702-732-6441; Stardust, 3000 Las Vegas Blvd S; ☾ 24hr; bus 301, 302

Though Wayne Newton (p147) has left the building, the Starlight's crowd is still vintage 1970s Vegas. You never know who or what tunes might be playing, with live local rock, swing, country and cover bands going on stage nightly after 9:30pm. Watch out for the stray karaoke night or late-afternoon show starting around 5pm.

TAILSPIN BAR & GRILL Map p260

☎ 702-436-7925; http://sincitysaloons.com; 6295 S Pecos Rd; ☾ 24hr; bus 111

Wondering what you will hear at the Tailspin? Consider the celebrities who have

LONG LIVE THE KING

Ladies and gentlemen, Elvis Presley left the building for that Great Stage in the Sky on August 16, 1977. A few fans allege that he faked his death at Graceland, slipping out to start a new life away from the pressures of fame and white jumpsuits. He's been spotted worldwide eating an extra-large pastrami on dark rye in a deli in Berlin, riding a double-decker bus in London and singing karaoke in a bar in Toronto. Alas, sightings are difficult to verify.

What isn't difficult is tracking down Elvis impersonators in Las Vegas. The Elvis-a-Rama Museum (p89) has daily tribute shows, while another Elvis look-alike gets the Imperial Palace's Legends in Concert (p146) all shook up.

Some say the best Elvis in Vegas is Steve Connolly, who currently does his Spirit of the King tribute show (www .spiritoftheking.com) at Fitzgerald's (Map p261; ☎ 702-388-2400; 2nd fl, 301 E Fremont St; admission free, one-drink minimum; ☾ 7:15 Thu-Mon). Then there's Pete 'Big Elvis' Vallee (www.bigelvis.biz), a leather-wearin', guitar-playin', former heavy-metal rocker from the East Coast who gives folks a taste of the King's '68 comeback special. At press time, Vallee was doing his tribute show at Barbary Coast (Map pp262-3; ☎ 702-737-7111; 3595 Las Vegas Blvd S; admission free; ☾ 3-6pm Tue-Fri; monorail Flamingo/Caesars Palace).

The Flying Elvi (www.flyingelvi.com), those wacky skydivers from Honeymoon in Vegas, are in town occasionally. Or you might glimpse an Elvis impersonator just walking down the street in his blue suede shoes. If not, you can always have the King guest star at your shotgun wedding by getting hitched at Viva Las Vegas Wedding Chapel (p85).

SEEING STARS

Headliners often appear at these casino showrooms and megaevent arenas:

Aladdin Theatre (Map pp262–3; ☎ 702-785-5000, 877-333-9474; www.planethollywood.com; Planet Hollywood [Aladdin], 3667 Las Vegas Blvd S; monorail Bally's & Paris) Acts at the old Aladdin's upgraded 7000-seat performing arts auditorium range from musical blockbusters to comedy kingpins.

Caesars Palace (Map pp262–3; ☎ 702-731-7110; www.caesarspalace.com; 3570 Las Vegas Blvd S; monorail Flamingo/Caesars Palace) It's not just for Céline Dion. Elton John, Stevie Nicks and other musical giants have burned up the 4000-seat Colosseum stage, too.

Clark County Amphitheater (Map p261; ☎ 702-455-8200; www.seeyouattthecca.com; 500 S Grand Central Pkwy; bus 106) Summer jazz concerts in the park and multicultural outdoor music festivals.

Flamingo (Map pp262–3; ☎ 702-733-3333; www.flamingolasvegas.com; 3555 Las Vegas Blvd S; monorail Flamingo/Caesars Palace) Gladys Knight, Frankie Valli and the Four Seasons and other R&B and oldies groups fill this 1200-seat showroom.

Las Vegas Hilton (Map p265; ☎ 702-732-5755, 800-222-5361; www.lvhilton.com; 3000 Paradise Rd; monorail Las Vegas Hilton) Where Elvis staged his Las Vegas comeback, the 1600-seat Hilton Theater carries on the tradition of big-name acts like Wayne Newton and other shows rotating in the Shimmer Cabaret.

Mandalay Bay Events Center (Map pp262–3; ☎ 702-632-7580, 877-632-7400; www.mandalaybay.com; 3950 Las Vegas Blvd S; tram to Luxor & Excalibur) Major touring acts, often country-and-western flavor, regularly fill the 12,000-seat arena. Summer concerts at Mandalay Beach have tempted the Go-Gos and Lyle Lovett to visit Sin City.

MGM Grand (Map pp262–3; ☎ 702-891-7777, 877-880-0880; www.mgmgrand.com; 3799 Las Vegas Blvd S; monorail MGM Grand) When pop stars like U2 and Alicia Keys come to town, they play the 17,0000-seat Grand Garden Arena. David Copperfield and Chris Isaak have appeared in the more intimate 740-seat Hollywood Theatre.

Orleans (Map pp262–3; ☎ 702-365-7075, 888-234-2334; www.orleansarena.com; 4500 W Tropicana Ave; free Strip shuttle) The sounds of Englebert Humperdinck, Dionne Warwick, Air Supply and the like take over the 800-seat showroom weekly. Major touring shows, such as LeAnn Rimes, play in the adjacent 9000-seat Orleans Arena.

Thomas & Mack Center (Map p265; ☎ 702-739-3267, 866-388-3267; www.thomasandmack.com; 4505 S Maryland Pkwy; bus 108, 109, 201, 213, 804) A hub for megaconcert events, and for the circus, when it comes to town. The $30-million, 19,000-seat sports and entertainment facility boasted Frank Sinatra and Dean Martin at its gala opening in 1983. Thomas & Mack also tickets events at the adjacent 3000-seat **Cox Pavilion** and the 15,000-seat **Sam Boyd Stadium** (Map p260; 7000 E Russell Rd; bus 107, or 201A during special events only) off the Boulder Hwy.

Coast Casinos (p202), **Station Casinos** (p202), the **Silverton** (p203) and **Primm Valley Resorts** (p228) host mostly country-and-western headliners.

dropped by, like Whitesnake and Steven Adler of Guns N' Roses. The jukebox rocks hard, the bands even harder. Local rock takes over on the weekends; open jams are held on Tuesday and Thursday for blues and beyond. No cover, and lotsa pool tables.

THE JOINT Map p265
☎ 702-693-5066; www.hardrockhotel.com; Hard Rock, 4455 Paradise Rd; most tickets $25-100; schedule varies; bus 108
Opened in 1995, the Joint has become a beacon for rock bands. Concerts at this intimate venue (capacity 1400) feel like private shows, even when Bob Dylan or the Rolling Stones are in town. Most shows are standing room only, with some reservable VIP balcony seats upstairs.

THEATRE BALLROOM Map p261
☎ 702-385-7111, 866-946-5336; www.goldennugget.com; 2nd fl, Golden Nugget, 129 E Fremont St; schedule varies; bus 301, 302
Vintage-style crooners like Tony Bennett, Julio Iglesias and Matt Dusk (of *Casino* reality-TV fame) fill up the Golden Nugget's gorgeous 2nd-floor Theatre Ballroom, which seats just 400 people. Headliners have only short engagements here, but always make for a great, sophisticated night out.

Luxor IMAX Theatre (opposite)

PERFORMING ARTS

Vegas is not a high-brow cultural mecca, so you'll have to ferret out the finer performing arts. Click to www.lvpac.org for updates on construction of the city's multifacility center; see p157 for a list of other major performing arts and concert venues around town. The *Las Vegas Review–Journal*'s 'Neon' guide, which appears on Thursday, lists major performing-arts events.

CASHMAN CENTER THEATRE Map p261

☎ 702-386-7100; 850 Las Vegas Blvd N; tickets $20-55; bus 113

Major touring productions like the *Vagina Monologues* and *Les Miserables* stop at this 1900-seat performing-arts space downtown at the Cashman Convention Center.

COCKROACH THEATRE

www.cockroachtheatre.com; tickets usually $10-15

This theater group claims it does 'plays that shift the laws of time, descend into the depths of the human brain, journey through unknown regions of earth, and crawl into twisted perversions of love and family.' Whoa. These experimental insects play mostly to alternative crowds in the downtown arts district.

LAS VEGAS PHILHARMONIC

☎ 702-258-5438; www.lasvegasphilharmonic.com; tickets $25-66

Around for less than a decade, this 70-piece orchestra performs sold-out shows at Artemus Ham Concert Hall in the UNLV Performing Arts Center (opposite), as well as at casino-hotel grand openings, Fashion Show Mall recitals and the CineVegas (p10) film festival.

NEVADA BALLET THEATRE

☎ 702-243-2623; www.nevadaballet.com; tickets $30-65

Nevada's only professional dance company gives performances of classical and contemporary dances year-round, primarily at Judy Bayley Theatre in the UNLV Performing Arts Center (opposite).

SEAT THEATER Map p261

☎ 702-676-1111; www.theartsfactory.com; Arts Factory, 103 E Charleston Blvd; tickets $10-15; bus 108, 206

Theater groups off the deep end – and we mean that in a good way – take the stage inside this downtown laboratory, the Social Experimentation and Absurd Theater (SEAT), at the Arts Factory (p80).

UNLV PERFORMING ARTS CENTER

Map p265

☎ 702-895-2787; http://pac.nevada.edu; Cottage Grove St, off Maryland Pkwy; tickets $10-100; bus 109

The university performing arts center hosts hundreds of events on three main stages year-round. The 1870-seat Artemus Ham Concert Hall has great acoustics, while the 550-seat Judy Bayley Theatre hosts everything from ballet to experimental music fests. The Black Box Theatre presents smaller theatrical and dance productions. The box office is south of the UNLV North Parking Garage, next to the main concert hall.

CINEMAS

Check **Fandango** (☎ 800-326-3264, www.fandango.com) for show times and online ticketing. The free alternative tabloids *City Life* and *Las Vegas Weekly* have film reviews and schedules, including the occasional arthouse or revival film screening at UNLV or Clark County Public Library branches.

BRENDEN PALMS CASINO Map p264

☎ 702-507-4849; Palms, 4321 W Flamingo Rd; adult/senior & child 3-12 $9.25/5.75, matinee shows before 6pm $6.25, IMAX films $9.25; bus 202

The swankest movieplex in town is outfitted with IMAX and Lucasfilm THX digital sound, plus rocker-chair stadium seating for superior sightlines. First-run Hollywood movies are the usual fare, except when the CineVegas film festival (p10) is in town.

CENTURY ORLEANS 18 Map p264

☎ 702-227-3456; Orleans, 4500 W Tropicana Ave; adult/senior & child 3-11 $9.25/5.75, matinee shows before 6pm $6.25; free Strip shuttle

This cluster of theaters features stadium-style seating. Its other casino multiplexes include **Century 18 Sam's Town** (☎ 702-547-7469; Sam's Town, 5111 Boulder Hwy; free Strip & downtown shuttles) and **Century Suncoast 16** (☎ 702-341-5555; Suncoast, 9090 Alta Dr, at Rampart Blvd).

CINEDOME 12 HENDERSON Map p260

☎ 702-564-5155; 851 S Boulder Hwy; adult/senior & child 3-11 $9.25/5.75, matinee shows before 6pm $6.25; bus 107

Once upon a time, domed-roof movie houses were all the rage from coast to coast. Although their curved screens can be small, try to catch a flick here before Vegas' retro domes disappear off the map for good.

CROWN NEONOPOLIS 14 Map p261

☎ 702-383-9600; 450 E Fremont St; adult/senior & child 3-11 $8.50/5.50, matinee shows before 6pm $5.50

Vegas' only downtown movie theater is also the cheapest first-run cinema in town. All 14 screens sport digital THX sound and high-backed, stadium-style seating. Babies are welcome at special 'Movies for Mom' showings on Wednesday mornings. There's free three-hour validated parking in the Neonopolis garage (enter off 4th St, north of Fremont St).

LAS VEGAS DRIVE-INS Map p260

☎ 702-646-3565; 4150 W Carey Ave, east of N Rancho Dr; admission per adult $6, discount Tue admission $4, children under 12 always free; ⊙ gates open at 6pm

One of the only two remaining in the entire state of Nevada, this old-fashioned place screens up to six double features daily. Bring your buddies, grab a bucket of popcorn and put your feet up on the dashboard – ah, heaven.

LUXOR IMAX THEATRE Map pp262-3

☎ 702-262-4555, 800-557-7428; Luxor, 3900 Las Vegas Blvd S; tickets $9, d/tr feature $13.50/17; ⊙ hourly 9am-11pm; tram to Excalibur & Mandalay Bay

Luxor's IMAX theater projects onto a seven-story, wall-mounted screen, but the images are 10 times more detailed than in conventional cinemas. With only 312 seats and a 15,000-watt digital surround-sound system, you'll always be close to the action. For the IMAX ridefilms, see p61.

REGAL VILLAGE SQUARE STADIUM 18 Map p260

☎ 702-221-2283; 9400 W Sahara Ave; adult/senior & child 3-11 $9.25/$5.75, matinee shows before 6pm $6.50; bus 204

Las Vegas doesn't have any truly independent or arthouse cinemas, but this multiplex way the hell out west of the Strip on Sahara Ave usually has at least a couple of indie flicks up on the marquee.

Soft toys, GameWorks (p61)

TROPICANA CINEMAS Map p265
☎ 702-450-3737; www.tropicanacinemas.com; 3330
E Tropicana Ave, cnr Pecos Rd; tickets before/after
6pm $1/2, special engagements $6; bus 111, 201, 804
The one discount movie theater near the
Strip charges just $1 to $2 to see its second-
run films. On weekends, 'midnight madness'
shows feature cult classics like *Dazed &
Confused* and *The Rocky Horror Picture Show*.

UNITED ARTISTS 8 SHOWCASE MALL
Map pp262-3
☎ 702-221-2283 ext 8; Showcase Mall, 3785
Las Vegas Blvd S; adults/seniors & children 3-11
$9.50/5.75, matinee shows before 6pm $6.50;
monorail MGM Grand
This is the only place to see first-run films
on the Strip, which means it's always
packed.

Entertainment

CINEMAS

Sports, Spas & Fitness

Sports, Spas & Fitness

Vegas has high-end spectator sports and spas ready to pamper your every whim, but you'll still get a workout just finding a place to work off that buffet belly, sugar. If working up a sweat outdoors is where your heart, mind and body are at, jump outside the city limits; see the Excursions chapter, p207.

WATCHING SPORTS

Although Vegas doesn't have any professional sports franchises, it's a sports-savvy town. Handicapping is one of the most popular activities and you can wager on just about anything at casinos' race and sports books. UNLV Runnin' Rebels (http://unlv.rivals.com) college teams enjoy a strong local following, but nothing stirs up the crowds as much as 'Fight Night.' Look for a new 4400-seat equestrian center opening at South Coast (p203) casino hotel in 2006. Ticketmaster (☎ 702-474-4000; www.ticketmaster.com) sells tickets for major sporting events.

BASEBALL
LAS VEGAS 51S

☎ 702-386-7200; www.lv51.com; Cashman Field, 850 Las Vegas Blvd N; tickets $7-12; ☽ Apr-Aug; bus 113

The Las Vegas 51s (you know, as in alien-friendly Area 51), the AAA franchise of the Los Angeles Dodgers, play at least a 70-game home schedule at Cashman Field (Map p261). Triple-A ball is just one step down from Major League Baseball, so the standard of play is high. Call for game times.

BASKETBALL
UNLV RUNNIN' REBELS

☎ 702-739-3267, 866-388-3267; http://unlvrebels.collegesports.com; Thomas & Mack Center, 4505 S Maryland Pkwy; tickets $12-50; ☽ Nov-Mar; bus 108, 109, 201, 213, 804

The Runnin' Rebels of the University of Nevada, Las Vegas, won the national collegiate basketball title in 1990. Since the Rebels played their first game in 1958, UNLV has sent many players to the pros. The quality of play at the Thomas & Mack Center (Map p265) is outstanding. The Lady Rebels play a shorter season from January through March.

TOP FIVE LEGAL HIGHS

- AJ Hackett Bungy (p75)
- bathhouse (p164)
- Fight Night (below)
- National Finals Rodeo (opposite)
- Red Rock Canyon (p170)

BOXING

Las Vegas has hosted more championship fights than any other city in the world. World-class boxing still draws fans from all over the globe. Check out the news, ringside pics and upcoming fight schedules at www.lvboxing.com. Most tickets sell for $25 to $300, and more than $1000 for major bouts. Venues include the following:

Mandalay Bay Events Center (Map pp262–3; ☎ 702-632-7580; www.mandalaybay.com; 3950 S Las Vegas Blvd; tram to Luxor & Excalibur) Here 12,000 spectators can watch boxing, bull riding and sumo wrestling. If you're lucky, you can watch fighters weigh in on the afternoon of the fight inside M-Bay.

MGM Grand Garden Arena (Map pp262–3; ☎ 702-891-7777, 877-880-0880; www.mgmgrand.com; 3799 Las Vegas Blvd S; monorail MGM Grand) Boxing and tennis are the sporting mainstays at this 17,000-seat arena.

Orleans Arena (Map p264; ☎ 702-365-7075, 888-234-2334; www.orleansarena.com; Orleans, 4500 W Tropicana Ave; free Strip shuttle) This arena has 9000 seats for boxing, hockey, motor sports, arena football and more.

CAR RACING
LAS VEGAS MOTOR SPEEDWAY

Map p260

☎ 702-644-4444, 800-644-4444; www.lvms.com; 7000 Las Vegas Blvd N; tickets from $15; bus 113A during special events only

For auto racing, including Nascar, Indy, and dirt track– and drag races, check out the enormously popular 1600-acre complex featuring a 1.5-mile superspeedway, go-cart tracks and a racing school. Events are often held at this $200-million facility, with autograph sessions before start time. You can even get married here. For ride-alongs, see p92.

FOOTBALL

Catch college tournament action at the **Las Vegas Bowl** (p12).

LAS VEGAS GLADIATORS

☎ 702-739-3267, 866-388-3267; Thomas & Mack Center, 4505 S Maryland Pkwy; www.lvgladiators.com; tickets $6-60; 🕑 Jan-May; bus 108, 109, 201, 213, 804

The Gladiators play arena football, which is faster, leaner and more aggressive than regular NFL American-style football. It's played on a smaller, padded indoor field at the **Thomas & Mack Center** (Map p265).

UNLV RUNNIN' REBELS

☎ 702-739-3267, 866-388-3267; http://unlvrebels.collegesports.com; Sam Boyd Stadium, 7000 E Russell Rd, east of Boulder Hwy; tickets $15-28; 🕑 Sep-Nov; bus 201A during special events only

The UNLV Runnin' Rebels have never been ranked No 1 in the country, and in fact the team has had a losing record in recent years. It's easy to obtain good seats to their five annual home games played at the 15,000-seat **Sam Boyd Stadium** (Map p260).

HOCKEY

LAS VEGAS WRANGLERS

☎ info 702-471-7825, tickets 702-284-7777; www.lasvegaswranglers.com; Orleans Arena, 4500 W Tropicana Ave; tickets $12-30, youth $7-10; 🕑 Oct-Apr; free Strip shuttle

Affiliated with the Calgary Flames of the National Hockey League (NHL), this minor-league hockey team you've probably never heard of faces off at the **Orleans Arena** (Map p264). They're in the National Conference West Division, which stretches from Alaska to California. Their winning season in 2005 finished with the Kelly Cup playoffs.

RODEOS

There are a few large rodeo events in Las Vegas each year, all usually held at the **Thomas & Mack Center** (Map p265; ☎ 702-739-3267, 866-388-3267; www.thomasandmack.com; 4505 S Maryland Pkwy; bus 108, 109, 201, 213, 804).

The most spectacular is the **National Finals Rodeo** (p12), which ropes in the top money winners in the Professional Rodeo Cowboys Association and Professional Bull Riders, who compete for millions in prize money. The event spans 10 days and is held in December; tickets are difficult to come by. The good news is that the box office resells same-day tickets starting each morning around 10am. Cheaper 'Mad Dash' find-a-seat tickets let you scramble around to find

Rock climbing (p170)

no-show seats in the balcony area, with at least a guaranteed view of the action from the standing room-only concourse.

The **Professional Bull Riders** (www.pbrnow.com; tickets from $100) annual World Finals events in early autumn attract the world's best bull riders. The action is fast, furious and frightening as the riders compete at venues such as the Thomas & Mack Center and the **Mandalay Bay Event Center** (p157).

Laughlin (p228) plays host to several big-time rodeo events, including the professional bull riders' Built Ford Tough series in late September or early October, the team roping finals in mid-November and the PRCA Rodeo finals in March.

SPAS & BEAUTY

Spas are blossoming in Las Vegas. Most day spas offer registered massage therapy (RMT), facials, manicures and pedicures, waxing and tanning services. Both men and women are welcome, unless otherwise stated. Try to make appointments at least a day in advance. Some spas are reserved for hotel guests on weekends; others are guests-only at all times, including those at the Bellagio, MGM Grand and Wynn megaresorts.

Day-use spa passes start at $20 (up to $35 if you're not a hotel guest), but this fee is usually waived with a treatment to the value of $50 or more. Expect to pay upwards of $100 for an hour-long massage, at least $65 for a 'quickie' facial and from $30 for waxing. Tanning sessions start at $10. More exotic treatments run up to $200 per hour. Expect to pay at least $50 for a haircut and style. Do give a tip if a service charge is not already included. Fruit, juices and healthy snacks are usually gratis.

If all you want is a gym, see p168. For free mini makeovers, drop by the makeup counter of major department stores (p172). Free beauty tricks are demo'd on some nights while you sip your cocktails at downtown's **Beauty Bar** (p137). For professional makeup advice, drop by **MAC Cosmetics** in Caesars Palace's Forum Shops (p174).

AQUAE SULIS Map p260
☎ 702-869-7807, 877-869-8777; www.jwlasvegas resort.com; 211 N Rampart Blvd; day pass guests/ nonguests $20/35; ☽ 5:30am-8pm
A massive 40,000-sq-ft spa in the far north-west corner of the city has Vegas' only

hydrotherapy circuit and a co-ed sauna, steam room and whirlpool. On the menu are desert hot-stone therapy, Turkish scrubs, spicy cherry herbal mud wraps and detox seaweed body masks, along with yoga, tai chi and pilates classes and the occasional tango class or tarot-card reading. The spa also sells luxury products imported from Southern California to Sweden.

ART OF SHAVING Map pp262-3
☎ 702-632-9356; Mandalay Place, btwn Mandalay Bay & Luxor, 3930 Las Vegas Blvd S; ☽ 9am-11pm Sun-Thu, 10am-midnight Fri & Sat, barbers available till 4 or 5pm; tram to Mandalay Bay or Luxor
Barbers wielding straight razors can as easily dispense advice about aftershave as upmarket skin-care treatments and aroma-therapy grooming products. Services start at $10, with a shave and a haircut costing $65 (not two bits).

BATHHOUSE Map pp262-3
☎ 877-632-9636; www.mandalaybay.com; THE-hotel, Mandalay Bay, 3950 Las Vegas Blvd S; day pass guests/nonguests $30/35; ☽ 6am-9:30pm; tram to Luxor & Excalibur
Popular with both sexes, this $25-million minimalist space defines hip. Organic skin-care products include an 'aromapoth-ecary' of massage oils blended to match your personality. Inside the spa are flow-ing waterfalls, dramatic stone walls and chaise longues by pools. The redwood sauna is perfect for sweating out the sins of the night before. Asian tea baths, fruit pulp facials and mix-and-match packages will please all comers. Ask about seasonal sunrise yoga on Mandalay Beach.

CANYON RANCH SPACLUB Map pp262-3
☎ 702-414-3600, 877-220-2688; www.canyon ranch.com; 4th fl, Grand Canal Shoppes, Venetian, 3355 Las Vegas Blvd S; day pass $35, with treat-ment $15; ☽ 5:30am-10pm, café 7am-6pm; monorail Harrah's/Imperial Palace
Popular with couples for its side-by-side treatments, this healthy place focuses on nutrition and offers more than 100 differ-ent activities, even a rock-climbing wall, all of which are priced à la carte. Popular treatments include Ayurvedic massage, mango sugar body scrubs and soaks in the Royal King's Bath, a custom-made bronze

tub. The café serves spa cuisine and fruit smoothies. Day passes include use of the high-tech fitness facilities. To get here, take the private elevator located inside the Grand Canal Shoppes next to the spa's Living Essentials boutique.

DJANEL SPA & SALON Map p260

☎ 702-868-6000; www.djanelspa.com; 5150 S Pecos Rd; ✦ by appointment only; bus 111

For a quieter oasis, head far east of the Strip to this personally oriented spa. Sun yourself in the backyard after breezing through the meditation room and having a treatment, maybe a detox body mud mask or a massage with aromatherapy oils. Djanel has a full-service salon and offers one-day massage workshops.

EL CORTEZ BARBER SHOP Map p261

☎ 702-385-5200; 2nd fl, 600 E Fremont St; ✦ 9am-5pm Tue-Sat; bus 107, 301, 302

Old-school barbers sharpen their shears at this upstairs hangout inside a very vintage casino. You may even spy some *Playboy* magazines lying around while you wait for a chair. Haircuts (for men only, of course) start at just $10.

OASIS SPA Map pp262-3

☎ 702-730-5720, 800-258-9308; www.luxor.com; West Tower, Luxor, 3900 S Las Vegas Blvd; day pass guests/nonguests $20/25; ✦ 24hr, closed 11:30pm Tue-6am Wed; tram to Excalibur & Mandalay Bay

It's not quite pampering fit for Queen Nefertiti (the theme is Egyptian, naturally), but it's still relaxing. All the usual treatments are offered, plus Aveda facials and aromatherapy showers, but the real reason to come is because you can, at almost any hour (well, except for Tuesday nights).

PALMS SPA & AMP SALON Map p264

☎ 702-942-6937; www.palms.com; Palms, 4321 W Flamingo Rd; day pass guests/nonguests $20/25; ✦ 6am-8pm; bus 202

Ultrasoft 'cashwear' robes, 'margarita madness' cocktails for your skin and candlelight yoga – oh, it's trendy to the max (the glam factor is superhigh). Relax by the lushly landscaped pool with its signature lavender floor before enjoying a couple's massage or heading to the lighted tropical cabanas, fitness center or pilates studio.

ROCK SPA Map p265

☎ 702-693-5522; www.hardrockhotel.com; Hard Rock, 4455 Paradise Rd; day pass guests/nonguests $20/25; ✦ 6am-10pm; bus 108

Nothing that Sin City's Hard Rock does fails to be a success. In the salon, find a celebrity stylist who has tousled the locks of David Bowie and Isabella Rossellini. Among soothing wood, rock and water elements, the spa offers wraps, body scrubs and facials; the theme is 'recovery.' Work off your latest bender in the health club with free weights, the latest fitness equipment and, if you're feeling fiesty, boxing classes.

SAINTS & SINNERS Map p260

☎ 702-471-6800; 7700 Las Vegas Blvd S; ✦ by appointment only; bus 117, 303

An artistic hair salon near the **Las Vegas Outlet Mall** (p183), Saints & Sinners has a calm atmosphere and friendly service, which makes it a fantastic alternative to super-busy salons on the Strip. Don't forget to pick up some free club passes and VIP cards on your way out the door. It's beside the **Bootlegger Bistro** (p128).

SPA AT GREEN VALLEY RANCH
Map p260

☎ 702-617-7570, 866-782-9487; www.greenvalley ranchresort.com; 2300 Paseo Verde Pkwy, off I-215 exit Green Valley Pkwy, Henderson; day pass $30; ✦ 6am-8pm; bus 111, 114

Enjoy the panoramic views back over the city as you work out or swim in the pool, which is near an outdoor steam room. Inside the spa, herbal teas and trail mix are among the life-sustaining goodies offered before and after your fruit-inspired treatment. You can choose a massage therapy of any variety, including shiatsu, deep-tissue, Swedish and hot-stone therapy, even a peppermint foot treatment.

SPA BY MANDARA Map pp262-3

☎ 702-946-4366; www.mandaraspa.com; Paris–Las Vegas, 3655 Las Vegas Blvd S; day pass $25; ✦ 6am-7pm; monorail Bally's & Paris

With Matisse-styled tiling, this full-service salon and spa displays Balinese and European influences. The most luxurious treatment rooms have handcrafted tropical hardwood, artworks and silk carpets.

Mandara's specialities are facials and romantic couples' packages. Look out for two-for-one discount coupons, often in the city's free tourist magazines.

SPA MOULAY Map p260

☎ 702-567-6049; http://lakelasvegas.hyatt.com; Hyatt Regency Lake Las Vegas Resort, 101 Montelago Blvd, Henderson, 20mi east of the Strip; ⏱ 8am-8pm

Situated on beautiful Lake Las Vegas near Lake Mead, this gorgeous Moroccan-themed spa is for when you need a great excuse for a day trip off the Strip. Decadent, whimsically themed treatments (such as the Harem's Blend Wrap with spices, citrus and essential oils) are as enticing as the private massage in lakeview rooms. Entry to the spa is only by appointment.

TRUEFITT & HILL Map pp262-3

☎ 866-714-1115; Forum Shops, Caesars Palace, 3500 Las Vegas Blvd S; ⏱ 10am-11pm Sun-Thu, 10am-midnight Fri & Sat; monorail Flamingo/Caesars Palace

A true gentleman's barbershop, direct from 19th-century London, this establishment claims to 'groom men for greatness.' Which they should, considering the prices of up to $100 for a shave and a haircut. Barbers proffer advice and sell a range of personal grooming products. Whether you're getting married or entering the World Series of Poker finals, this is the place to get cleaned up right.

FITNESS & RECREATION

People do jog on the Strip, but only very early in the morning when it's not hot and Las Vegas Blvd isn't as crowded. They look like strange anomalies as they weave in between drunks stumbling out of casinos, then bounce up the escalators of pedestrian skybridges. A better place to run is on the outdoor track at the University of Nevada, Las Vegas (Map p265), off Swenson St in the northeast corner of campus. Elsewhere you'll see commuters cycling around town, but Vegas' busy streets and scarce bike lanes make cycling a headache.

Active travelers looking for an endorphin fix should either stop by AJ Hackett Bungy (p75) or take a quick trip outside the city for rock climbing, mountain biking and hiking around Red Rock Canyon (p213); river paddling below Hoover Dam (p208) and aquatic sports in Lake Mead National Recreation Area (p211); hiking and rock climbing in the Valley of Fire (p212); and hiking, skiing and snowboarding near Mt Charleston (p229). Southern Nevada is also ranching country, so horseback riding tours are rampant both here and in the nearby canyon country of Utah and Arizona (p207).

BOWLING & BILLIARDS

Bowling is huge in Las Vegas. Most bowling centers are in casino hotels, where you can work on your glide-and-release at any time. The bowling centers mentioned here all rent top-of-the-line equipment. Fees vary, but average $3 per game and $2.25

BODY ART

If you've been looking for a place that will emblazon your skin or pierce your southern regions, you've come to the right city. Hours are somewhat erratic, so call ahead for an appointment at the places listed below:

PussyKat Tattoo Parlor (Map p265; ☎ 702-597-1549; 4972 S Maryland Pkwy; bus 109) Dirk Vermin, a former bassist, excels in doing pinup babes. Piercings also available. This strip-mall shop is next to Vermin's own way-out Gallery Au Go-Go.

Hart & Huntington Tattoo Company (Map p264; ☎ 702-942-7777; http://hartandhuntingtontattoo.com; Palms, 4321 W Flamingo Rd; bus 202) This plush, leather-walled tattoo parlor is the first ever to be inside a casino. A Beastie Boy attended the grand opening of H&H, the lovechild of a freestyle motocross legend and a nightclub promoter. Turntablists may perform live while you get pierced or needled. Check out the bios of the tattoo artists (including women) online.

Atomic City Tattoo (Map p261; ☎ 702-678-6665; www.atomiccitytattoo.com; 1506 Las Vegas Blvd S; ⏱ noon-6pm Sun-Tue & Thu, noon-midnight Fri & Sat; bus 301) Favored by Goths and fetishists. Often holds events on First Fridays (p81) when you can get pierced for under $20, and tattooed from $30 all day. Be seduced by the green neon glow of the sign outside.

TPC Canyons golf course (p168)

for shoe rental. Lanes are regularly closed to the public for league bowling, so always call ahead to check.

GOLD COAST Map p264
☎ 702-367-4700; 4000 W Flamingo Rd; graveyard bowling midnight-8am per game $1; ☷ 24hr; free shuttle to the Strip & Orleans
Seventy lanes, a full-service pro shop, video arcade, bar and lounge, plus bumper bowling for kids. League bowling some weeknights. Cosmic bowling with disco lights and music between 9pm and 2am on Friday and Saturday nights.

ORLEANS Map p264
☎ 702-365-7111; 4500 W Tropicana Ave; graveyard bowling midnight-8am per game $1; ☷ 24hr; free shuttle to the Strip & Gold Coast
Often voted the best bowling alley in the city, with 70 lanes, a full-service pro shop, video arcade and bar. Watch out for PBA (www.pbatour.com) tournaments here.

SAM'S TOWN Map p260
☎ 702-456-7777; 5111 Boulder Hwy; ☷ 24hr; free Strip & downtown shuttles
More than 50 lanes out on the Boulder Strip. On Friday and Saturday nights from

just before midnight till 3am, the 'Extreme Bowling Experience' turns on a super-'70s groove with disco music, funky lights and fog drifting across the lanes.

SILVERTON Map p260
☎ 702-263-7777; 3333 Blue Diamond Rd, off I-15; ☷ 24hr; bus 117
In Hootie & the Blowfish's Shady Grove Lounge, which also has pool tables, you'll find coin-operated miniature bowling ($3) inside an Airstream trailer.

GOLF
There are dozens of golf courses in Las Vegas Valley, most within 10 miles of the Strip. Golf season is in full swing from autumn through spring, depending on the temperatures (summers are just too dang hot). Mornings are cooler year-round, but green fees are cheapest during the sweltering midday heat, so aim for a twilight tee time. Generally, reservations for tee times should be made as early as possible (that is, as soon as you book your plane ticket or hotel room).

Following is a partial list of golf courses in the Las Vegas metro area that are open to the public. Many of the best resort golf courses in town, including Wynn, are open

167

only to guests and haven't been reviewed. Call the following courses for greens fees, tee times and directions.

For novelty's sake, head west and play the lowest-elevation golf course in the world at Furnace Creek in Death Valley (p224).

ANGEL PARK

☎ 702-254-4653, 888-446-5358; www.angelpark .com; 100 S Rampart Blvd; green fees $70-155
Two Arnold Palmer–designed championship municipal golf courses, plus the 12-hole, par-three Cloud Nine course and an 18-hole, natural grass putting course for practice.

BALI HAI Map p260

☎ 702-450-8000, 888-427-6678; www.balihaigolf club.com; 5160 Las Vegas Blvd S; green fees $195-295
Tropical foliage, water features and an island green on the par-three, 16th hole. Most find it overpriced, especially with planes going overhead, but it's still relatively new (opened in 2000).

BEARS BEST

☎ 702-804-8500, 866-385-8500; www.bearsbest .com; 11111 W Flamingo Rd; green fees $110-150
Designed by Jack Nicklaus, this new course rebuilds some of the Golden Bear's most famous holes from around the world, specifically selected for a desert setting.

LAS VEGAS GOLF CLUB

☎ 702-646-3003; 4300 W Washington Dr; green fees $50-100
An inexpensive municipal golf course with lots of trees (and golfers) and little water.

LAS VEGAS PAIUTE GOLF RESORT

☎ 866-284-2833; www.lvpaiutegolf.com; 10325 Nu-Way Kaiv Blvd, off US95 exit Snow Mountain; green fees $70-215
Now for something totally different, head for these three scenic Pete Dye–designed courses, about 30 miles northwest of downtown in the Springs Mountains (p229).

NORTH LAS VEGAS GOLF COURSE

☎ 702-633-1833; 324 E Brooks Ave; green fees $6.50-18
A night-lighted municipal course for nine holes on very short fairways.

ROYAL LINKS

☎ 888-427-6678; www.waltersgolf.com; 5995 E Las Vegas Valley; green fees $175-295
A castle clubhouse leads on to an 18-hole course inspired by famous greens of the British Open tour. Tiger Woods set the record here, scoring 67.

THE LEGACY

☎ 702-897-2187; www.thelegacygc.com; 130 Par Excellence Dr, Henderson; green fees $75-155
Rated one of the top 100 golf courses in the US, with rolling landscaping, desert terrain and the tricky 'Devil's Triangle' on the back nine.

TPC CANYONS

☎ 702-256-2500; www.tpc.com; 9851 Canyon Run Dr; green fees $80-260
Often featured on the PGA Tour, this course in Summerlin, codesigned by Raymond Floyd, even has views of Red Rock Canyon. It's also a certified Audubon cooperative sanctuary.

GYMS

Many casino and hotel spas (p164) have workout rooms or occasionally full fitness facilities, access to which is included in the cost of a day pass. Upscale chain hotels (p199) aimed at business travelers usually have free but limited fitness facilities for guests. Most gyms found off the Strip require membership. They will, however, issue day passes (approximately $15) to visitors. Free trial memberships, which may require showing local ID, can be downloaded online. Alternatively, you can inquire at the club's front desk.

24 HOUR FITNESS

☎ 800-432-6348; www.24hourfitness.com; day pass from $10; ☽ 24hr
This national fitness chain has a number of outlets scattered throughout Las Vegas, including one at McCarran Airport (p233). The Las Vegas West (Map p264; ☎ 702-368-1111; 3055 S Valley View Blvd; bus 104) branch has rock climbing. Further off the Strip, the Las Vegas East (Map p265; ☎ 702-641-222; 2605 S Eastern Ave; bus 110) location has a swimming pool, sauna and steam room.

BALLY'S Map pp262-3

☎ 702-967-4366; www.ballyslasvegas.com; 3645 Las Vegas Blvd S; day pass $20; ☾ 6am-7:30pm; monorail Bally's & Paris

In the basement, but conveniently close to the monorail, Bally's spa has a glassed-in workout facility, so you can take a peek before you plunk down your moolah. It also has separate wet and dry sauna and eucalyptus steam rooms for men and women. For information on Bally's tennis courts and clinics, call the **pro shop** (☎ 702-967-4598).

EXECUTIVE FITNESS Map pp262-3

☎ 702-794-9441; 12th fl, South Tower, Riviera, 2901 Las Vegas Blvd S; day pass $12-17, 30min massage incl use of facilities $45; ☾ 7am-7pm; bus 301, 302

The most affordable casino-hotel gym on the Strip is in a convenient location for conventioneers. No swimming pool, but it does have a whirlpool, steam room, weights and cardio machines, plus tanning beds and an oxygen bar.

LAS VEGAS ATHLETIC CLUB Map p265

☎ 702-734-5822; www.lvac.com; 2655 S Maryland Pkwy; entry pass per day/week $15/35; ☾ 24hr; bus 109, 204, 805

This local chain has big aspirations, but only four locations so far. The most convenient to the Strip is this Central branch, which has women-only training areas, a swimming pool and spa, racquetball courts, tanning and a juice bar. The newest club is in Henderson at **Green Valley** (Map p260; ☎ 702-853-5822; 9065 S Eastern Ave; ☾ 24hr; bus 110).

NEW YORK–NEW YORK SPA Map pp262-3

☎ 702-740-6955; www.nynyhotelcasino.com; 3rd fl, Empire Tower, 3790 Las Vegas Blvd S; day pass $20, three-day pass $35; ☾ 6:30am-7pm; monorail MGM Grand

The women's side of the spa has private hydrotherapy tubs, while the men's side has a whirlpool. In the workout room, treadmills overlook the pool area and enjoy natural lights as you do your circuit training or cardiovascular workouts. Massages available.

VEGAS BOXING Map p260

☎ 702-457-8624; 7035 W Sahara Ave; ☾ 6am-9pm Mon-Fri, 9am-5pm Sat; bus 204

Become your own *Million Dollar Baby* here, with weights, punching bags and cardio facilities, plus boxing and kickboxing classes. Personal training is available. Call to ask about a free workout.

YMCA OF SOUTHERN NEVADA Map p264

☎ 702-877-9622; 4141 Meadows Lane; day pass adult/senior/student 8-20/family $15/5/10/25; ☾ 8am-9pm Mon-Fri, 8am-6pm Sat, noon-4pm Sun; bus 103, 104, 207, 402

The reliable YMCA has a branch by the Meadows Mall, where a supervised kids gym is available for a small fee to parents who want to work out by themselves. The Y's mammoth facilities include a 25m indoor heated lap pool; outdoor tennis and indoor racquetball courts; and an outdoor walking track and second swimming pool. Yoga, aerobics and tai chi classes available.

Spa and fitness centre, Hard Rock (p165)

ICE SKATING

FIESTA ICE ARENA Map p260

☎ 702-647-7465; Fiesta Rancho, 2400 N Rancho Dr; admission $6, skate rental $2.50; ☼ call for public skate hrs; bus 106, 210

A novelty in the desert, this ice rink has a magnetic attraction for families and others seeking to escape the heat. It has a full-sized, NHL-regulation rink, plus a pro shop for skaters of all types. Rental skates are available. It's inside the Fiesta casino hotel.

ROCK CLIMBING

The most popular outdoor climbing routes are at **Red Rock Canyon** (p213) and, to a lesser degree, **Valley of Fire State Park** (p212). There are indoor climbing walls at **GameWorks** (p61), New York–New York's **ESPN Zone** (p64), Circus Circus' **Adventuredome** (p75) and the Silverton's **Bass Pro Shops Outdoor World** (p183).

There are climbing facilities at some branches of **24 Hour Fitness** (p168). **Powerhouse Rock Climbing Center** (Map p260; ☎ 702-254-5604; 8201 W Charleston Blvd; ☼ 11am-10pm Mon-Thu, 11am-8pm Fri, 10am-8pm Sat &

Sun; bus 208) is a no-frills indoor spot to practice before heading out to Red Rock Canyon.

ROLLER SKATING

CRYSTAL PALACE Map p260

☎ 702-458-7107; 4680 Boulder Hwy; ☼ call for public skate hrs; bus 107

About a 20-minute drive from the Strip, the Crystal Palace is an old-school proponent of 'artistic skating,' with gorgeous maple floors and organ music. Its **North Las Vegas** (Map p260; ☎ 702-645-4892; 3901 N Rancho Dr; bus 106) location has special events like black-out glow nights and marathon skates.

SWIMMING

Casino-hotel pools are generally open only to guests, except during summer party events. For our top hotel pool picks, see p196. Just keep in mind that most casino-hotel pools are made for lounging, not exercising. If you want to swim laps, book yourself in at a biz-friendly hotel east of the Strip (p199).

Shopping ■

Shopping

In Las Vegas, consumption is as conspicuous as dancing fountains in the middle of the desert. The metropolitan area has more than 40-million sq ft of retail space, and that staggering number is growing all the time. It has almost reached the point where you can say that if it isn't available in Las Vegas, it simply isn't available. International haute purveyors cater to cashed-up clientele – you can find almost anything (name brand, at least) that you'd see in London or Los Angeles, plus a few unique high-roller items not likely to be sold anytime soon, like Ginger Rogers' 7.02 carat marquis diamond engagement ring and the world's largest carved emerald, both on display in **Fred Leighton** (p174) at the Bellagio.

Although Sin City is famous (perhaps infamous) for many things, it isn't known for any particular souvenir. Rather, it's a place where you can buy almost anything your heart has ever desired – if you have the money. Because so much merchandise is sold almost exclusively to tourists, most merchants can arrange to have your purchase shipped home if you just can't take it with you. Savvy shoppers may want to read the *Consumer* column in the free *Las Vegas Weekly* to score the latest finds. For tax information, see p244.

Shopping Areas

Malls dominate the scene, but the specialty shops are found at the megaresorts. The Strip is the focus of the shopping action, with upscale boutiques concentrated in the newer resorts from the Fashion Show Mall south to Mandalay Place. Downtown and west of the Strip are the places to cruise for wigs, naughty adult goods and trashy lingerie. The resurgent popularity of retro styles has repopularized thrift and vintage stores in the arts and antiques district, just a stone's throw south of downtown. East of the Strip, Maryland Pkwy is chock-a-block with hip shops catering to a university crowd. Outer Neighborhoods are where you'll find outlet shopping, plus a few trendy, one-off boutiques that are worth the trip out to Vegas' burgeoning suburbs.

CLOTHING SIZES

Measurements approximate only, try before you buy

Women's Clothing

Aus/UK	8	10	12	14	16	18
Europe	36	38	40	42	44	46
Japan	5	7	9	11	13	15
USA	6	8	10	12	14	16

Women's Shoes

Aus/USA	5	6	7	8	9	10
Europe	35	36	37	38	39	40
France only	35	36	38	39	40	42
Japan	22	23	24	25	26	27
UK	3½	4½	5½	6½	7½	8½

Men's Clothing

Aus	92	96	100	104	108	112
Europe	46	48	50	52	54	56
Japan	S		M	M		L
UK/USA	35	36	37	38	39	40

Men's Shirts (Collar Sizes)

Aus/Japan	38	39	40	41	42	43
Europe	38	39	40	41	42	43
UK/USA	15	15½	16	16½	17	17½

Men's Shoes

Aus/UK	7	8	9	10	11	12
Europe	41	42	43	44½	46	47
Japan	26	27	27½	28	29	30
USA	7½	8½	9½	10½	11½	12½

Opening Hours

Off-Strip retail shopping hours are 10am to 9pm (to 6pm Sunday). Casino malls and shopping promenades often stay open later, until at least 11pm. Christmas Day is one of the few holidays on which most shops close.

THE STRIP

Practically every megaresort includes some type of shopping mall. Listed here are places that stand out for their superb shops or interesting architectural design. Look for the new Shoppes at the Palazzo retail center to open inside the Venetian's expansion as soon as 2007. Beware that on the Strip, the artwork bearing price tags is typically of pedestrian quality; when it comes to art-world sophistication, Las Vegas still can't compare to Los Angeles or New York.

CENTER STRIP

APPLE STORE Map pp262-3 Computers & Electronics
☎ 702-650-9550; Fashion Show Mall, 3200 Las
Vegas Blvd S; 10am-9pm Mon-Fri, 10am-8pm
Sat, 11am-6pm Sun; bus 301, 302
It's the hub for your non-PC digital lifestyle.
Attend free hands-on demonstrations of
all things 'i.' Query the savvy salespeople
behind the Genius Bar about perplexing
tech issues. Be wowed by the latest computer innovations in the theater. Lust after the
newest shiny iPod.

DESERT PASSAGE Map pp262-3 Shopping Mall
☎ 888-800-8284; www.desertpassage.com;
Planet Hollywood (Aladdin), 3663 Las Vegas Blvd S;
10am-11pm, till midnight Fri & Sat; monorail
Bally's & Paris
Upscale North African–themed marketplace
with 140 retailers and more than a half-
dozen restaurants, plus a rainy harbor and
wandering street performers. The emphasis is on gifts, plus men's and women's
streetwear by Lucky Brand Jeans, French
Connection and other casual designers.
Pedicabs await to roll baggage-laden shoppers along the 1.2 mile length of the shopping arcade; after hours, the wildest drivers
turn into speed devils.

EXOTIC CARS Map pp262-3 Specialty Shop
☎ 702-893-4800; Forum Shops, Caesars Palace,
3500 Las Vegas Blvd S; 10am-11pm, till midnight Fri & Sat; monorail Flamingo/Caesars Palace
Almost more of an attraction than it is a
shop, bilevel Exotic Cars allows you to
peruse Porsche brand apparel, get your
photo taken inside a Ferrari and salivate
over a Rolls Royce lifestyle. Around 50 vehicles are on display at any one time, some
easily worth up to a million dollars. If you
hit a big jackpot, now you know exactly
how to roll home in style.

FAO SCHWARTZ Map pp262-3 Toys & Gifts
☎ 702-796-6500; Forum Shops, Caesars Palace,
3500 Las Vegas Blvd S; 10am-11pm, till midnight Fri & Sat; monorail Flamingo/Caesars Palace
Before you step inside this kiddie paradise
of toys, games and other collectibles, be
sure to look up and pay your respects to
the enormous animatronic Trojan Horse
standing guard outside. Las Vegas–themed
Monopoly board games are sold here.

FASHION SHOW MALL

Map pp262-3 Shopping Mall
☎ 702-369-0704; www.thefashionshow.com; 3200
Las Vegas Blvd S; 10am-9pm Mon-Fri, 10am-
8pm Sat, 11am-6pm Sun; bus 301, 302
The Strip's only mall is also the biggest
and flashiest in Nevada. Bloomingdale's,
Dillard's, Neiman Marcus, Nordstrom, Saks
Fifth Avenue, Robinsons-May and Macy's
department stores anchor the mall, which
boasts 250 mainstream storefronts. Models
hit the runway almost daily and movie
stars shop at Talulah G and Still boutiques.
Moms and kids' stores include designer-
happy Along Came a Spider and Sanrio for
that 'Hello Kitty lifestyle.' The mall recently
received a billion-dollar face-lift as part of
an expansion.

Jewelry and clothes, Via Bellagio (p175)

173

FORUM SHOPS Map pp262-3 Shopping Mall

☎ 702-893-4800; www.shopsimon.com; Caesars Palace, 3500 Las Vegas Blvd S; ☺ 10am-11pm, till midnight Fri & Sat; monorail Flamingo/Caesars Palace

Franklins fly out of Fendi bags faster here at the nation's most profitable consumer playground than in the adjacent high-roller casino. Caesars' fanciful re-creation of an ancient Roman market houses 160 designer shops. Included in the mélange are catwalk wonders like Armani, Versace, Bvlgari and MaxMara, and notable imports like Agent Provocateur lingerie. Don't miss the spiral escalator by the grand Strip entrance.

FRED LEIGHTON Map pp262-3 Jewelry

☎ 702-693-7050; Via Bellagio, Bellagio, 3600 Las Vegas Blvd S; ☺ 10am-midnight; monorail Bally's & Paris

Many Academy Awards night adornments are on loan from the world's most prestigious collection of antique jewelry, notably art deco and nouveau. In Las Vegas, unlike at the uptight NYC outlet, they'll let anyone try on finery that once belonged to royalty. Prices run from about $100 for a tiny but exquisite pin to well over $1 million.

GRAND CANAL SHOPPES

Map pp262-3 Shopping Mall

☎ 702-414-4500; www.venetian.com/shoppe; Venetian, 3355 Las Vegas Blvd S; ☺ 10am-11pm, till midnight Fri & Sat; monorail Harrah's/Imperial Palace

Living statues and jugglers perform in St Mark's Square while gondolas float past (p58) as mezzo-sopranos serenade 80 upscale shops, including unusual specialty purveyors like Horologio, with its antique timepieces, and a few art galleries. Cobblestone walkways pass by Ann Taylor, BCBG, Banana Republic, Godiva, Kenneth Cole and Jimmy Choo. The mall opens its doors to the public at 7am.

GUGGENHEIM HERMITAGE STORE

Map pp262-3 Art & Gifts

☎ 702-414-2490; Venetian, 3355 Las Vegas Blvd S; ☺ 9am-9pm; monorail Harrah's/Imperial Palace

The museum gift shop stocks items with themes tied to the current exhibition at the art gallery (p58). Perhaps it's a discerning spot to find an aesthetically pleasing souvenir, yet the selection can be disappointingly small.

IMPERIAL PALACE AUTO COLLECTION Map pp262-3 Specialty Shop

☎ 702-794-3174; www.autocollections.com; 5th fl, Imperial Palace, 3535 Las Vegas Blvd S; adult/senior & child 3-12 $7/3; ☺ 9:30am-9:30pm; monorail Harrah's Imperial Palace

Car buffs could easily pass an hour viewing one of the world's largest privately owned auto collections. Among the wonderful vehicles on hand (all of which are for sale – sorry, no test drives) are more Rolls-Royces than you can toss a chauffeur at. Free admission coupons are widely available in the free tourist glossies or you can print one out from the website.

LE BOULEVARD Map pp262-3 Casino Arcade

☎ 702-946-7000; Paris, 3655 Las Vegas Blvd S; ☺ most shops 10am-11pm Sun-Thu, till midnight Fri & Sat; monorail Bally's & Paris

Bally's and Paris are connected via this chichi cobblestone replica of the Rue de la Paix. The winding promenade features French restaurants, lounges and boutiques. Highlights include fashion-forward Lunettes eyewear, Les Enfants for French children's fashions, La Vogue designer lingerie, Clio Blue jewelry, Presse newsstand, Cigars du Monde and La Cave's gourmet French nibbles and wine.

METROPOLITAN MUSEUM OF ART STORE Map pp262-3 Art & Gifts

☎ 702-691-2506; www.metmuseum.org/store; Desert Passage, 3663 Las Vegas Blvd S; ☺ 10am-11pm Sun-Thu, 10am-midnight Fri & Sat; monorail Bally's & Paris

NYC's savvy Met is known for its reproductions and singular gift items selected by expert curators, art historians, craftspeople and designers. Sales of books, scarves, stationery, prints and jewelry support the museum's educational mission and encyclopedic collections.

SONY STYLE

Map pp262-3 Computers & Electronics

☎ 702-697-5420; Forum Shops, Caesars Palace, 3500 Las Vegas Blvd S; ☺ 10am-11pm Sun-Thu, 10am-midnight Fri & Sat; monorail Flamingo/Caesars Palace

Highly conceptual and designed for savvy technogeeks, the Sony store is a candyland if you love nothing better than holding a new piece of innovative high-tech visual, audio or computer gear in your hot little hands. Demos are free.

STREET OF SHOPS Map pp262-3 Casino Arcade
☎ 702-791-7111; Mirage, 3400 Las Vegas Blvd S; ☺ most shops 9am-midnight; tram to TI (Treasure Island)

Splashing out on fancy feminine duds is all the rage at Actique, d.fine, La Perla and DKNY boutique and shoe salon. Leave the poodle at home, bring your movie-star shades and never lose track of time again with a signature Cartier timepiece from the Watch Boutique.

TI (TREASURE ISLAND) SHOPS
Map pp262-3 Casino Shops
☎ 702-894-7111; TI (Treasure Island), 3300 Las Vegas Blvd S; ☺ 10am-11pm; tram to Mirage

The small stable of fashion-conscious gift shops and boutiques carry Calvin Klein apparel, Cirque du Soleil merchandise and Sirens of TI–style clothing and lingerie, in case you or someone you love was actually titillated by the Sirens of TI (p58).

VIA BELLAGIO Map pp262-3 Casino Arcade
☎ 702-693-7111; Bellagio, 3600 Las Vegas Blvd S; ☺ most shops 10am-midnight; monorail Bally's & Paris

Bellagio's swish indoor promenade is home to the who's who of fashion-plate designers: Armani, Chanel, Dior, Gucci, Hermés, Prada, Tiffany & Co and Yves Saint Laurent – and, lest we forget, Fred Leighton (opposite). It also houses The Intimate Collection, vending La Perla and other tip-top lingerie, plus the Bellagio's own line of signature fragrances.

WYNN ESPLANADE
Map pp262-3 Casino Arcade
☎ 702-770-7000; 3131 Las Vegas Blvd S; ☺ 10am-11pm Sun-Thu, 10am-midnight Fri & Sat; bus 301, 302

Wynn has lured high-end retailers such as Oscar de la Renta, Jean-Paul Gaultier, Chanel, Cartier and Manolo Blahnik to this naturally lit concourse, which also boasts an art gallery (p59). In the process, he's created 75,000 sq ft of consumer bliss. Elsewhere in the resort are specialty shops like La Flirt beauty shop and Gizmos tech toys for adults. After you hit the jackpot, take a test drive at Wynn's Ferarri-Maserati dealership.

TOP FIVE CASINOS FOR SHOPPING ON THE STRIP
- Forum Shops (Caesars Palace; opposite)
- Grand Canal Shoppes (Venetian; opposite)
- Mandalay Place (Mandalay Bay; p176)
- Via Bellagio (Bellagio; left)
- Wynn Esplanade (Wynn; left)

SOUTH STRIP
55° WINE + DESIGN
Map pp262-3 Wine & Gifts
☎ 702-632-9355; www.55degreeslasvegas.com; Mandalay Place, 3930 Las Vegas Blvd S; ☺ 10am-11pm Sun-Thu, 10am-midnight Fri & Sat; tram to Mandalay Bay or Luxor

A wine shop extraordinaire, brought to you by the director of the four-story wine tower at Aureole (p115). Bottles out front are stacked in white mod fiberglass pods above handmade glassware and accessories. Knowledgeable staff handle the wine-tasting bar out back by the refrigerated wine cellar that stocks 2000 truly international wines. Prices are high, but every bottle gets its own pillowed bag for safe take-out.

HARLEY-DAVIDSON CAFE
Map pp262-3 Logo Shop
☎ 702-740-4555; http://www.harley-davidsoncafe.com; 3725 Las Vegas Blvd S; ☺ 11am-midnight; monorail Bally's & Paris

A shrine to all things Harley. A conveyor belt carries a dozen 'hogs' overhead in the café, where the walls are covered with photos of racers and celebrities. The official Harley-Davidson store carries a big selection of motorcycle and bomber jackets, collectors' pins, chrome shot glasses and scary belt buckles. Other Harley-Davidson shops are west of the Strip (Map p264; ☎ 702-252-5130; Rio, 3700 W Flamingo Rd; free Strip shuttle) and downtown (Map p261; ☎ 702-383-1010; 328 E Fremont St; bus 301, 302).

HOUDINI'S MAGIC SHOP
Map pp262-3 Toys & Gifts
☎ 702-740-6969, 877-346-4946; www.houdini.com; New York–New York, 3790 Las Vegas Blvd S; ☺ 9am-midnight; monorail MGM Grand

The legacy of this legendary escape artist lives on at this shop packed with gags,

Shopping

THE STRIP

pranks, magic tricks and 'zines. Magicians perform for wide-eyed crowds and each purchase includes a free private lesson. There are other Houdini's branches on the Strip – including the one at the Venetian's Grand Canal Shoppes (Map pp262–3) that displays authentic memorabilia – but the energetic staff here at New York–New York make the magic come alive.

M&M'S WORLD Map pp262-3 · Logo Shop
☎ 702-736-7611; Showcase Mall, 3785 Las Vegas Blvd S; ⏰ 9am-11pm Sun-Thu, till midnight Fri & Sat; monorail MGM Grand

Dedicated to the famous candy, M&M's World sells a rainbow of colors not available elsewhere, along with truckloads of one-of-a-kind souvenirs. On the 3rd floor, visitors are ushered into a theater to watch a short, complimentary 3-D movie.

MANDALAY PLACE
Map pp262-3 · Shopping Mall
☎ 702-632-7777; Mandalay Bay, 3930 Las Vegas Blvd S; ⏰ 10am-11pm Sun-Thu, 10am-midnight Fri & Sat; tram to Mandalay Bay or Luxor

M-Bay's airy commercial promenade, poised on the skybridge between Mandalay Bay and Luxor, houses a few dozen unique and upscale boutiques like Samantha Chang, GF Ferre, Nike Golf, Mulholland leather, Sauvage

swimwear, Max & Co, Urban Outfitters and Oilily for European children's clothing.

READING ROOM Map pp262-3 · Books & Gifts
☎ 702-632-9374; Mandalay Place, 3930 Las Vegas Blvd S; ⏰ 8am-11pm Sun-Thu, 8am-midnight Fri & Sat; tram to Mandalay Bay or Luxor

The love child of an Iowa Writers Workshop graduate, Vegas' newest indie bookshop is also its best. Bookworms will be entranced by the thoughtfully chosen selection of local-interest titles, as well as the fine collectible and rare editions in glass-fronted cases. Author readings and book signings occasionally take place. Regional guidebooks and maps are sold.

STUDIO WALK & STAR LANE SHOPS
Map pp262-3 · Casino Arcade
☎ 702-891-1111; MGM Grand, 3799 Las Vegas Blvd S; ⏰ most shops 10am-10:30 or 11pm; monorail MGM Grand

What to give the wannabe starlet who has everything? The Hollywood-themed shops at Star Lane, just off the grand hotel lobby, may hold the answer; designer luggage, costume jewelry and logo items are in the mix. On the short but fashionable Studio Walk concourse, you can drop by CBS Television City (p63) or shop for jewelry, luggage and apparel (especially for men).

BEST VEGAS SOUVENIRS

If all you really want is a T-shirt, a snow dome or a coffee mug announcing that you've been to 'Fabulous Las Vegas,' they're everywhere you turn. But if you're looking for something a tad more unusual, read on.

If you fancy shoving coins into a slot machine, consider buying one. New and reconditioned vintage electronic slot and video poker machines generally sell for $600 to $1000, though prices can climb much higher. Head for the Gamblers General Store (p178) or Showcase Slots (p182). Before you buy, ask if owning a one-armed bandit is legal in your home state or country.

Peruse the vintage collections of gaming chips, decks of cards, ashtrays and other casino memorabilia at downtown's Lost Vegas Historic Gambling Museum Store (p178). Be aware that rare beauties from legendary casinos of the past, such as the Sands, go for sky-high prices.

Every casino on the Strip has gift shops chockful of themed souvenirs, and some carry their own logo product lines. The Flamingo, for example, sells lots of doodads with flamingos on them (duh). Excalibur vends wizard sculptures and all things medieval. At Luxor you'll find Egyptian handicrafts. Ad infinitum.

It's kitschy, clichéd and unclassy as hell, but how can you go home without a souvenir drink glass? Maybe one shaped like the Eiffel Tower from Paris–Las Vegas, a sphinx from Luxor, a Stratosphere tower with a roller coaster–shaped straw or an almost tiki-style showgirl ceramic mug from Bally's.

In a town with as many strip clubs as gas stations, it should come as little surprise that the adult apparel business is ba-bah-booming. All those hard-working beefy guys and sultry women obviously don't have time to make their own G-strings and tasseled undies. Besides specialty shops reviewed in this chapter, there are also full-service lingerie shops inside some strip clubs (p154).

Bonanza Gifts (below)

EVERYTHING COCA-COLA

Map pp262-3   Logo Shop
☎ 702-597-3122; Showcase Mall, 3785 Las Vegas Blvd S; ☾ 10am-11pm; monorail MGM Grand
Nope, you can't miss that giant Coca-Cola bottle standing right on the Strip, can you? Inside, modern reproductions of nostalgic Coke memorabilia and more stuff are for sale. Upstairs the soda fountain has old-fashioned appeal.

NORTH STRIP

BONANZA GIFTS

Map pp262-3   Souvenirs & Gifts
☎ 702-385-7359; www.worldslargestgiftshop.com; 2440 Las Vegas Blvd S; ☾ 8am-midnight; monorail Sahara
If it's not 'the World's Largest Gift Shop,' it's damn close. Technically speaking, it's a series of interconnecting gift shops totaling 40,000 sq ft. The kitschy selection of only-in-Vegas souvenirs includes entire aisles of dice clocks, sassy slogan T-shirts, shot glasses and XXX gags. But beware, prices are higher than at B-list casino souvenir shops or downtown's Fremont St.

NASCAR CAFE Map pp262-3   Logo Shop
☎ 702-737-2897; 2535 Las Vegas Blvd S;
☾ 10am-9pm; monorail Sahara
A mecca for race-car fans, this signature shop sells racing collectibles, leather jackets, even ladies' wear. During race week events,
get your Nascar loot autographed by a real live driver during special appearances. The shop is next to the **Carzilla bar** (p77).

WELCOME TO FABULOUS LAS VEGAS STORE Map pp262-3   Souvenirs & Gifts
☎ 702-733-0013; 3055 Las Vegas Blvd S; ☾ 9am-11pm Sun-Thu, 9am-midnight Fri & Sat; bus 301, 302
The North Strip is almost as much of a gold mine for kitschy souvenirs as Fremont St downtown. This shop capitalizes on the newfound popularity of its namesake sign (p62). If you can't find the tourist crap you're anxious to buy, check at **Slots A' Fun** (p78) or the shops inside **Stardust** (p78).

DOWNTOWN

Shopping in the Fremont Street Experience, a pedestrian zone stretching from Main St east to the Neonopolis, is defined by kitschy souvenirs at unbeatably low prices, including at the Hawaii-born **ABC Store** (Map p261; ☎ 702-380-3098; 23 Fremont St; ☾ 7:30am-1am; bus 301, 302). In the arts district south of downtown and elsewhere around the Naked City, you'll need your own car or bus navigation skills and serious street smarts, as some blocks can be quite menacing to solo pedestrians.

A SLIGHTLY SINFUL ADVENTURE

Map p261   Clothing
☎ 702-387-1006; 1232 Las Vegas Blvd S;
☾ 10am-10pm Sun-Thu, 10am-midnight Fri & Sat; bus 301, 302
Many of the really mischievous outfits here are layered: think tiny outer garments followed by microscopic undergarments. For voyeurs, admiring the goods in the presence of the professional entertainer clientele can make a visit worth the effort.

ANTIQUES DISTRICT

Map p261   Art & Antiques
Colorado Ave, btwn Main & 3rd Sts; ☾ most shops 10am-5pm; bus 108, 207, 301
Antiques in Las Vegas? Yes indeed and lots of them, including retro objects from a rainbow of 20th-century decades and an infinite number of offbeat items that could easily fit in a suitcase. There's a dizzying array of unusual older furniture, some pieces are unique castoffs from casino

Shopping   DOWNTOWN

hotels. As the saying goes, one person's trash is another person's treasure. Helter-skelter shops include the **Funk House** (☎ 702-678-6278; 1228 S Casino Center Blvd) and shabby-chic **Gypsy Caravan Antique Village** (☎ 702-868-3302; 1302 S 3rd St).

ATTIC Map p261
Clothing

☎ 702-388-4088; www.atticvintage.com; 1018 S Main St; 🕑 9am-5pm Mon-Sat; bus 108, 206
A $1 'lifetime pass' (going toward your first purchase) is required to enter this fantastic retro emporium once featured in a Visa commercial. It's worth it, even if you don't buy. The first floor is mostly furnishings and hippie-chic clubwear. Upstairs is a 1960s and '70s stronghold, with a smaller selection from the '50s and before, plus a cool coffee bar for Greek grub.

D'LOE HOUSE OF STYLE
Map p261
Clothing

☎ 702-382-5688; 220 E Charleston Blvd; 🕑 11:30am-6pm Mon-Fri, by appt only Sun; bus 105, 206
You know it's fabulous from the instant you catch sight of its hot-pink and blue exterior. It's owned by Cirque du Soleil costume designer Mario D'Loe, who hoards unique fashions from the pre-WWII era to the 1970s, including evening wear, bejeweled accessories and more casual items.

GAMBLER'S BOOK SHOP
Map p261
Books

☎ 702-382-7555, 800-522-1777; www.gamblersbook.com; 630 S 11th St; 🕑 9am-5pm Mon-Sat; bus 109, 206
Longtime owner Edna Luckman (no joke) stocks just about every book ever written on gambling and Las Vegas. The amiable older gentlemen who staff the store dispense valuable edge-beating advice, though they're a bit suspicious of female customers, asking us once, 'So, you ladies are either librarians or FBI agents, right?'.

TOP FIVE ADULTS-ONLY SHOPS

- A Slightly Sinful Adventure (p177)
- Adult Superstore (p181)
- Bare Essentials (p181)
- Paradise Electro Stimulations (p182)
- Strings by Judith (p182)

GAMBLERS GENERAL STORE
Map p261
Souvenirs & Gifts

☎ 702-382-9903; www.gamblersgeneralstore.com; 800 S Main St; 🕑 9am-5pm; bus 105, 108, 207
Even if you're not the slightest bit tempted to buy a gaming device, take a look inside. This superstore has one of the largest inventories of slot machines in Nevada, with new models and beautiful vintage machines. Also available are roulette, craps and blackjack tables identical to those in casinos, and loads of gambling parapher-nalia such as coin changers, dice, custom-ized poker chips, handheld casino games, collectible decks of cards, automatic card shufflers and fuzzy dice.

LAS VEGAS PREMIUM OUTLETS
Map p261
Shopping Mall

☎ 702-474-7500; www.premiumoutlets.com; 875 S Grand Central Pkwy; 🕑 10am-9pm Mon-Sat, 10am-8pm Sun; bus 106, 108
The biggest ticket outlet mall in Vegas features 120 mostly high-end names like Armani Exchange, Calvin Klein, Dolce & Gabbana, Guess, Kenneth Cole and Ralph Lauren, alongside casual brands like Levi's. The **CAT** (☎ 702-228-7433, 800-228-3911; www.catride.com) Downtown Shoppers Express bus serves the mall every 20 minutes from 10am until 5pm.

LOST VEGAS HISTORIC GAMBLING MUSEUM STORE Map p261
Souvenirs & Gifts

☎ 702-385-1883; www.neonopolis.com; Neonopolis, 450 E Fremont St; 🕑 10am-8:45pm; bus 301, 302
Downtown at the **Neonopolis** (p84), this claustrophobic museum sells real pieces of Sin City's checkered past, from antique slot machines to vintage poker chips, match-books and photographs and the usual assorted kitsch.

MODIFY Map p261
Art & Antiques

☎ 702-384-6555; 8 E Charleston Blvd; 🕑 call for hrs; bus 108, 206
Step inside a time machine and journey back to when modern meant new instead of retro. This store, which mostly stocks used furniture, is like a museum of the mid-20th century, with owner-designed and handcrafted accessories like throw pillows that would be oh so stylish on the plane ride home.

Shopping

DOWNTOWN

NEW ROCK Map p261   Shoes
☎ 702-614-9464; www.newrockstore.com; 804 Las Vegas Blvd S; ☽ 11am-7:30pm Mon-Sat; bus 206, 301, 302
Tough guys and grrrls go for the almost all-black footwear here. Boots are equally suitable for anime heroes, motorcycle gangs, fetish clubs or the bridge of a sci-fi starship. Be prepared to plop down a couple of Benjamins if you want to stalk like a Goth in a hard-heeled pair of your own.

RAINBOW FEATHERS
Map p261   Specialty Shop
☎ 702-598-0988; www.rainbowfeatherco.com; 1036 S Main St; ☽ 8am-4pm Mon-Fri, 8am-noon Sat; bus 108, 206
Need turkey, chicken, duck, goose, pheasant, ostrich or peacock quills? Rainbow stocks a positively fabulous selection of fine feathers and fans for showgirl costumes in every possible shade. Feather boas (from $5) hang on racks by the front windows.

RED ROOSTER ANTIQUE MALL
Map p261   Art & Antiques
☎ 702-382-5253; 1109 Western Ave; ☽ 10am-6pm Mon-Sat, 11-5pm Sun; bus 108, 206
A one-stop antique-shopping extravaganza, where the vintage tiki wares draw shoppers from all over. Keep a sharp eye out for art-deco estate jewelry and Rat Pack–era memorabilia. It's tricky to get here by car: take Wyoming Ave west across the railroad tracks, turn right on to Western Ave and drive north until the street dead-ends.

TOYS OF YESTERYEAR
Map p261   Antiques & Toys
☎ 702-598-4030; 2028 E Charleston Blvd; ☽ 11am-4:30pm Mon-Sat; bus 110, 206, 715, 908
A fun little place specializing in toys of the not-so-distant past. The inventory is constantly changing but generally includes several lovely old train sets, carnival dolls and wind-up toys. In the same small strip mall, savvy antique hounds can also ferret out secondhand books, clothing and furniture.

VALENTINO'S ZOOTSUIT CONNECTION Map p261   Clothing
☎ 702-383-9555; 906 S 6th St; ☽ 11am-5pm Mon-Sat; bus 206, 301, 302
A sweet (and stylish!) husband-and-wife team outfits party-goers with upscale vintage apparel: fringed Western wear, felt hats, tie pins, snappy shoes and custom dresses. Rentals and custom swinging zootsuits are a speciality.

WILLIAMS COSTUME COMPANY
Map p261   Specialty Shop
☎ 702-384-1384; 1226 S 3rd St; ☽ 10am-5:30pm Mon-Sat; bus 105
Friendly staff have supplied the Strip's starlets with DIY costuming goods since 1957. Check out the headshots in the dressing rooms, then pick up some rhinestones, sequins, feathers, etc – you go, girl. Costume rentals available.

UNLV & EAST OF THE STRIP

Left your shopping till the last minute? **McCarran International Airport** (p233) has an eclectic collection of shops, including casino-hotel logo vendors; Las Vegas Gaming Supply, for handheld casino games, casino chips and full-sized slot machines; Area 51, a sci fi–themed collectibles store; the I Can't Believe It's Made in Nevada emporium; and multiple newsstands and book- and music sellers.

ALBION BOOKS Map p265   Books
☎ 702-792-9554; 2466 E Desert Inn Rd; ☽ 10am-6pm; bus 112
Though secondhand bookshops are as rare as million-dollar slot payoffs in Sin City, this fine establishment is worthy of collectors. Even if you have of a more pop culture bent or are shopping for young readers, you'll find plenty to keep your brains fed here, too.

ALTERNATE REALITY COMICS

Map p265   Books & Gifts

☎ 702-736-3673; 4800 S Maryland Pkwy;
⊙ 11am-7pm Mon-Sat, noon-6pm Sun; bus 109

An unbelievably cool comics shop for adults, with shelves artistically displaying the hippest graphic novels from *Stuck Rubber Baby* to Japanese *manga* to collectible editions such as *In the Shadow of No Towers*. Special artist events and signings occasionally happen here. It's in the same Strip mall as a tattoo parlor and Balcony Lights, a vinyl record shop.

BIG B'S Map p265   Music

☎ 702-732-4433; 4761 S Maryland Pkwy;
⊙ 10am-9:30pm Mon-Sat, 11am-7:30pm Sun; bus 109

A small indie record store where the friendly clerks don't effect that *High Fidelity* snobbery. Anyone from an off-shift showgirl to a UNLV football player might be found rummaging through the rare vinyl bins, which embrace rock, jazz and blues.

BUFFALO EXCHANGE Map p265   Clothing

☎ 702-791-3960; 4110 S Maryland Pkwy;
⊙ 10am-8pm Mon-Sat, 11am-7pm Sun; bus 109, 202, 213, 807

Trade in your nearly new garb for cash or credit at this hip secondhand chain that runs comfortably closer to the mainstream. They've combed through the dingy thrift-store stuff and culled only top-notch '40s to '70s vintage fashions, clubwear, streetwear and designer duds. It's a real bargain, too.

TOP FIVE VINTAGE SHOPS

- Attic (p178)
- Buffalo Exchange (left)
- D'Loe House of Style (p178)
- Lost Vegas Historic Gambling Museum Store (p178)
- Valentino's Zootsuit Connection (p179)

COWTOWN BOOTS

Map p265   Clothing & Shoes

☎ 702-737-8469; www.cowtownboots.com; 2989 Paradise Rd; ⊙ 10am-7pm Mon-Sat, 10am-5pm Sun; bus 108

It's a Western-wear wonderland to steer your horse toward, especially for a pair of ostrich, crocodile, rattlesnake, eel or even more exotic skinned boots. An expertly crafted and hand-trimmed pair is easily worth the $100 or more you'll pay, and they've got thousands in stock. Don't forget a cowboy shirt and a big silver belt buckle either, pardner.

DEEP SPACE NINE PROMENADE

Map p265   Casino Arcade

☎ 888-697-8735; www.startrekexp.com; Las Vegas Hilton, 3000 Paradise Rd; ⊙ 11am-11pm; monorail Las Vegas Hilton

It's no accident that the **Star Trek: The Experience** (p87) exit puts visitors on the Deep Space Nine Promenade, where Trekkers may think they've died and gone to Sto-vo-kor. Authentic TV and movie props, stuffed tribbles, Klingon ale and autographed col-

FAO Schwartz (p173)

lectibles found nowhere else in the Alpha or even Delta quadrants cost from just a few Earth dollars up to several hundred bars of gold-pressed latinum.

GUN STORE Map p265 — Specialty Shop
☎ 702-454-1110; www.thegunstorelasvegas.com; 2900 E Tropicana Ave; ⏲ 9am-6:30pm; bus 201, 711
Gun enthusiasts can fire off an M16 or AK47 submachine gun at this high-powered indoor shooting range for just $25. If you want to feel the heft of a Beretta, Colt or Glock in your hand, it'll cost $10 per handgun rental, plus a $5 range fee; ammo is extra. The shop also offers security and safety classes, not to mention a wide range of firearms for sale.

HARD ROCK Map p265 — Casino Arcade
☎ 702-693-5000; Hard Rock, 4455 Paradise Rd; ⏲ most shops 10am-11pm Sun-Thu, 10am-2am Fri & Sat; free Strip shuttle
The casino gift shop has lots of limited-edition rock 'n roll collectibles and spiffy stuff with the hotel's logo, but why stop there? Other top-notch consumer heavens are Love Jones for imported lingerie; the cigar humidor at Cuba Libre, with a bar serving specialty martinis, vintage scotch and cognac; and Rocks, a 24-hour jewelry store, so you can pick up that diamond watch right after your big win at poker.

RECORD CITY Map p265 — Music
☎ 702-735-1126; 300 E Sahara Ave; ⏲ 10am-5pm Mon-Sat, noon-5pm Sun; bus 108
Old-skool DJs love this local chain because it's got the best selection of used vinyl in town. There are multiple locations, each with its own 'licious flavor, including this one just a couple blocks east of the Strip.

SERGE'S SHOWGIRL WIGS
Map p265 — Specialty Shop
☎ 702-732-1015, 800-947-9447; Commercial Center, 953 E Sahara Ave; ⏲ 10am-5:30pm Mon-Sat; bus 204
Definitely one of America's largest wig showrooms, Serge's has been around for decades. The staff of stylists readily help Vegas showgirls, drag queens and even little ol' you find the glamour girl inside. As you enter the strip mall, it's immediately on the right.

THE JEWELER Map p265 — Jewelry
☎ 702-893-9979; Las Vegas Hilton, 3000 Paradise Rd; ⏲ 24hr; monorail Las Vegas Hilton
Nevada's largest discount jewelry chain stocks a selection of rings and necklaces. To accommodate that 3am urge for a solid-gold chain, the Hilton's branch stays open around the clock. There's another branch on the Center Strip (Map pp262–3; ☎ 702-731-3700; Flamingo, 3255 Las Vegas Blvd S; ⏲ 9am-12:30am; monorail Flamingo/ Caesars Palace).

WEST OF THE STRIP
The vast grid of interlocking streets west of I-15 are only if you're sure you know what you're looking for – you'll find some of Vegas' most unusual specialty shops here.

ADULT SUPERSTORE Map p264 — Toys & Gifts
☎ 702-798-0144; 3850 W Tropicana Ave; ⏲ 24hr; bus 201, 804
Popular with couples, this enormous, well-lit porn warehouse is a sexual candyland of toys, books, magazines, videos, less-than-tasteful 'marital enhancement products' and titillating accessories. Guys flying solo gravitate toward the XXX arcade upstairs.

BARE ESSENTIALS Map p264 — Clothing
☎ 702-247-4711; 4029 W Sahara Ave; ⏲ 10am-7pm Mon-Sat, noon-5pm Sun; bus 204
Pros swear by BE for its workaday attire. It's heavy on theme wear – lots of cheerleader and schoolgirl outfits. Slip down to nearby Bad Attitude Boutique (Map p264; ☎ 702-646-9669; www.badattitude.com; 4011 W Sahara Ave; ⏲ noon-7pm Mon-Sat), for custom-made corsets, goth fetish wear or burlesque fashions. Red Shoes (Map p264; ☎ 702-889-4442; 4011 W Sahara Ave; ⏲ 10:30am-8pm Mon-Sat, noon-7pm Sun) stocks knee-high boots and glittery platform shoes. To find this strip mall, look for the miniature Statue of Liberty standing just to the west.

FIELD OF DREAMS Map p264 — Specialty Shop
☎ 702-221-9144; www.fieldofdreams.com; Masquerade Village, Rio, 3700 W Flamingo Rd; ⏲ 11am-midnight Tue-Fri, 10am-midnight Sat-Mon; free Strip shuttle
There's really only one name in sports and celebrity memorabilia in Las Vegas, and

it deserves a look whether you're buying or not. Among the items that have been sold here are a thank-you note signed by JFK, a poster of the Beatles autographed by all four band members and a basketball signed by Michael Jordan. There's another branch inside Caesars' **Forum Shops** (p174).

MASQUERADE VILLAGE

Map p264   Casino Arcade

☎ 702-252-7777; Rio, 3700 W Flamingo Rd; ☽ 10am-11pm; free Strip shuttle
Stroll replica 200-year-old Tuscan-tiled streets past midrange retailers like La Valize (luggage, handbags and accessories), Fortune Cookie (Asian-inspired gifts), Elegant Pretenders (faux jewelry), Roland's (evening and bridal wear) and tie-dyed HippyChic.

PARADISE ELECTRO STIMULATIONS

Map p264   Specialty Shop

☎ 702-474-2991, 800-339-6953; www.peselectro.com; 1509 W Oakey Blvd; ☽ 9am-5:30pm Mon-Fri; bus 105
This self-proclaimed Tiffany's of fetish boutiques is tucked discreetly away on the wrong side of the tracks. Its sworn mission is to 'bring human sexuality into the 21st century.' This gallery is the exotic dungeon-esque setting for owner Dante Amore's legendary $4000 auto-erotic chair, which you must see (and feel) to believe.

SHOWCASE SLOTS

Map p264   Souvenirs & Antiques

☎ 702-740-5722, 888-522-7568; www.showcaseslots.com; 4305 S Industrial Rd; ☽ 9am-5pm Mon-Sat; bus 202
Save your spare quarters in your own stylish piggy bank by buying an antique or modern 'one-armed bandit' or video poker machine. Nostalgic game-room antiques such as Wurlitzer jukeboxes and retro candy machines are also sold. Fun!

STRINGS BY JUDITH Map p264   Clothing

☎ 702-873-7820; 4970 Arville St; ☽ 10am-9pm; bus 104, 201, 804
This industrial strip-mall warehouse stocks adult and fetish fashions. It dresses go-go dancers from head to toe with jewelry, platform shoes, the shortest skirts you have ever seen and, yes, of course, G-strings.

TOWER RECORDS Map p264   Music

☎ 702-364-2500; Wow! Superstore, 4580 W Sahara Ave; ☽ 10am-midnight; bus 204, 805
Indie record stores come and go so fast in the Las Vegas scene that you may have to retreat to this chain megastore with its collection of 100,000 CDs and almost as many DVDs, magazines and books combined. Call ahead for schedules of in-store events like shows by live bands and celebrity signings.

WINE CELLAR Map p264   Wine & Gifts

☎ 702-777-7614; Masquerade Village, Rio, 3700 W Flamingo Rd; ☽ 3-11pm Mon-Thu, till midnight Fri, noon-midnight Sat & Sun; free Strip shuttle
Rio's classy subterranean tasting room stocks 50,000 bottles, worth more than $10 million, from the world's top wine-producing regions. The cellar's $2-million Chateau d'Yquem vertical collection, with bottles from every vintage produced between 1855 and 1990, is museum-worthy. More than 100 wines are poured by the glass, with wine-tasting flights, international cheeses and exotic chocolates rounding out the impressive if unevenly priced collection.

OUTER NEIGHBORHOODS

What's the next big thing? Maybe the $350-million gargantuan Town Square complex on Las Vegas Blvd S at Sunset Rd, which is set to open in 2006.

ANTIQUES AT THE MARKET

Map p260   Art & Antiques

☎ 702-307-3960; 6665 S Eastern Ave; ☽ 10am-7pm Mon-Sat, noon-5pm Sun; bus 110
Where have all the antique dealers gone? The answer: southeast of the airport. Dozens upon dozens of vendors have set up shop inside the 24,000 sq ft of warehouse space here, dealing in anything from high-

---

TOP FIVE SPECIALTY SHOPS

- **55° Wine + Design** (p175)
- **Bass Pro Shops Outdoor World** (opposite)
- **Field of Dreams** (p181)
- **Gun Store** (p181)
- **Houdini's Magic Shop** (p175)

end European furnishings you could never take home with you to emporiums of kitsch collectibles and costume jewelry.

BASS PRO SHOPS OUTDOOR WORLD

Map p260 — Specialty Shop

☎ 702-730-5200; Silverton, 3333 Blue Diamond Rd; ☽ 9am-10pm Mon-Sat, 10am-7pm Sun; bus 117

Attached to the Silverton casino resort (p203), this paradise for fishers, hunters and campers stakes a claim on more than 165,000 sq ft spread over two levels, with a 32ft-high climbing wall, archery and pistol ranges, a 40,000-gallon aquarium and a meandering in-store stream stocked with native Nevadan species. Eye the historical prints and handcrafted wildlife chandeliers, too, at this hillbilly superstore.

BELLIES AND BLOSSOMS

Map p260 — Clothing

☎ 702-255-1100; suite 115, Siena Promenade, 10271 S Eastern Ave, Henderson; ☽ 10am-6pm Mon-Sat, noon-3pm Sun; bus 110

A fabulous shop for moms-to-be. Inside, you certainly won't find your own mother's maternity wear. Hip mamas come here for playful tees, but also for designer dresses, pants, swimsuits and active wear, plus stylin' diaper bags and skin-care products.

DISTRICT Map p260 — Shopping Mall

☎ 702-564-8595, 877-564-8595; www.thedistrictat gvr.com; Green Valley Ranch, 2220 Village Walk Dr, Henderson, off I-215 exit Green Valley Pkwy; ☽ 10am-9pm Mon-Sat, 11am-6pm Sun; bus 111, 114

An off-Strip locals' magnet, the open-air District often sponsors free live music, especially on weekend evenings. It has a variety of shops, such as Anthropologie, Ann Taylor Loft, Pottery Barn, Sharper Image and REI, the premier West Coast retailer of indoor and outdoor activity equipment.

FASHION OUTLETS OF LAS VEGAS

Shopping Mall

☎ 702-874-1400, 888-424-6898; www.fashionout letlasvegas.com; 32100 Las Vegas Blvd S, off I-15 exit 1, Primm; ☽ 10am-8pm, holiday hrs vary; shopper shuttle (one-way/round-trip fare $7/13) from MGM Grand & Desert Passage

About a 45-minute drive southwest of Vegas, this outlet mall is in Primm at the California state line. There's a good mix of more than a hundred high-end (Coach, Escada, Versace, Neiman Marcus, Last Call) and everyday (Banana Republic, Guess, Sketchers) brands. Discount coupons for the Strip shuttle are available online; call the toll-free number for reservations. See p228.

FRY'S ELECTRONICS

Map p260 — Computer & Electronics

☎ 702-932-1400; 6845 Las Vegas Blvd S, cnr I-215; ☽ 8am-9pm Mon-Fri, 9am-9pm Sat, 9am-7pm Sun; bus 105, 301

A mecca for geeks and computer nerds from around the world, this Silicon Valley export has any piece of high- or low-tech gadgetry you need, whether it's an adapter for your hair drier or a new operating system for your laptop, plus new DVDs.

LAS VEGAS OUTLET CENTER

Map p260 — Shopping Mall

☎ 702-896-5599; www.premiumoutlets.com; 7400 Las Vegas Blvd S; ☽ 10am-9pm Mon-Sat, 10am-8pm Sun; bus 117, 303

One of America's largest factory-outlet malls, a short drive south of Mandalay Bay, the Outlet Center boasts more than 130 shops, including clothing (Billabong, Levi's, Tommy Hilfiger) and shoes (Reebok, Sketchers, Vans), and, for the kiddies, there's a full-sized carousel.

Grand Canal Shoppes (p174)

MUSETTE Map p260   Clothing
☎ 702-309-6873; Village Square Shopping Center,
9420 W Sahara Ave; ☽ 10am-7pm Mon-Fri, 10am-
8pm Sat, 11am-6pm Sun; bus 204, 213
Sexy and sophisticated, this boutique
looks as if it were airlifted out of Los
Angeles, except that it has more of a
Southwestern flair. Come here for denim-
friendly fashionista threads of labels from
Juicy Couture to Dolce & Gabbana, and
for designers from California and beyond
whom you may not have heard of yet, but
will. The staff do their best to make you
feel like a princess.

ZIA RECORD EXCHANGE Map p260   Music
☎ 702-735-4942; 4225 S Eastern Ave; ☽ call for
hrs; bus 202, 807
Calling itself the 'last real record store'
(though Californian devotees of Amoeba
Music may disagree), this Arizona indie
records chain has opened a Vegas megastore that sells new and used vinyls, CDs
and more.

Sleeping

Sleeping

Vegas hits the jackpot, with a grand total of over 130,000 guest rooms. If a bankroll isn't burning a hole in your pocket, a little luxury here can be had more cheaply than almost anywhere else in the world. Of course, an exquisite penthouse villa overlooking the Strip with perks like 24-hour butler service costs $10,000 per night. However, even in most megaresorts' standard rooms you'll find luxurious bathrooms with marble tubs, high-tech bells and whistles, and attention lavished on detail. Impeccable service 24/7, a concierge with a can-do attitude, and expedited airport check-in are par for the course.

The time-tested low-roller strategy is to stay in less-luxurious places next to the casinos where you plan to spend most of your time. Stepping down in price doesn't require forfeiting all amenities, though. Slightly smaller rooms at a midrange hotel can lock in much lower rates. Casino hotels along the Strip may offer fabulous rooms for almost the same price as dingy digs at downtown hotels, because the Strip properties make back big bucks in their gaming areas, whereas downtown joints don't have enough blackjack tables and slot machines to recoup all of their losses on accommodation.

How to choose, when every place is currying your favor? On your first trip to Vegas, almost any property on the Strip will dazzle you. That said, you'll still want to get a little bang for your buck, so don't go only by name recognition. Some of the vintage names on the North Strip have the most disappointing rooms and locations. The Center Strip is where all of the action is, and you'll pay for it. The South Strip is a perfect compromise: you can get the full-on Vegas experience, plus the monorail line stops there, and yet you'll almost always pay less. Downtown is mostly for local gamblers, visitors who've tired of the Strip scene, and penny-pinchers, although it's experiencing a revival. Outlying area hotels offer some amazing deals, if you're willing to make the drive.

In the end, every casino hotel has its own personality, described in reviews here and in the Sights chapter. It's smart to invest time surfing the Web and phoning a few hotels weeks in advance of your trip. Otherwise, you may find yourself stuck in a wham-bam-thank-you-ma'am at the seamy edges of downtown, which is not the way to live it up in Sin City.

Check-in time is 3pm (earlier only if your room happens to be ready). Check-out is before noon, and good luck asking the front-desk staff for an extension. Upscale hotels offer in-room Internet access for a fee (typically $10 per 24 hours) via high-speed connections for laptops and WebTV keyboards; cheaper accommodations may not have data ports on phones for dial-up Internet connections. The swimming pool icon (🏊) is used for hotels with indoor or outdoor pools. The latter are typically closed from November to March or April, but heated indoor pools are available for a dip year-round.

Finally, don't be surprised to find many of the amenities you're used to are missing, as many hotel rooms do not have coffeemakers, refrigerators or climate control. This is to drive you out of your room and back into the casino. For the same reason, room service can be agonizingly slow – it's often faster to go downstairs to the hotel's coffee shop.

Reservations

Whatever you do, don't arrive in town without a reservation, at least for the first night. If you just stroll in the hotel's front door, you may find that the only thing available is a

HOTEL ROOM ROULETTE

If you're not happy with the room you've been assigned at check-in, all you have to do is ask. Sweet-talking the front-desk clerks (or even tipping, some people swear) can work wonders. Generally speaking, you want an upper-floor room with a view of the Strip or the mountains. Corner rooms are often bigger, not to mention quieter. Always ask when making reservations if a hotel is currently under construction and either demand a room away from the noise or stay elsewhere. Choose which tower you'll stay in carefully. Decide whether it's more important to be close to the parking garage or the main casino action, and remember that newly built or renovated rooms are always better in Vegas.

BEAT THE CLOCK

You're all fired up to head for Sin City, but you can't seem to find anywhere decent to stay. If time's running out, try the following:

- Online travel booking agencies reserve rooms in bulk and pass on volume discounts; they're useful when everything is supposedly sold out. You can phone them, too.
- **Las Vegas Convention & Visitors Authority** (LVCVA; ☎ 800-332-5333; www.vegasfreedom.com) can help out in a pinch. Ask about last-minute specials.
- Last-minute travel specialists, such as www.site59.com, www.lastminutetravel.com, www.priceline.com and www.travelworm.com, which book air, hotel and car-rental packages on short notice.
- Share and share alike in a Strip room with two double beds or a suite, which usually fits up to four people sleeping in shifts, sharing beds and/or crashing on the floor. If you're lucky, there'll be a queen-sized sofa bed.
- Nongaming hotels and off-Strip accommodations may have vacancies when no casino hotels, including the older places downtown, have any rooms. Reliable hotel and upscale motel chains are found on Paradise Rd, a short cab ride from the Strip.
- Outlying accommodations around Las Vegas (p202) can be fantastic places to stay, and less crowded to boot.
- Cheap motels might do for a night if you're desperate. Motels in Boulder City near Hoover Dam (p211) don't rent by the hour like those south of downtown Las Vegas or on Fremont St east of Glitter Gulch.
- Cast your net further afield to Laughlin or other casino hotels near the California, Arizona and Utah state lines (p203).

Failing that, there's no better place to stay up all night than Vegas!

---

two-bedroom suite at a nightly rate exceeding your entire month's rent or mortgage at home. Always call ahead, even if it's just from the airport or the interstate as you drive into town.

You'd be amazed how often every standard room in the Las Vegas metro area is occupied. If you're planning your trip during major holidays (p240) or special events (p8), all of the desirable rooms (and even the undesirable ones) will be booked out months in advance. During the biggest conventions, Laughlin (about 100 miles south of Vegas, and at least a 90-minute drive) is booked solid.

These days savvy travelers make their reservations online, either via the hotel's own website or using an online travel booking agent. It may pay to phone the hotel and ask to negotiate a better deal, especially if you're making reservations for groups of 10 or more. Always ask about discounts for seniors, AAA members etc when you reserve your room.

When you show up to check in, don't lose your cool if the hotel has lost or mistaken your reservation. Maybe you requested a nonsmoking suite in the new high-rise tower, but they're cheekily trying to give you a smoking room with twin beds in an old wing that's ready to be demolished. All is not lost, because the front-desk clerk has the discretion to change or even upgrade your room. Chat them up and watch what happens. For tips on scoring top-notch rooms, see p191.

Rates

As with so many things in life, timing is everything, and that's true for hotel rooms here. Rates fluctuate wildly according to demand, which is always high. Midweek (Sunday to Thursday) tariffs are up to 50% lower than on weekends (Friday and Saturday nights), but some places still charge slightly more on the shoulder nights of Thursday and Sunday than they do Monday to Wednesday. Staying more than one night may keep costs down (most places require a two-night minimum stay on weekends, in fact). Or you might find better bargains staying in different hotels every night. The lowest rates are generally offered during the week after a big holiday weekend, during the hottest summer months (July and August) and in the winter doldrums after New Year's.

What all this means is that the rates shown here should be viewed only as approximate (ie the average weekday vs weekend rates for a standard double). The amount you are quoted by the hotels could be appreciably higher; it's unlikely they will be substantially lower, as prices quoted here are the lowest standard rates – that is, when it's not a recognized holiday

GETTING AN EDGE OVER THE HOUSE

If you're looking for a rate that's unavailable now or you want to stay at a hotel that's sold out, check back in a few days or a week or two. Sometimes you can suddenly reserve great rooms at much less than you had formerly expected to pay. Hotels hold back blocks of rooms that they can then release to the general public later if others cancel.

It also often pays to check with the hotel where you'll be staying a week or so in advance to see if the rates you were quoted when you booked a room have changed. If they've fallen, you can keep the difference if you ask that your quoted rate be changed. The savings can be substantial: let's say that on July 1 you booked a room at the Luxor for the first week of August, at a cost of $119 a day. On July 21, you call the Luxor and learn that the rate for a room for the first week of August is now going for $79. If you tell the reservations agent that you reserved a room for that week at $119 a night and want your rate changed to $79, they'll often make the adjustment – and you'll save over $250.

and there are no big conventions in town. It may be worth searching for accommodations even before booking your plane ticket. If your travel dates are even the tiniest bit flexible, you could save yourself hundreds of dollars. The 'Cheap Sleeps' sections list places that usually have rooms starting at under $100, even on weekends.

Almost all hotels have websites that allow you to instantly check room rates and availability. Some properties will try to lure you in with heavily discounted rates during slow periods – double-check if these are 'all-inclusive' to avoid hidden charges. That said, the special promotional rates and packages offered online are often fantastic. For less than you'd regularly pay for a standard room, the hotel might give you a mini-suite upgrade and throw in perks like free passes to the spa or other casino attractions, discounted show tickets, and breakfast may even be on the house.

But how do you know if you're getting the best deal? You don't, until you've shopped around. The good (and the bad) news is that almost all hotels raise and lower their prices in perfect sync, which means that on busy weekends you've got to keep a sharp eye out for the few places that are dealing bargains. Start by checking the rates offered by major online travel booking agents, such as **Expedia** (☎ 800-397-3342; www.expedia.com), **Orbitz** (☎ 888-656-4546; www.orbitz.com) and **Travelocity** (☎ 888-872-8356; www.travelocity.com). These sites can find you a vacant room when the hotel says they're all booked up. Sometimes their rates will beat the house, other times not. You can save time by comparing deals being offered on multiple sites with search engines **QIXO** (www.qixo.com) and **SideStep** (www.sidestep .com) for free. Online travel bidding sites, such as **Priceline** (www.priceline.com), may save you money but they won't let you specify the property you want to stay in, which makes it all a crapshoot – just imagine ending up in a chain hotel or motel down by noisy McCarran Airport. Discounts travel news from www.smartertravel.com and www.travelzoo.com can alert you to great deals, either in advance or at the last minute. All of the major travel booking sites offer air, hotel and/or car-rental packages, as do airlines and tour operators (p232).

Last but not least, count on adding a room tax of 9% to all rates quoted here, plus expect miscellaneous fees such as a 'daily energy use surcharge' and a charge for local phone usage. Cancellation fees, typically up to the entire first night's charge (and sometimes the full cost of your entire stay), may be waived if you call to cancel at least 48 hours in advance.

THE STRIP

Much like the popular-kids' lunch table in high school, everyone wants to stay near the Center Strip area, focused just north of Flamingo Rd. But the South Strip can be just as much of a blast, not to mention affordable, and it's just as convenient to the monorail. Avoid the dead North Strip past the Fashion Show Mall unless you've secured a special deal or you really love dives (in which case, why aren't you going downtown?).

See p48 for detailed descriptions of these casino hotels. But construction on the Strip never stops, so by the time you read this, expect to see an even more crowded Strip skyline with more new casino hotels, condos and perhaps megaresorts. Advance check-in at the airport is available at many of these hotels, too.

Especially on weekends, when hotel rates skyrocket, you'll likely find better rates at hotels just off the Strip, either over I-15 to the west (p201) or east toward Paradise Rd (p199). Many places have free Strip shuttles, which makes them a good deal.

CENTER STRIP

Viva Las Vegas, baby! This is where all the action is, and rates rise to match. Most of the fantasy casino hotels are built on lavish spreads, while midrange and so-called budget places are crowded up against one another, mostly on the east side of Las Vegas Blvd. Traditionally, the center of it all has been the 'Four Corners' intersection with Flamingo Rd, but these days the properties further north toward Spring Mountain Rd are just as hot.

On foot it's about 1½ miles from Planet Hollywood's Aladdin north to the Fashion Show Mall. If you're driving, traffic snarls are common. Only a few hotels provide back entrances to their parking garages off Audrie Lane to the east or Industrial Rd to the west. If you plan to ride the monorail, two pieces of advice. First, most monorail station entrances are found at the very back of the casino, which entails a lot of walking and possibly getting lost, so it's not worth taking it just one stop. Second, the station names can be deceptive (eg the Flamingo/Caesars Palace stop is not on the same side of the street as Caesars).

BALLY'S Map pp262-3   Casino Hotel
☎ 702-739-4111, 888-742-9248; www.ballyslasvegas.com; 3645 Las Vegas Blvd S, back entrance off Audrie Lane; r weekday/weekend from $69/129, ste from $180; monorail Bally's & Paris; 🖳
Bally's aims to be tasteful, but comes perilously close to being cheesy, just like its topless revue Jubilee! (p145). Both appeal to an older, more sedate crowd of gam-

TOP FIVE LUXE SLEEPS ON THE STRIP

When money's no object, indulge yourself at the following:
- **Bellagio** (below)
- **Caesars Palace** (p190)
- **THEhotel** (p193)
- **Venetian** (p191)
- **Wynn** (p191)

An honorable mention goes to the **MGM Grand** (p193), another magnificent megaresort.

blers. Blissfully theme-free towers house spacious rooms and suites; the latter have another queen Murphy bed and a whirlpool tub. Extras include tennis courts and a top-notch health club in the spa. It's possible that Harrah's may overhaul or even demolish this property in the near future, so stay tuned.

BELLAGIO Map pp262-3   Casino Hotel
☎ 702-693-7111, 888-987-3456; www.bellagio.com; 3600 Las Vegas Blvd S, side entrance off Flamingo Rd; r weekday/weekend from $159/329, ste from $775; monorail Bally's & Paris; 🖳
If anything in Vegas is truly spectacular, this five-diamond destination built by Steve Wynn is it. Guest rooms are styled out with artwork, lavish bathrooms and views of the lush, landscaped grounds. Do the rooms still seem small? That's because the bathrooms and closets are oversized. Lake-view rooms looking onto the famous fountains are in demand. A new luxury Spa Tower is the lavish icing atop the five-diamond cake. Alas, as at any Strip megaresort, the service can be impersonal.

Handy room at the Viva Las Vegas Wedding Chapel (p85)

CAESARS PALACE Map pp262-3 Casino Hotel
☎ 702-731-7110, 877-427-7243; www.caesars
palace.com; 3570 Las Vegas Blvd S, back entrance
off Frank Sinatra Dr; r weekday/weekend from
$140/220, ste from $300; monorail Flamingo/
Caesars Palace; 🔊
Decadence still reigns here. A new all-suite
tower overlooks the huge 'Garden of the
Gods' swimming-pool complex. Smaller
rooms have subtle elements such as wood
cabinets trimmed in Greek designs and wall
treatments inspired by Pompeian murals. All
feature whirlpool tubs. The only problem is
that Caesars is built for gods, not mortals,
who may end up running a marathon just
navigating the gargantuan grounds.

FLAMINGO Map pp262-3 Casino Hotel
☎ 702-733-3111, 888-308-8899; www.flamingolas
vegas.com; 3555 Las Vegas Blvd S, back entrance off
Audrie Lane; r weekday/weekend from $80/150, mini-
ste from $160; monorail Flamingo/Caesars Palace; 🔊
The stuff of Bugsy Siegel's dreams, the
Flamingo sure has history. But charm? Not
so much. For faithful regulars and wide-
eyed visitors, a prime location trumps the
downsides at this legendary casino hotel.
Miami-style color schemes and flimsy
furnishings dominate the tall towers. In
standard rooms, bathrooms are woefully
undersized, so it's worth spending more for
a mini-suite. Parking is a nightmare.

HARRAH'S Map pp262-3 Casino Hotel
☎ 702-369-5000, 800-427-7247; www.harrahs.com
/our_casinos/las; 3475 Las Vegas Blvd S, back
entrance off Audrie Lane; r weekday/weekend from
$59/129; monorail Harrah's/Imperial Palace; 🔊
Abandoning its usual riverboat theme, Harrah's Las Vegas casino hotel tries to evoke
the ambience of Mardi Gras, although it's

nothing like the partyin' **Rio** (p202). Some
rooms located in the Carnival Tower overlook the Mirage's erupting volcano. Staff
are remarkably friendly.

MIRAGE Map pp262-3 Casino Hotel
☎ 702-791-7111, 800-627-6667; www.mirage.com;
3400 Las Vegas Blvd S, back entrance off Spring
Mountain Rd; r weekday/weekend from $99/199, ste
from $259; tram from TI (Treasure Island); 🔊
The faux-Polynesian Mirage has a white
tiger's share of attractions. Check-in happens
by the lobby aquarium. Gone are the original tropical colors, but your room, although
small, *is* refined. There are one- and two-
bedroom suites, as well as eight villa apartments and six lanai bungalows, each with
a private pool and garden. Renting a suite
might entitle you to airport limo service,
fresh flowers and priority restaurant seating.

PARIS–LAS VEGAS
Map pp262-3 Casino Hotel
☎ 702-946-7000, 877-796-2096; www.parislasvegas
.com; 3655 Las Vegas Blvd S, back entrance off Audrie
Lane; r weekday/weekend from $149/199, premier-
view r add $40; monorail Bally's & Paris; 🔊
Rooms at this Hotel de Ville replica are
comfortable with armoires enhancing the
Gallic feel. But like almost anywhere else
in Vegas, rates climb for upper-floor rooms
with views. Rooms facing the half-scale Eiffel Tower and the dancing fountains of Bellagio across the street also cost more than
those facing the property's ugly derriere.

PLANET HOLLYWOOD (ALADDIN)
Map pp262-3 Casino Hotel
☎ 702-785-9474, 877-333-9474; www.planetholly
wood.com; 3667 Las Vegas Blvd S, enter off Harmon
Ave; r weekday/weekend from $99/169, Strip-view r
add $30, ste from $199; monorail Bally's & Paris; 🔊
The Arabian fantasy of the Aladdin was
swimming in a sea of debt when Planet
Hollywood bought it. At press time, the new
corporate owners were slowly making over
and expanding the resort. Previously each
room or suite was nothing extraordinary,
except for its spacious marble bathroom
and in-room computers wired for Internet
access. Unless Planet Hollywood lowers the
rates, however, you probably can do better
elsewhere, at least until the new Sheraton-
run hotel venture gets on its feet in 2006.

TOP FIVE THEME HOTELS
Fantasies take flight at the **Venetian** (opposite), **Bel-
lagio** (p189) and **Caesars Palace** (above). But the
following are the top five value-conscious hotels that
still give you a taste of another place:
- **Luxor** (p192)
- **New York–New York** (p193)
- **Rio** (p202)
- **Paris–Las Vegas** (right)
- **TI** (Treasure Island; opposite)

TOP FIVE HOTELS FOR FOODIES

- **Bellagio** (p189)
- **Caesars Palace** (opposite)
- **MGM Grand** (p193)
- **Paris–Las Vegas** (opposite)
- **Venetian** (below)

TI (TREASURE ISLAND)

Map pp262-3   Casino Hotel

☎ 702-894-7111, 800-288-7206; www.treasure island.com; 3300 Las Vegas Blvd S, side entrance off Spring Mountain Rd; r weekday/weekend from $89/159, tower deluxe r with view add $30, ste from $199; tram from Mirage; ☒

Once a family-friendly Caribbean theme hotel, Treasure Island has reinvented itself as adults-only TI. While it's more laughable than erotic, you can still be seduced by its sexy location. Cream-colored rooms are hidden away from the casino action, when you need to take a break. Floor-to-ceiling windows make small rooms seem bigger than they are, but those balconies are just props.

VENETIAN Map pp262-3   Casino Hotel

☎ 702-414-1000, 888-283-6423; www.venetian.com; 3355 Las Vegas Blvd S; ste weekday/weekend from $149/219; monorail Harrah's/Imperial Palace; ☒

Fronted by canals and graceful bridges, the five-star Venetian's 'standard' suites are anything but. In fact, they are the largest and most luxurious in town. Every suite is at least 650 sq ft, with wrought-iron railings and a marble foyer, a canopy-draped bedchamber, and a sunken living-room salon with a modern entertainment center. The new Venezia Tower has a private pool and its own exclusive check-in and concierge level.

WYNN Map pp262-3   Casino Hotel

☎ 702-770-7100, 888-320-9966; www.wynnlas vegas.com; 3131 Las Vegas Blvd S; r weekday/weekend from $219/299, ste from $359; bus 301, 302; ☒

The Strip's newest, copper-tinted high-rise has deluxe resort rooms bigger than some studio apartments, with high thread-count linens, sofas with ottomans, flat-screen high-definition TVs, Turkish towels and all the little luxuries. Salon suites have prime floor-to-ceiling views and private massage rooms; all suites have private VIP check-in. Desert tones pervade and service is fabulous. The only drawback is being off the monorail line.

Cheap Sleeps

BARBARY COAST Map pp262-3   Casino Hotel

☎ 702-737-7111, 888-227-2279; www.barbarycoast casino.com; 3595 Las Vegas Blvd S, cnr Flamingo Rd; r weekday/weekend from $60/110; monorail Bally's & Paris

With cheap rooms smack-bang mid-Strip, the Barbary is Las Vegas' worst-kept secret. The casino's charming, turn-of-the-20th-century–Victorian decor transfers seamlessly to the basic rooms with brass beds, lace curtains, floral carpets and gaslight-style lamps. It's often tough to secure a bed, not to mention a self-parking space in the garage.

ALWAYS A ROOM AT THE TOP

If you drop wads of cash around the casino, you may just be comped a sumptuous suite. But let's assume you're not a high-rolling 'whale' being courted by the casino. As many people have said, someone has to get the best room in the house. Why not you?

If you intend to do some serious gambling, enroll in the players' club (it's free) and ask to be rated. Then, as you gamble, the amount you gamble will be tallied. Members of a players' club don't need to gamble very much before many hotels (especially those downtown on Fremont St) will upgrade them to a suite or offer them a discounted rate on their standard room.

Deluxe suites are reserved for invited guests but occasionally are available on a walk-in basis. If you've just got to have one, say so at the reception desk, and vow to gamble like there's no tomorrow. They've heard it all before, but it never hurts to try.

Frequent casino hotel guests get preferred treatment. You can gain status instantly by signing up for a hotel-branded credit card. A low-roller's way to find out in advance about special deals is to sign up online for the casino hotel's free email newsletters and offers.

IMPERIAL PALACE Map pp262-3   Casino Hotel
☎ 702-731-3311, 800-634-6441; www.imperial palace.com; 3535 Las Vegas Blvd S; r weekday/weekend from $65/85, ste from $94; monorail Harrah's/Imperial Palace; 🖭

This riff on a royal Asian theme thankfully never takes itself too seriously. Given the mid-Strip location and often low rates, it's awfully good value. Standard rooms are nothing special, but some deluxe ones have been renovated recently. Each 'Luv Tub' suite features a spacious bedroom with an ego-stroking mirror and a 300-gallon sunken tub in a heavily mirrored bathroom. Narcissists, rejoice! Note that Harrah's has acquired this property.

SOUTH STRIP

Definitely more convenient than the far North Strip, the South Strip spreads just south and north of Tropicana Ave. Many people prefer staying here because it's easier to drive around, room rates are better and the nightlife is stimulating. Like anywhere else on the Strip, it's a longer walk than you might think between hotels. The free Mandalay Bay–Luxor–Excalibur tram system and elevated pedestrian walk-

ways make it easier to get around. The monorail stop at the MGM Grand can zip you up to the Center Strip. Coming attractions include the MGM Mirage's Project City Center, abutting the old Boardwalk casino hotel; and the equally high-rise Cosmopolitan condo, hotel and casino complex, a joint Grand Hyatt venture, next door to the Bellagio.

EXCALIBUR Map pp262-3   Family Casino Hotel
☎ 702-597-7777, 877-750-5464; www.excalibur .com; 3850 Las Vegas Blvd S, back entrance off Frank Sinatra Dr; r weekday/weekend from $55/110, spa ste from $130; tram to Mandalay Bay & Luxor; 🖭

For better or worse, the relentless Arthurian motif doesn't stop in the casino. Two towers total 4000-plus rooms, all on the small side. On the plus side, they do have nonsmoking, family-friendly rooms and spa suites. Kids under 13 stay free with their parents, so you can imagine how boisterous it gets.

FOUR SEASONS
Map pp262-3   Nongaming hotel
☎ 702-632-5050, 877-632-5000; www.fourseasons .com/lasvegas; 3960 Las Vegas Blvd S, cnr Four Seasons Dr; r from $245; tram to Luxor & Excalibur; 🖭

Private elevators whisk guests away to exclusive rooms on Mandalay Bay's 35th through 39th floors. The overpriced nongaming resort provides comfort, quiet and concierges who coddle guests. A full-service spa, workout room, garden pool, 24-hour business center and twice-daily housekeeping seal the deal. There's also an early-arrival and late-departure lounge.

LUXOR Map pp262-3   Casino Hotel
☎ 702-262-4100, 888-777-0188; www.luxor.com; 3900 Las Vegas Blvd S, back entrance off Frank Sinatra Dr; r weekday/weekend from $80/150, Jacuzzi ste from $99; tram to Excalibur & Mandalay Bay; 🖭

All guest rooms feature art-deco and Egyptian furnishings, plus marble bathrooms. If you're staying in the pyramid rooms (no bathtubs), you can ride the Luxor's unusual high-speed elevators, called 'inclinators,' because they must travel at a 39-degree angle to ascend. Newer tower rooms often have better views. You should ask for a room that faces Mandalay Bay, not Excalibur.

TI, Treasure Island (p191)

MONTE CARLO Map pp262-3   Casino Hotel

☎ 702-730-7777, 888-529-4828; www.montecarlo
.com; 3770 Las Vegas Blvd S, cnr Rue De Monte
Carlo, back entrance off Frank Sinatra Dr; r week-
day/weekend from $79/149, ste from $159; monorail MGM Grand; ☑

It's hardly Monaco, but an American re-
interpretation of European style infuses
every room, where large marble tubs lend
themselves to therapeutic soaks. The swimming pool (with a slow-moving river ride
and wave pool) and spa are impressive, but
in terms of theme hotels, this one's a flop.
Tram service to and from the Bellagio was
suspended at press time, making it a long-
ish walk here from the monorail.

NEW YORK–NEW YORK

Map pp262-3   Casino Hotel

☎ 702-740-6969, 888-693-6763; www.nynyhotel
casino.com; 3790 Las Vegas Blvd S, back entrance
off Frank Sinatra Dr; r weekday/weekend from
$79/159; monorail MGM Grand; ☑

The art-deco rooms are classy and freshly
remodeled with black marble-topped bathroom sinks and comfy beds. The cheapest
rooms are rather tiny (just what one would
expect in NYC), but pay a few dollars more
for a Broadway or Park Avenue Deluxe (the
latter have flat-screen TVs) and you'll have
plenty of legroom. Avoid noisy lower-level
rooms facing the roller coaster.

THEHOTEL Map pp262-3   Casino Hotel

☎ 702-632-7777, 877-632-7800; www.thehotelat
mandalaybay.com; 3950 Las Vegas Blvd S, cnr road
to Mandalay Bay, back entrance off Frank Sinatra
Dr; ste weekday/weekend from $169/279; tram to
Luxor & Excalibur; ☑

Kick back with your entourage at what
is truly THE hotel of the moment in Las
Vegas. Once you enter the high-ceilinged

MANDALAY BAY Map pp262-3   Casino Hotel

☎ 702-632-7777, 877-632-7800; www.mandalay
bay.com; 3950 Las Vegas Blvd S, cnr Road to
Mandalay Bay, back entrance off Frank Sinatra Dr;
r weekday/weekend from $129/219, ste from $179;
tram to Luxor & Excalibur; ☑

Hip House of Blues theme rooms on the
34th floor feature art naïf motifs. Otherwise,
a watered-down South Seas theme persists throughout the plain, yet generously
sized rooms. Many well-tanned guests feel
it's worth a stay just to gain access to the
sprawling pool complex with its artificial
beach. Suites have imported-stone entries,
big-screen TVs, whirlpool tubs and brand-
name spa products.

MGM GRAND Map pp262-3   Casino Hotel

☎ 702-891-7777, 800-929-1111; www.mgmgrand
.com; 3799 Las Vegas Blvd S, enter off Tropicana
Ave; r weekday/weekend from $90/200, ste from
$140; monorail MGM Grand; ☑

There's plenty to choose from at the
world's largest hotel (5000-plus rooms in
four 30-story towers), but is bigger better?
Luxurious suites, with multiple bathrooms
and patio whirlpools, can be a bargain;
rooms have plain art-deco–themed Hollywood bungalow decor, but those in the
Grand Tower are a knockout. It's the entertainment that makes the MGM shine, plus a
spa (open to guests only) and the convenience of a monorail station.

TOP FIVE HOTELS AFTER DARK

If you crave Vegas' hottest nightlife, stay at the
following:
- Hard Rock (p199)
- MGM Grand (left)
- THEhotel (above)
- Treasure Island (p191)
- Bellagio (p189) and Caesars Palace (p190) are
  tied for fifth place.

lobby off Mandalay Bay, you'll know you've finally arrived. Expansive art-deco suites (no rooms) come with high-speed Internet, wet bars, plasma TVs, living areas, chic decor and deep soaking tubs.

TROPICANA Map pp262-3   Casino Hotel
☎ 702-739-2222, 888-826-8767; www.tropicanalv
.com; 3801 Las Vegas Blvd S, back entrance off E
Reno Ave; r weekday/weekend from $45/120, Island
Tower r add $10, Paradise Tower r add $30; monorail
MGM Grand; ⛭
World famous since it debuted in 1957, the Trop is poised to make a comeback. But not yet. The Island Tower keeps its kitschy Polynesian theme, while the newer Paradise Tower (where rooms have refrigerators) tries for French provincial. Don't go for the more cramped 'garden rooms,' but do take advantage of the poolside wi-fi hot spot. At press time, the future of the Trop was uncertain, so call ahead to check on renovations or a closing date.

Cheap Sleeps
HOOTERS (SAN REMO)
Map pp262-3   Casino Hotel
☎ 702-739-9000, 800-522-7366; www.sanremolas
vegas.com, www.hooterscasinohotel.com; 115
E Tropicana Ave, back entrance off E Reno Ave;
r weekday/weekend from $29/115
This often-overlooked casino hotel isn't quite on the Strip, but it's only a short walk from it. Its convenient location – behind the Tropicana, across the street from the MGM Grand – is probably what prompted the Hooters chain to take it over as of early 2006. At press time, small standard rooms were still disappointingly tacky.

NORTH STRIP
You'll notice that the Strip starts to peter out north of the Fashion Show Mall. Partly it's because the more modest properties found here tend to be older. Some are sadly worn, although they may have the last remaining rooms in Vegas with windows that actually open onto fresh-air balconies. If you're betting on which casino hotel is next to be demolished, look no further. Rumor has it that the former Wet 'n Wild theme park just south of the Sahara is being redeveloped into a theme megaresort. A new luxury

---

TOP FIVE (ALMOST) THEME-FREE STRIP HOTELS
- Bally's (p189)
- MGM Grand (p193)
- Monte Carlo (p193)
- THEhotel (p193)
- Wynn (p191)

---

high-rise Conrad Hotel (www.conradhotels .com) owned by Hilton will soon rise north of the Riviera.

Transportation is a downside here. The Sahara monorail station is barely within striking distance of the Stratosphere. For all of the other casino hotels, however, you'll have to either walk up from the Center Strip or get off the monorail at the Las Vegas Convention Center, then hop in a cab. It makes more sense to drive instead, except for the fact that the corner of Las Vegas Blvd and Sahara Ave is one of the most notoriously slow and tangled intersections in the whole city. Avoid driving on Las Vegas Blvd and instead look for rear entrances to casino parking garages off Industrial Rd (on the west side of the Strip), Riviera Blvd (for the Riviera) or Paradise Rd (for the Sahara).

CIRCUS CIRCUS
Map pp262-3   Family Casino Hotel
☎ 702-734-0410, 800-634-3450; www.circuscircus
-lasvegas.com; 2880 Las Vegas Blvd S, cnr Circus
Circus Dr, back entrance off Industrial Rd; r weekday/
weekend from $50/100; bus 301, 302; ⛭
At this family-friendly favorite, most of the low-cost standard rooms have sofas and balconies or patios; those in the 30-story Skyrise Tower have advantageous access to two swimming pools. Suites, like clowns, come in varying shapes and sizes. Motel-style Manor rooms out back aren't very appealing, but they do have refrigerators.

NEW FRONTIER Map pp262-3   Casino Hotel
☎ 702-794-8200, 800-634-6966; www.frontierlv
.com; 3120 Las Vegas Blvd S, cnr Desert Inn Rd, side
entrance off Fashion Show Dr; r weekday/weekend
$45/105, ste from $65/135; bus 301, 302; ⛭
Another way to slum it on the North Strip, but at least there are some diversions here like infamous Gilley's (p151). Rooms have basic amenities, while 'deluxe' suites with

all the charm of Astroturf encircle an open-air atrium out back. It may be the most country-and-western-style casino hotel on the Strip, but you're not likely to run into many real cowgirls here.

RIVIERA Map pp262-3   Casino Hotel

☎ 702-734-5110, 800-634-6753; www.rivierahotel .com; 2901 Las Vegas Blvd S, cnr Riviera Blvd; r weekday/weekend from $84/159, deluxe r add $40; bus 301, 302; 🖫

At this aging lady of the Strip, rooms are subpar – soft floral decor, cable TV, nothing fancy. For these rates, you'd expect much more. 'Deluxe' rooms in the Mediterranean South Tower have refrigerators; so do those in the Monte Carlo Tower (between the casino and its convention center), which also has bay windows.

SAHARA Map pp262-3   Casino Hotel

☎ 702-737-2111, 888-696-2121; www.saharavegas .com; 2535 Las Vegas Blvd S, enter off Paradise Rd; r weekday/weekend from $50/90; ste from $155; monorail Sahara; 🖫

A relentless, but delightful Moroccan theme pervades this 1950s hotel, where each room in the Tangiers Tower comes with a wooden desk topped with a brass lamp and chairs with camel designs. Sadly, the rest of the rooms aren't done up in the same vintage style. Although it's not an exciting place to put up your feet, some of the city's better bargains are here, plus a handy monorail station and a pool with old-school glamour.

STARDUST Map pp262-3   Casino Hotel

☎ 702-732-6441, 866-642-3120; www.stardustlv .com; 3000 Las Vegas Blvd S, cnr Desert Inn Rd, back entrance off Industrial Rd; r weekday/weekend from $50/100, ste from $110; bus 301, 302; 🖫

A spread-out property with parking lots you wouldn't want to be caught in late at night. The 1500-plus rooms aren't going to appear in *Architectural Digest* anytime soon. However, in the same way that a chintzy dress can look pretty at night, so too can these rooms. There's little attention to detail, and the hotel staff, perhaps cognizant that their rooms don't measure up, are friendly. By and large, the guests found here are big fans of the Vegas of yesteryear.

STRATOSPHERE Map pp262-3   Casino hotel

☎ 702-380-7777, 888-236-7495; www.stratosphere hotel.com; 2000 Las Vegas Blvd S, enter off Baltimore Ave; r weekday/weekend from $35/90; monorail Sahara; 🖫

Warning! Your room is *not* in the tower but rather in a much smaller building at the base of the spire. The main drawback to staying here is that it's far from the rest of the Strip, although the Sahara monorail station is nearby. Lower rates guarantee crushing crowds. Perks include a fitness center and free self-service laundry. Ask for an upper-floor Premier Tower room with a view. A mandatory $5-per-day 'resort fee' includes use of the fitness center, huge swimming pool and guest laundry machines, plus free tower admission (🕙 10am-noon).

Cheap Sleeps

If you've brought your Winnebago to Vegas, Circus Circus (opposite) has a KOA-operated **RV park** (☎ 702-733-9707, 800-562-7270; www .koa.com; 500 Circus Circus Dr, off Industrial Rd; RV sites with full hook-ups $22-82) behind the casino with a swimming pool and sauna, self-service laundry, pet runs, wi-fi and nearly 400 sites with 24-hour check-in.

WESTWARD HO Map pp262-3   Casino Hotel

☎ 702-731-2900, 800-634-6803; www.westwardho .com; 2900 Las Vegas Blvd S, south of Circus Circus Dr, back entrance off Industrial Rd; r weekday/ weekend $31/61; bus 301, 302; 🖫

On the downtrodden North Strip, you'll stumble drunkenly across the Westward Ho. It's cheap and no-frills, but not many thrills either (except for multiple pools). If you like dives, then this is the place for you. Think of it as a place to lay your head, nothing more, at least until new owners take over.

TOP FIVE HOTELS FOR KIDS

Family-friendly casino hotels are few in Vegas. Those that exist often let children stay for free in their parents' rooms and a few offer perks such as on-site child care (p237). Perennial faves include the following:

- **Circus Circus** (opposite)
- **Excalibur** (p192)
- **Green Valley Ranch** (p202)
- **Hyatt Regency Lake Las Vegas Resort** (p202)
- **Orleans** (p201)

COOL HOTEL POOLS

Las Vegas' sexy pool-party season kicks off just before the start of summer. While the city is home to some truly spectacular aquatic hangouts, not many are open year-round and most are reserved for guests only, which makes it especially worth booking in at the following:

Caesars Palace (p190) With its gorgeous lawns, Corinthian columns, magnificent palms and four marble-inlaid pools, Caesars Palace's stately **Garden of the Gods Oasis** (open year-round) is a divine sight to behold. Goddesses proffer frozen grapes in summer. Topless sunbathing is allowed at the Venus pool.

Hard Rock (p199) This très-hip **Beach Club** (open seasonally) features two pools with piped-in underwater music, grass-shack cabanas with personal misting systems, and a jungle of lush vegetation, plus swim-up blackjack at the exotic Palapa pavilion. **Rehab** (admission $10-30; noon-8pm Sun) summer pool parties are legendary, and open to all who pay the cover.

Mandalay Bay (p193) By an artificial beach, the seasonal wave pool features 1700 tons of California sand, 1.6-million gallons of water and surfing competitions. Need we say more? Well, you can also float away on a lazy river ride (also open seasonally). On summer nights, clothing-optional **Moorea Beach Club** (p152) morphs into an ultra lounge (admission $10-30).

Flamingo (p190) A multilevel, rejuvenating pool experience (Mar-Oct) with flamingos, waterfalls, lagoons and grottoes (water slides are open seasonally). For mobster-era purists, there's a small oval-shaped pool. During summer, the pool stays open late and high-energy, quasi-Hawaiian luaus happen twice nightly.

Tropicana (p194) For tropically landscaped grounds, head to the poor-man's Mirage, the Trop, where a 12,000-sq-ft main pool (Mar-Oct) is ringed by a lagoon, a picturesque waterfall and 60 varieties of flora. Swim up for blackjack during summer. Year-round a glassed-in heated indoor pool and poolside wi-fi hot spots are available.

If you're staying downtown, the prime Olympic-sized pool is at the **Golden Nugget** (opposite), where you can lounge inside retro red-and-white-striped cabanas (from $75 per day).

Note most hotel pools are shallow; the deepest (12ft) is at **Bally's** (p189). Other record-holders are the longest 'lazy river' ride (1000ft), at the **MGM Grand** (p193); biggest hot tub – it holds up to 50 party animals – at **TI** (Treasure Island; p191); best views and activities, at the **Hyatt Regency Lake Las Vegas Resort** (p202); highest-elevation pool, at the 25th-floor clothing-optional beach club inside the **Stratosphere** (p195); and coolest cabanas (literally – they've got air con), next to the octagon pool at **Paris–Las Vegas** (p190), where you can get poolside massages at **Spa by Mandara** (p165) in the shadow of the Eiffel Tower.

DOWNTOWN

If views are important to you, stay elsewhere. Otherwise, if you're a serious gambler or someone who likes to save your dough, there's nowhere like the Glitter Gulch corridor of Fremont St for a taste of old-school Vegas. See p79 for detailed descriptions of most of these properties. They're nothing fancy, except for the luxurious Golden Nugget, which sets a new standard.

There are suites at most of these hotels, but casino hosts control them; they're usually only available to members of the players' clubs (p191). Rooms facing Fremont St catch a lot of noise coming up from the Fremont Street Experience (p82), so bring a pair of earplugs.

Most of the middle-aged gamblers you'll find downtown drive here. The monorail does not extend to Fremont St, so visitors usually take a cab from the Strip. City buses (p234) stop at the Downtown Transportation Center (DTC), from where it's a short walk to the Fremont St casino hotels. From the Strip, take bus No 301 (local) or No 302 (express) to the DTC.

BINION'S Map p261   Casino Hotel
☎ 702-382-1600, 800-937-6537; www.binions.com; 128 E Fremont St, enter off Casino Center Blvd; r weekday/weekend from $50/75;
Y'all, this downtown icon has changed since legendary Texan wildman Benny Binion opened it as the Horseshoe in 1951. Harrah's briefly took the reins in 2004, but this troubled hotel recently switched owners yet again. Dark, run-down rooms featured almost zero amenities and the rooftop pool was closed at press time. We hope that things will look up soon.

CALIFORNIA Map p261   Casino Hotel
☎ 702-385-1222, 800-634-6255; www.thecal.com; 12 E Ogden Ave, enter off N 1st St; r weekday/weekend from $59/75;
Although it's neither particularly Californian nor Hawaiian (the Cal hosts many visitors

from Hawaii), this popular, friendly hotel has tropically colored rooms with white plantation shutters, mahogany furnishings and marble baths. Check out the rooftop pool.

FITZGERALD'S Map p261 Casino Hotel
☎ 702-388-2400, 800-274-5825; www.fitzgeralds lasvegas.com; 301 E Fremont St, enter off S 3rd St; r weekday/weekend from $39/59

Sky-high 'Club 21' rooms are worth an upgrade, as they're outfitted with leather ice buckets, electric shoeshine machines, fancy toiletries and nightly turndown service. Otherwise, this is just another cheap Fremont St casino, albeit with a happy-go-lucky Irish theme.

FOUR QUEENS Map p261 Casino Hotel
☎ 702-385-4011, 800-634-6045; www.fourqueens .com; 202 E Fremont St, enter off S 2nd St; r weekday/weekend from $34/64

If you don't get an upper-floor room, the raucous Fremont St scene is guaranteed to keep you awake all night long. So what's to love? Deluxe suites have a refrigerator, and Jacuzzi suites fit up to four people in a pinch. It's directly opposite the Golden Nugget, and has a brewpub (p137) downstairs.

FREMONT Map p261 Casino Hotel
☎ 702-385-3232, 800-634-6182; www.fremont casino.com; 200 E Fremont St, enter off Casino Center Blvd; r weekday/weekend from $50/70

The classic Fremont has been kickin' for over 50 years. Its rooms may be pint-sized, but they've been recently (and tastefully) renovated. You're welcome to sprint down

the street to swim in the California's rooftop pool.

GOLDEN GATE Map p261 Casino Hotel
☎ 702-385-1906, 800-426-1906; www.goldengate casino.net; 1 Fremont St, enter off Main St; r weekday/weekend from $39/65

Rooms at this century-old Frisco-themed casino are dark, dingy and often come with a racket next door. But they're big on security and guest elevators are only accessible with room keys. Other than that, the best thing is that it's perfectly perched at the busy corner of Fremont and Main.

GOLDEN NUGGET Map p261 Casino Hotel
☎ 702-385-7111, 800-846-5336; www.golden nugget.com; 129 E Fremont St, enter off S 1st St; r weekday/weekend from $59/79, ste from $275; 🖵

If you're hip to the downtown scene, relive the fabulous heyday of 1950s Las Vegas at this swank address. Relax in generously cut rooms with rich decor, including half-canopy beds, vanity tables and marble bathrooms. Each unique luxury spa-tower suite features a spiral staircase and private whirlpool bath, but most are reserved for major players on weekends.

LAS VEGAS CLUB Map p261 Casino Hotel
☎ 702-385-1664, 800-634-6532; www.vegasclub casino.net; 18 E Fremont S, enter off E Ogden Ave; r weekday/weekend from $59/79

This sports-themed casino is almost as popular as the Cal with visitors from Hawaii. Rooms aren't exactly the Ritz, but they're not bad on a budget; request one in the North Tower. Guests can use the rooftop pool at the Plaza, too.

MAIN STREET STATION
Map p261 Casino Hotel
☎ 702-387-1896, 800-465-0711; www.mainstreet casino.com; 200 N Main St, enter off Stewart Ave; r from $55

As handsome as the main casino, the 17-floor guest-room tower is all gussied up with tiled foyers, Victorian sconces and marble-trimmed hallways. Bright, cheerful rooms come with gilt mirrors and plantation shutters. A glassed-in pedestrian walkway crosses over to the Cal, also owned by Boyd Gaming, so you can take a dip in the rooftop pool.

TOP FIVE VINTAGE VEGAS HOTELS

- **Golden Nugget** (right) Stylish, sexy and smart, the Nugget has put the glitz back into downtown's Glitter Gulch.
- **Sahara** (p195) Nostalgic for Vegas' lost glamour? So is the Sahara.
- **Flamingo** (p190) Relive *Fear and Loathing in Las Vegas* at this gangsters' hideaway. Being bad never felt so good.
- **Stardust** (p195) Brilliant neon and retro lounge acts carry on, even though Wayne Newton has left the building.
- **El Cortez** (p198) Like dives? They've got 'vintage' 1940s rooms waiting just for you.

Sleeping

DOWNTOWN

PLAZA Map p261   Casino Hotel

☎ 702-386-2110, 800-634-6575; www.plazahotel casino.com; 1 Main St; r weekday/weekend from $59/79, deluxe r add $10; 🏊

Built in the early '70s, Jackie Gaughan's Plaza is attached to the Greyhound bus station. Rooms overlook downtown or the freeway spaghetti bowl; neither sight is lovely, and the casino is downright depressing. Do yourself a favor and at least book a 'deluxe' room. It has a rooftop pool, a workout room and tennis courts that the blue-haired ladies in the bingo room have never seen.

VIVA LAS VEGAS VILLAS Map p261   Motel

☎ 702-384-0771, 800-574-4450; www.vivalasvegas villas.com; 1205 Las Vegas Blvd S; standard r week-day/weekend from $59/75, theme r from $89/125, ste from $175; bus 301, 302

Come armed with a high tolerance for the no-tell motels nearby. But if you adore kitsch, this wedding fantasyland is the most inviting place between downtown and the Strip. Themed motel-style rooms aren't punched from a cookie cutter, and one of the suites has a Cadillac bed fit for the King. Just don't expect speedy service, as new couples tie the knot here every 15 minutes.

Cheap Sleeps

Warning: on the Strip, a 'cheap sleep' means anything starting under $100 per night. But downtown, scraping the bottom of the barrel will rarely cost that much. These places are only if you've got a high tolerance for dark, dingy rooms or you're flat-out broke with no car. Believe it or not, there are even rougher-edged places than the ones listed here.

TOP FIVE KITSCH HOTELS

In a city that celebrates the careers of Elvis and Liberace, there's some stiff competition when it comes to kitsch. Aficionados of terribly tasteless and truly tacky accommodations should stay at the following:

- **Circus Circus** (p194)
- **Excalibur** (p192)
- **Imperial Palace** (p192)
- **Stratosphere** (p195)
- **Viva Las Vegas Villas** (left)

EL CORTEZ Map p261   Casino Hotel

☎ 702-385-5200, 800-634-6703; www.elcortez hotelcasino.com; 600 E Fremont St, enter off 6th St; vintage r weekday/weekend from $20/32, tower r from $30/52

It's a few blocks east of the Fremont Street Experience, which may make pedestrians nervous. Then again, if that kind of thing bothered you, you wouldn't be staying at this seedy place, anyway. Upper-floor tower rooms are much better than the cheap 'vintage' 1940s-style queen-bed rooms only accessible by stairs from the casino.

SIN CITY HOSTEL Map p261   Hostel

☎ 702-868-0222; www.sincityhostel.com; 1208 Las Vegas Blvd S; dm from $18.50, r from $37, all-incl continental breakfast; ⏰ reception 6am-2am Apr–mid-Oct, 7am-11pm mid-Oct–Mar; bus 301

A few scary blocks north of the Stratosphere, this no-frills place has air con and DSL access. Sporty and high-tech diversions can help you avoid spending time in your room. Inquire about shuttle service to San Francisco, luggage storage and more. Be advised: prostitutes often can be found standing curbside a short way from the hostel.

Relaxing around the pool, Hard Rock (opposite)

Sleeping

DOWNTOWN

USA HOSTELS LAS VEGAS

Map p261   Hostel

☎ 702-385-1150, 800-550-8958; www.usahostels
.com/vegas; 1322 E Fremont St; dm $13-23, d $37-
54, all-incl breakfast; bus 107; ☒

This 24-hour hostel is so popular with
travelers (never mind its location in another crappy part of town) that the man-
agement is strict about who it's willing
to let stay here. American guests must
have an out-of-state college ID and may
be asked for proof of international travel.
Basic nonsmoking rooms have air condi-
tioning and a private bath. Daily excursions
head out to canyons, casinos and clubs,
or you can spend all day swimming in the
pool and Jacuzzi, hitting the billiards tables
and hooking up to high-speed Internet
access. Call for a free pick-up from the
Greyhound bus station.

UNLV & EAST OF THE STRIP

The hottest area for visitors is near the Hard
Rock at the intersection of Harmon Ave and
Paradise Rd, but other places are within
walking distance of the Strip. Paradise Rd
south of Harmon Ave is hairy, though it's
closer to the university. Chain hotels and
motels found heading north on Paradise Rd
feel isolated, though some are near the Las
Vegas Convention Center and its monorail
station. If you're not staying at the Hard
Rock, taking a cab to the Strip or waiting
for a local bus are your only transportation
options.

TOP FIVE BIZ HOTELS

If you're in town for a convention, chances are you'll
be staying at one of the Strip casino hotels with trade
show facilities, such as Mandalay Bay. For the main
Las Vegas Convention Center, convenient hotels include the following:

- Las Vegas Hilton (right)
- Residence Inn Convention Center (p200)
- Embassy Suites Hotel Convention Center (right)
- Renaissance Las Vegas (p200)
- Westin Casuarina (p200) The Westin is handy to
  the Flamingo's monorail station, which can speed
  you to the convention center.

CARRIAGE HOUSE

Map p265   Nongaming Hotel

☎ 702-798-1020, 800-221-2301; www.carriagehouse
lasvegas.com; 105 E Harmon Ave, enter off Audrie
Lane; r/ste from $80/110; bus 105, 301; ☒

Around the corner from the old Aladdin, this hotel makes its money selling
timeshares. If you get a deal on a vacation
rental, you'll get a small room with a kitchenette or a double-sized suite with a fully
stocked kitchen. The lowest rates are fair
for this location.

EMBASSY SUITES HOTEL CONVENTION CENTER

Map p265   Nongaming hotel

☎ 702-893-8000, 800-362-2779; http://embassy
suites.hilton.com; 3600 Paradise Rd, north of E
Twain Ave; ste incl breakfast weekday/weekend
from $129/145; bus 108; ☒

Down the road from the convention center,
this welcoming place's rates are lower than
at newer all-suite hotels because you won't
get a full kitchen – just a refrigerator, cof-
feemaker and microwave. If you're not here
on business or don't have a big family, look
elsewhere.

HARD ROCK Map p265   Casino Hotel

☎ 702-693-5544, 800-473-7625; www.hardrock
hotel.com; 4455 Paradise Rd, cnr Harmon Ave;
r weekday/weekend from $99/259, ste from $300;
free Strip shuttle; ☒

Oversized guest-rooms are as hip as the rest
of this vainglorious shrine to rock 'n' roll,
which pulls in a moneyed crowd mostly
from Southern California. Each room affects
a modern Euro style, with French doors and
a state-of-the-art Bose stereo system. Sexier
suites boast a half-moon couch, wet bar and
a jet tub with spa amenities. Some caveats:
service at this party hotel can be half-assed,
and overbooking is common.

LAS VEGAS HILTON Map p265   Casino Hotel

☎ 702-732-5301, 888-732-7117; www.lvhilton.com;
3000 Paradise Rd, cnr Riviera Blvd; r weekday/week-
end from $59/115; monorail Las Vegas Hilton; ☒

There's nothing particularly memorable
about this upscale contemporary hotel
near the convention center, but it's quiet,
convenient to the monorail and without
artifice. Sprawling standard rooms have
deeper-than-usual bathtubs; those on

upper floors with windows facing east have panoramic views of the mountains. Relive 1920s Hollywood, set sail for the Bahamas or go on safari in one of the themed suites.

MARRIOTT SUITES

Map p265   Nongaming Hotel

☎ 702-650-2000, 800-244-3364; http://marriott .com; 325 Convention Center Dr; ste weekday/weekend from $145/160; monorail Convention Center;

On a side road squeezed between the convention center and the North Strip, this reliable chain is a few steps above the run-down casinos nearby. Guest rooms have a pull-out sofa, if you're traveling in a group, and living/sleeping areas separated by French doors. For the location and price, it's overrated.

RENAISSANCE LAS VEGAS

Map p265   Nongaming Hotel

☎ 702-733-6533, 866-352-3434; www.renaissance lasvegas.com; 3400 Paradise Rd; r/ste from $109/229; monorail Convention Center;

A shiny high-rise on Paradise Rd, the alluring Renaissance courts business travelers with free high-speed Internet access and flat-screen TVs in every room. The best bonus is eating at Envy (p124).

RESIDENCE INN CONVENTION

CENTER Map p265   Nongaming Hotel

☎ 702-796-9300, 800-331-3131; http://marriott .com; 3225 Paradise Rd; ste incl breakfast from $125; monorail Convention Center;

A home away from home for executives, here even studio suites come with full kitchens and an extra sofa bed, plus free high-speed Internet access. This low-lying complex is more popular than the recently remodeled high-rise Residence Inn Hughes Center (☎ 702-650-0040; 370 Hughes Center Dr; ste incl breakfast from $145), about a mile away.

TUSCANY SUITES Map p265   Casino Hotel

☎ 702-893-8933, 877-887-2261; www.tuscanylas vegas.com; 255 E Flamingo Rd, east of Koval Lane; r weekday/weekend from $70/145; bus 105, 202;

Away from the hectic Strip, this Italianated hotel can be downright dead. But it has loads of privacy, with oversized but plain rooms (classed as 'suites') that all have mini-kitchens.

Curved balcony, Bellagio (p189)

WESTIN CASUARINA Map p265   Casino Hotel

☎ 702-836-9775, 888-625-5144; www.westin.com; 160 E Flamingo Rd, cnr Koval Lane; r weekday/weekend from $130/160; bus 105, 202;

Be near the Strip without giving up any business-class amenities at this refined high-rise. Quite like the Las Vegas Hilton (p199), this upscale chain hotel throws in a few Vegas-style perks, such as casino gaming and a showroom.

Cheap Sleeps

See the boxed text on opposite for more cheap motels off the Strip.

SOMERSET HOUSE Map p265   Motel

☎ 702-735-4411, 888-336-4280; www.somerset -house.com; 294 Convention Center Dr, west of Paradise Rd; s weekday/weekend $35/44, d $44/55; monorail Convention Center

OK, it's hardly luxurious, but even considering the shabby rooms, it's hard to beat these bargain-basement rates so close to the North Strip. Some guests complain about the deserted area after dark, but it's safer and quieter than the shady motels stranded in the Naked City. Discounts for seniors and weekly stays; children aged under 11 stay free.

TERRIBLE'S Map p265   Casino Hotel

☎ 702-733-7000, 800-640-9777; www.terrible
herbst.com; 4100 Paradise Rd, cnr Flamingo Rd;
r $40-100; bus 108, 202, 807; 🖭

A casino run by a chain of gas stations –
wait, don't stop reading yet. This off-Strip
cheapie may be a slots 'n video poker kind
of place, but who cares when you've got
clean rooms, a 24-hour workout room and
free airport shuttles.

WEST OF THE STRIP

All of these casino hotels are just off I-15,
and most provide free shuttles to the Strip.
Otherwise, it's a short drive on Flamingo
Rd east to the 'Four Corners' area of the
Center Strip. From the Orleans, drive east on
Tropicana Ave across the Strip and turn left
into the MGM Grand's parking garage, from
where it's a short walk to the monorail.

GOLD COAST Map p264   Casino Hotel

☎ 702-367-7111, 888-402-6278; www.goldcoast
casino.com; 4000 W Flamingo Rd, cnr S Valley View
Blvd; r weekday/weekend from $50/99; free shuttle
to the Orleans & the Strip; 🖭

It's a local scene at this Coast Casinos hotel.
If you can't score the cheapest rates for
only-average rooms, though, it's not worth
staying here. It has a free fitness center and
outdoor pool, plus a popular Chinese eatery
(p127) for the many Asian package tourists.

ORLEANS Map p264   Family Casino Hotel

☎ 702-365-7111, 800-675-3267; www.orleans
casino.com; 4500 W Tropicana Ave, cnr Arville St;
r weekday/weekend from $50/120; free airport &
Strip shuttles; 🖭

It's supposed to be Mardi Gras all year
round at the Orleans, a family-friendly
casino hotel with on-site child care (p237).
Hundreds of tastefully appointed French-
provincial rooms are actually 450-sq-ft
'petite suites,' which come with oversized
bathroom tubs. A spa, a fitness center, an
arcade and a bowling alley add the finish-
ing touches.

PALMS Map p264   Casino Hotel

☎ 702-942-7777, 866-942-7777; www.palms.com;
4321 W Flamingo Rd, cnr Wynn Rd; r weekday/week-
end from $89/329, ste from $139/409; bus 202; 🖭

Twentysomethings still love the Palms of
MTV's *Real World* fame. Spacious, under-
stated rooms with divinely comfortable
beds have window-side sitting areas with
a sofa and coffee table, plus a desk in
rooms with a king-sized bed. Staff can be
attitudinous, but try talking your way into
an upper-floor room with a Strip view.
Sultry suites vary: playpens for bachelor/
bachelorette parties; high-ceiling bedrooms
with extra-long beds for NBA players; or the
2900-sq-ft 'Real World' suite with a working
kitchen and full bar – the only of its kind in
Las Vegas.

SLEEPING WITH THE CHAIN GANG

Sometimes there are just no bargains to be had in Las Vegas, and you have to fall back on a chain motel. Where it's
located makes all the difference, since rates are likely to be more than you'd pay for a cookie-cutter room in any other
US city. Any advantages to these motels? Easy parking, free (or low-cost) local calls and amenities like refrigerators and
in-room coffeemakers that are otherwise missing at most Vegas hotels.

    Motel 6 Tropicana (Map p265; ☎ 702-798-0728, 800-466-8356; www.motel6.com; 195 E Tropicana Ave, 0.5 miles
east of the Strip; s weekday/weekend from $48/67, d from $54/73; bus 201; 🖭) Tiny rooms are basic; small pets are
allowed. The next-closest branch, on Industrial Rd, on the west side of I-15, may be cheaper, but it's not within walking
distance of the Strip. A third, less-expensive branch is out on the Boulder Strip.

    Super 8 Motel (Map p265; ☎ 702-794-0888, 800-800-8000; www.super8vegas.com; 4250 Koval Lane, cnr Fla-
mingo Rd; r weekday/weekend from $59/91; free airport shuttle, bus 105, 202; 🖭) Adjacent to the rowdy Ellis Island
Casino & Brewery, rooms vary, but access to the Strip is easy. There's a more expensive branch downtown, but it's a
few too many blocks east of Glitter Gulch for comfort.

    Best Western Mardi Gras Inn (Map p265; ☎ 702-731-2020, 800-634-6501; www.mardigrasinn.com; 3500 Para-
dise Rd, south of E Desert Inn Rd; r weekday/weekend from $65/105; bus 108; 🖭) With a facade that recalls the French
Quarter, this faded chain motel ups the ante with slot machines. Other Best Westerns near the airport or in North Las
Vegas aren't recommended, but the chain's Lighthouse Inn & Resort in Boulder City near Hoover Dam has views.

    More upscale motel and hotel chains cluster near the convention center.

Sleeping

WEST OF THE STRIP

RIO Map p264   Casino Hotel

☎ 702-777-7777, 800-752-9746; www.harrahs.com /our_casinos/rlv; 3700 W Flamingo Rd, cnr S Valley View Blvd; r weekday/weekend from $79/159; free Strip shuttle; ⓢ

The all-suites Rio leaves guests raving about the spaciousness of its rooms, which have a cocktail table, crescent-shaped couch and fully detailed bathroom. Unfortunately some rooms are windowless, so ask for one with a view. Masquerade suites add a Jacuzzi tub, dining room, wet bar and 180-degree views of mountains or the Strip.

Cheap Sleeps

WILD WILD WEST Map p264   Casino Motel

☎ 702-740-0000, 800-634-3488; www.wwwest hotelcasino.com; 3300 W Tropicana Ave, off I-15; r weekday/weekend from $30/70; bus 201, 804; ⓢ

Owned by Station Casinos, this gambling hall popular with truckers has cheap motel rooms within spitting distance of the Strip, but you can't walk there, especially at night. You get what you pay for, so don't expect too much, but they do have WebTV. Solo women may want to look elsewhere.

OUTER NEIGHBORHOODS

All of these places have something winning about them that makes them worth a trek away from the Strip. If it's your first and only trip to Vegas, then by all means stay near the Strip. But outlying accommodations can be amazing value. You'll also get more local flavor and more attentive service, especially at smaller casino hotels. Some offer infrequent shuttle services to the Strip and/or downtown. Otherwise, you'll have to drive yourself.

South of the Strip near outlet malls, you'll find some bargains, but the chains near the

---

TOP FIVE HOTELS WORTH A TRIP

- Green Valley Ranch (right)
- JW Marriott Las Vegas Resort (opposite)
- Sam's Town (opposite)
- Silverton (opposite)
- Hyatt Regency Lake Las Vegas Resort (right)

---

airport have nothing to recommend them. Favored by locals and RV-drivin' retirees, casino hotels on the Boulder Strip of the Boulder Hwy hark back to Nevada's Old West. The affluent suburbs of Henderson (southeast of the Strip and the airport) and Summerlin (northwest of downtown) are at least a 20-minute commute. It takes a half hour or longer to get to Lake Las Vegas, a tranquil oasis. North Las Vegas, near the Las Vegas Motor Speedway and Nellis Air Force Base, is known for being down on its luck.

Coast Casinos (www.coastcasinos.com) and Station Casinos (www.stationcasinos.com) operate a chain of local casino hotels in a number of locations around town. Some of the best are reviewed here, but in general the rule is that the newer the property, the better the accommodations. In Summerlin, Station Casinos promises its Red Rock resort and spa will open to much fanfare soon.

GREEN VALLEY RANCH

Map p260   Casino Hotel

☎ 702-617-7704, 866-782-9487; www.greenvalley ranchresort.com; 2300 Paseo Verde Dr, off I-215 exit Green Valley Pkwy, Henderson, 10 miles southeast of the Strip; r from $189; free Strip & airport shuttles; ⓢ

Join a country-club crowd of execs, locals and families here, where cowboy flavor meets upscale Mediterranean-hotel style, with twice-daily housekeeping, down comforters and great robes. It's a quieter, classy alternative to the Strip.

HYATT REGENCY LAKE LAS VEGAS RESORT Map p260   Casino Hotel

☎ 702-567-1234, 888-591-1234; http://lakelasvegas .hyatt.com; 101 Montelago Blvd, Henderson, 20 miles east of the Strip; r weekday/weekend from $159/179, lake-view r add $30; round trip Strip shuttle per person $40; ⓢ

A gorgeous lakeside setting makes this tranquil oasis worth the drive, especially if you have kids with boundless energy. Many of the Moroccan-themed rooms have balconies. The mandatory daily resort fee ($15) added to all quoted rates covers some of the myriad recreational activities on offer. To get here, take I-215 eastbound to Lake Mead Dr, then turn left and follow Lake Las Vegas Pkwy; it's about a 30-minute trip.

Facade, Paris–Las Vegas (p190)

rooms have satellite TV and face either an interior waterfall garden bounded by a glass-atrium roof or the twinkling city lights set against the desert mountains. Ranchers, locals and RVers flock here, and there's a lot of good stuff to keep them amused.

SILVERTON Map p260 — Casino Hotel

☎ 702-263-7777, 866-946-4373; www.silverton casino.com; 3333 Blue Diamond Rd, off I-15, 4 miles south of the Strip; r/ste from $80/250; free Strip & shopping shuttles; 🔁
Built for the same crowd as the **Bass Pro Shops Outdoor World** (p183) next door, the large lodge-style rooms at this conservative casino resort feature the same beds found at the Bellagio but for a fraction of the price. That way you can afford all of those jellybeans in the mini-bar.

SOUTH COAST Map p260 — Casino Hotel

☎ 702-796-7111, 800-675-3267; www.southcoast casino.com; 9777 Las Vegas Blvd S, 5.5 miles south of the Strip; rates unavailable at press time; 🔁
Set to open in mid-2006, this ambitious Coast Casino will be just a quick drive south of the Strip. Oversized guest-rooms with plasma-screen TVs and high-speed Internet are promised. A family-oriented development, it'll have a pool complex and sand volleyball court, movie theaters, a bowling center and child care, plus an equestrian center.

JW MARRIOTT LAS VEGAS RESORT
Map p260 — Casino Hotel

☎ 702-869-7777, 877-869-8777; www.jwlasvegas resort.com; 211 N Rampart Blvd, 11 miles north-west of the Strip; r from $179, ste from $239; 🔁
A beautiful oasis away from the Strip, this Mediterranean-style resort is the most popular for families, golfers and other active types who want the best of the urban jungle and the desert. Each suite-sized room has a bathroom with a separate whirlpool tub and a raindrop shower. On summer weekends, arrive in time for tequila sunset happy hour.

PALACE STATION Map p264 — Casino Hotel

☎ 702-367-2411, 800-634-3101; www.palacestation .com; 2411 W Sahara Ave, off I-15, 1 mile west of the Strip; r weekday/weekend from $40/100, luxury-tower r add $30; free Strip & airport shuttles; 🔁
Getting lower marks than other railroad-themed Station Casinos, this locals' favorite will do in a pinch. It's got a handy location close to the Strip. Not all rooms are created equal, though. Avoid the older 'value' courtyard rooms and go for 'luxury' tower rooms instead.

SAM'S TOWN Map p260 — Casino Hotel

☎ 702-456-7777, 800-634-6371; www.samstownlv .com; 5111 Boulder Hwy, 6 miles east of the Strip; r weekday/weekend from $40/110, ste from $100; free Strip & downtown shuttles; 🔁
This is the major player on the Boulder Strip. Here giant Southwestern-themed

---

RUNS FOR THE BORDER

If you're driving to Nevada and suddenly find out that every hotel in Vegas is full when you call ahead, don't panic. You can pull over just after the California state line at the family-friendly casino hotels in **Primm** or **Jean** (p228). If you're coming from Arizona, there are retro motels in **Boulder City** (p211) near Hoover Dam, as well as a slew of casino hotels a helluva lot further south in **Laughlin** (p229).

Off I-15 at the Utah state line, the burgeoning, low-key town of **Mesquite** (☎ 877-637-7848; www.visitmesquite.com) is just over an hour's drive from downtown Las Vegas. **CasaBlanca** (☎ 800-459-7529; www.casablancaresort.com; r weekday/weekend from $39/69, high season add $20) casino hotel, golf course and spa is the most popular place to stay, but a few inexpensive motels are found on the main street, too.

SUITE DEALS

The most popular all-suite hotels for extended stays are directly across from the Hard Rock, just west of Paradise Rd. Upscale 'European' **Alexis Park Villas** (☎ 702-796-3322, 800-582-2228; www.alexispark.com; 375 E Harmon Ave; ste incl breakfast from $79; ⚑) and less frilly **St Tropez** (☎ 702-369-5400, 800-666-5400; www.sttropezlasvegas .com; 455 E Harmon Ave; ste incl breakfast from $99; ⚑) serve business travelers and airline flight crews. Spacious, but very well-used suites (some accommodate up to four people) are in two-story buildings around swimming pools. Being close to the Hard Rock keeps them full.

Lining Paradise Rd north of Harmon Ave are dozens of chain all-suite hotels that all advertise rates around $100 per night, slightly less for extended stays. But traffic can be a headache. Plus, service and room standards are unpredictable. To be near the convention center, pay more to stay at one of the places listed in 'Top Five Biz Hotels' (p199).

Note that almost all extended-stay hotels offer daily rentals if space is available. To spend less on a room or suite with a kitchenette or fully equipped kitchen, search further away from the Strip. The most convenient lineup is along Las Vegas Blvd S, a few miles south of Tropicana Ave, down by the outlet malls and Blue Diamond Rd. Decent chains with branch locations there and elsewhere around town include the following:

- **Budget Suites of America** (☎ 866-877-2000; www.budgetsuites.com; ste per week/month from $199/749) The daily rates at this far-less-attractive chain are nothing to sing about, but for longer stays on a shoestring, it's worth a try.
- **Emerald Suites** (☎ 866-847-2002; www.emeraldsuites.com; ste per week from $435) A small, local enterprise aimed at business travelers, repeat visitors to Vegas and people who are just moving to town. Free high-speed Internet.
- **Homestead Studio Suites** (Map p265; ☎ 800-804-3724; 3045 S Maryland Pkwy; studio ste per night from $60) A middle-of-the-road choice, with locations east of the Strip and on the Boulder Hwy.

SUNCOAST Map p260   Casino Hotel

☎ 702-636-7111, 877-677-7111; www.suncoast casino.com; 9090 Alta Dr, 10 miles northwest of the Strip; r weekday/weekend from $69/129; free airport & Strip shuttles; ⚑

Can't afford the Marriott in Summerlin, but still want proximity to Red Rock Canyon and nearby golf courses? Try the farthest-flung branch of the Coast Casinos chain. Giant rooms have floor-to-ceiling windows, some with mountain views. Families will feel right at home here with a bowling center, multiplex movie theater and on-site child care.

SUNSET STATION Map p260   Casino Hotel

☎ 702-547-7777, 888-786-7389; www.sunsetstation .com; 1301 W Sunset Rd, Henderson, 10 miles south-east of the Strip; r weekday/weekend from $70/109; free Strip & airport shuttles; ⚑

A favorite with Henderson locals, this one tops the Station Casinos chain. Granted, it's a long way to go off the Strip. But on the weekends, you'll get much more than you would for the same price on the tattered edges of the Strip.

Cheap Sleeps

If you've brought your Winnebago to Vegas, the **Silverton** (p203; sites with full hook-ups $36-55) is closest to the Strip. But most people head for RV parks along the Boulder Hwy; there's one at **Sam's Town** (p203; sites with full hook-ups $13-21).

Can't find a cheap room for the night? Avoid the rent-by-the-hour motels on the Boulder Strip and in North Las Vegas. If you want a decent motel, you may have to make the drive all the way out to Boulder City, near Hoover Dam.

CANNERY Map p260   Casino Hotel

☎ 702-507-5700, 866-999-4899; www.cannery casinos.com; 2121 E Craig Rd, off I-15, 10 miles northeast of the Strip; r weekday/weekend from $60/90; bus 403; ⚑

This fruity casino hotel – which boasts walls adorned with WWII-era pin-ups – in down-and-out North Las Vegas sees a lot of traffic from the nearby speedway and Nellis Air Force Base. Rates soar during Nascar week-ends, but otherwise it simply plays to the local crowd.

Excursions ▪

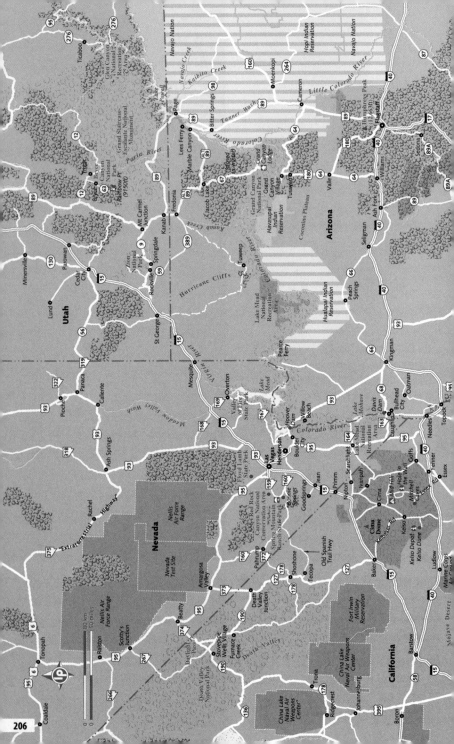

Excursions

Las Vegas is the antithesis of a naturalist's vision of America. Yet it's near some of the Southwest's most spectacular attractions. Beautiful Red Rock Canyon is just outside town. Also within easy striking distance of Sin City are imposing Hoover Dam, the cool oases of Lake Mead National Recreation Area, brilliant Valley of Fire State Park and the popular gambling gulch of Laughlin. Even the forests and snowfields of Charleston Peak are less than an hour's drive away.

For those with more than an afternoon to spare, the most incredible natural wonders beckon. Just over the California state line are the geological wonderlands of Death Valley and the oft-overlooked Mojave National Preserve. Longer drives bring you to Arizona's famed Grand Canyon or to the otherworldly duo of Utah's Zion and Bryce Canyon National Parks. You could visit any of these grand places in an excruciatingly long day trip. But overnighting in the desert to see the sunset and tomorrow's sunrise, when the pastel palette of the landscape shows off exquisite hues, is an opportunity you shouldn't miss. Otherwise, a time-saving option is to view these sights by air (p208), which can easily be done from Las Vegas.

The following sections provide basic information for getting away from the neon of the Strip and into this almost indescribable country. The day-trip destinations can be done on the spur of the moment, as long as you've got your own transportation (for car rentals, see p235), but for overnight trips, advance reservations are essential. Always check the forecast before heading out by calling the **National Weather Service** (☎ 702-736-3854). If you came to Vegas unequipped for the Great Outdoors, West Coast outfitter **REI** (☎ 702-896-7111; 🕙 10am-9pm Mon-Sat, 11am-6pm Sun) is nearby at the **District** (p183) shopping mall in Henderson.

In-depth coverage of the areas beyond Las Vegas can be found in Lonely Planet's *Southwest USA, Grand Canyon National Park, Zion & Bryce Canyon National Parks, California* and *Road Trip: Route 66* guidebooks.

THE BEST DAM DAY TRIPS
To get the most bang out of your day in the desert, make a grand loop east of Las Vegas. Stop off in old-fashioned **Boulder City** (p210) en route to magnificent **Hoover Dam** (p209), then backtrack and slowly wind north beside **Lake Mead** (p211), timing your drive perfectly to finish up in **Valley of Fire State Park** (p212) during the last hours before sunset.

If you don't want to make a whole dam day of it, then head west to **Red Rock Canyon** (p213), which is amazingly close to the Strip. Spend a cool morning or late afternoon horseback riding, mountain biking or just driving on the scenic loop through this national conservation area. Kids may like Bonnie Springs nearby.

CALIFORNIA, HERE WE COME
One in four visitors to Las Vegas happens to be from Southern California, which should tell you just how easy it is to visit the Golden State from Sin City.

You can do a western driving loop through **Death Valley National Park** (p224) in a day, but only if you get an early start. A better idea is to roll out of Vegas after brunch, then stay overnight at Furnace Creek, Stovepipe Wells village or Beatty. Explore this giant park the next day before high-tailing it back to the Strip. A quicker excursion is to head south into the **Mojave National Preserve** (p227), in the no-man's land between I-15 and I-40, just west of the Nevada state line.

If you're driving from Los Angeles to Las Vegas, the quickest route is to take I-10 east to I-15, then take I-15 north all the way to the Strip. For driving distances, times and highway information, see p234. A slower, more scenic option is to detour off I-15 at Baker and head north through Death Valley National Park or trace a smaller loop south through the Mojave National Preserve.

CANYONS DEEP, DESERT HIGHS

Ooh, baby: it doesn't get much bigger or more impressive than **Grand Canyon National Park** (p215). The national park is split by the Colorado River, which means you've got two choices: either visit the **South Rim** (p216) or the **North Rim** (p219). You've got to decide before leaving Las Vegas, though. An action-packed, multiday option would be to head northeast from Las Vegas to Utah's St George, the jumping-off point for trips to the canyon's North Rim and also **Zion National Park** (p220) and **Bryce Canyon National Park** (p223).

To visit the more popular South Rim, cross over **Hoover Dam** (opposite), then take US 93 southeast to Kingman. Follow I-40 east to Williams and then head north to Grand Canyon Village. You can overnight in the park or back in Flagstaff. If you're not in a hurry, though, take the scenic **Route 66** (p217) from Kingman to Williams via Seligman. Then on the way back to Sin City, avoid retracing your route over Hoover Dam by following Route 66 west from Kingman over the California state line to Needles, then head north on US 95 or detour further west through the **Mojave National Preserve** (p227).

ORGANIZED TOURS

Most organized tours appeal to seniors who prefer to leave the driving to others. It's easy enough to escape the city with a rental car, but Hoover Dam package deals can save a lot of ticketing headaches and adventure outfitters can ease logistic hassles. Free hotel pick-up and drop-off from the Strip are included in many rates. Check online and in Vegas' free tourist glossy magazines (p242) for frequent promotions.

Black Canyon River Adventures (☎ 702-294-1414, 800-455-3490; www.blackcanyonadventures.com; Hacienda Hotel, off Hwy 93 east of Boulder City; adult/child 5-12/child 13-15 $73/45/70, plus transportation from Las Vegas $106/103/78) Three-hour motor-assisted raft floats down the Colorado River. Boats launch from the base of Hoover Dam, stopping for swimming and lunch en route to Willow Beach Marina.

Desert Eco-Tours (☎ 702-647-4685; www.lasvegaszoo.org; half-day tour $130, full-day tours $110-230) Offers nonprofit small-group tours of ghost mining towns, geological wonders, petroglyphs, and gemstone collecting areas.

Down River Outfitters (☎ 702-293-1190, 800-748-3702; www.downriveroutfitters.com; guided tour $150, canoe & kayak rentals per person per day $45-55) Small-group canoe and kayak trips from the base of Hoover Dam to Willow Beach. All-day guided trips stop at caves and canyons along the way and include a picnic lunch and free shuttle service to/from the Strip. Canoe or kayak rentals only include shuttle service from the staging area to the Hoover Dam launch site and later pickup at Willow Beach.

Escape Adventures (☎ 702-296-2953, 800-596-2953; www.escapeadventures.com/las_vegas/; weekend & multiday trips from $385) Letting you escape the neon jungle for a single-track mountain-bike and/or hiking tour of stunning Red Rock Canyon, Death Valley, the Grand Canyon, Utah's national parks and beyond. Tours (from $99) of Red Rock Canyon and the Spring Mountains with subsidiary **Las Vegas Cyclery** (Map p260; ☎ 702-838-6966; 8221 W Charleston Blvd; www.lasvegascyclery.com) include free hotel transfers to/from the Strip.

Gray Line (☎ 702-384-1234, 800-634-6579; www.grayline.com; tours $35-140) Reputable bus tour operator offers a variety of excursions to Hoover Dam, Red Rock Canyon, Lake Mead (including a cruise) and the Grand Canyon.

Papillon Helicopter Flights (☎ 702-736-7243, 888-635-7272, toll-free in the UK 0800 404 9767, in Ireland 1-800-625-009; www.papillon.com; Grand Canyon tours per person $240-350; ☯ departures 7am-4:15pm), Vegas' oldest helicopter-flightseeing outfitter does luxury tours all over the Southwest. The Grand Canyon Celebration flight experience includes a touchdown on the canyon floor. Departures from McCarran Airport's Executive Terminal.

Pink Jeep Tours (☎ 702-895-6777, 888-900-4480; www.pinkjeeplasvegas.com; half-day tours $75-100, full-day tours $120-320) Small-group, off-road adventure alternatives to Hoover Dam, Valley of Fire, Red Rock Canyon, Mt Charleston and Eldorado Canyon. The 'Ultimate Grand Canyon Combo' includes brief helicopter and pontoon boat rides.

Rocky Trails Adventure Tours (☎ 702-869-9991, 888-846-4747; www.adventurelasvegas.com; tours $100-500; ☯ reservations 24hr) A one-stop shop for outdoor adventure tours. Arranges everything from guided kayak floats below Hoover Dam to soaring glider rides and off-road 4WD explorations of ghost towns and mines.

WAY OFF THE BEATEN PATH

Almost everybody who makes an excursion from Vegas visits Hoover Dam, Red Rock Canyon, the Grand Canyon or Zion and Bryce Canyon National Parks.

To escape the crowds, you can visit the same spots but make lesser-known detours along the way, like stopping first at **Boulder City** (p210) en route to Hoover Dam or following **Route 66** (p217) to the Grand Canyon's South Rim.

Or you can chuck the popular itineraries entirely in favor of more odd and off-beat places. Leave the desert behind for the alpine highs of Charleston Peak in the **Spring Mountains** (p229), which can be combined with a trip to Red Rock Canyon, or go UFO-watching outside **Area 51** along the **Extraterrestrial Highway** (p225).

HOOVER DAM

The 726ft-high, concrete Hoover Dam was once the tallest dam in the world. It has a striking beauty, with its imposing, graceful curve filling a dramatic red rock canyon, backed by the brilliant blue waters of Lake Mead. A simple, strong form and art-deco design and embellishments contrast beautifully with the stark landscape. A New Deal project, construction of the dam in the 1930s provided much-needed employment as the country struggled through the Great Depression. When the dam opened in 1936, it was possibly America's only public-works project completed ahead of schedule: by two years and under budget by $14 million.

Originally called Boulder Dam, the edifice was officially renamed by Congress in 1947 to honor President Hoover, under whose administration the land compromise that made the dam possible was worked out. The dam was built primarily to control

> ### TRANSPORTATION
>
> **Distance from Las Vegas** to Hoover Dam visitor center 35 miles
> **Direction** Southeast
> **Travel Time** 45 minutes
> **Bus** Coach tours from Vegas are a bargain (from about $35) and guarantee tickets to the basic dam tour. CAT (p234) bus 116 goes only as far as Boulder City.
> **Car** From the Strip, take I-15 south to I-215, then take I-515/US 93 & 95 and continue southeast of Henderson over Railroad Pass, then past Boulder City to Hoover Dam. Expect possible traffic delays until the new bypass is completed by 2008. As you approach the dam, park in the multilevel parking lot ($5, cash only; ☺ 8am-6pm) *before* you reach the visitor center and the Arizona state line.

floods on the lower Colorado River. The hydroelectricity and water supply were bonuses that enabled Las Vegas to grow. The waters of the lower Colorado irrigate some one million acres of land in the USA and almost half a million in Mexico; provide water to 18 million people primarily in Las Vegas, Los Angeles, San Diego, Phoenix and Tucson; and generate 4 billion kilowatt hours a year for Southern California, Nevada and Arizona.

Hoover Dam (above)

To some people, Hoover is only a dam, but to many it's the best nongambling attraction in Nevada. The **visitor center** has interesting exhibits as well as a great rooftop view of the dam. (Incidentally, the visitor center at Hoover Dam cost taxpayers $125 million – only $40 million less than the dam itself.) A free walk across the dam allows you and more than 1.3 million other people every year to cross the Arizona–Nevada border, where clocks announce the time-zone change.

The National Park Service's highly recommended **Discovery Tour** starts below ground with a short video presentation, followed by a guided tour into the bowels of the dam. Ride the elevators more than 50 stories down to Black Canyon tunnel to view the dam's massive power generators, each of which alone could power a city of 100,000 people. Then race back up top for a self-guided tour of flood-preventing spillways, historic exhibit halls and outdoor interpretive sites. Even if you don't pay for the tour, you can still eavesdrop on the fascinating talk near the 30ft-high **Winged Figures of the Republic**, a memorial to the men who built this triumph of sweat and engineering.

When you tire of admiring the vertiginous views and pretending to jump the railing (no terrorist jokes, please – that sort of thing is taken very seriously around here) make a beeline for the refrigerated gift shop, where you can pick up unique, all-American novelties for your loved ones: 'Got Power?' T-shirts, 'Dam Proud to Be An American' bumper stickers, Hoover Dam–shaped refrigerator magnets – you name it, bub.

Most visitors don't turn around and head right back to the Strip right after visiting the dam. If you get an early start, you can make a day of it by rafting or paddling down the Colorado River. Otherwise the usual day-trip route backtracks to the gateway to **Lake Mead** (opposite) and ends up in **Valley of Fire State Park** (p212).

Information

Boulder City Chamber of Commerce (☎ 702-293-2034, 866-297-4547; www.bouldercitychamber.com; 465 Nevada Way, Boulder City; ☻ 9am-5pm Mon-Fri) Opposite the Boulder Dam Hotel.

Hoover Dam Visitor Center (☎ information 702-294-3517, tour reservations 702-597-5970, 866-291-8687; www.usbr.gov/lc/hooverdam; Hwy 93; tour adult/child 7-16/senior & military $10/5/8; ☻ 9am-5pm, last tickets sold 4:45pm, closed Thanksgiving & Christmas) Avoid weekends and arrive early in the day to avoid long lines (before 10:30am or around 3pm).

Sights & Activities

Black Canyon River Adventures (p208) Organized group float trips downriver from Hoover Dam to Willow Beach Marina.

Boulder City Outfitters (☎ 702-293-1190, 800-748-3702; http://bouldercityoutfitters.com; half-/full-day tours $100/150) Mountain-biking and hiking trips around Lake Mead and Boulder City.

Down River Outfitters (p208) Canoe and kayak trips launch below Hoover Dam; guided tours and self-guided trips available.

Hoover Dam Museum (☎ 702-294-1988; www.bcmha.org; upstairs, Boulder Dam Hotel, 1305 Arizona St, Boulder City; adult/senior & child $2/1; ☻ 10am-5pm Mon-Sat, noon-5pm Sun, closed on some holidays) Interactive exhibits and a 20-minute film about the dam's construction.

DETOUR: BOULDER CITY

On the way to Hoover Dam, about 25 miles from the Strip, divert on to Business 93 to loop through quaint downtown Boulder City, which sprang up in the early 1930s to house and feed thousands of dam construction workers. Charmingly, not a whole lot has changed since then.

Turn right at Arizona St for the **Boulder Dam Hotel**. Upstairs is the engagingly hands-on **Hoover Dam Museum**, which narrates the surprising social history of the everyday folks who built the dam. You'll appreciate the Hoover Dam tour much more if you detour here first. Just down the street is the historic **Boulder Theatre**, also built by the New Deal–era Works Progress Administration (WPA). Back on the main street are hodge-podge **antique shops** and a handful of busy restaurants. When you're ready to continue to Hoover Dam, follow Nevada Way out of town.

Alternatively, you can always stop in Boulder City for dinner on the way back from the dam if you get a late start from Vegas. On weekend nights, local indie bands often play at **Matteo's Underground Lounge** in the basement of the Boulder Dam Hotel. Retro **Boulder Bowl** is a block further east. In fact, the only entertainment missing from this peculiarly quiet town is gaming, which has been illegal here since the 1950s.

Eating & Entertainment

Boulder Bowl (☎ 702-293-2368; 504 California Ave, Boulder City; ☺ hours vary) By the Central Market.

Chiarelli's Deli & Market (☎ 702-293-6600; 1224 Arizona St, Boulder City; lunch $6-10; ☺ 9.30am-6pm Mon-Fri) Home-cooked pasta, toothsome sandwiches and iced tea.

Matteo's Dining & Underground Lounge (☎ 702-293-0098; Boulder Dam Hotel, 1305 Arizona St, Boulder City; breakfast & lunch $4-8, dinner mains $10-25; ☺ breakfast, lunch & dinner) For the lounge, see p156.

Milo's (☎ 702-293-9540; 534-8 Nevada Way, Boulder City; meals $5-20; ☺ café 6am-3pm, restaurant 11am-10pm) Wine cellar, sidewalk café and espresso bar.

Snacketeria (☎ 702-293-4364; at Nevada spillway on north side of Hoover Dam wall; ☺ 9am-5pm) Cafeteria-quality food, bottled water, film, souvenirs and books.

LAKE MEAD

It's less than an hour's drive from Las Vegas to the most visited northern section of the 1.5-million-acre **Lake Mead National Recreation Area (NRA)**. Within this area are Lake Mead, which extends 110 miles toward the Grand Canyon; 67-mile-long Lake Mohave, which runs along the Arizona–Nevada border; and miles of spectacular desert around the lakes. Admission to Lake Mead NRA costs $5 per car (free for annual national parks pass holders), and is valid for five days.

When Hoover Dam was built between 1931 and 1935, it backed up the Colorado River, forming Lake Mead. In 1953 the smaller Davis Dam was completed, forming Lake Mohave. The Colorado River and the two lakes form a natural border with Arizona to the east. Lake Mead has 550 miles of shoreline and a capacity of 9.1-trillion gallons, equal to two years of the normal flow of the Colorado River. A favorite vacation spot for local families, the lake is set in peaceful surrounds, most of which are undeveloped and protected as part of the recreation area.

There are few facilities of any kind, so stock up on food, drink and other supplies such as sunscreen before heading out this way. Most day-trippers approach Lake Mead outside Boulder City via the turn-off to Lakeshore Scenic Dr, 4 miles west of Hoover Dam. Stop off at **Alan Bible visitor center**, a wellspring of information on recreational options, camping and natural history that shows a free documentary on the history and construction of Hoover Dam. The **north entrance station** is 2 miles beyond the visitor center.

Popular year-round activities include swimming, fishing, boating, waterskiing, kayaking and even scuba diving. The main route winds north, then east, passing lovely beaches and bays, multiple marinas, scenic viewpoints and short hiking trails along the way. Boat tours depart from a landing just north of the turn-off to **Boulder Beach**. About 10 miles beyond the north entrance station, the road curves west toward **Lake Las Vegas**.

Turn northward past the **Wetlands Trail** for bird-watching, then drive east along Northshore Rd. Before the 25-mile marker is the **Northshore Summit** trailhead for views of the **Bowl of Fire**. Next up is gorgeous **Redstone Dune Trail** picnic area, a good place to get out of the car and stretch. Further north past **Echo Bay** and **Overton Beach** is the turn-off to **Valley of Fire State Park** (p212).

Sleeping

Best Western Lighthouse Inn & Resort (☎ 702-293-6444, 800-937-8376; www.bestwestern.com; 110 Ville St, off US 93, outside Boulder City; r weekday/weekend from $65/80) Perched above Lake Mead with beautiful views.

Boulder Dam Hotel (☎ 702-293-3510; www.boulderdamhotel.com; 1305 Arizona St, Boulder City; r/ste incl breakfast from $100/140) Bette Davis, FDR and Howard Hughes have all slept here. Rooms are hot, small and noisy.

El Rancho Motel (☎ 702-293-1085; 725 Nevada Hwy, Boulder City; s/d $65/80) Boulder City's main street has plenty of comfy vintage motels like this one.

Sands Motel (☎ 702-293-2589; http://sandsmotelbouldercity.com; 809 Nevada Hwy, Boulder City; s/d from $59/69, add $10 Fri & Sat) Clean, friendly, family-owned 1950s motel.

TRANSPORTATION

Distance from Las Vegas to Alan Bible Visitor Center 30 miles; to Las Vegas Bay 25 miles; to Echo Bay 55 miles; to Overton Beach 70 miles

Direction Southeast

Travel Time 45 to 75 minutes

Car From the Strip, take I-15 south to I-215, then take I-215 to I-515/US 93 & 95 and continue southeast of Henderson over Railroad Pass, then past Boulder City. About 4 miles before Hoover Dam, turn left on to Lakeshore Scenic Dr near the visitor center. The lake is also accessible from Las Vegas via Lake Mead Dr (NV 146), which heads east from Henderson and crosses the Boulder Hwy. The west entrance station is before the intersection with Lake Las Vegas Pkwy.

Information

Alan Bible Visitor Center (☎ 702-293-8990; www
.nps.gov/lame; off Lakeshore Scenic Dr at Hwy 93;
🕑 8:30am-4:30pm, closed Thanksgiving, Christmas &
New Year's Day) Free exhibits, brochures, ranger talks
and cactus garden walks, plus books and maps for sale.

Sights & Activities

Lake Mead Cruises (☎ 702-293-6180; www.lakemead
cruises.com; Hemenway Harbor, 90min midday cruise per
adult/child $20/9; brunch & dinner cruises from $33/15;
🕑 departures daily) Operates sightseeing trips on Lake
Mead.

Las Vegas Boat Harbor (☎ 702-293-1191; www.boating
lakemead.com; Hemenway Harbor; boat or waverunner

VALLEY OF FIRE STATE PARK

Near the northern end of Lake Mead National Recreation Area, this park is a masterpiece of desert scenery, a fantasyland
of wondrous shapes carved in psychedelic
sandstone by the erosive forces of wind and
water. The fiery red rocks are similar in
appearance and geology to the desert landscapes of Utah, Arizona and New Mexico,
but are easily accessible from Las Vegas and
not crowded with tourists.

Early residents included basket-making
and pueblo-building tribes. Several petro-
glyphs survive throughout the park as a reminder of these early Native Americans. Some
of the most interesting formations are **Elephant Rock** and the **Seven Sisters**. Especially scenic is
the winding side road past the visitor center out to **White Domes**. This road passes **Rainbow Vista**
and the three-mile roundtrip hiking trailhead to **Fire Canyon** and **Silica Dome** (incidentally where
Captain Kirk perished in *Star Trek: Generations*). On the other side of the main road from
the petrified logs, **Atlatl Rock** has some distinct and artistic petroglyphs. Migratory birds also
stop over in the park.

rental per hour $30-50, per day $180-360) Most of the
marinas on Lake Mead offer personal watercraft rental,
including this one.

Eating & Sleeping

Echo Bay Resort (☎ 702-394-4000, 800-752-9669; www
.sevencrown.com; RV sites $12-18, d $60-115) Simple
motel, marina, restaurant and cocktail lounge near Overton.

Hyatt Regency Lake Las Vegas Resort (p202)

Lake Mead Resort (☎ 702-293-2074, 800-752-9669;
d $55-85, kitchen ste $100-175) Basic motel, marina, floating restaurant and cocktail lounge near Boulder Beach.

NPS Campgrounds (☎ 800-752-9669; tent & RV sites
$10) Shoreline sites open year-round at Boulder Beach, Las
Vegas Bay (tents only), Callville Bay and Echo Bay.

TRANSPORTATION

Distance from Las Vegas to state park visitor center
55 miles
Direction Northeast
Travel Time 1 hour
Car The quickest route from Las Vegas is via I-15 to
NV 169. For those coming from Hoover Dam, the drive
along the western shore of Lake Mead is more scenic;
turn west toward the Valley of Fire when you're
1 mile past the Overton Beach turn-off from
Northshore Rd.

Valley of Fire State Park (above)

Spring and fall are the best times of year to visit; daytime summer temperatures typically exceed 100°F. The valley looks most vibrant at dawn and dusk, though most of its wildlife is nocturnal. There's a $6 day-use fee per vehicle, payable at the visitor center just off NV 169, which curves gently through the park west of **Lake Mead** (p211). The center has excellent exhibits, provides general information, sells books and maps, and the staff can make hiking suggestions. Free ranger programs incorporate fossil hunting, interpretive hikes and moonlight astronomy.

Information

Valley of Fire State Park Visitor Center (☎ 702-397-2088; http://parks.nv.gov/vf.htm; ☽ 8:30am-4:30pm) Call for ranger program schedules.

Sights

Lost City Museum (☎ 702-397-2193; http://dmla.clan .lib.nv.us/docs/museums/lost/lostcity.htm; 721 S Moapa Valley Blvd, Overton; adult/senior $3/2, child under 18 free; ☽ 8:30am-4:30pm) Worth a detour.

Eating

Inside Scoop (☎ 702-397-2055, 395 S Moapa Valley Blvd, Overton; items $3-6; ☽ 10am-8pm Mon-Sat, 11am-7pm Sun) Friendly ice-cream parlor and café. Take-out available.

DETOUR: LOST CITY

Eight miles north of the turn-off west to Valley of Fire State Park from Lake Mead, the modest **Lost City Museum** tells the story of a 'lost' pueblo that existed here from 300 BC until around 1150 AD. Interior displays of excavated ruins aren't as captivating as the Pueblo Revival–style building itself, constructed of sun-dried adobe bricks by the Civilian Conservation Corps during the 1930s. You can peek inside replicas of original Native American dwellings behind the museum, which stands at the south end of the small town of Overton.

Sugar's Home Plate (☎ 702-397-8084; 309 S Moapa Valley Blvd, Overton; meals $4-12; ☽ closed Mon) Head for this sports bar and restaurant for barbecue and homemade pies.

Sleeping

Best Western North Shore Inn (☎ 702-397-6000, 800-937-8376; www.bestwestern.com; 520 N Moapa Valley Blvd; r incl breakfast from $70) Basic rooms, outdoor heated pool.

Plaza Motel (☎ 702-397-2414; 207 S Moapa Valley Blvd, Overton; r $35-65) Cheaper, but not as scenic as the Lake Mead motels (opposite).

State Park Campgrounds (tent & RV sites incl day-use entry fee $14) First-come, first-served campsites with water, outdoor grills, restrooms and showers.

RED ROCK CANYON

The startling contrast between the artificial neon glow of Las Vegas and the awesome natural forces of Red Rock Canyon can't be exaggerated. Only **Valley of Fire State Park** (opposite) can compete in showing off the rugged, artistic beauty of the Southwest.

The canyon is actually more like a valley, with the steep, rugged red rock escarpment rising 3000ft on its western edge. It was created about 65 million years ago when tectonic plates collided along the Keystone Thrust fault line, pushing a protective plate of limestone up and over younger red sandstone, slowing its eventual erosion.

The 130-sq-mile Red Rock Canyon National Conservation Area should be on the must-see list of every visitor to Las Vegas, but – perhaps fortunately – it often isn't. A 13-mile, one-way **scenic loop** allows visitors to drive past some of the area's most striking features, gain access to the hiking trails and rock-climbing routes or simply be entranced by the panoramic vistas. Pay the day-use fee

TRANSPORTATION

Distance from Las Vegas to Red Rock Canyon visitor center 20 miles
Direction West
Travel Time 30 minutes
Bicycle You can cycle all the way to Red Rock Canyon from Las Vegas (for now, Charleston Blvd has bike lanes), but you're better off renting from McGhie's Bike Outpost in Blue Diamond.
Car There are two routes to Red Rock Canyon from Las Vegas. From the Strip, take I-15 south, exit Blue Diamond Rd (NV 160), drive west, then after 10 miles veer right on to NV 159. For the return trip, drive east along NV 159, which turns into Charleston Blvd.

(per car/motorcycle $5/2) at the entrance station, where rangers hand out copies of the helpful 'Keystone Visitor's Guide.' Next, stop by the excellent **visitor center**, which has free maps and brochures, natural history exhibits and information about all kinds of activities, from nature walks to challenging hikes, world-class rock-climbing routes, and 4WD roads.

Calico Hills is the premier spot for sport climbing. The hardest rock-clambering trail for hikers is the 5-mile, four-hour round-trip trek up **Turtlehead Peak**, which starts at the **Sandstone Quarry** parking lot. **Willow Springs** picnic area has several trailheads, including for the easy 4.5-mile walk round trip to **White Rock**, as well as the short **Children's Discovery Lost Creek Trail**. The parking lot for **Ice Box Canyon** is an alternate starting point for a 2.5-mile round-trip trail across open desert and into the canyon, where you can do some tricky boulder scrambling for another 1.5 miles each way to reach an upper pool with a seasonal waterfall.

Information

Red Rock Canyon Interpretive Association (☎ 702-515-5367; www.redrockcanyonlv.org) Informative website. Also operates the nonprofit bookstore and gift shop at the visitor center. Call between 8am and 4pm for scheduled interpretive programs (such as yoga, rock climbing, hikes, birding and wildflower walks); reservations recommended.

Red Rock Canyon National Conservation Area Visitor Center (☎ 702-515-5367; www.redrockcanyon.blm.gov; ☽ 8:30am-4:30pm, scenic loop open 6am-5pm winter, till 7pm spring & fall, till 8pm summer) Junior ranger activity booklets for kids also available.

Sights & Activities

Bonnie Springs (☎ 702-875-4191; www.bonniesprings.com; 1 Gunfighter Lane, Blue Diamond; admission per car weekday/weekend $7/10; ☽ 10:30am-5pm, to 6pm in summer) Horseback rides per hour $30 (children must be at least six years old).

McGhie's Bike Outpost (☎ 702-875-4820; www.bikeoutpost.com; 16 Cottonwood Dr B, Blue Diamond; full-suspension mountain bike rental per day $35, multiday and weekly discounts available; ☽ Wed-Sun, call for seasonal hours) Guided road and off-road tours (per person $110-130) include bike rental, helmet, water and hotel pickup.

Silver State Tours (☎ 702-798-7788; www.silverstatetours.com; 1hr ride $28, half-day ride incl box lunch $115) Horseback trips departing from inside Spring Mountain Ranch State Park (entrance fee waived). Also offers covered wagon and stagecoach rides.

Spring Mountain Ranch State Park (☎ 702-875-4141; http://parks.nv.gov/smr.htm; off NV 159, Blue Diamond; day-use fee per vehicle $6; ☽ 8am-dusk, visitor center 10am-4pm) Call for daily guided-tour schedules.

Eating

Bonnie Springs Ranch Restaurant (☎ 702-875-4191; meals from around $10, parking $7-10; ☽ usually open 8am-11pm) Your only option near Red Rock; don't expect much from the all-American menu.

Plush (p152) The perfect place for sunset drinks on the return trip, a short detour north of Charleston Blvd.

Rosemary's Restaurant (p128) On the way back from Red Rock, stop by Las Vegas' best eatery (clean yourself up a bit first, though – it's a classy crowd).

Sleeping

Bonnie Springs Motel (☎ 702-875-4400; www.bonniesprings.com; 1 Gunfighter Lane, Blue Diamond; d $60-80, kitchen ste $95-100) Basic motel rooms. Pets welcome, except in specialty theme rooms. Guests-only morning horseback ride ($30) includes breakfast.

Red Rock Canyon Campground (☎ 702-515-5352; 2 miles east of visitor center on NV 159; ☽ Sep-May) First-come, first-served camping with water and pit toilets. Backcountry camping elsewhere requires a permit (call ☎ 702-515-5050).

DETOUR: BLUE DIAMOND

En route to Red Rock Canyon from the south, you'll pass the tiny town of Blue Diamond, where **McGhie's Bike Outpost** is a one-stop shop for mountain bike rentals, equipment and guided tours around Red Rock Canyon, as well as quick access to 125 miles of single-track in the Cottonwood Valley and Black Velvet areas.

Northwest on NV 159, **Bonnie Springs** has been the scene of countless B-movie shoots. Designed for kiddies, it has the works: Old West melodramas, simulated hangings and gunfights, miniature train rides, a wax museum, a cactus garden and a sad petting zoo. The ranch was once a refueling point for wagon trains on the Old Spanish Trail to California, but it's been strictly a tourist attraction since the 1950s.

More peaceful and authentic is **Spring Mountain Ranch State Park**, just up the road from Bonnie Springs. Inside the national conservation area, this family-friendly picnic park sprawls beneath the Wilson Range. The cool mountain ranch was once owned by Howard Hughes. Today it offers short nature walks, small historical exhibits inside the ranch house, and guided tours and summer 'Theater Under the Stars.'

GRAND CANYON NATIONAL PARK

The Grand Canyon is Arizona's most famous sight – indeed, it is arguably the best-known natural attraction in the US. At 277 miles long, roughly 10 miles wide and a mile deep, it's an incredible spectacle of Technicolor rock strata. Carved by the Colorado River, the canyon's many peaks and buttes and its meandering rims give access to fantastic views. Popular flightseeing day trips from Las Vegas (often combined with flyovers of Hoover Dam and Lake Mead, and a ground tour of the South Rim) provide short-stay visitors with a brief introduction to this famous hole in the ground. Descending into the canyon on hiking and mule trails offers the best sense of the breathtaking variety in the landscape, wildlife and climate.

After first being dismissed as little more than an obstacle to exploration, the canyon drew 19th-century miners bent on exploiting its rich natural resources. Native American resistance and the lack of water slowed development, but by the time Frederick Jackson Turner declared the end of the American frontier in 1893, entrepreneurs had transformed the canyon into one of the country's most celebrated destinations. At the dawn of the industrial revolution, people flocked here in search of the romanticized wilderness ideal and embraced its sublime beauty. They still do; the park attracts four million visitors each year.

Today the rims are only 10 miles apart, as the crow flies, but it's a 215-mile, five-hour drive on narrow roads between the visitor centers on the South and North Rims. Thus, Grand Canyon national park is essentially two separate areas, and is treated as such here. The congested South Rim has more facilities and is the most visited, but the North Rim is closer to Utah's **Zion** (p220) and **Bryce Canyon National Parks** (p223).

In summer, there's no escaping the crowds. Peak season runs from about April to November, and the park is busiest from Memorial Day to Labor Day. On average, temperatures are 20°F cooler on the rim than at the bottom of the canyon, which often exceeds 100°F in summer. June is the driest month, and summer thunderstorms make July and August the wettest. Weather is cooler in fall; freezing overnight temperatures and snow are likely by November. Winter weather can be beautifully clear, but be prepared for fierce storms and extreme cold. Daylight Saving Time (p244) is not observed in Arizona, except by the Navajo Nation.

TRANSPORTATION

Air Rates for hour-long air tours start at around $130 per person; day-long air/ground/boat combos run $200 to $300 per person, and premier helicopter tours landing on the canyon's floor fetch $350 per person. Reputable Vegas-based flightseeing operators include: **Grand Canyon Express** (☎ 702-433-1677, 800-940-2550; www.airvegas.com), **Grand Canyon Tour Company** (☎ 702-655-6060, 800-222-6966, toll-free in the UK 0800 917 5156, in Ireland 1-800-702-022; www.grandcanyontourcompany.com), **Papillon Helicopter Flights** (p208) and **Scenic Airlines** (☎ 702-638-3300, 800-634-6801; www.scenic.com).

Car The Grand Canyon's North Rim is 215 miles (4½ to 5 hours) from the South Rim by car.

Shuttle For transfers from the South Rim to the North Rim and vice versa, try **Trans Canyon Shuttle** (☎ 928-638-2820; one-way/return $65/110; ☼ mid-May–mid-Oct) This is *not* a tour bus but a service for hikers. Reservations required; cash only.

Grand Canyon National Park (above)

Excursions

GRAND CANYON NATIONAL PARK

SOUTH RIM

About 90% of national-park visitors go to the South Rim, centered on **Grand Canyon Village**, which has both early-20th-century hotels and modern amenities. The foremost attraction is the rim itself, paralleled by a 33-mile scenic road with jaw-dropping views and hiking trails snaking along the rim and down into the canyon. To get away from the traffic, trek down to the river and stay at **Phantom Ranch** or at one of several campgrounds; reservations are a must. Mule rides also require advance planning.

Just north of Tusayan is the park's south entrance station. A short drive further ahead by **Mather Point** is **Canyon View Information Plaza**. After stretching your legs, continue to **Grand Canyon Village**. Duck inside the 100-year-old **Hopi House**, one of the park's many Native American–inspired designs by famed Western architect Mary Colter, as well as the equally historic **El Tovar Hotel** and cliffside **Kolb Studio**. At the northeastern end of the village, panoramic views of the canyon unfold at **Yavapai Observation Station**, which has a small geology museum.

When you're refreshed, strike out from either side of the village – **Hermit Rd** goes west; **Desert View Dr** goes east. The rim dips in and out of view as the road passes through the piñon-juniper and ponderosa stands of Kaibab National Forest. Pullouts along the way offer spectacular views and interpretive signs explain the canyon's features and geology. Seasonal shuttle buses parallel the 13-mile **Rim Trail**, which is the easiest walk in the park.

Crowds get thinner the further west you venture. **Mohave and Hopi Points** offer great views of the Colorado River. At the western terminus of the road, **Hermit's Rest** was once a Fred Harvey stagecoach stop. In the opposite direction, Desert View Dr rolls east of Mather Point for 25 miles to the park's eastern entrance station. En route, pause to walk the 800-year-old pueblo ruins at **Tusayan Museum**, then scramble up the five-story stone **Desert View Watchtower**, the highest point on the South Rim.

Exploring the canyon's backcountry is exhilarating. From the rim you can't appreciate the rich wilderness below. Dip toward the canyon floor along the main trails and you'll quickly be immersed in scenes of otherworldly beauty. Adventure enthusiasts should plan to spend at least a night or two deep in the inner gorge – walking the sandy banks of the Colorado River, exploring the side canyon tributaries, sleeping beneath the vast swath of stars and listening to the nightly serenade of chirping frogs – for which backcountry permits are required.

TRANSPORTATION

Distance from Las Vegas 275 miles
Direction Southeast
Travel Time 5 hours

Air In addition to tours, **Scenic Airlines** (p215) also offers scheduled flights from North Las Vegas to Grand Canyon Airport ($99 to $149 each way) in Tusayan, 7 miles from the South Rim.

Bus Most flightseeing companies also offer land-based coach tours, as does **Gray Line** (p208). Narrated bus tours with **Xanterra Parks & Resorts** (☎ 303-297-2757, 888-297-2757; Bright Angel Lodge; www.grandcanyonlodges.com; tours $13-35, children 16 and under free with paying adult) leave from Grand Canyon Village. Reservations advised.

Car Drive to Hoover Dam (see p209), then cross the state line into Arizona and take US 93 south to Kingman, then I-40 east to Williams. Head north on AZ 64, which joins US 180 to Grand Canyon Village. Free parking lots are available. Note Hermits Rest road is closed to private vehicles from March to November.

Shuttle On the South Rim, free **shuttles** (☎ 928-638-0591; ☀ Mar-Nov) operate along three routes: around Grand Canyon Village; west along the rim to Hermits Rest; and east to the South Kaibab trailhead. Buses run every 15 minutes during the day and half-hourly from one hour before sunrise till 6:30am, and from dusk till one hour after sunset. Call the day prior to your visit for wheelchair-accessible shuttle reservations. The seasonal **Trans Canyon Shuttle** (p215) to the North Rim departs at 1:30pm from Bright Angel Lodge.

Train Diesel and steam passenger trains operated by **Grand Canyon Railway** (☎ 928-773-1976, 800-843-8724; www.thetrain.com; 233 N Grand Canyon Blvd, Williams; adult/child 2-10/youth 11-16 round-trip fare from $74/27.50/38) run year-round to the South Rim from Williams, west of Flagstaff. Rates include the park entrance fee; overnight accommodations packages available.

DETOUR: ROUTE 66

Sure, you can speed along the interstate. But America's 'Mother Road' is the most scenic and diverting way to reach the Grand Canyon's South Rim. In Kingman, less than 20 miles past the turn-off to Chloride mining town on US 93, the **Powerhouse Visitor Center** (☎ 928-753-6106, 866-427-7866; www.kingmantourism.org; 120 W Andy Devine Ave; 9am-5pm, to 6pm Mar-Nov), has information, maps and a Route 66 museum ($3).

Follow Andy Devine Ave east out of Kingman on to historic Route 66, passing Hackberry's general store, the tribal territory of Peach Springs, and the hokey family-vacation destination of Grand Canyon Caverns, finally cruising into **Seligman**, a vintage roadside town. Drop by historic **Angel Delgadillo's Route 66 Gift Shop & Visitor's Center** (☎ 928-422-3352; http://route66giftshop.com; 217 E Route 66), to spin yarns about the old days, then head on over to his late brother Juan's wacky **Snow Cap Drive-In** (☎ 928-422-3291; 301 E Route 66).

Savor the serene landscape and broad horizons as you motor out of town along Crookton Rd to Ash Fork, where you rejoin I-40 east to charming **Williams**, a town that's on the national register of historic places and was the last place on Route 66 to be bypassed by the interstate. From Williams, you take a vintage train or drive up to Grand Canyon Village.

On your way back to Vegas, zoom along I-40 to Kingman, turning off on to Oatman Rd, which corkscrews into the Black Mountains over Sitgreaves Pass. At century-old **Goldroad Mine** (☎ 928-768-1600; www.goldroadmine.com; 1hr mine tours adult/child 12 & under $12/6; 10am-4pm), have some chili-and-apple pie at the Prospector Cafe. Two miles further along is the Old West town of **Oatman**, where gunfight re-enactments are held on weekends. Squeezed among the antiques shops, the 1902 Oatman Hotel is where Clark Gable and Carole Lombard honeymooned in 1939.

A couple miles west of Oatman, veer left on to a historic byway leading through breathtaking high-desert landscape. In spring, the region comes alive with wildflowers, but watch out for flash floods. Keep going through Golden Shores and the **Havasu National Wildlife Refuge**, where desert trails wind along the Colorado River. After the railroad tracks, get back on to I-40 westbound to cross into California. The white-piped **Old Trails Arch Bridge**, which once carried Dust Bowl–era refugees, stands to the south. At Needles, head north to **Laughlin** (p228) or west into the **Mojave National Preserve** (p227) and back to Vegas – eventually.

A day hike down to the river and back is a death wish. Hundreds of young, healthy people who try it each year end up in life-threatening situations. While it's easy to stride down the trail for a few hours, the steep uphill return during the midday heat when you're tired can be fatal. For a hardy workout, take the well-graded **South Kaibab Trail**, which starts near Yaki Point, as far as **Skeleton Point**, a 6-mile round trip (in summer, turn around at **Cedar Ridge** instead). The less steep, but busier **Bright Angel Trail** begins at Grand Canyon Village. Day hikers go as far as **Indian Gardens** (9-mile round trip), but in summer if you didn't hit the trail at dawn, turn around at the **3-Mile Resthouse** instead.

Information

Services in Grand Canyon Village include a post office and bank. The closest gas station is south in Tusayan.

Backcountry Information Center (☎ 928-638-7875; Parking Lot E, Grand Canyon Village; 8am-noon & 1-5pm) This center offers information on hiking and overnight backpacking, though staff only answer the phone after 1pm Monday to Friday. Backcountry trail and campsite quotas are limited, so apply for a permit as far in advance as possible. If you arrive without one, put yourself on the waiting list – and pray.

Canyon View Information Plaza (☎ 928-638-7644; 1 mile from Grand Canyon Village; 8am-5pm, extended peak-season hrs) Ranger-staffed info desk and large bulletin boards with information about lodging, weather and more. Free programs include interpretive talks and guided walks (many are wheelchair-accessible). Ask about Junior Ranger activities for children aged four to 14.

Desert View Information Center (☎ 928-638-7893; 9am-6pm, winter hrs vary) Near the eastern entrance of the park.

Grand Canyon Association (☎ 928-638-2481; www .grandcanyon.org; Canyon View Information Plaza) Non-profit bookstore sells books, maps, trail guides and videos.

Grand Canyon National Park – South Rim (☎ 928-638-7888; www.nps.gov/grca/grandcanyon/south-rim; 7-day entry pass per vehicle $20) 24-hour recorded information on everything from weather conditions to applying for permits. At the south and east entrance stations, rangers hand out *The Guide*, which has detailed information on everything from interpretive programs to shuttle-bus routes.

Medical Clinic (☎ 928-638-2551; Grand Canyon Village; 9am-6pm Mon-Fri, 10am-2pm Sat, extended summer hrs) Offers walk-in medical care.

Williams–Grand Canyon Chamber of Commerce (☎ 928-635-0273; http://williamschamber.com; 200 W Railroad Ave, cnr Grand Canyon Blvd, Williams; 8am-5pm, till 6.30pm in summer) Has exhibits, books, maps and brochures. Kaibab National Forest rangers help sift through outdoor recreation opportunities.

Sights & Activities

Canyon Village Marketplace (928-638-2262; 8am-7pm, later in summer) Hiking, camping and backpacking equipment rentals and sales.

Desert View Watchtower (928-638-2736; Desert View; 9am-5pm)

Hopi House Gallery (928-638-3458; Grand Canyon Village; 8am to 6pm, later in summer) Sells Native American art and crafts.

Kolb Studio (928-638-2771; Grand Canyon Village; 8am-5pm, later in summer) Bookstore and temporary art exhibits.

Tusayan Museum (928-638-2305; 3 miles west of Desert View; 8am-5pm, free tours 11am & 1:30pm)

Xanterra Parks & Resorts (303-297-2757, 888-297-2757; www.grandcanyonlodges.com) Offers mule trips year-round. Choose from the seven-hour day trip (including box lunch $133) or overnight trip to Phantom Ranch ($367, 2nd person $297), which includes a night's lodging and all meals. Riders must be at least 55 inches tall and weigh less than 200lbs. Reserve up to 23 months in advance.

Yavapai Observation Station (928-638-1890; 1 mile east of Market Plaza, Grand Canyon Village; 8am-5pm, later in summer)

Eating

Arizona Room (928-638-2631; east of Bright Angel Lodge, Grand Canyon Village; mains $10-25; 11:30am-3pm & 4:30pm-10pm Mar-Dec) Steaks and seafood with antler chandeliers and canyon-view windows.

Charly's Pub & Grille (928-779-1919; Hotel Weatherford, 23 N Leroux St, Flagstaff; mains $8-20; 11am-10pm) Stand-out Southwest cuisine and live music.

Deli at Marketplace (928-638-2262; Market Plaza, Grand Canyon Village; dishes $5-8; 8am-6pm, extended hrs in summer) Fresh take-out sandwiches and hot dishes.

El Tovar Dining Room (928-638-2631; El Tovar Hotel; lunch mains $10-20, dinner mains $30-35; 6.30am-2pm & 5pm-10pm, lounge 11am-11pm) Quality food in an elegant, historic setting; dinner reservations essential.

Hermits Rest (928-638-2351; Hermit Rd; 9am-5pm, later in summer) Snack bar and gift shop.

Old Smokey's Pancake House (928-635-1915; 624 W Route 66, Williams; meals under $10; 6am-1pm Mon-Sat) Stop here for breakfast.

Pine Country Restaurant (928-635-9718; 107 N Grand Canyon Blvd, Williams; meals around $10; 6am-9pm) For a slice of heavenly pie.

Sleeping

About 1000 rooms are available on the South Rim in lodges run by **Xanterra** (303-297-2757, 888-297-2757; www.grandcanyonlodges.com). Reservations are essential in summer. Cancellations provide a few with last-minute rooms; call 928-638-2631 to check same-day availability. If you can't find accommodation inside the park, try Tusayan (5 miles south), Williams (60 miles south) and Flagstaff (80 miles southeast).

Bright Angel Lodge & Cabins (Grand Canyon Village; r $55-70, cabins $85-110) Built in 1935, offers rustic charm.

Canyon Motel & RV Park (928-635-9371, 800-482-3955; www.thecanyonmotel.com; 1900 E Rodeo Rd, Williams; cottages from $60) On the eastern outskirts of Williams, with a pool. Cheaper 1940s motels downtown fill up quickly in summer.

DuBeau Route 66 International Hostel (928-774-6731, 800-398-7112; www.grandcanyonhostel.com; 19 W Phoenix St, Flagstaff; dm $16-18, r $34-41, all incl breakfast) Also runs the lively Grand Canyon International Hostel nearby.

El Tovar Hotel (Grand Canyon Village; d $125-285) Quintessential national-park lodge with renovated rooms, inviting porches, arts-and-crafts–style chairs, stained glass and exposed beams.

NPS Campgrounds (reservations 301-722-1257, 800-365-2267; http://reservations.nps.gov; sites $10-15) In Grand Canyon Village, year-round Mather Campground books up fast; campers should be prepared for freezing winter nights. Near the eastern entrance, Desert View Campground (mid-May–mid-Oct) has fewer facilities; first-come, first-served sites are often full by early morning.

Phantom Ranch & Canteen (dm $27) At the bottom of the canyon. Try showing up at the Bright Angel Lodge transportation desk at 6am (some people queue up even earlier) to snag a canceled bunk.

Red Garter Bed & Bakery (928-635-1484, 800-328-1484; http://redgarter.com; 137 W Railroad Ave, Williams; r $80-145) Inside a restored Victorian bordello.

NORTH RIM

On the Grand Canyon's North Rim, more than 8000ft above sea level, solitude reigns supreme. Rugged and remote, it boasts meadows thick with wildflowers and dense clusters of willowy aspen and spruce trees. The air is often crisp, the skies vast and blue. If crowds make you cringe, this is where to head for wild isolation. There is only one road in, so you must backtrack more than 60 miles after your visit. It's colder and wetter here, too, and the North Rim is open for business from mid-May to mid-October only. However, the views are spectacular and the lack of huge crowds makes visiting the North Rim a more peaceful, if more spartan, experience of the canyon's majesty.

Hwy 67 takes you through the Kaibab Plateau and thick forest. Most visitor facilities are clustered around Grand Canyon Lodge, including the adjacent North Rim Visitor Center. The paved half-mile trail to **Bright Angel Point** and back is a must. Beginning from the parking lot or the lodge, the trail wraps up, down and out along a narrow finger of an overlook that dangles between the Transept and Roaring Springs Canyon. The sensation of being suspended in the air above the canyon is uplifting. The 1.5-mile **Transept Trail** goes north from the lodge through forest to the campground.

There are excellent canyon views from Bright Angel Point, but to reach other overlooks you need to take the signed turn east, about 3 miles back north on Hwy 67, to **Point Imperial** and **Cape Royal**. It's 9 miles to Point Imperial, which is the highest overlook in the entire park and has stunning views. Backtrack about 4 miles from Point Imperial and drive 15 miles south to Cape Royal where there are more great views and some short hiking trails. With 4WD and high clearance, you can take unpaved roads to several other outlooks along the North Rim. One of the most spectacular of these remote overlooks is the **Toroweap Overlook** at **Tuweep**, far to the west of the main park facilities.

The **North Kaibab Trail** plunges down to **Phantom Ranch** (opposite) on the Colorado River, 5750 feet below and 14 miles away. This is the only maintained rim-to-river trail from the North Rim and it connects with trails to the South Rim. The first 4.7 miles are the steepest, dropping well over 3000 feet to **Roaring Springs** – a popular all-day hike and mule-ride destination. If you prefer a shorter day hike below the rim, you can walk just three quarters of a mile down to **Coconino Overlook** or 2 miles to the **Supai Tunnel**, 1400 feet below the rim, to get a flavor of steep inner-canyon hiking. Hikers wishing to continue to the river will need backcountry permits. Because the river is about two times further from the North Rim than the South Rim, rangers suggest three nights for a rim-to-river and return hike, staying at Cottonwood and Bright Angel campgrounds. For trans-canyon hikes, you'll need to make shuttle reservations (p215).

TRANSPORTATION

Distance from Las Vegas 265 miles
Direction Northeast
Travel Time 5½ hours
Car From the Strip, take I-15 north across the Utah state line. Just past St George, take UT 9 east to US 89 south, then pick up Alt US 89 (Hwy 89A) at Fredonia south to AZ 67, which heads 40 miles south to the North Rim. Alternatively, take UT 9 east to **Zion National Park** (p220) before continuing south on US 89A and AZ 67 to the North Rim.
Shuttle A hikers' shuttle (first person $5, each additional person $2) to the North Kaibab Trail departs at 5:20am and 7:20am from Grand Canyon Lodge; purchase tickets the night before at the lodge's front desk. The seasonal **Trans Canyon Shuttle** (p215) to the South Rim departs at 7am from the lodge.

Information

All North Rim services, accommodations and restaurants are open from mid-May to mid-October only, including the gas station (☼ 7am-7pm), post office and general store.

Arizona Department of Transportation (ADOT; ☎ 888-411-7623; www.dot.state.az.us) To check road conditions and closures.

Backcountry Information Center (☎ 928-638-7875; North Rim ranger station, near campground; ☼ 8am-noon & 1-5pm) Apply for permits as early as possible. If you don't have a reservation, put yourself on the waiting list as soon as you arrive, although chances of a next-day permit for Cottonwood or Bright Angel Campgrounds are slim.

Grand Canyon Association (☎ 800-858-2808; www.grandcanyon.org; ☼ 8am-6pm) Nonprofit bookstore located in the lodge complex.

Grand Canyon National Park – North Rim (☎ 928-638-7888; www.nps.gov/grca/grandcanyon/north-rim) 24-hour recorded information.

North Rim Visitor Center (☎ 928-638-7864; ☯ 8am-6pm mid-May–mid-Oct) Next to the Bright Angel Peninsula parking lot. Seasonal interpretive programs, info and maps.

Activities

Canyon Trail Rides (☎ 435-679-8665; www.canyonrides .com; 1hr rim ride $30, half-day canyon ride $55, full-day canyon tour incl lunch $105) All mule trips have maximum-weight limits and minimum-age requirements. Advance reservations recommended, or check availability at the company's desk in the Grand Canyon Lodge.

Eating

Deli in the Pines (☎ 928-638-2611; dishes $4-6; ☯ 7am-9pm) Small cafeteria beside the lodge serves surprisingly good made-to-order sandwiches, pizza and ice cream.

Grand Canyon Lodge Dining Room (☎ 928-638-2611; mains $5-28; ☯ 6:30-10am, 11:30am-2:30pm, 4:45-9:45pm) A wonderful spot with panoramic views; solid

menu has vegetarian options. Dinner reservations (call ext 160 between mealtimes) required.

Rough Rider Saloon (☎ 928-638-2611; ☯ 5:30am-10:30am & 11:30am-11pm) Also serves morning coffee and pastries. The stone patio offers rough-hewn rocking chairs facing the rim and a blazing fire on chilly nights. Inside is Teddy Roosevelt memorabilia.

Sleeping

If these are booked, try your luck 85 miles northeast in Marble Canyon and Lees Ferry or backtrack along Hwys 67 and 89A to Jacob Lake, Fredonia or Kanab, Utah.

Grand Canyon Lodge (☎ 928-638-2611, reservations 303-297-2757, 888-297-2757; www.grandcanyonnorth rim.com; d $90-115) The canyon views are stunning at this historic lodge. Rustic yet modern cabins comprise the majority of accommodations. Reserve months in advance.

North Rim Campground (reservations ☎ 301-722-1257, 800-365-2267; http://reservations.nps.gov; 1.5 miles north of Grand Canyon Lodge; tent & RV sites $15-20) Pleasant sites blanketed in pine needles. Dump stations but no hookups. Reservations accepted, or else show up before 10am and hope for the best.

ZION NATIONAL PARK

The first national park established in Utah is so overpowering that it is at once a shutterbug's dream and despair, as no photo can do justice to the breathtaking scenery. The highlight of the park is **Zion Canyon**, a half-mile-deep slash formed by the Virgin River cutting through the sandstone. Everyone wants to follow the narrow paved road at the bottom, straining their neck to take in the vistas of looming cliffs, domes and mountains. So popular is this route that it became overcrowded with cars and a shuttle-bus service was implemented. Other scenic drives are less crowded but just as magnificent. For all its awe-inspiring majesty, Zion also offers more delicate beauties, too – weeping rocks, tiny grottos, hanging gardens and meadows of wildflowers – that lend it a meditative quality.

Almost half of the park's annual 2.5 million visitors arrive between Memorial Day and Labor Day. Summers are hot (over 100°F), though overnight temperatures drop into the 60°s F. Beware of short but heavy rainstorms from mid-July to mid-September. Spring weather is variable and hard to predict. The bug season peaks in summer – bring insect repellent. Autumn is ideal, with warm days and cool nights.

Spring to fall, the shuttle stops at all major trailheads along the 6.2-mile road through Zion Canyon, the park's centerpiece. In the off-season, you can park at the shuttle stops and several scenic pullouts. Less than a mile from the park's southern entrance is the **Zion Human History Museum**, which presents the geological and human history of Zion and its birth as a park. For those with the time and energy, day and overnight hikes can take you into spectacularly wild country. In order of increasing difficulty, the best trails accessible from Zion Canyon scenic drive are briefly mentioned here. All have superb views; distances are one-way. Inquire about trail conditions before setting out.

The paved **Pa'rus Trail** parallels the road for almost 2 miles from South Campground to the main canyon junction. The ever-wonderful, paved, mile-long **Riverside Walk** begins at the end of the scenic drive. From the trail's end, you can continue along (and in) the Virgin River for several miles; this is the final portion of the Narrows. The quarter-mile **Weeping Rock Trail** climbs 100 feet to hanging gardens. **Emerald Pools** is another favorite; a paved half-mile trail

TRANSPORTATION

Distance from Las Vegas 160 miles
Direction Northeast

Travel Time 3 hours

Bicycle Allowed only on the Zion Canyon scenic drive and Pa'rus Trail. Rentals from Springdale bike shops run $10/22/35 per hour/half day/full day. **Springdale Cycle Tours** (☎ 435-772-0575, 800-776-2099; www.springdale cycles.com; 1458 Zion Park Blvd) does repairs, rentals and offers guided tours ($50-250).

Car From the Strip, take I-15 north across the state line. Just past St George, Utah, take UT 9 east past Springdale to the southern park entrance. You can drive the Zion–Mt Carmel Hwy through the park year-round. The tunnel east of Zion Canyon is so narrow that escorts ($15) must accompany oversized vehicles (some are prohibited); call ahead to check.

Parking The visitor-center parking lot is typically full from 10am to 3pm. Park in Springdale and ride the shuttle into the park instead.

Shuttle From late March through October, the park operates two free shuttle loops: the Zion Canyon Loop, which makes nine stops between the visitor center and the Temple of Sinawava at the end of the scenic drive; and the Springdale Loop, which makes six regular stops and three flag stops along Hwy 9 between Springdale and the giant-screen theatre, from where you can walk to the park entrance. In summer, shuttles operate 5:45am to 11pm, spring and fall 6:45am to 10pm. Shuttles run every 6–10 minutes, 9am to 8pm, and every 15–30 minutes early and late in the day. Tune to 1610AM for current shuttle information.

leads to the lower pool and waterfall, while a mile-long unpaved trail leads to the upper pool. The mile-long **Hidden Canyon Trail** has several steep drop-offs and climbs 850ft to a narrow, shady canyon. More strenuous is the 4-mile **Observation Point Trail** (2150ft ascent), which is less exposed than the **Angels Landing** trail but also offers great views.

Travelers can backpack and wilderness camp along more than 100 miles of trails in Zion National Park. The most famous backpacking trip is through the **Narrows**, a 16-mile journey into canyons along the Virgin River's north fork. The easiest and busiest of the backcountry hikes, it's unforgettable. Plan on getting wet (much of the hike is in the river) and for it to take two days. Day hikers without permits are allowed to wade up upriver as far as Big Springs, so the final miles can get distressingly crowded. The hike is best done in early summer or fall; it may close anytime between July and September due to flash floods.

If there's one sport that makes Zion special, it's **canyoneering**. Rappel over the lip of a sandstone bowl, swim icy pools, trace a slot canyon's curves – canyoneering is beautiful, dangerous and sublime all at once. And it's easy to learn. Guided trips are prohibited in the park, so courses are held outside Zion, after which students can try out their newfound skills in the park. The park service sets day-use limits. Among the easiest routes are the **Subway** and **Orderville Canyon**, which ends at the Narrows. If you can use a harness, the challenging, all-day **Mystery Canyon** trek lets you be a rock star – the last 115ft rappel drops into the Virgin River before admiring crowds day-hiking the Narrows.

The 10-mile road east from Zion Canyon to the park's eastern entrance station is an engineering feat, with switchbacks and a mile-long tunnel, after which the geology quickly changes into slickrock, with many carved and etched formations, of which the mountainous **Checkerboard Mesa** is a memorable example. Of several parking areas along the road, only one has a marked trail – the half-mile **Canyon Overlook Trail**, which climbs over 150ft to offer fine views into Zion Canyon.

Information

Backcountry Desk (☎ 435-772-0170; Zion Canyon Visitor Center; ⏲ 7am-6pm spring & fall, till 7pm summer) Overnight permits cost $10 to $20 and are issued on a walk-in basis on the day prior to, or of, your hike. Some permits are issued by lottery or online at http://zionpermits.nps.gov.

Canyon Trail Rides (☎ 435-679-8665, 435-772-3810; www.canyonrides.com; 1hr/half-day horseback ride $30/55; ⏲ Mar-Oct) Has a desk at Zion Lodge.

Zion Adventure Company (☎ 435-772-0990; www .zionadventures.com; 36 Lion Blvd, cnr Hwy 9, Springdale; ⏲ 9am-9pm Mar-Nov) Leads rock-climbing and canyoneering trips and classes.

Excursions **ZION NATIONAL PARK**

Zion Canyon Medical Clinic (☎ 435-772-3226; 120 Lion Blvd, Springdale; ☻ call for hrs) Urgent care walk-in clinic. The nearest 24-hour emergency room is in St George.

Zion Canyon Visitor Center (☎ 435-772-3256; Hwy 9; ☻ 8am-5pm, till 6pm spring & fall, till 7pm summer) Near the park's southern entrance, the central source for all park info.

Zion Human History Museum (☎ 435-772-0168; admission free; ☻ 8am-5pm, till 6pm spring & fall, till 7pm summer) Good introductory film shown every half hour.

Zion National Park (www.nps.gov/zion; 7-day entry pass per car $20) South and east entrance stations are located at either end of the Zion–Mt Carmel Hwy.

Zion Natural History Association (☎ 435-772-3265, 800-635-3959; www.zionpark.org) Runs the visitor center's excellent bookstore.

Zion Outdoor Center (☎ 435-772-1001; 868 Zion Park Blvd, Springdale; ☻ 8am-8pm Mar-Nov) Sells and rents rock-climbing equipment.

Eating

Summer opening hours are listed here. Restaurants may close additional days or keep shorter hours in the off-season.

Bit & Spur Restaurant & Saloon (☎ 435-772-3498, 1212 Zion Park Blvd, Springdale; mains $10-25; ☻ 5-10pm, bar till midnight) A local institution that's the liveliest spot in town. Southwest-influenced seafood and steak specials.

Bumbleberry Restaurant (☎ 435-772-3611; 897 Zion Park Blvd, Springdale; meals $5-15; ☻ 7:30am-9pm Mon-Sat) Nothing-special family dining, but very special bumbleberry pie.

Castle Dome Cafe (☎ 435-772-7700; Zion Lodge; dishes $3-6, pizza $11-15; ☻ 10am-7pm) Sandwiches, burgers, salads, soups, Asian-ish rice bowls and ice cream.

Pentimento (☎ 435-772-0490; Driftwood Lodge, 1515 Zion Park Blvd, Springdale; breakfast dishes $4-7, dinner mains $9-20; ☻ 7am-noon & 5-10pm) A simple, classic menu of NY Strip steak, rack of lamb and wild mountain trout.

Red Rock Grill (☎ 435-772-7760; Zion Lodge; breakfast buffet adult/child $8.50/4.50; lunch sandwiches & salads $6-8, dinner mains $12-21; ☻ 6:30-10am, 11:30am-3pm & 5:30-9pm) The window-lined dining room has magnificent views. Dinners are decent steaks and grilled fish (reservations required).

Sol Foods Market & Deli (☎ 435-772-0277; 95 Zion Park Blvd, Springdale; items $5-8; ☻ 7am-10pm, deli till 9pm) For quick eats. Has falafel and gyros, fish and chips, burritos and wraps, and a great riverside patio, plus wi-fi.

Spotted Dog Café & Pub (☎ 435-772-3244; Flanigan's Inn, 428 Zion Park Blvd, Springdale; mains $12-25;

☻ 7-11am & 5-9pm) High-end, Western-style cooking includes buffalo and elk meatloaf, blackened tuna, rabbit and steaks; there's a full bar.

Springdale Fruit Company (☎ 435-772-3222; 2491 Zion Park Blvd, Springdale; sandwiches $5; ☻ 8am-8pm, closed winter) Sandwiches, smoothies and a lovely picnic area.

Zion Pizza & Noodle Company (☎ 435-772-3815; 868 Zion Park Blvd, Springdale; pizza $9-14, salads & pasta $8-10; ☻ 4-10pm) Serves up Utah microbrews.

Sleeping

Springdale sits on Hwy 9, outside the park's southern entrance. A few miles further west, Rockville has several B&Bs. **Zion Canyon Visitors Bureau** (☎ 888-518-7070; www.zionpark.com) has accommodations listings for both. East of Zion, a few towns dot Hwy 89, the largest being Kanab. Nearer Nevada, St George has chain motels and hotels.

Canyon Ranch Motel (☎ 435-772-3357, 866-946-6276; www.canyonranchmotel.com; 668 Zion Park Blvd, Springdale; r $48-92; ☻) Detached plain but comfy cottages, and a small pool. Some rooms have kitchens (add $10). Free wi-fi.

Desert Pearl Inn (☎ 435-772-8888, 888-828-0898; www.desertpearl.com; 707 Zion Park Blvd, Springdale; d $128-153, tr/q add $10/20) Stylish rooms have suede sofas, handwoven Oaxacan bedspreads, pressed-tin tables, wet bars, wi-fi and sleeper sofas.

NPS Campgrounds (☎ 800-367-2267; http://reservations.nps.gov; sites $16-20) Near the southern entrance are two year-round campgrounds: Watchman (reservations taken mid-Mar–Oct); and first-come, first-served South. Both have water and toilets, no showers.

Zion Lodge (☎ 435-772-3213, reservations 303-297-2757, 888-297-2757; www.zionlodge.com; d $80-150) The park's only lodge has well-appointed motel rooms and cabins with gas fireplaces. All cabins have wooden porches and stellar views, but no TVs. Book months in advance, or try for a same-day reservation by calling ☎ 435-772-7700.

Zion Ponderosa Ranch Resort (☎ 435-648-2700, 800-293-5444; www.zionponderosa.com; Mt Carmel; tent per person $42, cabin s/d $85/125, cabin ste $160/200, per child 3-11 add $75) This all-inclusive resort is an ideal spot for families. Rates include all meals and a wide variety of activities. The turnoff is 2 miles from Zion's east entrance.

Zion River Resort (☎ 435-635-8594, 888-822-8594; www.zionriverresort.com; 730 E Hwy 9, Virgin; tent site $30, RV sites $38-45, cabin $65-75) Pristine RV Park has camping cabins, a pool, free wi-fi and shuttles to Springdale.

BRYCE CANYON NATIONAL PARK

The Grand Staircase – a series of steplike uplifted rock layers stretching north from the Grand Canyon – culminates in the **Pink Cliffs** formation at this popular park. These cliffs were deposited as sediment in a huge prehistoric lake some 50 to 60 million years ago, slowly lifted above sea level, then eroded into wondrous ranks of pinnacles and points, steeples and spires, cliffs and crevices, and oddly-shaped hoodoos.

The park's most famous sights are at the cliff-eroded **Bryce Amphitheater**, just south of the visitor center. The park's 18-mile scenic **Rim Road** roughly parallels the canyon rim, passing the visitor center, lodge, viewpoints (don't miss Inspiration and Bryce Points) and trailheads, ending at **Rainbow Point** (9115ft).

You can whisk in and out in a few hours, but, for a richer experience, numerous trails will take you out among the spires and deeper into the heart of the landscape. The easiest is the 5.5 mile **Rim Trail**, which skirts Bryce Amphitheater from Fairyland Point to Bryce Point. At Rainbow Point, the one-mile **Bristlecone Loop** is an easy walk with 100-mile vistas on clear days. Outside the park boundaries, off Hwy 12 toward Tropic, the easy half-mile walk along **Mossy Cave Trail** takes you to a waterfall.

Moderately difficult trails descend below the rim. The most popular is **Queen's Garden**, which drops from Sunrise Point, combined with the **Navajo Loop Trail**, which descends from Sunset Point and passes through the famous slot canyon 'Wall Street.' This 2.5-mile combo hike sees lots of traffic and may remain open in winter. Down on the canyon floor, you can hike among berry-laden Rocky Mountain junipers and towering pines while marveling at the elegant, ancient rock above. The 23-mile **Under-the-Rim Trail** from Bryce Point to Rainbow Point is the park's longest.

Though the smallest of southern Utah's national parks, Bryce receives more than 1.7 million visitors annually, with most arriving between May and September. During summer, daytime temperatures may reach into the 80°s F – and even hotter below the rim – but nighttime lows often dip below freezing. June is relatively dry, but July and August see sudden torrential storms. Snow blankets the canyon from November to April, when a few of the park's roads are unplowed to allow cross-country skiing and snowshoeing.

Sights & Information

Ruby's Inn has a post office, ATM, general store, gasoline and Internet access.

Bryce Canyon National Park (www.nps.gov/brca; 7-day entry pass per car $20) The park's free newspaper, the *Hoodoo*, lists hikes, ranger-led activities and shuttle routes.

Bryce Canyon Natural History Association (☎ 435-834-4600, 888-362-2642; www.brycecanyon.org) Operates the bookstore at the visitor center.

NPS Visitor Center (☎ 435-834-5322; Hwy 63; ☽ 8am-4:30pm, till 6pm spring & fall, till 8pm summer) Maps, information, natural history exhibits and backcountry permits.

TRANSPORTATION

Distance from Las Vegas 250 miles
Direction Northeast

Travel Time 4½ to 5 hours
Car From the Strip, travel north on I-15 across the Utah state line. Approximately 50 miles past St George, take UT 14 east for 40 miles, then turn left on to US 89 north. Turn right on to UT 12 and drive east to UT 63, which heads south to the Zion National Park entrance. From the park, it takes approximately two hours to drive 85 miles to Bryce Canyon. Follow UT 9, then turn left on to US 89 north and continue as above.
Shuttle During summer, leave your car at the shuttle-bus terminus, just south of the UT 12/63 junction, and ride the bus into the park.

Activities

Canyon Trail Rides (☎ 435-679-8665; www.canyonrides .com; Hwy 63, Bryce Canyon Lodge; 2hr/half-day ride $40/55) Trips into Bryce Amphitheater on horses and mules.

Scenic Rim Trail Rides (☎ 435-679-8761, 800-679-5859; www.brycecanyonhorseback.com; 1hr/2hr ride $23/30, half-day ride $51)

Eating & Sleeping

Most visitors stay north of the park in Bryce, near the junction of Hwys 12 and 63, or 7 miles east in Tropic.

Best Western Ruby's Inn (☎ 435-834-5341, campground 435-834-5301, reservations 866-866-6616; www.rubysinn .com; 1000 & 1280 S Hwy 63; meals $5-30, tent/RV sites from $18/29, tipis/cabins from $26/45, r $55-150, ste $100-175; ☺ restaurants 6:30am-10pm) A gargantuan motel complex serving assembly-line food, just north of the park.

Bryce Canyon Lodge (☎ 435-834-5361, 888-297-2757; www.brycecanyonlodge.com; inside the park; meals $8-25, d $110-140; ☺ dining room 6:30-10:30am, 11am-3:30pm & 5:30-9:30pm, lodge & dining room Apr-Oct only) This 1920s lodge exudes rustic mountain charm, offering modern hotel-style units and romantic, slightly dated cabins. It's by far the best place to eat (dinner reservations essential).

Bryce Canyon Pines Resort (☎ 435-834-5441, 800-892-7923; www.brycecanyonmotel.com; milepost 10, Hwy 12, Bryce; meals $5-16, tent/RV site $15-24, s $30-75, d $40-85, kitchenettes $65-95; ☺ restaurant 6:30am-9:30pm) Known for its homemade soups and pies, the Bryce Canyon Pines Resort also has simple motel rooms.

NPS Campgrounds (☎ 800-365-2267; www.reserveusa .com; tent & RV sites $10) Year-round North Campground is near the visitor center. About 2 miles south, first-come, first-served Sunset Campground (☺ late spring-early fall) has fewer amenities.

Stone Canyon Inn (☎ 435-679-8611, 866-489-4680; www.stonecanyoninn.com; off Fairyland Lane, Tropic; r incl breakfast $80-155, cottages $275) The top choice for savvy travelers, with gorgeous views, delicious breakfasts and wi-fi Internet access.

DEATH VALLEY

Its name as seductive as it is intimidating, Death Valley is a crazy-quilted geological playground. With the lowest elevation in the United States, boulders that appear to race across the sun-baked desert floor, mosaic canyons, rolling sand dunes, extinct volcanic craters and palm-shaded oases, the actual valley is about 100 miles north to south and 5 miles to 15 miles wide. **Death Valley National Park** covers a much larger area – more than 5000 sq miles – which includes several other valleys and mountain ranges to the north.

The rock formations you see today were created by geological events that occurred as long ago as 500 million years. Limestone and sandstone were formed on an ancient seabed and slowly lifted by movement in the earth's crust. The rock strata were bent, folded and cracked as converging tectonic plates pushed up mountain ranges. These stresses led to a period of volcanic activity, explosively distributing ash and cinders that provided much of the rich coloring seen in the valley.

The Timbisha Shoshone lived in the Panamint Range for centuries, visiting the valley every winter to gather acorns, hunt waterfowl, catch pupfish in marshes and cultivate small areas of corn, squash and beans. The fractured geology of Death Valley left many accessible minerals, and the earliest miners in the 1860s sought gold, silver, copper and lead. The most sustained mining operation was the Harmony Borax Works, which extracted borate, an alkaline mineral used to make detergents. By the late 1920s, most of the mining had ceased.

The peak season to visit is in the cooler winter months or early spring when wildflowers bloom. Death Valley used to be practically empty in summer, but recently it's become popular with European visitors keen to experience temperatures above 120°F. Starting out early in the morning – always a good thing to do in the desert – is absolutely essential if you want to cram everything into a day trip from Vegas. A peaceful overnight stay inside or near the park, however, ensures you see the gorgeous sunset and sunrise.

The lowest point accessible by road is **Badwater**, at the south end of the valley, where you can walk on the constantly evaporating bed of salty, mineralized water. As you drive north, look west across the valley floor at the **Devil's Golf Course**, which is filled with lumps of crystallized salt. Further north is the turnoff for the **Artist's Drive** scenic loop. Six miles north is **Golden Canyon**, which you can hike up to see the sandstone cliffs of **Red Cathedral**.

TRANSPORTATION

Distance from Las Vegas 145 miles to Furnace Creek
Direction West
Travel Time 3 to 3½ hours
Car The most direct route from Las Vegas is to take US 95 north 85 miles to NV 373 south, which becomes CA 127 at the state line and leads to Death Valley Junction, from which it's a 30-mile drive west on CA 190 to Furnace Creek. But the scenic route is to take I-15 south of the Strip to the Blue Diamond exit, then NV 160 west. After 35 miles, turn left on to Tecopa Rd/Old Spanish Trail Hwy through Tecopa, then CA 127 north 8 miles to Shoshone. Turn left and follow Hwy 178 northwest 55 miles to Badwater.

DETOUR: AREA 51

The most way-out excursion from Sin City is a helluva detour on the way to Death Valley or back from the national park via Tonopah, north of Beatty. Yet die-hard alien freaks and conspiracy theorists will want to visit infamous Area 51.

To get there, drive north from Las Vegas on US 93 for about 85 miles. Past the hot-springs enclave of Ash Springs, turn left on to NV 318, then left again on to NV 375, aka the 'Extraterrestrial Highway.' From there, it's 40 miles west to Rachel, NV. Stop in for a burger and beer at the **Little A'le'Inn** (☎ 775-729-2515, fax 775-729-2551; www.littlealeinn .com; meals $5, RV & tent sites $12, r from $40; ☺ diner usually 8am-9pm). The gift shop sells alien bobbleheads, self-published books and invaluable maps of the area.

Skywatchers gather on the south side of NV 375, back west near the 29-mile marker. There you'll find the black (now white) mailbox, which marks the beginning of a dirt road into Groom Lake's military base. Stay straight at the first three-way intersection, then turn right on to Groom Lake Rd. Warning! Only travel as far as the boundary of the base, which is marked by signs but no fences. Otherwise, you'll be arrested and fined hundreds of dollars (or worse), promise.

Many UFO hunters say that the nexus of otherworldly visitation has headed north to Utah (click to www.aliendave .com for full disclosure). Judge for yourself at Rachel's three-day annual **UFO Friendship Campout**, held over Memorial Day weekend, where paranormal investigations may leave you more convinced of the existence of alien life. For a virtual visit to Area 51, surf to www.dreamlandresort.com.

Back on Hwy 190, continue north to Furnace Creek. Branch right and drive more than 20 miles up to **Dante's View** (5475ft), which is absolutely brilliant at sunrise or sunset. Heading down towards the central valley, **Twenty Mule Team Canyon** is a windy one-way driving loop. Alternatively, take a short walk out to **Zabriskie Point**, which is a great place to see lava-capped formations and eroded badlands. Back at Furnace Creek, the **Borax Museum** will tell you all about the stuff, and there's a big collection of old coaches and wagons out the back. Just up the road is the **Furnace Creek Visitor Center** and, further on, the ruins of the **Harmony Borax Works**. From there, Hwy 190 heads north past Beatty Cut-Off Rd, which climbs to **Hell's Gate** to meet Hwy 374, which heads over **Daylight Pass** out of the park toward **Rhyolite** ghost town, 3 miles west of the historic mining settlement of **Beatty**.

If you have time, first keep going north on Hwy 190 to the main junction, then curve west to see the majestic **sand dunes**, seemingly airlifted straight out of the Sahara, opposite a field of arrowweed clumps called the **Devil's Cornfield**. Further west is the village of **Stovepipe Wells**. Backtrack to the junction, then turn left and take Hwy 267 north past the turn-off to awe-inspiring **Titus Canyon** all the way to the north end of the valley. Detour west to **Ubehebe Crater**, caused by the explosive meeting of superheated volcanic lava with cool groundwater, and smaller **Little Hebe Crater**. To the east is **Scotty's Castle**, nearly 3000ft above sea level and noticeably cooler than the valley floor. Walter E Scott, alias 'Death Valley Scotty', was the quintessential tall-tale teller who captivated people with his stories of gold. His most lucrative friendship was with Albert Johnson, a wealthy insurance magnate from Chicago, who bankrolled this elaborately constructed desert oasis.

Information

Furnace Creek has most of the facilities. Satellite towns outside the park include Shoshone (south entrance), Beatty (north) and lonely Death Valley Junction (east). Gas stations are open 24 hours in Furnace Creek and Beatty.

Beatty Chamber of Commerce (☎ 775-553-2424, 866-736-3716; www.beattynevada.org; 119 Main St, Beatty; ☺ usually 10am-2pm) Info on local accommodations and attractions.

Furnace Creek Visitor Center & Museum (☎ 760-786-3200; Hwy 190; ☺ 8am-5pm) Excellent books for sale, plus free maps, brochures and ranger-led interpretive programs.

Sights & Activities

Borax Museum (☎ 760-786-2345; Furnace Creek Ranch, Hwy 190; admission $2; ☺ 9am-4pm Oct-May)

Death Valley National Park (www.nps.gov/deva; 7-day entry pass per vehicle $10; ☺ 24hr) Not all park entrances have a fee-collection station, but you're still expected to pay. Rangers have better things to do than chase you, and besides the NPS needs the funding.

Furnace Creek Golf Course (☎ 760-786-2345; Furnace Creek Ranch, Hwy 190; greens fees $55; ☺ mid-Oct–early May) The world's lowest-elevation course.

Horseback riding (☎ 760-786-3339; Furnace Creek Ranch, Hwy 190; 1-/2-hour rides $35/50; ☺ Oct–mid-May)

Excursions
DEATH VALLEY

225

Scotty's Castle (☎ 760-786-2392; adult/child 6-15/senior $11/6/9, child 5 & under free; ☾ 8:30am-6pm, tours 9am-5pm) Historical home also known as Death Valley Ranch. Call ahead for tour reservations.

Tecopa Hot Springs Resort (☎ 760-852-4420; www.tecopahotsprings.org; Tecopa Hot Springs Rd, Tecopa; entry $5; ☾ call for hrs, closed summer) Sex-segregated bathhouses with natural hot springs.

Timbisha Shoshone Tribe (http://timbisha.org) Tribal homelands near Furnace Creek.

Eating

There are general stores at Furnace Creek and Stovepipe Wells.

Burro Inn Café (Burro Inn, Beatty; meals $3.25-14; ☾ 24hr) Unforgettably good steak and eggs, pancake breakfasts, lunch sandwiches and surf-and-turf or pasta dinners.

Café Çest Si Bon (☎ 760-852-4307; 118 Hwy 127, Shoshone; dishes $2-6; ☾ 7am-5pm Wed-Mon) Solar-powered Internet café for espresso drinks, baked goods and gourmet vegetarian fare.

China Ranch Date Farm (☎ 760-852-4415; www.chinaranch.com; Furnace Creek Rd, off Old Spanish Trail Hwy, east of Tecopa; ☾ 9am-5pm) Mmmm, fresh-baked date bread.

Exchange Club Casino (☎ 775-553-2368; 119 Main St, Beatty; breakfast specials $2, most meals under $15; ☾ 24hr) Restaurant serves large portions of burgers, steaks, sandwiches, or belly up to the 1890s bar.

Forty Niner Cafe, Wrangler Steak House & Corkscrew Saloon (☎ 760-786-2345; Furnace Creek Ranch; mains $8-25; ☾ cafe 7am-9pm Oct-May, 10am-9pm May-Oct, steakhouse 5-9pm Oct-May, 6-9:30pm Jun-Sep) Long waits for only average food, but it's convenient. Avoid the buffet.

Furnace Creek Inn (☎ 760-786-2345; Hwy 190, Furnace Creek; lunch $10, dinner $20-30; ☾ lunch & dinner mid-Oct–mid-May) An elegant dining room atop the oasis. So-so food is best enjoyed at the casual bar. Good wine list.

Toll Road Restaurant & Bad Water Saloon (☎ 760-786-2387; Stovepipe Wells Village; breakfast & lunch $5-8, dinner mains $10-23; ☾ 7-10am, 11:30am-2pm & 5:30-9pm, bar 4:30-11pm) Above-par cowboy cooking inside a ranch house. The saloon next door has Skynnard on the jukebox and pool tables.

Sleeping

Amargosa Opera House & Hotel (☎ 760-852-4441; www.amargosa-opera-house.com; Death Valley Junction; r $49-66) 1920s Mission-style arcade has well-worn but clean motel rooms (no TVs or phones) and eccentric management. Reservations required.

Burro Inn (☎ 775-553-2445, 800-843-2078; www.burroinn.com; 851 Hwy 95 S, Beatty; RV sites $15, r $35-80) Old West–style motel rooms (pets OK).

Exchange Club Motel (☎ 775-553-2368, 888-561-2333; www.exchangeclubcasino.com; 119 Main St, Beatty; r $41-68) A historic place, since 1906. Decent rooms with fridge, phone and cable TV.

Furnace Creek Inn & Ranch (☎ 760-786-2345, reservations 303-297-2757, 888-297-2757; www.furnacecreekresort.com; Hwy 190, Furnace Creek; ranch cabins $105-125, motel r $135-180, inn r $255-335, inn ste $350-390; ☾ inn closed mid-May–mid-Oct, ranch open year-round) The ranch has ordinary cabins and motel rooms. Further east, the hilltop inn has plain rooms in palm-shaded Spanish-style stone buildings and a springwater-fed pool.

NPS Campgrounds (☎ 800-365-2267; http://reservations.nps.gov; sites $10-16) Furnace Creek (crowded, little shade, mostly RVs), Mesquite Spring (near Scotty's Castle) and Wildrose (high in the Panamint Range) campgrounds are open year-round.

Shoshone Inn (☎ 760-852-4335; www.shoshonevillage.com; Hwy 127, Shoshone; d incl tax $64-80) Basic 1950s motel rooms with TV and phone (some have kitchenettes).

Stovepipe Wells Village (☎ 760-786-2387; www.stovepipewells.com; Hwy 190; r $83-103) Roadside motel with a small pool. Slightly tired rooms are the cheapest in the park.

Zion National Park (p220)

MOJAVE NATIONAL PRESERVE

This sprawling preserve contains 1.5 million acres of sand dunes, Joshua trees, volcanic outcroppings and stunning rock formations – sort of like Death Valley and Joshua Tree National Parks rolled into one, but with blessedly fewer people. Bighorn sheep, desert tortoise and wily coyote are frequently sighted, especially around dusk and in the early morning. One drawback is the lack of facilities, plus abnormally strong winds are the norm. Daytime temperatures hover near or above 100°F from May to September, then hang around 50°F for most of the winter, when snowstorms are not unheard of.

You can spend an entire day or just a few hours driving around the free preserve, taking in its sights and getting out and exploring some of them on foot. Visible to the south from I-15, **Cima Dome** is a 1500ft hunk of granite spiked with volcanic cinder cones and crusty outcroppings of basalt left by lava that flowed from over seven-million years to around 10,000 years ago. Kelbaker Rd, which goes south from Baker, is a good place from which to see this anciently charred landscape up close. At one point the number of cones is so great that they are protected as the **Cinder Cones National Natural Landmark**.

> ## TRANSPORTATION
>
> **Distance from Las Vegas** 95 miles to Baker
> **Direction** South
> **Travel Time** 90 minutes
> **Car** From the Strip, take I-15 south across the California state line. Several paved and unpaved access roads branch south off of the interstate into the preserve, making it a short, spectacular side trip for visitors headed to or from LA.

Also off Kelbaker Rd, about 7 miles south of the information center at the restored 1920s **Kelso Depot**, are the **Kelso Dunes**, fabulously shaped sand dunes that rise to 600ft by the **Devil's Playground**. The 'booming' dunes can produce a musical noise as sand blows up their windward side and then sweeps down the 'slip-face' of the dunes. Hiking around these sand heaps is fun and less taxing than you might imagine, as the sand gets compressed by the wind. The trailhead is at the end of a 4-mile graded access road.

On the eastern side of Kelbaker Rd, the Providence Mountains create an impressive wall of rocky peaks. Accessible from Essex Rd off I-40 are **Mitchell Caverns**, known for their drip-like formations called speleothems. North of the caverns, on Black Canyon Rd (which extends north from Essex Rd), stands the **Hole-in-the-Wall** formation. These vertical walls of tuff (pronounced 'toof'), which look something like cliffs made of unpolished terrazzo marble, are thought to be from a powerful volcanic eruption that blasted rocks into the air and across the landscape some 18.5 million years ago. Ask at the **information center** to check if **Wild Horse Canyon Rd**, a gorgeous 10-mile driving loop from Hole-in-the-Wall up to **Mid Hills**, is currently passable by car. North of Mid Hills, Black Canyon Rd intersects with a section of the old **Mojave Road**, a trading and military supply route once trekked by camels in the mid-19th century.

In the far northeastern corner of the preserve, but quite close to the Nevada state line, is the historic railway town of **Nipton** (population 28), which has all the peace and quiet you'd ever need. An overnight stop here will rejuvenate your spirit. It has a quaint 1940s trading post, hotel and café, but they tend to roll up the sidewalks awfully early.

Information

Hole-in-the-Wall Information Center (☎ 760-928-2572; www.nps.gov/moja; off Black Canyon Rd, 20 miles north of I-40; ☽ 9am-4pm Fri-Sun year-round, also 9am-4pm Wed & Thu Oct-Apr) Information, maps, books and interpretive programs.

Kelso Depot Visitor Center (☎ 760-252-6161; Kelso-Cima Rd, at Kelbaker Rd; ☽ 9am-5pm) Interpretive displays, excellent maps and books for sale, and on-duty rangers provide current road and weather information.

Nipton Trading Post (☎ 702-856-2335; 107355 Nipton Rd, Nipton; ☽ 8am-6pm) Books, maps, information, groceries, artisan jewelry and a 24-hour self-serve laundromat.

Sights

Mitchell Caverns (☎ 760-928-2586; www.calparks mojave.com; adult/child 6-16 $4/2, child under 6 free; ☽ tours daily Sep-May, weekends Jun-Aug) Tours often sell out. Call for current schedules; make reservations at least two weeks in advance.

DETOUR: CALIFORNIA STATE LINE

Southern Californians bombing along I-15 to Las Vegas may mistake the bright lights of **Primm** for a suburb of Las Vegas. No such luck, but it's only a 40-minute drive from the Strip on the Nevada side of the state line. Pause for outlet shopping (p183) at **Primm Valley Resort**, where you can see the 1934 getaway car fatefully used by Bonnie and Clyde, and Al Capone's more smartly bullet-proofed vehicle. Next-door **Buffalo Bill's** casino hotel is the place for amusement thrill rides, such as the Desperado roller coaster, one of the nation's tallest and fastest. Country music megastars occasionally perform at Star of the Desert Arena.

On the way south to Primm, you'll pass the small enclave of **Jean**, about 10 miles north of the California border on I-15. Turn off at **Nevada Landing**, a steamboat-style casino hotel, for the 7-mile trip west on NV 161 to the almost ghost town of **Goodsprings**, where the tin-shack **Pioneer Saloon** (☎ 702-874-9362; ⏱ 11am-late) dates from 1913 (which makes it the oldest still-standing bar in southern Nevada). Riddled with bullet holes, it still manages to serve up cold drinks atop its vintage cherrywood bar. Admire the vintage poker tables and movie-star memorabilia before driving back east to I-15.

Eating

There are dozens of predictable dining options at all of the casino hotels (see below).

Mad Greek (☎ 760-733-4354; 72112 Baker Blvd, Baker; dishes $4-12; ⏱ 24hr) Gyros, Greek salads, strawberry shakes and desserts galore – easily the best food along I-15.

Whistlestop Oasis (☎ 760-856-1045; 107355 Nipton Rd, Nipton; lunch $4.50-8.50, dinner $8-25; ⏱ usually open 10am-7pm) Gourmands' haven with ice-cold beer, pool tables and scrumptious pork chops.

Sleeping

Hotel Nipton B&B (☎ 760-856-2335; www.nipton.com; 107355 Nipton Rd, Nipton; tent sites $15, eco-lodge d incl breakfast $60, hotel d incl breakfast $70; ⏱ check in before 6pm at the trading post) Its slogan is 'conveniently

located in the middle of nowhere.' Historic B&B rooms and eco-tents (with electricity and platform beds) share garden hot tubs. Free wi-fi for guests.

Nevada Landing (☎ 800-628-6682; www.stopatjean .com; off I-15 exit 12, Jean; r Sun-Thu/Fri/Sat from $20/35/55) Ragged casino hotel that may have rooms when Primm is full.

NPS Campgrounds (☎ 760-928-2572; tent & RV sites $12; ⏱ open year-round) First-come, first-served sites with pit toilets and running water. Hole-in-the-Wall is surrounded by rocky desert landscape, while Mid Hills is set among pine and juniper trees.

Primm Valley Resort (☎ 800-386-7867; www.prima donna.com; 31900 Las Vegas Blvd S, Primm, off I-15 exit 1; r from $43). Polished hotel and casino also handles reservations for family-friendly **Buffalo Bill's** (r from $36) and well-worn **Whiskey Pete's** (r from $27).

LAUGHLIN

Nevada's little gambling gulch by the river, Laughlin is even more oddly situated in the middle of nowhere than Las Vegas once was. In fact, it feels a lot like Vegas circa 1975. While Sin City has zoomed into the 21st century, Laughlin is entrenched in the gambling culture of yester-year. Active types love its proximity to miles of recreational shoreline in the southern section of **Lake Mead National Recreation Area** (p211). Otherwise, you'll earn a keen sense of irony to appreciate the time warp here. If you roll into town straight from the Strip, you may get a sense of déjà vu. There's a well-worn Flamingo Laughlin, a glitzy Golden Nugget Laughlin and more casino hotels.

Your first stop is Don Laughlin's original **Riverside Resort**, where it all began. Peruse the classic-cars collections, restored antique slot machines and the unluckiest hall of fame in the Loser's Lounge. Also opened in the 1960s was the Bobcat Club casino, which eventually became today's **Golden Nugget**, with a tropical atrium. Move on to

TRANSPORTATION

Distance from Las Vegas 100 miles
Direction Southeast
Travel Time 2 hours
Bus Some bus tour companies advertise free day-return coach trips to Laughlin.
Car From the Strip, take I-15 south to I-215, then take I-215 to I-515/US 93 & 95 southeast of Henderson over Railroad Pass, then turn right on to US 95 before Boulder City. Take US 95 south for 60 miles past Searchlight. Turn left on NV 163 and drive east for 20 miles to Laughlin, 25 miles north of Needles, CA.

the next decade at the faux–Old West **Pioneer Hotel & Gambling Hall**, which opened as the Colorado Club, and the kitschy **Colorado Belle**, a riverboat-themed casino. The unexpected fave is **Ramada Express**, which has a free miniature train around the property.

What is there to do here? Well, you can gamble, lounge around with a cocktail, gamble some more, escape the brutal heat on the river, and then top it all off with a bit more gambling. Detour west of Davis Dam, which forms Lake Mohave, to see **Grapevine Canyon** and its Native American rock-art petroglyphs and spring wildflowers. It stands in the shadow of 5600ft **Spirit Mountain**. To reach the canyon, take Christmas Tree Pass Rd, 5 miles west of town off NV 163, and drive 2 miles north. **Big Bend of the Colorado State Recreation Area**, for swimming, boating, bird-watching and hiking, is 5 miles south of town off the Needles Hwy.

For major events taking place in Laughlin, see p8.

Information

Big Bend of the Colorado SRA (☎ 702-298-1859; http://parks.nv.gov/bb.htm; entry fee per vehicle $3)

Lake Mohave Ranger Station (☎ 928-754-3272; www.nps.gov/lame; Katherine Landing; ⌚ 8am-4pm)

Laughlin Visitors Bureau (☎ 702-298-3321, 800-452-8445; www.visitlaughlin.com; 1555 S Casino Dr; ⌚ 8am-4:30pm) Maps, information and accommodations bookings.

Eating & Sleeping

Boarding House (☎ 702-298-2442; www.pioneerlaughlin.com; Pioneer Hotel & Gambling Hall, 2200 S Casino Dr; meals from $2; ⌚ 24hr) The cheapest meal deals in town.

Colorado Belle (☎ 702-298-4000, 877-460-0777; www.coloradobelle.com; 2100 S Casino Dr) Good grub, including the **Boiler Room** microbrewery.

Don Laughlin's Riverside Resort (☎ 702-298-2535, 800-227-3849; www.riversideresort.com; 1650 S Casino Dr; RV sites $21-22, r weekday/weekend $32/59) A movie theater, bowling alley, supervised kids' center and boat cruises ($10).

Golden Nugget Laughlin (☎ 702-298-7111, 800-950-7700; www.goldennugget.com; 2300 S Casino Dr; r weekday/weekend from $29/69) Posh rooms and dining at Jane's Grill and the riverside Deck.

Ramada Express (☎ 702-298-4200, 800-243-6846; www.ramadaexpress.com; 2121 S Casino Dr; r weekday/weekend from $21/50) Not on the river, but has adults-only rooms.

SPRING MOUNTAINS

The Spring Mountains form the western boundary of the Las Vegas valley, with higher rainfall, lower temperatures and fragrant pine, juniper and mahogany forests – a total escape from the desert valley, as it's usually about 30°F cooler at these elevations.

Driving west on NV 157 (Kyle Canyon Rd), you'll pass the misleadingly named **Mt Charleston Hotel**, a popular stop for Sunday brunch. Just past the NV 158 turnoff is the **USFS Kyle Guard & Information Station**, where you can pick up essential outdoor activity information, including free trail-guide brochures. The village of **Mt Charleston** gives access to several hikes. Curve left on to Old Park Rd and drive up the mountain. The demanding 16.5-mile round trip **South Loop Trail** up **Charleston Peak** (11,918ft) starts from the **Cathedral Rock** picnic area. An easier, 3-mile round trip trail leads to Cathedral Rock for views over Kyle Canyon. Nearby is the rustic **Mt Charleston Lodge** with its chalet-style dining room and lounge. Back downhill at the end of **Echo Rd** are more trailheads, including for twin **Mary Jane Falls** (2.5 miles return).

Heading north on NV 158, the alpine road winds past scenic campgrounds and even more trailheads. Turn left on to NV 156 (Lee Canyon Rd) to eventually reach the 40-acre, **Las Vegas Ski & Snowboard Resort**, with four lifts, 10 trails (longest run is 3000ft) and a 1000ft vertical drop for intermediate alpine skiing, plus a half pipe and terrain park for snowboarding. Surprised? Don't be. 'Nevada' is derived from the Spanish word for snow, and over 120in of the powdery stuff falls on these slopes each year.

> ## TRANSPORTATION
>
> **Distance from Las Vegas** 40 miles to Mt Charleston
> **Direction** Northwest
> **Travel Time** 45 minutes
> **Car** From the Strip, take I-15 north to US 95. Continue along US 95 north to NV 157 (Kyle Canyon Rd). NV 158 connects Kyle Canyon Rd to NV 156 (Lee Canyon Rd), which loops back east to US 95.

Excursions

SPRING MOUNTAINS

DETOUR: TULE SPRINGS

Barely out of the Las Vegas metro area, 2000-acre **Floyd Lamb State Park** is on the site of historic Tule Springs, a watering hole for Native American tribes and early mining prospectors. Transformed into a dude ranch in the 1940s, it gained notoriety as the place where movie stars came to get their quickie divorces by waiting out Nevada's six-week residency requirement in style. These days the park has picnic areas, small lakes for fishing and a band of resident peacocks, plus the Las Vegas Gun Club (as seen in the film version of *Fear & Loathing in Las Vegas*). To get there, follow the signs from the Durango Dr turnoff on the east side of US95, less than 3 miles south of NV 157 (Kyle Canyon Rd).

Information

USFS Information Station (☎ 702-872-5486; www
.fs.fed.us/r4/htnf/districts/smnra.shtml; Kyle Canyon Rd;
⟳ hrs vary)

Sights

Floyd Lamb State Park (☎ 702-486-5413; http://parks
.nv.gov/fl.htm; 9200 Tule Springs Rd; day-use fee per
vehicle $6; ⟳ 6am-dusk)

Las Vegas Ski & Snowboard Resort (☎ 702-593-9500;
www.skilasvegas.com; half-day pass adult/senior & child
under 13 $28/18, full day $38/25) Season is usually mid-
November till March/April. Ski and snowboard equipment
($30) and clothing ($25) rental is first-come, first-served.

Eating & Sleeping

Mt Charleston Hotel (☎ 702-872-5500, 800-794-3456; 2
Kyle Canyon Rd; www.mtcharlestonhotel.com; r $110-124,
ste $230) Hoity-toity lodging and dining.

Mt Charleston Lodge (☎ 702-872-5408; 800-955-1314;
www.mtcharlestonlodge.com; 1200 Old Park Rd; lunch
$10-18, dinner mains $6-20, cabins $125-220; ⟳ restau-
rant 8am-9pm, lounge 24hr) Rustic, romantic log cabins
with fireplaces, whirlpool tub and private decks. The family
restaurant has killer views.

USFS Campgrounds (reservations ☎ 518-885-3639, 877-
444-6777; www.reserveusa.com; tent & RV sites $15-35;
⟳ mid-May–Oct, some open year-round) Of the several
campgrounds, Hilltop has the best views.

Directory

Directory

TRANSPORTATION

Las Vegas is readily accessible from every major North American city, and from most of the world's metropolises, too. How you move around Sin City says a lot about who you are; low-rollers stick to the free or cheap public-transportation options, while high-rollers cruise along in an exotic convertible or stretch Hummer limo.

Gridlock along the Strip and freeways around central Las Vegas makes driving a chore. The best way to get around is on foot, in conjunction with the occasional mono-rail, shuttle bus or taxi ride (avoid the slow trolleys, though). The Strip has movable walkways and elevated crosswalks. Don't jaywalk – more people are injured while crossing the street than in auto accidents. Limited city bus services go further afield.

For organized tours, see p48. For transportation options for trips out of town, see the Excursions chapter (p205).

AIR

Deals on airfares can be found almost year-round, especially in the low seasons: December and January (except for Christmas and New Year's) and summer (June to August). Many airlines offer deals via their websites and sell flight packages that include accommodations and/or rental cars.

Online travel agents and websites that can help you find discounted flights, hotels and car-rental deals, include the following:

> ### THINGS CHANGE...
>
> The information provided in this section is particularly vulnerable to change. Check directly with the airline or a travel agent to make sure you understand how a fare (and ticket you may buy) works and shop carefully. Be aware of the security requirements for international travel. The details given in this chapter should be regarded as pointers and are not a substitute for your own careful, up-to-date research.

11thHour.com (www.11thhourvacations.com)

Cheap Tickets (www.cheaptickets.com)

Expedia.com (www.expedia.com)

Hotels.com (www.hotels.com)

Hotwire (www.hotwire.com)

LowestFare.com (www.lowestfare.com)

Orbitz (www.orbitz.com)

Priceline (www.priceline.com)

QIXO (www.qixo.com) Airfare search engine.

Sidestep (www.sidestep.com) Online travel search engine.

Site 59 (www.site59.com) Last-minute travel specialist.

SmarterTravel.com (www.smartertravel.com)

STA Travel (www.sta.com) Student and youth budget travel agent.

Travelocity (www.travelocity.com)

Travelzoo (www.travelzoo.com)

Yahoo! Travel (www.travel.yahoo.com)

THE MORE, THE MERRIER (AND THE CHEAPER)

The vast majority of package tours appeal to senior citizens who enjoy gambling in Las Vegas for a couple of days at a time and prefer to leave the driving or flying to others. Transportation, accommodations and airport shuttles are generally included in the price of these tours; meals are generally not. Some tours are led by a director; others are unaccompanied.

Round-trip transportation and two nights' stay can cost as little as $129. Air travel is always a bit more expensive than bus. Most quoted prices are based on double occupancy; solo travelers may pay a surcharge.

You can book directly with many hotels or airlines. **America West Vacations** (☎ 800-235-9298; www.americawestvacations.com) and **Southwest Airlines Vacations** (☎ 800-435-9792; www.swavacations.com) offer package tours from many US destinations. Online travel agents (above) offer even more options. Package-tour wholesalers, such as **Funjet Vacations** (☎ 800-558-3050; www.funjet.com), advertise in the travel sections of major US newspapers and alternative weeklies.

GETTING TO/FROM THE AIRPORT

Taxi fares to Strip hotels (30 minutes or more in heavy traffic) run from $10 to $20, cash only. Fares to downtown average $15 to $25. By law, an airport pickup surcharge of $1.20 applies. Fare gouging ('long-hauling') through the 'airport connector' tunnel to the interstate is common; tell your driver to use the Paradise Rd surface route unless time is of the essence or you're going to the south end of the Strip.

Many megaresorts on the Strip and some off-Strip hotels offer airport shuttles. Otherwise, airport shuttles such as **Bell Trans** (☎ 702-739-7990, 800-274-7433; www.bell-trans.com) charge about $4.75 per per person to the Strip, $6 to downtown or off-Strip hotels. Shuttles operate from around 7am to midnight, but some run 24 hours.

From the airport, it costs from $34 per hour for a chartered sedan or from $41 for a luxury six-person stretch limo – either is a good deal for groups. It rarely takes more than an hour to reach the Strip or downtown, unless there's heavy (weekend) traffic.

If you're pinching pennies, staying downtown and traveling light, hop aboard **CAT** (p234) bus No 109 and ride it north along Maryland Pkwy all the way to the **Downtown Transportation Center** (DTC; Map p261; 300 N Casino Center Blvd) in about 35 minutes. The bus operates every 10 to 30 minutes around the clock. It takes about 45 minutes from the airport to reach downtown on bus No 108, which stops at the convention center, Las Vegas Hilton and Sahara monorail stations.

For car rentals, see p235.

Airlines

Airlines serving Las Vegas' McCarran International Airport include those listed below:

Aeromexico (☎ 800-237-6639; www.aeromexico.com)

Air Canada (☎ 888-422-7533; www.aircanada.com)

Air Transat (☎ 877-872-6728; www.airtransat.com)

AirTran Airways (☎ 800-247-8726; www.airtran.com)

Alaska Airlines (☎ 800-252-7522; www.alaskaair.com)

Allegiant Air (☎ 800-432-3810; www.allegiantair.com)

Aloha Airlines (☎ 800-367-5250; www.alohaairlines.com)

America West Airlines (☎ 800-235-9292; www.americawest.com)

American Airlines (☎ 800-433-7300; www.aa.com)

American Trans Air (ATA; ☎ 800-435-9282; www.ata.com)

BMI (☎ 800-788-0555; www.flybmi.com)

Continental Airlines (☎ 800-523-3273; www.continental.com)

Delta Air Lines (☎ 800-221-1212; www.delta.com)

Frontier Airlines (☎ 800-432-1359; www.flyfrontier.com)

Harmony Airways (☎ 866-868-6789; www.hmyairways.com)

Hawaiian Airlines (☎ 800-367-5320; www.hawaiianair.com)

Hooters Air (☎ 888-359-4668; www.hootersair.com)

Independence Air (☎ 800-359-3594; www.flyi.com)

Japan Airlines (JAL; ☎ 800-525-3663; www.japanair.com)

Jet Blue (☎ 800-538-2583; www.jetblue.com)

Mexicana Airlines (☎ 800-531-7921; www.mexicana.com)

Midwest Express (☎ 800-452-2022; www.midwestexpress.com)

Northwest Airlines/KLM (☎ 800-225-2525; www.nwa.com)

Philippine Airlines (☎ 800-435-9725; www.philippineair.com)

Song (☎ 800-359-7664; www.flysong.com)

Southwest Airlines (☎ 800-435-9792; www.southwest.com)

Spirit Air (☎ 800-772-7117; www.spiritair.com)

Sun Country Airlines (☎ 866-359-6786; www.suncountryairlines.com)

Ted (☎ 800-225-5833; www.flyted.com)

TMA (☎ 866-435-9862; www.iflytma.com)

United Airlines (☎ 800-864-8331; www.united.com)

US Airways (☎ 800-428-4322; www.usairways.com)

Virgin Atlantic (☎ 800-862-8621; www.virgin-atlantic.com)

If you'll be arriving in the USA on a flight that isn't nonstop, you first must clear customs at a gateway airport (eg New York, Miami, Los Angeles, Honolulu) and then board a domestic flight bound for Las Vegas.

Airport

Just a crap shoot from the southern end of the Strip, **McCarran International Airport** (LAS; Map p260; ☎ 702-261-5211; www.mccarran.com) is one of the USA's 10 busiest airports, yet it's easy to navigate. It's notorious for late flights; however, self-service check-in kiosks ease headaches. Domestic flights use

Directory

TRANSPORTATION

Terminal 1; international and charter flights depart from Terminal 2. A free shuttle links both terminals.

McCarran offers ATMs, a full-service bank, free wi-fi Internet access, tourist information desks, a police substation, a post office, notary services and a first-aid station. Left-luggage lockers are unavailable currently due to post-9/11 security concerns. Airport diversions include slot machines, free historical aviation displays, **24 Hour Fitness** (☎ 702-261-3971; day pass $10) and a kids' play area. Advance check-in is available for some Strip hotels, though skip them if lines are long.

Short-term metered airport parking costs 25¢ per 10 minutes (change machines are available). Long-term covered parking at Terminal 1 costs $10 per day. Uncovered long-term parking at Terminal 2 costs $8 per day. If both garages are full, you'll be directed to a remote overflow lot. Free shuttles run between the overflow lot and the airport. Long-term parking is limited to 30 days.

BUS

Long-distance **Greyhound** (☎ 800-231-2222; www.greyhound.com) buses arrive at the **Greyhound bus station** (Map p261; ☎ 702-384-9561; 200 S Main St) downtown. Discounts on standard fares are given to ISIC cardholders, seniors, children and pairs traveling together. Buy tickets at least a week in advance for the best advance-purchase fares. Special nonrefundable 'casino' fares for adults could save you 50%.

Local buses with **Citizens Area Transit** (CAT; ☎ 702-228-7433, 800-228-3911; www.catride.com) operate daily from around 5:30am to 1:30am, with the most popular Strip and downtown routes running 24/7. The fare is $1.25, except on bus Nos 301 and 302 ($2); exact change is required. Free transfers, timetables with maps (25¢) and day passes ($5) are available from bus drivers, the **Downtown Transportation Center** (DTC; Map p261; 300 N Casino Center Blvd; ☉6am-6:45pm) or **South Strip Transfer Terminal** (SSTT; Map p260; 6675 S Gilespie St; ☉9am-5pm). Useful tourist routes are No 108 (Paradise/Fremont Street Experience–Monorail Connector), No 109 (Maryland Pkwy–Airport Connector), No 113 (Las Vegas Blvd North), No 202 (Flamingo) and No 301 (Strip), plus No 302 (Strip Express). Buses during rush hours can be standing room only.

CAR & MOTORCYCLE

Las Vegas makes for a great road trip. In the desert some vehicles may overheat when temperatures outside top 90°F. If you're driving around on a hot day, keep the air con off to avoid taxing the engine.

Auto-club members enjoy 24-hour emergency roadside assistance anywhere in the USA. If you have an accident, break down or lock your keys in your car, you're entitled to free service within a given radius of the nearest service center. Members also receive a range of discounts, for example, on car rentals and at hotels.

Auto clubs include the following:

American Automobile Association (☎ 800-874-7532; www.aaa.com) AAA offers travel insurance, free maps and popular tour books. Has reciprocal membership agreements with several international auto clubs (check first and bring your membership card).

Better World Club (☎ 866-238-1137; www.betterworld club.com) An eco-friendly alternative to AAA.

Driving

The only document that you'll legally need to operate a car or motorcycle for up to 12 months is a license from your home country. You may be required to show an international driving permit if your license isn't written in English.

Buckle up: seat belts are mandatory for all passengers. Helmets are required for motorcyclists. Drive on the right-hand side of the road. Right-hand turns at a red light are OK after making a full stop, but avoid blocking intersections. Pedestrians legally have the right of way at all times. Drivers must stop for pedestrians at crosswalks. Beware of jaywalkers – too many people are injured while crossing the street.

Most motorists drive conservatively due to the constant presence of traffic cops and harsh fines. The legal blood alcohol level is 0.10%. Driving under the influence (DUI) of drugs or alcohol is punished by mandatory jail time, revocation of driving privileges, court fines, raised insurance premiums and expensive lawyers' fees.

Gasoline costs upwards of $2 per gallon. The main roads into and out of Las Vegas are I-15 and US Hwy 95. US Hwy 93 leads east from downtown to Hoover Dam; I-215 goes by McCarran Airport. Traffic moves along at a decent clip, except during morning and afternoon rush hours and at night on weekends, especially along the Strip. When traffic is snarled on the highways, stick to surface routes instead, such as Industrial Rd along the west side of the Strip. Listen to KNUU 'K-News' (970AM) for traffic and weather updates every 10 minutes.

To reach Las Vegas, it takes about four to five hours from Los Angeles (270 miles); 4½ to 5½ hours from San Diego (330 miles); and nine to 10 hours from San Francisco (570 miles). On weekends and holidays, these trip times can double or even triple. For recorded updates on road conditions, dial ☎ 877-687-6237 for Nevada or ☎ 800-427-7623 for California. Along the I-15 corridor, Highway Radio (Barstow 98.1FM, Baker 99.7FM) broadcasts Mojave traffic and weather updates every half hour.

Parking

There's free self-parking everywhere on the Strip. For valet parking, there's usually no charge either, but tip the attendant $2 when your keys are returned. Downtown casino hotels offer free parking (maximum stay for non-guests is usually four hours), but remember to get your parking stub validated inside the casino before exiting.

Rental

Rates go up and down like the stock market, so it's worth surfing the Web and phoning around to see what's available. Booking ahead normally gets you the best rates, with

---

NO WHEELS? NO PROBLEM!

California-based **Green Tortoise** (☎ 415-956-7500, 800-867-8647; www.greentortoise.com) leads adventure bus tours for alternative-minded twenty-somethings. The week-long 'Canyons of the West' itinerary ends in Las Vegas. Departures are from San Francisco or Los Angeles. The cost ($670) includes ground transportation, park entrance fees and 70% of meals. You must arrange and pay for your own transportation to/from the departure city.

Party-hardy **Contiki** (www.contiki.com) leads one-week bus tours that roll through California, Arizona and Nevada, including Las Vegas. Most of the non-American travelers are aged 18 to 35. Lodging, ground transportation and some meals are included in the cost (from £395), but airfare to/from the departure city (Los Angeles) is extra.

---

the airport often being cheaper than downtown or on the Strip. Typically, renting a small car might cost $25 to $50 per day, or from $125 per week. But after adding insurance, taxes and fees, you could receive a surprising bill. Most companies add local sales taxes of up to 7.5% and governmental-service fees of 10% to their advertised rates; a customer facility charge ($3 per day) plus a 10% airport surcharge are often applied.

Most companies require a major credit card, and some require that the driver be at least 21 or 25 years old. Especially for weekend rentals, make reservations at least two weeks in advance. Car seats, which are legally required for young children, rent for $10 or less per day, but you'll need to reserve them in advance, too.

Car-rental agencies with airport desks include the following:

Alamo (☎ 877-252-6600; www.alamo.com)

Avis (☎ 800-230-4898; www.avis.com)

Budget (☎ 800-922-2899; www.budgetvegas.com)

Dollar (☎ 800-800-4000; www.dollar.com)

Enterprise (☎ 800-261-7331; www.enterprise.com)

Hertz (☎ 800-654-3131; www.hertz.com)

Payless (☎ 702-736-6147; www.paylesscarrental.com)

Savmor (☎ 800-634-6779; www.bnm.com/savmor.htm)

Thrifty (☎ 800-367-2277; www.thrifty.com)

US Rent-A-Car (☎ 800-777-9377; www.us-rentacar.com)

Major hotels also have car-rental desks.

For something glamorous, ring **Rent-A-Vette** (Map p265; ☎ 800-372-1981; www.rent-a-vette.com; 5021 Swenson St; ☺8am-5pm). Corvettes and exotic convertibles easily fetch $200 or more per day. **Las Vegas Motorcycle Rentals** (Map p265; ☎ 877-571-7174; www.lvhd.com; 2605 S Eastern Ave; ☺8am-5pm Mon-Fri, 8am-4pm Sat, 10am-4pm Sun) rents brand-new Harleys from $90 to $155 per day, including unlimited mileage, a helmet and rain suit. For longer hauls, **Cruise America** (☎ 800-784-7368; www.cruiseamerica.com) specializes in RV and camper rentals.

MONORAIL

The **Las Vegas Monorail** (☎ 702-699-8299; www.lvmonorail.com; ☺7am-2am) links properties along the Strip's resort corridor. Currently monorail stations are found at: the MGM Grand; Bally's & Paris; the misleadingly named Flamingo/Caesars Palace, which has no direct access to Caesars Palace; Harrah's/Imperial Palace; Las Vegas Convention Center; Las Vegas Hilton; and the Sahara. A one-way ride costs $3. A discounted 10-ride ticket ($20) can be used by multiple people. It costs $10/25 for a one-/three-day pass, a good idea if you're staying on the Strip.

SHUTTLE

Most off-Strip casino hotels offer free shuttle buses to and from the Strip. Handy services for tourists run between the Rio and Harrah's (10am to 1am, every 20 to 30minutes); the Gold Coast, the Orleans and Barbary Coast (9:30am-midnight, every 20min); and from the Stardust (every 90min, 9:50am-9:50pm), Harrah's (every 90min, 9:30am-9:30pm), Bourbon Street (every 100min, 9:30am-9:10pm) or San Remo on Tropicana Ave (every 100min, 10am-9:40pm) to Sam's Town on the Boulder Hwy, from where you can catch another shuttle headed downtown to the California and Fremont (every 1¼ hours, 9am-10:45pm).

For airport shuttles, see p233.

TAXI

Taxi stands are found at almost every casino hotel; it's almost impossible to hail one on the street. Fares (cash only) are metered: flagfall is $3.20, plus $1.80 per mile and 40¢ per minute while waiting. Vegas is surprisingly compact, so taxis are reasonable on a per-trip basis. A 4 to 5-mile lift from one end of the Strip to the other will run $10 to $15, depending on traffic. Other approximate fares include: mid-Strip to downtown, $12 to $15; and downtown or mid-Strip to the convention center, $10 to $12. Don't forget to tip the driver 10%, rounded up to the nearest dollar. By law, all companies must have at least one wheelchair-accessible van. Reputable cab companies include **Desert Cab** (☎ 702-386-9102), **Western Cab** (☎ 702-736-8000) and **Yellow/Checker/Star** (☎ 702-873-2000). File complaints via http://taxi.state.nv.us.

TRAIN

Talk of reviving **Amtrak** (☎ 800-872-7245; www.amtrak.com) train services persists, but for now the closest stations are in Kingman, Arizona (105 miles away), and in Needles (115 miles) and Barstow (155 miles), in

California. **Greyhound** (p234) provides a daily connecting Thruway bus service between Las Vegas and all three cities. A high-speed MagLev (magnetic levitation) rail link between Southern California and the Vegas Valley has been studied, but no dice yet.

TRAM

Free private tram systems connect a few casino hotels on the Strip, including TI (Treasure Island) and the Mirage; and the Excalibur, Luxor and Mandalay Bay.

TROLLEY

Frequent stops make trolleys the slowest way to get around. Be advised these vehicles aren't wheelchair-friendly either. Private air-con trolleys (☎ 702-382-1404) ply the length of the Strip, stopping at most hotels (including the Stratosphere). The only detour is to the Las Vegas Hilton near the convention center on Paradise Rd. Trolleys operate every 15 to 20 minutes, 9:30am to 1:30am daily. The single-ride fare is $1.75, and day passes cost $5 each (exact change is required).

PRACTICALITIES
ACCOMMODATIONS

Accommodation listings in this book are arranged alphabetically, with Cheap Sleeps (budget options) listed at the end of each neighborhood section. Count on adding a city room tax of 9% to all rates quoted in this book. See the Sleeping chapter for typical amenities, weekday vs weekend rates and advice about great deals.

LIGHT ME UP, BABY

A common complaint registered by tourists is cigarette smoke. 'Smoke-free' and 'Las Vegas' are rarely in the same sentence: there are ashtrays at every telephone, elevator, pool and shower, in toilets and taxis, and at the movies. Token nonsmoking sections exist in most restaurants and most hotels claim to offer nonsmoking rooms, but don't expect the air to be free of a whiff (or much more) of cancer sticks. If that worries you, ask when making reservations for places that are *entirely* nonsmoking or guarantee their nonsmoking rooms and areas are legit.

Unless you're on a junket yourself, avoid visiting during big conventions. Colossal crowds can be annoying and costly, since hotels jack up room rates and standard rooms are scarce. Contact the **Las Vegas Convention & Visitors Authority** (LVCVA; ☎ 702-892-7575, 877-847-4858; www.lasvegas24hours .com) for a list of convention dates. If you're claustrophobic, bypass New Year's Eve and other holidays (p240), as well as major special events (p8). The slowest times of year are usually the hottest summer months (July and August) and the winter doldrums (January and February).

BUSINESS HOURS

At casino hotels, open for business 24/7 is the rule – many places don't even bother with locks on their doors. Normal business hours for government offices are 9am to 5pm weekdays. Some postal outlets may stay open later and on weekends. Banks usually keep shorter hours; certain branches are open Saturday morning. Retail shopping hours are 10am to 9pm (to 6pm Sunday). Shopping malls and promenades in the casinos often stay open until 11pm or later. Christmas Day is one of the few holidays on which most shops close. Restaurants are usually open for lunch on weekdays from 11am to 2:30pm. They serve dinner from 5:30pm until 10pm from Sunday to Thursday, later on weekends. If restaurants take a day off, it's Monday or Tuesday. Most production shows are closed one day a week; the 'dark' day, as showbiz folks call it in Las Vegas, varies from show to show. Dance clubs open around 10pm until 3am (some stay open until 6am) but may be closed earlier in the week. It's not a problem finding 24-hour convenience stores or pharmacies.

CHILDREN

Las Vegas exists primarily for gamblers. Because the legal gambling age is 21, many casinos would rather you left little ones at home. State law prohibits people under age 21 from being in gaming areas and under 18s from being on the Strip after 9pm on weekends or holidays unless accompanied by a parent or guardian. With increasing frequency, casino hotels are prohibiting strollers on their grounds.

But not every gaming establishment looks upon children as so many sewer rats. **Circus Circus** (p75) was the first to appeal to families, providing free children's entertainment within earshot of the casino. Many casino hotels have followed suit (see 'Top Five Hotels for Kids,' p195), and these days, despite the ever-present gaming, Las Vegas is a family-vacation destination. There are several spectacular roller coasters in town, and no shortage of arcades, movie theaters and animal attractions where discounts for children are readily available. There are even child-friendly production shows (p146). Turn to p77 for our list of recommended family-friendly attractions and activities. For more about how to enjoy travel with young ones, read Lonely Planet's *Travel with Children*. Surf to www .lasvegaskids.net for city-specific advice and information.

Babysitting

Always ask for a licensed and bonded babysitting service, which hotel concierges can recommend. Many agencies send someone right to your hotel room. **Around the Clock Child Care** (☎ 702-365-1040, 800-798-6768; http://aroundtheclock.homestead.com) has a four-hour minimum of $60 per child and $12 for each additional hour.

All Coast Casinos and Station Casinos hotels have on-site child-care centers (but parents must remain on the casino hotel premises), including at the **Orleans** (p90; per child per hr $6; ☽ 9am-midnight, to 1am Fri & Sat), where a five-hour maximum daily visit applies and kids aged 2½ to 12 are welcome. Other properties in these chains are Green Valley Ranch, South Coast, Sunset Station, Gold Coast and Palace Station; see the Sleeping chapter.

At the **Hyatt Regency Lake Las Vegas Resort** (p202), the Camp Hyatt recreational programs (per session $27 to $40) are open to guests' children aged three to 12.

CLIMATE

Every year Las Vegas enjoys over 300 sunny days and receives just over 4in of rainfall. January and August are Las Vegas' wettest months, averaging just over a half inch of rain. The otherwise dry weather acts as a magnet for sun-starved retirees and others seeking refuge from blizzards at home. The mercury hovers above 100°F June through August. Tourism officials are quick to note it's a 'dry heat,' which is relatively true. Due to the billions of tons of concrete and asphalt in Las Vegas, temperatures in the city often exceed 75°F well after nightfall. That said, chilly days and cold nights (even snow!) fall upon southern Nevada during winter, so bring a jacket. See p8 for the best times to visit Las Vegas. Call the **National Weather Service** (☎ 702-736-3854) for forecasts and current conditions.

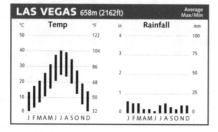

LAS VEGAS	658m (2162ft)				Average Max/Min

COURSES

For tourists, some casinos offer free gambling lessons. Las Vegas has dozens of trade schools for bartenders, card dealers and slot-machine mechanics; see the Work section on p246. Most courses require a multi-week commitment, and tuition runs anywhere from a couple hundred dollars into the thousands, but they'll help with job placement afterward. Gun certification and training classes are another draw in Nevada; ask at the **Gun Store** (p181).

CUSTOMS

You can import, duty free, 1L of alcohol, if you're over 21 years old; 200 cigarettes, 50 cigars (not Cubans) or 2kg of tobacco, if you're over 18; and gifts totaling $100 ($800 for US citizens). Travelers with more than $10,000 in US and/or foreign currency, traveler's checks or money orders must declare these upon entry. Dispose of any perishable items, such as fruits, vegetables or plants, in the bins provided. There are heavy penalties for attempting to import illegal drugs or drug paraphernalia. Counterfeits of trademarked brand-name items and currently any goods made in Cuba, Iran, North Korea or Sudan are prohibited. For the latest regulations, contact **US Customs & Border Protection** (☎ 202-354-1000, 877-227-5511; www.cbp.gov).

DISABLED TRAVELERS

Las Vegas is a very accommodating place for people with reduced mobility. Nearly every casino in town is on the ground floor. The **Imperial Palace** (p54) caters to guests with disabilities or mobility issues. Because so many gamblers are senior citizens, most casinos, hotels, restaurants and public restrooms are wheelchair-accessible. Request the free *Access Las Vegas* pamphlet from the LVCVA's **ADA Coordinator** (☎ 702-892-7413, voice relay 800-326-6888, TTY 800-326-6868; www.lasvegas24hours.com)

Las Vegas has the most ADA-accessible guest rooms in the US. Where stairs exist, so does an elevator or a ramp. Several resort pools have special lifts to enable water access. At most showrooms wheelchair seating and assisted listening devices are available. Guide dogs may legally be brought into restaurants, hotels and businesses. Many public-service phone numbers and some pay phones are adapted for the hearing-impaired.

Elevated pedestrian crosswalks on the Strip are elevator-equipped. Automatic doors and shaved curbs are standard everywhere. Taxi companies are required by law to have at least one wheelchair-accessible van. Most public transport (including the monorail) and some private airport shuttles are also lift-equipped. For hand-controlled rental cars, reserve well in advance. With any paratransit certification card, you can use **CAT ADA Paratransit** (☎ 702-228-4800, TTY 702-676-1834) services for up to 21 days. If you're driving, bring your disabled parking permit from home or apply for a 90-day temporary permit at **City Hall** (Map p261; ☎ 702-229-6431; 400 Stewart Ave; ☻ 8am-5pm Mon-Fri). Valet parking is readily available on the Strip and downtown.

Many local tour operators cater to the needs of disabled travelers, including on excursions to the Grand Canyon and Hoover Dam.

DISCOUNTS

The biggest discounts are 'comps' handed out by casinos to members of slot clubs and 'rated' gamblers. Full 'RFB' (room, food and beverage) is the coveted treatment lavished on the highest rollers (aka 'whales'). See p36 for the low-down on getting comped and rated – the more you lose, the more you save...

Freebie magazines distributed at the airport, tourist information centers and in most hotel rooms are the source of the biggest discounts (often half-price or two-for-one admission) on shows, dinner and attractions.

Casino 'fun books,' usually given to guests but sometimes available just for the asking, get the traveler a range of discounts, starting with a free souvenir from the gift shop, but are valid only for that hotel and its sister properties. You can print out coupons in advance from websites like www.lasvegasinsider.com, www.vegas4locals.com and www.lasvegasfunbook.com, or by searching online for 'Las Vegas fun book.'

ELECTRICITY

Electric current in the USA, like in Canada and Mexico, is 110 volts, 60 Hz AC. Gadgets built for higher voltage and cycles (such as 220/240V, 50-cycle appliances from Europe) will function poorly. North American electrical goods have plugs with two (flat) or three (two flat, one round) pins. Otherwise, you will need to use a converter or adapter.

EMBASSIES & CONSULATES

All embassies are in the nation's capital, Washington DC; dial ☎ 202-555-1212 for directory assistance. Some consulates are found in Los Angeles or San Francisco.

EMERGENCY

For hospital emergency rooms and clinics see p241.

Police, fire & ambulance ☎ 911

Police (nonemergency) ☎ 311

GAY & LESBIAN TRAVELERS

Queer Las Vegas exists, but it's largely unmapped. Public displays of affection (whether gay or straight) aren't very common or appreciated by the moral majority in this conservative town.

The flamboyant Fruit Loop area, a mile east of the Strip near the intersection of E Harmon Ave and Paradise Rd, is Sin City's queer epicenter. Las Vegas has several gay and lesbian bars and clubs

HELPFUL HOTLINES
These crisis hotlines are available 24 hours.

Alcoholics Anonymous ☎ 702-598-1888

Centers for Disease Control ☎ 800-842-2437

Gamblers Anonymous ☎ 702-385-7732

Narcotics Anonymous ☎ 702-369-3362

Poison Center ☎ 702-732-4989

Planned Parenthood ☎ 800-322-1020

Rape Crisis Center ☎ 702-366-1640

SAFE House (Domestic Violence) ☎ 702-451-4203

Suicide Prevention ☎ 702-731-2990

Youth Crisis Hotline ☎ 800-448-4663

(p151), and there are a few drag shows in town. Big annual events include **Las Vegas Pride** (☎ 702-615-9429; www.lasvegaspride.org; ☷ late May) and the Gay New Year's Eve party. **Lambda Business & Professional Association** (Map p265; ☎ 702-593-2875; www.lambdalv.com; Suite B-25, Commercial Center, 953 E Sahara Ave), the queer chamber of commerce, organizes monthly social mixers around town. **The Center** (Map p265; ☎ 702-733-9800; www.thecenter-lasvegas.com; Suite B-25, Commercial Center, 953 E Sahara Ave) hosts queer social groups and special events.

To plug into the scene, read **Bugle QVEGAS** (www.qvegas.com) and **Out Las Vegas** (www.outlasvegas.com). Pick up free copies of these magazines at the **Pride Factory** (Map p265; ☎ 702-444-1291; Suite E-1B, Commercial Center, 953 E Sahara Ave; www.pridefactory.com; ☷ 10am-midnight), a gift shop and Internet café, or **Get Booked** (Map p265; ☎ 702-737-7780; www.getbooked.com; 4640 S Paradise Rd, cnr Naples Dr; ☷ 10am-midnight, to 2am Fri & Sat), an older gay and lesbian retailer. Other community websites are www.gayvegas.com and www.outinlasvegas.com.

Civil unions and same-sex marriages aren't recognized by the state of Nevada, but gay-owned **Viva Las Vegas Villas & Wedding Chapel** (p85) arranges same-sex commitment ceremonies and overnight stays in its kitschy theme motel (p198).

The **Gay & Lesbian National Hotline** (☎ 888-843-4564; www.glnh.org; ☷ 4pm-midnight Mon-Fri, noon-5pm Sat) offers counseling, information and referrals.

Directory

PRACTICALITIES

HOLIDAYS

During national public holidays, all banks, schools and government offices (including post offices) are closed, and transportation, museums and other services are on a Sunday schedule. Holidays marked with an asterisk (*) below are widely kept; some are observed the following Monday if they fall on a weekend.

January 1 New Year's Day*

3rd Monday January Martin Luther King Jr Day

3rd Monday February Presidents' Day

March/April Easter

Last Monday May Memorial Day*

July 4 Independence Day*

1st Monday September Labor Day*

2nd Monday October Columbus Day

November 11 Veterans' Day

4th Thursday November Thanksgiving*

December 25 Christmas Day*

See p8 for major events, festivals and peak travel seasons.

INTERNET ACCESS

Most travelers make constant use of Internet cafés and free Web-based email such as **Yahoo** (www.yahoo.com) or **Hotmail** (www.hotmail.com).

If you're traveling with a notebook or hand-held device, be aware that your modem may not work once you leave your home country. The safest option is to buy a reputable 'global' modem before you leave home, or buy a local PC-card modem if you're spending an extended time in any one country. For more information, see www.teleadapt.com.

Major Internet service providers (ISPs) have local dial-up numbers, but not all budget hotels or motels have phones with data ports, and those that do often charge $1 per local phone call with a time limit of 30 minutes. Better hotels offer in-room high-speed Internet access, typically for $10 or so per 24 hours; WebTV keyboards may be provided. Hotel business centers charge outrageous rates for high-speed connections.

Internet kiosks around town come and go, but wireless (wi-fi) Internet is slowly spreading, including at lower-end casino hotels like the **Tropicana** (p194). At press time,

the best free wi-fi hotspots are at McCarran Airport, outside the **Apple store** (p173) at the Fashion Show Mall or at urban branches of the **Clark County Public Library** (☎ 702-734-7323; www.lvccld.org; 833 Las Vegas Blvd N; ☺ 9am-9pm Mon-Thu, 10am-6pm Fri-Sun), which provides free guest library cards to out-of-state residents with picture ID so that you can also use their Internet workstations (reservations recommended).

Otherwise, if you've left your laptop at home, the following are convenient:

Cyber Stop (Map pp262–3; ☎ 702-736-4782; www.cyberstopinc.com; Hawaiian Marketplace, Polo Towers Plaza, 3743 Las Vegas Blvd S; per 30min $8, hr $12; ☺ 7am-2:30am; monorail MGM Grand) The most reliable among dozens of cheap Internet cafés found inside gift shops on the Strip, most offering access from 20¢ per minute.

FedEx Kinko's (Map p265; ☎ 702-951-2400; www.fedexkinkos.com; 395 Hughes Center Dr, off Paradise Rd; per min 20¢; ☺ 24hr; bus 108, 202) Between the Strip and the convention center, with a T-Mobile wi-fi hotspot.

FedEx Kinko's (Map p261; ☎ 702-383-7022; www.fedexkinkos.com; 830 S 4th St; per min 20¢; ☺ 7am-10pm Mon-Fri) Near downtown, with a T-Mobile wi-fi hotspot.

FedEx Kinko's (Map p265; ☎ 702-735-4402; www.fedexkinkos.com; Suite 107, 4440 S Maryland Pkwy; per min 20¢; ☺ 7am-11pm) Near the UNLV campus, with a T-Mobile wi-fi hotspot.

LEGAL MATTERS

In a tourist-dependent city like Las Vegas, cops are on their best behavior. However, if a police officer gives you an order, don't seize upon that moment to start a public debate.

The drinking age of 21 is strictly enforced. Always carry photo ID to satisfy bartenders, bouncers and the like. In Las Vegas, it is legal to purchase alcohol at any time of day or night. It's against the law to have an open container of alcohol while walking down the street, but this rule is generally waived in the spirit of good public relations. However, if you're *staggering* down a street with a drink in your hand, you may be thrown in the 'drunk tank' (ie local jail) to sober up. There is zero tolerance at all times for any kind of illegal drug use. If police find marijuana, cocaine or any other illegal substance on you, you will get a free ride to the local jail.

Having an open container of alcohol in a car is always a big no-no, whether or not the driver is drinking. You could incur stiff

IS IT LEGAL?

Carrying a concealed weapon Yes (with a Nevada-issued permit).

Drinking Yes (if you're 21 years old).

Drugs No (except with a prescription).

Gambling Yes (if you're 21 years old).

Getting married fast Yes (p85).

Prostitution No (not in Clark County).

Sex Yes (age of consent is 16 for heterosexual sex, 18 for homosexual sex).

Smoking in public Yes (if you're 18 years old; see 'Light Me Up, Baby', p236).

fines, jail time and penalties if caught driving under the influence (DUI) of alcohol or any illegal substance (eg marijuana). The blood-alcohol limit over which you are considered legally drunk is 0.10%, which is often reached after just two beers. Penalties include throwing you in jail overnight, followed by a court appearance, heavy fine(s) and/or further incarceration.

If you are arrested for any reason, you have the right to remain silent. You are not legally required to speak to a police officer if you don't want to. However, never walk away from law-enforcement personnel without permission. Anyone who is arrested has the right to make one phone call. If you're from overseas and don't have a lawyer, friend or family member to help you, call your consulate (the police will provide the number upon request). **Clark County Legal Services** (Map p261; ☎ 702-386-1070, TTY 702-386-1059; http://clarkcountylegal.com; 800 S 8th St; ⏲ 8:30am-5pm Mon-Fri) provides free legal aid and services.

MAPS

The detailed maps in this guide are all you're likely to need. More detailed maps of the city and its sprawling suburbs are widely sold at hotels, gas stations and newsstands. Compass Maps' *Las Vegas* ($6.95) shows every single street in the city and also the metro area (including Henderson) on a large fold-out map, with a road index. The comprehensive, spiral-bound *Thomas Guide: Las Vegas & Clark County* ($24.95) extends all the way to Boulder City, Laughlin and Mesquite.

The **Nevada Commission on Tourism** (p245) widely distributes a free *Official State Map*. One side has a detailed map of the state, a Las Vegas regional map, a distance chart, and a list of recreational areas and campgrounds. The flip side has information about the state's history, attractions and tourism offices.

MEDICAL SERVICES

Excellent medical care is readily available, but if you are not properly insured, a collision with the US health-care system could prove fatal to your budget. The need for medical insurance when visiting the USA cannot be overemphasized. Doctors often expect payment on the spot for services rendered, after which your insurance company may reimburse you. Americans should check carefully with their insurer at home to see what conditions are covered in their policy. This is especially true for HMO members, who may have to call a special number to get approval for health care away from home.

Clinics

For minor ailments, it's almost always less expensive to go to a walk-in clinic than a hospital ER. Just east of the Strip, **Harmon Medical Center** (HMC; Map p265; ☎ 702-796-1116; www.harmonmedicalcenter.com; 150 E Harmon Ave; ⏲ 24hr) offers courtesy vans and translation services.

University Medical Center (UMC) operates a **Quick Care Network** (www.umc-cares .org/quickcares/) of urgent-care clinics that have x-ray and laboratory services. These clinics include the following:

Boulder Quick Care (Map p260; ☎ 702-383-2300; 5412 Boulder Hwy; ⏲ 8am-7:30pm Mon-Fri, 8am-4pm Sat & Sun)

McCarran Quick Care (Map p265; ☎ 702-383-3600; 1769 E Russell Rd, east of McCarran International Airport; ⏲ 8am-7:30pm)

Sunset Quick Care (Map p260; ☎ 702-383-6210; 525 Marks St, west of I-515, Henderson; ⏲ 8am-7:30pm)

If you chip a tooth or require emergency dental attention, contact the **Southern Nevada Dental Society** (☎ 702-733-8700; www.snds online.org) for referrals.

Emergency contraception services are available from **Planned Parenthood** (Map p265;

☎ 702-547-9888; www.pprm.org; Suite 54, Renaissance 3 Shopping Center, 3320 E Flamingo Rd; ✆ closed Sun; bus 202, 807).

Emergency Rooms

For medical emergencies dial ☎ 911. Hospitals with 24-hour ERs include the following:

Desert Springs Hospital (Map p265; ☎ 702-733-8800, emergency ☎ 702-369-7647; 2075 E Flamingo Rd)

Sunrise Hospital & Medical Center (Map p265; ☎ 702-731-8000, emergency ☎ 702-731-8080; 3186 Maryland Pkwy)

University Medical Center (UMC) of Southern Nevada (Map p264; ☎ 702-383-2000, emergency ☎ 702-383-2661; 1800 W Charleston Blvd) With the most advanced trauma center in Nevada.

Valley Hospital Medical Center (Map p264; ☎ 702-388-4000, emergency ☎ 702-388-4544; 620 Shadow Lane)

Pharmacies

CVS (Map p260; ☎ 702-262-9028; 3758 Las Vegas Blvd S; ✆ 24hr; monorail MGM Grand)

Walgreens (Map pp262–3; ☎ 702-739-9645; 3765 Las Vegas Blvd S; ✆ 24hr; monorail MGM Grand)

Walgreens (Map p261; ☎ 702-385-1284; 495 E Fremont St; ✆ 9am-7pm Mon-Fri, 9am-6pm Sat, 10am-6pm Sun; bus 301, 302)

MONEY

Nothing works like cash, but in Las Vegas you will find that most forms of payment are welcome. Most Americans do not carry large amounts of cash for everyday use, relying instead on credit cards, ATMs and direct debit cards. Personal checks (even from out of state) are commonly accepted with photo ID. All prices quoted in this book are in US dollars ($) and do not include taxes, unless otherwise noted. For exchange rates, see the inside front cover of this book. See also p16.

ATMs

Interbank ATM exchange rates usually beat traveler's checks or exchanging foreign currency. ATMs are everywhere, even right inside casino gaming areas, but transaction fees are often high (at least $3 at casino hotels), and your home bank may charge another fee on top of that. You can avoid these surcharges by using your debit card to get cash back when making a purchase at a non-casino business, such as Walgreens.

Changing Money

Casinos exist to separate you from your dough and thus will facilitate that end any way they can 24/7. Fees to exchange foreign currency tend to be higher than at banks but lower than at exchange bureaus. **American Express** (Map pp262–3; ☎ 702-739-8474; Fashion Show Mall, 3200 Las Vegas Blvd S; ✆ 9am-9pm Mon-Fri, 10am-8pm Sat, 11am-6pm Sun) changes currencies at competitive rates.

Credit Cards

Visa, American Express and MasterCard are widely accepted, Discover and Diners Club less so. All casinos will advance cash against plastic, but fees are sky-high.

Currency

US currency (the dollar) is divided into 100 cents (¢). Coins come in 1¢ (penny), 5¢ (nickel), 10¢ (dime), 25¢ (quarter), 50¢ (half-dollar; these are rare) and $1 denominations. Notes come in $1, $2 (also rare), $5, $10, $20, $50 and $100.

Traveler's Checks

Checks issued by **American Express** (☎ 800-221-7282), **Visa** (☎ 800-227-6811) and **Thomas Cook** (☎ 800-287-7362) are accepted by most businesses and can be replaced if lost or stolen. Restaurants, hotels and most shops readily accept US dollar checks. Fast-food restaurants and smaller off-Strip businesses will sometimes refuse to accept them.

NEWSPAPERS & MAGAZINES

Nevada's largest daily newspaper is the conservative **Las Vegas Review-Journal** (www.lvrj .com), which hits the streets every morning and publishes the Friday *Neon* entertainment guide. The **Las Vegas Sun** (www .lasvegassun.com) is the afternoon rag. On Sunday, the newspapers publish jointly. Free tabloid weeklies include **CityLife** (www .lvcitylife.com) and **Las Vegas Weekly** (www .lasvegasweekly.com).

An information-packed tourist magazine that's distributed freely to guest rooms is

What's On (www.ilovevegas.com), a weekly guide to current and upcoming shows and events. Other free tourist-oriented guides also available at casino hotels and the LVCVA (p245) include **Showbiz Weekly** (www.lvshowbiz.com) and **Today in Las Vegas** (www.todayinlv.com), which both have valuable discount coupons.

The glossy monthly **Las Vegas Life** (www.lvlife.com) has an affluent locals-only readership, while **Casino Player** (www.casinoplayer.com) magazine targets gaming enthusiasts. Popular websites for the latest news and updates, aimed at die-hard Vegas visitors, include www.lasvegasinsider.com, www.lasvegasadvisor.com and www.cheapovegas.com.

PHOTOGRAPHY & VIDEO

Photography is prohibited at McCarran Airport and strongly discouraged inside casinos. Print film is widely available at hotel gift shops, supermarkets and drugstores, but for digital-camera memory cards, sticks and photo printing visit a specialty camera shop. Casino hotels such as Caesars Palace and the Venetian have them in their shopping arcades, or try **Millennium Foto** (Map pp262–3; ☎ 702-696-9430; Carnaval Court, 3475 Las Vegas Blvd S; ☺ 9am-midnight). Camera shops also stock B&W and 35mm slide film. If you purchase a video, note that the US uses the NTSC color TV standard, which is not compatible with international standards like PAL and Secam.

POST

For US postal information (including poste-restante/general-delivery mail), visit www.usps.com or call ☎ 800-275-8777. Convenient full-service post offices are found **downtown** (Map p261; Suite 100, 201 Las Vegas Blvd S; ☺ 8:30am-5pm Mon-Fri); just **west of the Strip** (Map pp262–3; 3100 S Industrial Rd; ☺ 8:30am-6pm Mon-Fri, 9am-3pm Sat); and at **McCarran Airport** (Map p265; 5795 Paradise Rd; ☺ 9am-1pm & 2-5pm Mon-Fri).

Domestic rates are 37¢ for letters up to 1oz (plus 23¢ for each additional ounce) and 23¢ for postcards. International airmail rates are 80¢ (Canada or Mexico 60¢) for letters of the same size or postcards. Most casino hotels sell stamps and will mail letters and packages for you.

Important letters or packages can be sent overseas via **Federal Express** (☎ 800-463-3339; www.fedex.com) or **UPS** (☎ 800-782-7892; www.ups.com), which guarantee on-time delivery to other countries.

RADIO

Due to the city's status as a mecca for sports betting, there are no fewer than a half-dozen radio AM stations that broadcast sport on a regular basis, including the Fox sports network's 1460AM (KENO).

As you're driving around Las Vegas, flip the dial to these stations:

88.9FM (KNPR) National public broadcasting.

89.7FM (KCNV) Classical music.

91.5FM (KUNV) Jazz from the University of Nevada.

92.3FM (KOMP) Modern and classic rock.

98.5FM (KLUC) Hip-hop, R&B and Top 40.

102.7FM (KSTJ) '80s rock.

104.3FM (KJUL) Swingin' cocktail tunes and dusties.

107.5FM (KXTE) Headbanger 'X-treme Radio'.

Listen online before you go at www.vegastalkradio.com and www.lvrocks.com.

SAFETY

Despite the burgeoning population of the metro area and over 37-million visitors per year, there's less crime than ever reported in Las Vegas now. Police and private security officers are out in force and surveillance cameras are omnipresent. VIVA Patrol volunteers trained by the police act as roving ambassadors in busy tourist areas, ready to answer your questions and prevent crime.

Violent crime is not likely to affect many Las Vegas tourists (statistically you're more likely to be robbed in San Francisco or LA), but property theft is common, so use your common sense. Park in busy areas, remove valuables from sight and lock up. Utilize the in-room safes that most hotels provide, and make sure you never leave your valuables unattended, especially in casinos. Beware of pickpockets in crowds and on public transport. Having strangers thrust ads for strippers at you on the Strip can be annoying, but a simple 'No, thanks' will suffice.

In case of a life-threatening emergency, dial ☎ 911. To report a minor crime when immediate police response isn't required, dial ☎311. You will need a police report of the incident to file an insurance claim in most cases.

TAXES

There is no value-added tax in the USA. There is no state sales tax in Nevada but county and/or city taxes are added to most stated prices and fees. A sales tax of 7.5% applies to the retail price of goods and services (gasoline is an exception) and there's a 9% hotel tax added to room rates, including those quoted in this book. Car-rental agencies charge both taxes *and* fees (p235).

TELEPHONE

The area code for Clark County, including Las Vegas, is ☎702; for the rest of Nevada it's ☎775. Some toll-free numbers are good anywhere in North America, others can be dialed only within the USA, and still others work only inside (or outside) Nevada. If dialing a number outside your area code, dial ☎1 first. Beware that international rates apply for calls to Canada, even though the dialing code (☎1) is the same as for domestic long-distance calls. For all other overseas direct-dial calls, dial ☎011 followed by the country code. Pay phones are mostly coin-operated; some accept credit cards or have data ports for laptop or PDA Internet connections. Major carriers such as AT&T (☎800-321-0288) can facilitate long-distance and collect calls, as can the operator (dial ☎0 from a pay phone), but it's usually cheaper to use a phonecard. If you need to send a fax, ask at your hotel's front desk or business center (rates from $2).

Cell Phones

North America uses a variety of mobile-phone systems, most of which are incompatible with the GSM 900/1800 standard used in Europe, Asia and Africa. Check with your service provider about using your phone in Las Vegas. Calls may be routed internationally, while US travelers should beware of roaming surcharges; either way, it can become very expensive for a 'local' call. On the Strip, most hotel business centers rent cell phones to guests. Cyber Stop (p240) rents Nokia handsets (per day $5 plus 85¢ per minute for all calls). Using cell phones near casino race and sports books is prohibited.

Phonecards

Sold at convenience stores, private pre-paid phonecards almost always give rates superior to direct dialing from public pay phone or in-room hotel phones. Beware of phonecards that advertise the cheapest per-minute rates; they may charge hefty connection fees for each call, especially for using the toll-free access number (at pay phones you can deposit 35¢ and dial the local access number instead). You can avoid the hassle of bad connections by choosing a slightly more expensive phonecard from a major long-distance carrier, such as AT&T (☎800-321-0288), whose phonecards are available at many stores around town.

TELEVISION

Major broadcast networks (CBS, NBC, ABC and FOX) offer prime-time fare; alternatives include the university's public-access channel (UNLV-TV) and the national Public Broadcasting Service (PBS). Cable in most hotel rooms is limited to news, sports and pay-per-view movies.

TIME

Las Vegas uses Pacific Standard Time (PST), which is eight hours behind Greenwich Mean Time (GMT). The Pacific time zone is one hour behind Mountain Standard Time (MST), which is observed by Nevada's eastern neighbors Arizona, Utah and Idaho.

Daylight Saving Time (DST) starts on the first Sunday in April, when the clocks move forward one hour; it finishes the last Sunday in October. Nearby Arizona doesn't observe daylight-saving time, although the Navajo Nation within its borders does.

At noon in Las Vegas, it's 3pm in New York, 8pm in London, 9pm in Paris, and 7am (the following day) in Sydney.

TIPPING

Hotel and casino staffers rely on tips to bring their incomes up to decent levels. Fortunes have been made by valet parking concession owners. However, tips should only be given as a reward for good service. If you receive lousy service, leave a poor tip or, in exceptionally bad cases, none at all; to do otherwise defeats the purpose of tipping. Here is a guide to tipping in Las Vegas:

Airport skycaps Around $1 to $2 per bag.

Bartenders 15%, rounded up to the next dollar.

Bellhops & hotel porters $1 per bag, minimum total $2 ($5 if you have several bags).

Cocktail waitresses $1 per drink.

Concierges From $2 for making a phone call up to $20 for securing tickets to a sold-out show.

Doormen $1 to $2 for summoning you a cab, depending on the weather.

Limo Drivers $5 per person or 10 to 15% of the total fare, whichever is higher.

Maids $1 to $2 per night, left in an obvious place, usually under the card provided.

Restaurants 15 to 20% for good service; don't tip if a service charge (of 15 to 18% for groups of six or more) has already been included. See also p105.

Room Service 15%, minus any gratuity already charged on the bill.

Taxis 10%, then round total fare up to the nearest dollar.

Valet parking attendants $2 per car, paid when the keys are handed back to you.

It's not expected to tip cashiers, casino or slot hosts, ticket-booth vendors or hotel front-desk employees. For gamblers' tipping customs, see p36.

TOURIST INFORMATION

There are quite a number of tour operators around town with 'Tourist Information' signs posted out front, but the city's only true tourist office is the **Las Vegas Convention & Visitors Authority** (LVCVA; Map pp262–3; ☎ 702-892-7575, 877-847-4858; www.visit lasvegas.com; 3150 Paradise Rd, cnr Desert Inn Rd; ☾ 8am-5pm), opposite the convention center. Friendly, knowledgeable staff give away free brochures, magazines and maps. The hotline (☾ live operators 6am-9pm) has 24-hour recorded entertainment and convention schedules.

The **Nevada Commission on Tourism** (www .travelnevada.com) runs Nevada Welcome Centers statewide, including the following:

Mesquite (☎ 877-637-7848; off I-15 exit 122; ☾ 8am-4:30pm) Near the Utah state line.

Primm (☎ 702-874-1360; off I-15 exit 1; ☾ 9:30am-6:30pm) By the California state line. If you have out-of-state ID, get 20 minutes of free Internet access.

Tourist information offices operated by LVCVA abroad include the following:

Australia (☎ 02-9328-5440; www.lasvegasfreedom .com.au)

France (☎ 0825 83 13 73; www.lasvegasfreedom.fr)

Germany (☎ 089-2366-21-30; www.lasvegasfreedom.de)

Japan (☎ 3-3358-3265; www.lasvegasfreedom.jp)

Mexico (☎ 01-55-5281-4923; www.lasvegasfreedom .com.mx)

South Korea (☎ 02-777-9282; www.lasvegasfreedom .co.kr)

UK (☎ 01564-79-4999; www.lasvegasfreedom.co.uk)

VISAS

Check with **US Citizenship and Immigration Services** (USCIS; ☎ 800-375-5283; www.uscis.gov) and the **US Department of State's Bureau of Consular Affairs** (☎ 202-663-1225; www.travel.state .gov/visa) for the latest information about entering the USA. Information here and in the Travel Links section of www.lonely planet.com is highly subject to change. It is up to you to verify it with the relevant government agencies before traveling.

Under the US visa-waiver program, visas currently aren't required for citizens of the EU, Australia and New Zealand for visits up to 90 days, as along as you present a machine-readable passport upon arrival. Under the visa-waiver program, you cannot change or extend your non-immigrant status at a later date. Temporary visitors from Canada do not normally need a visa, but must bring their passport. Citizens of Mexico need to have a non-immigrant visa or a B1/B2 Visa/Border Crossing Card (aka 'laser visa'). Citizen of other countries must apply in advance for a non-immigrant visa.

All exit and entry procedures are controlled by the Department of Homeland Security (www.dhs.gov) with its US-VISIT program. A passport and/or visa does not guarantee entry. A return ticket is normally required. Immigration officials have the authority to deny admission to anyone for any reason, except those seeking asylum.

WOMEN TRAVELERS

On the Strip, drunk men may make obnoxious comments, but most don't take this behavior further if ignored. Though prostitution is illegal in Clark County, prostitutes (aka 'escorts,' 'call girls,' 'working girls' or 'weekend warriors') are a part of Nevada's high-rolling culture. Solo women may occasionally find themselves subjected to uninvited propositions by men.

If you are sexually assaulted, you don't have to call ☎ 911 or even talk to the police in order to get help. If your life isn't in immediate danger, you can call the **Rape Crisis Center** (RCC; ☎ 702-366-1640) hotline. Staff act as a link between medical, legal and social-service systems, advocating on behalf of survivors to ensure their rights are respected and needs are addressed. After calling the hotline, assault survivors can go to the nearest hospital where an advocate and/or specially trained nurse will be available. If you decide to pursue legal action, the police can be called at that time instead.

WORK

Las Vegas is a convention town. Trade shows and expos bring in millions of visitors (and billions of dollars) annually. The **LVCVA** (p245) has all the resources and information you'll need to plan a meeting or take care of business while you're in town. Upmarket hotel business centers have sky-high rates, but they're convenient. For more reasonably priced Internet access and basic business services, try **FedEx Kinko's** (p240).

Las Vegas has one of the highest job-growth rates in the country, but most jobs only pay minimum wage ($6.15 per hour). State law prohibits an employer from applying tips against the minimum wage. To work at any hotel-casino in Las Vegas, a prospective employee may need to obtain a 'sheriff's card' from the police department. For more information and other employment resources, visit the online Career Center of the **Las Vegas Chamber of Commerce** (☎ 702-735-1616; www.lvchamber.com).

US law makes it difficult for foreign citizens to work in the country without a prearranged permit from an employer. If you are caught working illegally, you can be immediately deported and barred from the US for five years.

Directory

PRACTICALITIES

Behind the Scenes

THE LONELY PLANET STORY

The story begins with a classic travel adventure: Tony and Maureen Wheeler's 1972 journey across Europe and Asia to Australia. There was no useful information about the overland trail then, so Tony and Maureen published the first Lonely Planet guidebook to meet a growing need.

From a kitchen table, Lonely Planet has grown to become the largest independent travel publisher in the world, with offices in Melbourne (Australia), Oakland (USA) and London (UK). Today Lonely Planet guidebooks cover the globe. There is an ever-growing list of books and information in a variety of media. Some things haven't changed. The main aim is still to make it possible for adventurous travelers to get out there – to explore and better understand the world.

At Lonely Planet we believe travelers can make a positive contribution to the countries they visit – if they respect their host communities and spend their money wisely. Every year 5% of company profit is donated to charities around the world.

THIS BOOK

This 3rd edition of *Las Vegas* was researched and written by Sara Benson. Scott Doggett wrote the 1st and 2nd editions. The Gambling chapter was cowritten by Jonathan Grotenstein. Some text in the book was adapted from Andrew Dean Nystrom's *Best of Las Vegas*, and the 'Got Lucky' boxed text was cowritten by Luci Yamamoto. This guide was commissioned in Lonely Planet's Oakland office and produced by the following:

Commissioning Editor Suki Gear

Coordinating Editor Simon Williamson

Coordinating Cartographer Herman So

Coordinating Layout Designer Jim Hsu

Managing Cartographer Alison Lyall

Proofreaders Nigel Chin, Lucy Monie

Assisting Cartographers Hunor Csutoros, James Ellis, Kusnandar

Assisting Layout Designers Laura Jane, Jacqui Saunders

Cover Designer Brendan Dempsey

Project Managers Charles Rawlings-Way, Celia Wood

Cover photographs by Lonely Planet Images: colored neon lights, Chris Mellor (top); a showgirl display at Madame Tussauds Wax Museum, Venetian, Richard Cummins (bottom); old Neon Museum on Fremont St, Richard Cummins (back).

Internal photographs by Ray Laskowitz/Lonely Planet Images except for the following: p74 (#2) Michael Aw/Lonely Planet Images; p2 (#4), p11, p17, p36, p57, p68 (#3), p68 (#4), p69 (#2), p69 (#4), p71 (#3), p71 (#4), p73 (#1), p73 (#2), p100, p126, p131, p163, p183, p203 Richard Cummins/Lonely Planet Images; p2 (#2), p2 (#3), p67 (#2),

p86, p200 Lee Foster/Lonely Planet Images; p2 (#1), p70 (#2), p82 Ryan Fox/Lonely Planet Images; p67 (#4) Kevin Foy/Alamy Images; p74 (#1) Roberto Soncin Gerometta/Lonely Planet Images; p68 (#2), p70 (#1), p70 (#3), p167 Mark & Audrey Gibson/Lonely Planet Images; p74 (#3) Ralph Lee Hopkins/Lonely Planet Images; p69 (#3), p71 (#2) Dennis Johnson/Lonely Planet Images; p12, p69 (#1) Christina Lease/Lonely Planet Images; p53, p226 James Lyon/Lonely Planet Images; p72 (#2) Eastham & Max Paoli/Lonely Planet Images; p68 (#1) Mark Parkes/Lonely Planet Images; p212, p215 Carol Polich/Lonely Planet Images; p72 (#1) Trinette Reed/Alamy Images; p29 Emily Riddell/Lonely Planet Images; p74 (#4) Cheyenne L. Rouse/Lonely Planet Images; p67 (#3) Toby Skinner/Alamy Images. All images are the copyright of the photographers unless otherwise indicated. Many of the images in this guide are available for licensing from Lonely Planet Images: www.lonelyplanetimages.com.

THANKS
SARA BENSON

Thanks to all the PR folks, especially Stephanie Heller, Gina Boccadoro, Kate Turner, Victoria Kent, Marc Jay and Jana Blackburn. But if there's anyone who deserves to strike it rich in Vegas, it's editrix Suki Gear. Becca Blond and Kim Grant generously gave tip-top advice and shared valuable research. While keeping me company on the road, Amy Lowe and Josh Lucas also kept me sane. Last but not least, thanks to Elvis, Dean Martin and Frank Sinatra for always being just a download away.

ACKNOWLEDGMENTS

Many thanks to the following for the use of their content: Las Vegas Monorail Route Map © Las Vegas Monorail Company 2005; thanks also to David Gonzalez from MGM Mirage for providing the casino source maps.

OUR READERS

Many thanks to the travelers who used the last edition and wrote to us with helpful hints, useful advice and interesting anecdotes:

Virginia Arrieta, Anthony Bailey, Tina Barnes, Jim Beffa, Samantha Blyth, Lewis Brown, Bob Carroll, Michael Chang, Rob Ciampa, Lucy Dallas, Sue Dodds, Glenn Dodson, Vicki Edmunds, Victoria Embs, Fabio Falchi, Kathy Farr, Tami Fichter, Joe Ganesh, Jude Harrison, Lisa Haun, Chris & Rose Hunneyball, Jane James, Christopher Jones, Teresa Kamieniak, Bas Kempen, Karen Kester, Frank Lodewick, Youval Marks, Minouche Martins, Patricia Maud, Rich Mick, Dana Miller, Caroline Mitchell, Bruce Mocking, Heather Monell, Roberta Murray, Joe Nekrasz, Eric Nowitzky, Jo Philip, Linda Rafferty, Julie Reefer, Donna Regan, Brian Russell, Jane Salty, Ronald Schlosberg, Stacey Sefton, Mary Sheesley, Val Shingleton, Claire Snel, Andy Sparrow, Sarah Tilley, Aison To, Dawn Toles, Wendy Tucker, Fredrik Tukk, Huub van der Linden, Stijn van Rest, Erica van Zon, Sally Wade, Andrew Wignall, Rachael Woodcock, Andrew Young.

ACKNOWLEDGMENTS

Many thanks to the following for the use of their content: Las Vegas Monorail Route Map © Las Vegas Monorail Company 2005; thanks also to David Gonzalez from MGM Mirage for providing the casino source maps.

SEND US YOUR FEEDBACK

We love to hear from travelers — your comments keep us on our toes and help make our books better. Our well-traveled team reads every word on what you loved or loathed about this book. Although we cannot reply individually to postal submissions, we always guarantee that your feedback goes straight to the appropriate authors, in time for the next edition. Each person who sends us information is thanked in the next edition — and the most useful submissions are rewarded with a free book.

To send us your updates — and find out about Lonely Planet events, newsletters and travel news — visit our award-winning website: www.lonelyplanet.com /feedback.

Note: We may edit, reproduce and incorporate your comments in Lonely Planet products such as guidebooks, websites and digital products, so let us know if you don't want your comments reproduced or your name acknowledged. For a copy of our privacy policy visit www.lonelyplanet.com/privacy.

Notes

Index

See also separate indexes for Eating (p256), Drinking (p257), Shopping (p258) and Sleeping (p258).

000 map pages
000 photographs

MAP LEGEND

ROUTES

	Tollway		One-Way Street
	Freeway		Mall/Steps
	Primary Road		Tunnel
	Secondary Road		Walking Tour
	Tertiary Road		Walking Tour Detour
	Lane		Pedestrian Overpass

TRANSPORT

	Monorail		Tram

HYDROGRAPHY

	River, Creek		Canal
	Intermittent River		Water

BOUNDARIES

	State, Provincial

AREA FEATURES

	Airport		Cemetery, Christian
	Area of Interest		Land
	Building, Featured		Mall
	Building, Information		Park
	Building, Other		Sports
	Building, Transport		Urban

POPULATION

●	Large City	●	Medium City
●	Small City	●	Town, Village

SYMBOLS

Sights/Activities	Drinking	Information
Christian	Drinking	Hospital, Medical
Museum, Gallery	Café	Information
Zoo, Bird Sanctuary	**Entertainment**	Internet Facilities
Eating	Entertainment	Post Office, GPO
Eating	**Transport**	Toilets
Shopping	Airport, Airfield	**Geographic**
Shopping	Bus Station	Lookout
Sleeping	General Transport	Mountain, Volcano
Sleeping	Parking Area	Pass, Canyon

Maps

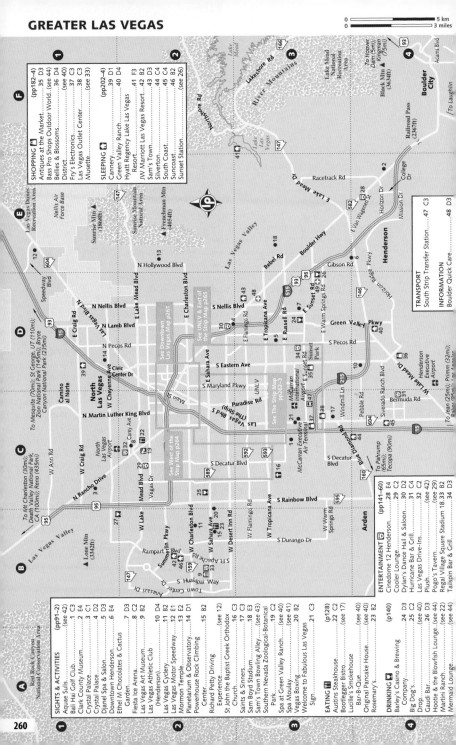

0 _____ 5 km
0 _____ 3 miles

Henderson

Boulder
City

North
Las Vegas

Arden

DOWNTOWN LAS VEGAS

0 — 800 m
0 — 0.5 miles

THE STRIP

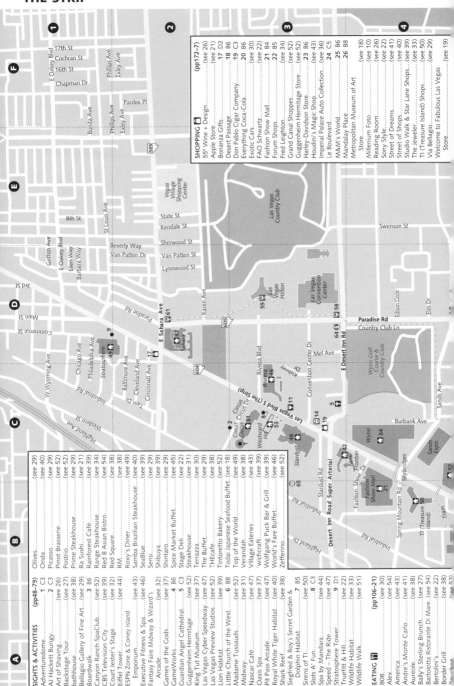

263

WEST OF THE STRIP

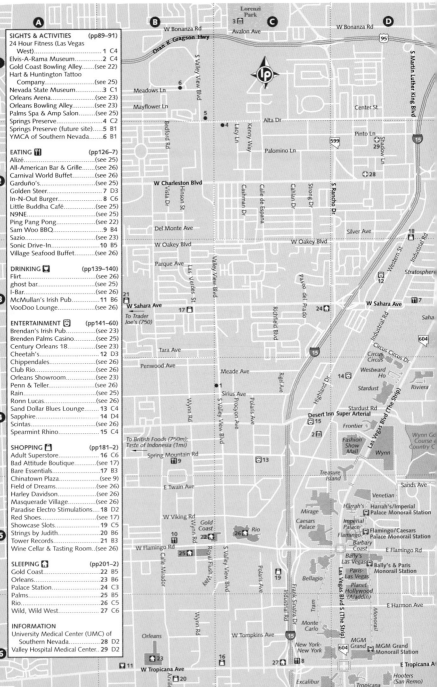

UNLV & EAST OF THE STRIP

| | | 1 km |
| | | 0.5 miles |

SHOPPING (pp179–81)
Albion Books....................................34 C2
Alternate Reality Comics...............35 B4
Big B's...36 B4
Buffalo Exchange............................37 B3
Cowtown Boots...............................38 B2
Deep Space Nine
    Promenade..............................(see 52)
Get Booked.....................................39 B4
Gun Store..40 D4
Havana Cigar Co...........................(see 13)
Record City......................................41 B1
Retro Vintage Clothing...................42 B3
Serge's Showgirl Wigs....................43 B1
The Jeweler...................................(see 52)
Zia Record Exchange.......................44 C3

SIGHTS & ACTIVITIES (pp86–9)
24 Hour Fitness...............................1 C1
Atomic Testing Museum..................2 B3
Haunted Vegas Tours..................(see 49)
Las Vegas Athletic Club..................3 B1
Las Vegas Convention Center.4 B2
Liberace Museum............................5 C4
Plane Watchers' Parking Lot.6 C5
PussyKat Tatttoo Parlor...7 B4
Rock Spa......................................(see 50)
Star Trek: The Experience...........(see 52)
UNLV Special Collections
    (Lied Library)..............................8 B3
Welcome to Fabulous
    Downtown Las Vegas Sign..9 B1
Winchester Cultural Center...10 D2

EATING (pp123–6)
AJ's Steakhouse...........................(see 50)
Battista's Hole in the Wall............11 A3
Cafe Heidelberg.............................12 B1
Envy...(see 55)
Firefly...13 B1
Hamburger Mary's.........................14 B3
Lotus of Siam.................................15 B1
Metro Pizza....................................16 C4
Metro Pizza................................(see 60)
Mistral...(see 52)
Mr Lucky's...................................(see 50)
Nobu..(see 50)
Paymon's Mediterranean
    Café...17 B3
Pink Taco....................................(see 50)
Quark's Restaurant.....................(see 52)
Rainbow's End................................18 B1

Simon Kitchen & Bar...................(see 50)
Sweet Georgia Brown's...............19 D3
Tillerman.......................................20 C3

DRINKING (pp138–9)
Crown & Anchor............................21 C4
Cuba Libre...................................(see 50)
Double Down Saloon...................(see 39)
Ellis Island Casino & Brewery....(see 60)
Gordon Biersch..............................22 B3
Hofbräuhaus...................................23 B3
Hookah Lounge...........................(see 17)
International Vintage Wine
    Cellar.......................................(see 13)
Quark's Bar.................................(see 52)

ENTERTAINMENT (pp141–60)
Apollo Spa.....................................24 B1
Beacher's Madhouse....................(see 50)
Body English.................................(see 50)
Buffalo..25 B4
Club Paradise.................................26 B3
FreeZone......................................(see 23)
Gipsy...27 B3
Goodtimes......................................(see 5)
Hilton Theatre................................28 B2
Ice...29 A3
Shimmer Cabaret.........................(see 28)
The Beach.......................................30 B2
The Joint......................................(see 50)
Thomas & Mack Center.................31 B4
Tribute to Frank, Sammy,
    Joey & Dean..............................(see 49)
Tropicana Cinemas........................32 D4
UNLV Performing Arts Center....33 B3

SLEEPING (pp199–201)
Alexis Park Villas............................45 A3
Best Western Mardi Gras Inn.......46 B2
Carriage House...............................47 A3
Embassy Suites Hotel Convention
    Center..48 B2
Greek Isles.....................................49 B3
Hard Rock.......................................50 B3
Homestead Suites...........................51 B2
Las Vegas Hilton.............................52 B2
Marriott Suites................................53 A2
Motel 6 Tropicana..........................54 A4
Renaissance Las Vegas..................55 B2
Residence Inn Convention Center..56 B2
Residence Inn Hughes Center........57 A3
St Tropez...58 B3
Somerset House..............................59 A2
Super 8 Motel.................................60 B3
Terrible's..61 B3
Tuscany Suites................................62 A3
Westin Casuarina...........................63 A3

TRANSPORT
Las Vegas Motorcycle Rentals....(see 1)
Rent-a-Vette..................................64 B4

INFORMATION
Clark County Public Library...........65 C3
Desert Springs Hospital..................66 C3
FedEx Kinko's.................................67 B3
FedEx Kinko's.................................68 B3
Harmon Medical Center (HMC)....69 A3
Lambda Business & Professional
    Association...............................(see 72)
McCarran Quick Care.....................70 C5
Planned Parenthood.......................71 C3
Pride Factory...................................72 B3
Sunrise Hospital & Medical Center..73 B2
The Center....................................(see 72)

265

LAS VEGAS TRANSPORT MAP

LAS VEGAS MONORAIL

IT'S MORE THAN TRANSPORTATION. **IT'S A REAL TRIP.**™

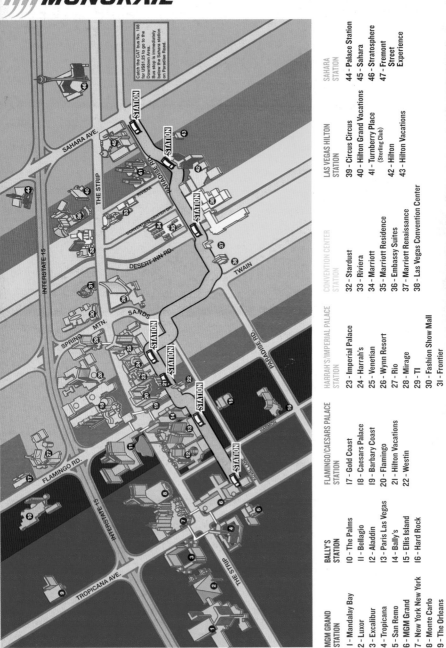

Catch the CAT bus No. 108 for US#1.25 to go to the Downtown Area. Bus stop is immediately below the Sahara station on Paradise Road.

MGM GRAND STATION
1 - Mandalay Bay
2 - Luxor
3 - Excalibur
4 - Tropicana
5 - San Remo
6 - MGM Grand
7 - New York New York
8 - Monte Carlo
9 - The Orleans

BALLY'S STATION
10 - The Palms
11 - Bellagio
12 - Aladdin
13 - Paris Las Vegas
14 - Bally's
15 - Ellis Island
16 - Hard Rock

FLAMINGO/CAESARS PALACE STATION
17 - Gold Coast
18 - Caesars Palace
19 - Barbary Coast
20 - Flamingo
21 - Hilton Vacations
22 - Westin

HARRAH'S/IMPERIAL PALACE STATION
23 - Imperial Palace
24 - Harrah's
25 - Venetian
26 - Wynn Resort
27 - Rio
28 - Mirage
29 - TI
30 - Fashion Show Mall
31 - Frontier

CONVENTION CENTER STATION
32 - Stardust
33 - Riviera
34 - Marriott
35 - Marriott Residence
36 - Embassy Suites
37 - Marriott Renaissance
38 - Las Vegas Convention Center

LAS VEGAS HILTON STATION
39 - Circus Circus
40 - Hilton Grand Vacations
41 - Turnberry Place (Sterling Club)
42 - Hilton
43 - Hilton Vacations

SAHARA STATION
44 - Palace Station
45 - Sahara
46 - Stratosphere
47 - Fremont Street Experience